William Francis Collier

History of the British Empire

William Francis Collier

History of the British Empire

ISBN/EAN: 9783743307827

Manufactured in Europe, USA, Canada, Australia, Japa

Cover: Foto ©ninafisch / pixelio.de

Manufactured and distributed by brebook publishing software (www.brebook.com)

William Francis Collier

History of the British Empire

HISTORY

OF

THE BRITISH EMPIRE.

BY

WILLIAM FRANCIS COLLIER, LL.D.,

TRINITY COLLEGE, DUBLIN;

Author of "Great Events of History," "History of English Literature," &c.

LONDON:
T. NELSON AND SONS, PATERNOSTER ROW;
EDINBURGH; AND NEW YORK.

MDCCCLXVI.

PREFACE.

This book aims at giving a clear outline of British History, retaining those details only, upon which the life and colour of the story depend.

The earlier Periods, during which settlers of various names and races continued to pour from the mainland of Europe upon these shores, have been sketched less minutely than those later times, when the nation, already formed and rooted, began to grow from within and to expand her mighty energies.

At the beginning of each Period is given an Outline, intended to serve as a framework for the study of the succeeding chapters. Each Period closes with a picture of the daily life and manners of the people, which, it is hoped, will be considered both attractive and useful.

It has been thought best to condense the Literary and Artistic History into a list of eminent men, with notes of their chief works. For convenience' sake the leading men of the Brunswick Period, whose names grow very numerous, are given at the end of each reign.

Since the exactness of historical knowledge depends greatly upon Chronology and Genealogy, these have been made prominent features of the work. While the leading dates are given with the text in the order of time, they are also grouped under certain heads; in which form they may be made the foundation of most interesting lessons. In the Genealogical Trees the line of descent from Egbert and Malcolm Canmore to Victoria can be clearly traced, with all its collateral branches.

Instead of the usual host of questions for examination, a few questions are given by which any reign may be fully analyzed. A list of Colonies, with notes upon their situation, their history, and their value, will be found at the end of the book.

Although written for Schools, this book will be found to contain all that is necessary to work a British History Paper for the Government Certificate of Merit, for the Middle Class Degree of A.A., or for most of the Civil Service Examinations.

CONTENTS.

Chap.
    Introduction, ...

ROMAN PERIOD.

  I. Roman Period, ...
    Leading Dates, ...

SAXON PERIOD.

    I. Time of the Heptarchy, ...
   II. Early Saxon Kings, ...
  III. Time of Danish Rule, ...
  IV. Saxon Line restored, ...
   V. Scotland and Ireland during the Saxon Period,
  VI. Social Condition of the Anglo-Saxons,   ...
    Leading Authors, ...
    Leading Dates, ...
    Genealogical Trees, ...

EARLY NORMAN KINGS.

    I. William I., ...
   II. William II., ...
  III. Henry I., ...
  IV. Stephen, ...
   V. Scotland during the Norman Period,   ...
  VI. Social Condition of the Normans,   ...
    Leading Authors, ...
    Leading Dates, —   ...   .
    Genealogical Tree, ...

PLANTAGENETS PROPER.

    I. Henry II., ...
   II. Richard I., ...
  III. John, ...
  IV. Henry III., ...

CONTENTS.

Chap.		Page
V.	Edward I.,	90
VI.	Edward II.,	94
VII.	Edward III.,	97
VIII.	Richard II.,	103
IX.	Scotland and Ireland during the first Seven Plantagenet Reigns,	107
X.	Social Condition of the People under the Plantagenets Proper,	113
	Leading Authors,	116
	Leading Dates,	116
	Genealogical Tree,	118

HOUSE OF LANCASTER.

I.	Henry IV.,	119
II.	Henry V.,	123
III.	Henry VI.,	127

HOUSE OF YORK.

I.	Edward IV.,	133
II.	Edward V.,	138
III.	Richard III.,	139
IV.	Social Condition of the People under the Houses of York and Lancaster,	142
	Leading Authors,	144
	Leading Dates,	144
	Genealogical Tree,	145

TUDOR PERIOD.

I.	Henry VII.,	146
II.	Henry VIII.,	157
III.	Edward VI.,	169
IV.	Mary I.,	173
V.	Elizabeth,	177
VI.	Stuart Sovereigns of Scotland—Ireland,	185
VII.	Social Condition of the People under the Tudors,	193
	Leading Authors,	199
	Leading Dates,	201
	Genealogical Tree,	202

STUART PERIOD.

I.	James I.,	203
II.	Charles I.,	209
III.	Commonwealth,	220
IV.	Charles II.,	227
V.	James II.,	238
VI.	William III. and Mary II.,	247
VII.	Anne,	253

Chap.		Page
VIII. Social Condition of the People under the Stuarts, ...		259
Leading Authors, ...		263
Leading Dates, ...		267
Genealogical Tree, ...		269

GUELPH PERIOD.

I. George I., ...		270
Leading Authors, ...		276
II. George II., ...		277
Leading Authors, ...		287
III. George III., ...		289
IV. George III. (continued), ...		296
Leading Authors, ...		308
V. George IV., ...		310
Leading Authors, ...		313
VI. William IV., ...		315
Leading Authors, ...		318
VII. Victoria, ...		319
Leading Authors, ...		331
VIII. The British Constitution and Government, ...		334
Leading Dates, ... -		337
Genealogical Tree, ...		339
British Colonies and Dependencies, ...		340

I. Give the Period to which the reign belongs—its place in the Period—its opening and closing Dates.
II. Trace the Descent of the Sovereign from the Conqueror—name the father, mother, brothers, sisters, husband or wife, sons and daughters.
III. Describe the personal life, character, and death of the Sovereign.
IV. Describe the Foreign Policy of the reign—giving especially the Wars and Alliances.
V. Describe the Domestic Policy of the reign.
VI. Name and describe all important Laws, and other Constitutional Changes.
VII. Give any Dominions acquired or lost, and Colonies planted, &c.
VIII. Name the leading Statesmen, Warriors, Authors, Men of Science, &c.—and tell for what they are famous.
IX. Give and explain any Historical Names or Titles—such as **Triers, Ordainers, Field of the Cloth of Gold,** &c.
X. State and describe the leading Events, classifying them as religious, political, social, commercial, literary, &c.

In describing an event there are six things always to be given: 1. The Causes 2. The Time. 3. The Place. 4. The Persons concerned. 5. The Circumstances. 6. The Consequences.

HISTORY

OF

THE BRITISH EMPIRE.

INTRODUCTION.

The British Isles.	Their condition in Cæsar's
Etymology of names.	time.
Earliest inhabitants.	Druidism.

THE British Isles lie to the north-west of the Continent of Europe; the larger, Great Britain, being situated near the Continent; the smaller, Ireland, lying further west in the Atlantic Ocean. Great Britain, called by the ancients Albion and Britannia, comprises the three countries, England, Wales, and Scotland.

The origin of the names, Britain, Albion, Wales, and Scotland, is wrapped in much obscurity. Some have supposed that the name Britain was derived from Brutus, a son of Ascanius the Trojan. The name Albion—still used in the form Albyn, or Alpin, as the Highland term for Scotland—is supposed to have been given to the island by the Gauls, from the chalk cliffs of the south-eastern coast. It is a Celtic word, meaning 'White Island,' and is most likely connected with *albus* and *Alp*. Wales, or Weallas, is thought to have been so named from a Saxon word, meaning 'wanderers' or 'foreigners,' because it was peopled by British refugees. It was also called Cambria. The Welsh have always called themselves Cymri, a name which probably connects them with the ancient Cimbri. Scotland took its name from a tribe called Scoti,—perhaps akin to the Scythians of Northern Europe,—who, early in the Christian era, passed from the north of Ireland into Britain, and, many centuries afterwards, gave their name to their new country. At the time of the Roman invasion the southern Britons called the inhabitants of the northern part of the island *Caoill daoin*, or 'people of the woods.' Hence the Latinized name Caledonia. The etymology of the word England admits of no doubt. It is another form of Angleland, and was derived from the Angli, the chief of the Saxon tribes. The smaller island was anciently called Ierne, a name which seems to have been formed from the Celtic word *eire*, meaning 'west.' The Romans called it Hibernia and Insula Sacra. Its present names are Ireland and Erin, in which can still be traced its old appellation.

These two islands, lying almost in the centre of the land hemisphere, with the great colonies of British America, Australia, and Cape Colony, with India, and numerous smaller dependencies in every quarter of the globe, form the British Empire. The object of this work is to trace, from the earliest time, of which we have any sure knowledge, to the present day, the events which have united under one Sovereign so many scattered lands.

The original inhabitants of the British Isles were Celts. The population now consists of two well-defined races— the Celtic and the Gothic, branches of the great Indo-European or Japhetic stock. The former are found in Wales, Cornwall, the Isle of Man, the Highlands of Scotland, and the south and west of Ireland,—in all places speaking the same language, though in different dialects, and still retaining in manners and dress many peculiarities of the ancient race; while the latter hold the lower and more fertile districts. Akin to the Celts of Britain are the Bretons, or people of Bretagne, anciently Armorica, the most westerly part of France.

Many centuries before the Christian era, Phœnician sailors from the colonies in Africa and Spain visited the British Islands, led thither by their rich tin mines. Herodotus, writing about four centuries and a half before Christ, mentions the Cassiterides or Tin Islands (supposed to be the

Scilly Isles); but the Greeks then knew nothing of them beyond their existence.

From Cæsar, Tacitus, Diodorus Siculus, and others, we learn a little about ancient Britain. The country seems to have been then full of marsh and forest, with a few patches of rudely tilled ground on the shore next Gaul. The natives of the interior sowed no corn, but lived on milk and flesh. Those far north were often obliged to feed on the roots and leaves which grew wild in the woods. They clad themselves in skins, leaving their limbs bare; and these they stained blue with the juice of a plant called woad. They were a brave and hardy people, and had some knowledge of war. Cæsar describes them as fighting on foot, on horseback, and in chariots, which, from blades that have been dug up on ancient battle-fields, seem to have been armed with scythes attached to the axle. Although divided into many tribes, they chose a single leader when danger menaced their common country; and, thus united, they were most formidable. Those who lived in the south were, from their intercourse with Gaul, more civilized than the rest. They wore a dress of woollen cloth, woven in many colours; and were adorned with chains of gold, silver, or bronze. Golden and silver ornaments for the arms, neck, and head; rings of various metals, which Cæsar says were the only sort of money they used; spear and arrow heads of flint and bronze, shaped with a delicacy which, with all our machinery, we cannot excel; and great works of rudely piled stone, such as Stonehenge in Wiltshire and Stennes in Orkney, are almost the only memorials by which we can judge of this ancient people.

The religion of the Celts was Druidism; their priests were called Druids; and their chief sanctuary was the Island of Mona, now Anglesea. The word Druid seems to be connected with *drus*, the Greek name of the oak, their sacred tree. In addition to their priestly duties, the Druids were the bards, the lawgivers, and the teachers of the people. They wore long white robes and flowing beards, to distinguish them from the people, over whom they had complete control. They believed in the transmigration of souls, and taught the worship of one God; but the serpent, the sun and moon, and the oak, shared their veneration; and their altars were stained with the blood of men and women, whom, as Cæsar tells, they burned in large numbers, enclosed in immense cages of wicker work. These victims were generally men who had been convicted of theft or some other crime, their sacrifice being deemed peculiarly acceptable to the gods; but in the absence of such, they never hesitated to immolate the innocent. The circles of stone already referred to are supposed by some to have been the scenes of these fearful rites; but it is more probable that they were sepulchral monuments erected in honour of departed chiefs. The oak groves were the dwellings of the Druids, and the temples for their daily worship. Their three chief feasts had reference to the harvest: one was held after the seed was sown, another when the corn was ripening, and a third when the crop was gathered in. Besides these, a solemn ceremony took place on the sixth day of the moon nearest to the 10th of March, which was their New-year's-day, when the Archdruid with a golden knife cut the mistletoe from its parent oak; while attendant priests, with their white robes outspread, caught the sacred plant as it fell. The traces of these customs linger still, especially in the south of England, where the sports of May-day, the fires of Midsummer-eve, the harvest-home, and the cutting of the mistletoe at Christmas, are duly observed.

ROMAN PERIOD.

55 B.C. to 410 A.D.—465 years.

Leading Features: **THE DAWN OF CIVILIZATION, AND THE INTRODUCTION OF CHRISTIANITY.**

CHAPTER I.

Julius Cæsar lands.	Boadicea.	Christianity introduced.
His return.	Agricola.	Withdrawal of the Romans.
Intentions of Augustus and Caligula.	Roman walls. Severus.	Scotland and Ireland during Roman period.
Lieutenants of Claudius.	Roman division of Britain.	
Caractacus.	Caurausius and Allectus.	Roman roads and towns.

JULIUS CÆSAR, having subdued the tribes of Gaul, desired to add Britain to his conquests. He had left a legion under Publius Crassus to guard the Venetic Isles, the group of which Belle-isle is chief; and from the soldiers he learned the course, long and carefully kept a secret, by which the Gallic merchants reached the coast of Britain. The valuable pearl fisheries, and the mineral wealth of the island, were inducements additional to the glory which he expected to reap. He first called together a number of Gallic merchants, but could learn nothing of value from them; then, having sent an officer with a ship of war to reconnoitre, he crossed the Strait of Dover, called in Latin 'Fretum Oceani,' with 80 ships, having on board two legions, or 12,000 troops. He found the high, white cliffs of Kent studded with bands of Britons, and had much difficulty in landing; however, the eagle-bearer of the tenth legion led the way, and Roman discipline prevailed. Four days after, a storm shattered the fleet; and Cæsar, having repaired his vessels, thought it best to return to Gaul. He had been absent seventeen days. *55 B.C.*

Next summer he landed on the Kentish shore with five legions, comprising 30,000 foot and 2000 horse. The British tribes had united their forces, and were led by Cassivelaunus, whose territory lay along the Thames. He proved himself a brave and skilful general, and kept the Romans in check for some time, by taking advantage of the woods and rivers. However, Cæsar forced his way across the Thames, and came up with his foe, intrenched in the midst of thick woods and treacherous marshes. Here the British chief held out for a while, in hopes that the leaders of the Kentish tribes would take the Roman camp and burn the fleet; but, when he heard that they had been foiled in this attempt, he came to terms with Cæsar. Hostages were given, the amount of yearly tribute settled, and Cæsar went back to Gaul.

43 A.D. Until the reign of the Emperor Claudius, the Romans did not return to Britain. Augustus, first Emperor of Rome, had formed a plan to do so, but its execution was prevented. The foolish Caligula led his troops to the shore of Gaul, opposite to Britain; where, having shown them the faint outline of the hills in the distance, he set them to gather shells in their helmets, as the spoils of the conquered ocean. This he celebrated on his return to Rome with a triumph.

Plautius and Vespasian, the lieutenants of Claudius, after hard fighting, gained a footing on the island. Plautius, supplied from Gaul with all necessaries, drove the Britons across the Thames; but further he could not go, until the Emperor joined him with new forces. Then, having crossed the river, the Romans penetrated Essex, where they founded their first colony—Camalodūnum, now Colchester or Maldon. Vespasian fought more than thirty battles, before he subdued the tribes of Hampshire and Wight.

Plautius was succeeded by Ostorius Scapula, who disarmed all the Britons within the Roman bounds. This act roused the spirit of the natives. The Silures, a tribe of South Wales, took the lead; and under their chief, Caractacus, they kept the Romans in constant war for nine years. But at last the Romans, having forced their way into the British strongholds, routed the army of Caractacus; who, fleeing to his step-mother, Cartismandua, Queen of the Brigantes, was by her betrayed into their hands. He was led in triumph through the streets of Rome, and was doomed to die; but his dauntless bearing in the Emperor's presence won for him a free pardon.

Another leader of the Britons was Boadicea, who, in Nero's reign, was Queen of the Iceni, a tribe inhabiting Norfolk and Suffolk. She, having suffered shameful wrongs and insults from the Romans, called her countrymen to arms. She led them to battle, destroyed Camalodūnum and London, which was, even at this early date, a flourishing commercial town ; but, being defeated by Suetonius Paulinus, she killed herself.   **61 A.D.**

To Julius Agricola, lieutenant of Domitian, is due the honour of making Britain a Roman province in more than name. We have an account of his operations in the works of Tacitus, his son-in-law. While he upheld the terror of the Roman arms and checked all revolt, he adopted a milder policy. He taught the arts of peace to the conquered race, and many high-born Britons assumed the Roman toga, language, and manner of life. He did what no Roman general had yet done, in penetrating the pathless woods of Caledonia, and extending Roman rule to the shores of the Moray Frith. In this expedition he had to contend with many fierce foes, and fought a battle at Mons Grampius, with the Caledonian chief Galgacus, before passing that great natural barrier. The scene of this battle is uncertain : many name Ardoch in Perthshire as the probable place. While cruising upon the northern coasts, the sailors of Agricola discovered Britain to be an island.   **78 A.D**   **84 A.D.**

This great general built two lines of forts from sea to sea, for the protection of the southern provinces ; one from the Tyne to the Solway Frith; the other, two years after, from the Frith of Forth to the Frith of Clyde. The Emperor Adrian, unable to hold the northern ramparts, raised that called Vallum Adriani, or the Picts' Wall, close to the first chain of forts built by Agricola. In the reign of Antonine the Romans, under Lollius Urbicus, pushed their territory far north, and restored Agricola's second wall, which was then called Vallum Antonini, and at a later date Graham's Dyke.   **79 A.D.**   **120 A.D.**   **138 A.D.**

More than once a Roman governor of Britain assumed the imperial purple. This happened in one case during the reign of Severus, when Albinus led the British legions into Gaul to contest the Empire. Severus, victorious over his rival, divided the government of Britain between two of his lieutenants; but he was soon obliged, by the incursions of the Caledonians, to visit the island in person. He marched to attack his fierce foes in their mountain fastnesses. They, whose only weapons were a dirk, a heavy sword slung around them by an iron chain, and a lance with a bell at one end, and whose sole protection was a rude target of hide, soon yielded to the skill and valour of disciplined legions. Severus traversed their forests, and, having inflicted heavy punishment for their ravages, built, a few yards from the wall of Adrian, a strong stone wall, requiring a garrison of 10,000 men. He had scarcely turned south when the Caledonians rose again; and in his northward march to reduce them he died at York, then Eborăcum. His son Caracalla yielded to the native chiefs all the territory north of the wall built by his father.

211 A.D.

By the Romans, Britain was divided into six provinces. These were as follow:—

I. **BRITANNIA PRIMA**, including all the country south of Gloucestershire and the Thames.
II. **FLAVIA CÆSARIENSIS**, the central counties, forming a square whose angles rest on the Wash and the mouths of the Dee, the Severn, and the Thames.
III. **BRITANNIA SECUNDA**, Wales and that part of England west of the Severn and the Dee.
IV. **MAXIMA CÆSARIENSIS**, from the Wash and the Dee on the south to the wall of Adrian on the Tyne.
V. **VALENTIA**, the country between the walls of Adrian and Antonine.
VI. **VESPASIANA** or **CALEDONIA**, the tracts north of Antonine's wall.

The first four provinces were completely reduced; the fifth was partially subdued by Agricola, Urbicus, Severus, and Theodosius, who lived in the reign of Valentinian, and gave his sovereign's name to the district; the last was merely traversed by the Roman troops, but never conquered.

INTRODUCTION OF CHRISTIANITY.

Our knowledge of Britain during the latter years of the Roman period is very scanty. For twelve years the island was an independent state. Carausius, appointed Count of the Saxon Shore by the Emperors Diocletian and Maximian, commanded a fleet, which was sent to defend the British coasts from the Scandinavian pirates. He established himself as Ruler of Britain, and actually forced the Emperors to acknowledge his claim to the title. He fell at York by the dagger of a Briton named Allectus, who seized the throne; but, three years after, he too fell in battle with the Emperor Constantius Chlorus, and Roman ascendency was restored. This prince married Helena, a British lady, by whom he had a son, afterwards called Constantine the Great.

288 A.D.

297 A.D.

300 A.D.

It is an unfailing rule in history, that, when a civilized nation subdues one less advanced, the ultimate benefit derived by the conquered people far outweighs any temporary loss at first suffered. The early years of Roman rule in Britain were but the dark hour before the dawn. Christianity was introduced into Britain about the latter end of the first century; some say by Peter or Paul. The Britons suffered persecution for the Cross in the reign of Diocletian. St. Alban, the first British martyr for Christ, gave his name to the town of Hertfordshire at which he suffered. Constantine the Great, having been born at York, honoured Britain as his birth-place, and greatly encouraged the teaching of the Christian faith in the island. Thus the Britons received from their Roman conquerors the greatest boon that could be conferred on a nation, —'to know Christ and him crucified.'

303 A.D.

At last the incursions of the Goths and other northern tribes became so frequent, and so fierce, that the Roman soldiers were withdrawn from Britain to guard the heart of the Empire. Levies of the British youth were employed in the Roman service in Gaul, and elsewhere on the Continent. Soon, the Emperor Honorius, finding it advisable to contract the limits of the Empire, released the Britons from Roman sway, and withdrew all signs of authority.

410 A.D.

Little can be said of Scotland and Ireland during this period. The remains of Roman baths and forts at Burgh-head, Ardoch near Dunblane, and other places, clearly prove that the Romans penetrated as far north as the Moray Frith. But the wild forests north of the Forth were too dense for the manœuvres of disciplined troops, and the Roman legions made no permanent conquest of their savage denizens. The Orkney and the Shetland Islands, with the northern counties, were, during the latter years of this period, seized by the Scandinavians, whose descendants may still be found there. Ireland, or the Sacred Isle, maintained intercourse with the Welsh, and was the abode of the older Celtic tribes, who long preserved the Druidical worship in its original forms.

The Romans taught the Britons to develop the resources of their country. They opened up the island by making roads paved with stone. These were called *Strata;* whence our word Street. They also laid the foundation of a lucrative trade, Rome and her continental provinces affording a good market for British produce. The chief exports at this time were corn, cheese, lime, chalk, oysters, and pearls. British cattle, horses, and dogs, were much prized; and large supplies of tin, lead, iron, with some gold and silver, were drawn from the island. A gold coinage was in use shortly after Cæsar's time. Specimens have been found stamped with the figures of cattle, like the Latin *pecunia* (from *pecus*). The Romans being essentially a military nation, the words introduced by them, and still used by us, relate to their position in the island, as an army in occupation of a conquered land. Their towns were military stations, strongly fortified; and were called in Latin, *castra,* or 'camps.' This word can be recognised in various forms in such names as Chester, Winchester, Leicester, and Doncaster. The Latin word *colonia* can be traced in Lincoln, and Colchester; and the city of Bath, although not now called by a Roman name, was a leading Roman watering-place, as recent discoveries of long-buried temples and statues have shown.

LEADING DATES OF THE ROMAN PERIOD.

Landing of Julius Cæsar,	B.C. 55
Return of the Romans in the reign of Claudius,	A.D. 43
Death of Boadicea,	61
Agricola begins his government,	78
Agricola builds his walls,	79
Battle of Mons Grampius,	84
Adrian's Wall built,	120
Antonine's Wall built,	138
Death of Severus at York,	211
Britain independent,	288
Roman rule restored,	300
Martyrdom of St Alban,	303
Romans leave Britain,	410

SAXON PERIOD.

410 A.D. to 1066 A.D.—656 years.

CHAPTER I.

TIME OF THE HEPTARCHY.

410 A.D. to 827 A.D.—417 years.

Leading Features: BLOODSHED AND CHANGE.

Miserable state of the Britons.	Establishment of the Heptarchy.	Revival of Christianity.
Arrival of Saxon tribes.	Prince Arthur. Bretwalda.	Heptarchy reduced to three. Wessex survives.

The Britons, who had lived in peace under Roman protection, were in a wretched plight when that was withdrawn. The Picts and Scots, breaking through the unguarded walls, pillaged the northern country; the pirates of the Danish and German coasts, who had hardly been kept in check by the Roman fleets, descending upon the east and south, sailed up the rivers in their light flat-bottomed skiffs, burning and slaying without mercy; while the land was torn by internal strife, between a Roman faction under Ambrosius and a British under Vortigern. The petty British states made a feeble attempt at union by the election of a monarch, whom they called Pendragon; but the contentions for this office only made things worse.

Vortigern asked the aid of the pirates, or sea-kings, as they called themselves. They were fierce men, of great size, with blue eyes, ruddy complexion, and yellow, streaming hair; practised in war, using the axe, the sword, the spear, and the mace. Their chief god was Odin, or Woden; their heaven was Valhalla. The story of their settlement in Britain, though true in some points, rests on uncertain tradition. It is, that two chiefs of the Jutes, or people of Jutland, named

Hengist and Horsa, were hired by Vortigern for the defence of his faction. They landed at Ebbsfleet, on the coast of Thanet in Kent; but, after they had repelled the enemies of Vortigern, they turned their arms against himself, seized Kent, and invited their kindred over to share the spoil. Another story, of British origin, makes Kent a gift to the Jutes from Vortigern, who fell in love with Rowena, the daughter of Hengist. For more than a century after this, bands of invaders, from the countries lying between the Elbe and the Rhine, continued to pour upon the south and east shores of Britain, driving the inhabitants west and north before them, and seizing all the lowland territory. These invaders were of three tribes, Jutes, Angles, and Saxons. **449 A.D.**

Seven kingdoms, called the Saxon Heptarchy, were thus founded. These were,—

I. **KENT**; founded by Hengist, 457 A.D.
II. **SOUTH SAXONY**, including Sussex and Surrey; founded by Ella, 490 A.D.
III. **WEST SAXONY**, or **WESSEX**, including all the counties west of Sussex and south of the Thames, Cornwall excepted; founded by Cerdic, 519 A.D.
IV. **EAST SAXONY**, including Essex and Middlesex; founded by Ercenwin, 527 A.D.
V. **NORTHUMBRIA**, the land north of the Humber, as far as the Forth; founded by Ida, 547 A.D.
VI. **EAST ANGLIA**, including Norfolk, Suffolk, and Cambridge; founded by Uffa, 575 A.D.
VII. **MERCIA**, including the midland counties, east of the Severn, north of the Thames, and south of the Humber; founded by Cridda, 582 A.D.

The chief opponent of the Saxon invaders was Arthur, King of the Silures of South Wales. He won twelve battles. The sixty 'Knights of the Round Table' were his principal officers. He was slain by his nephew, Mordred; and was buried at Glastonbury, where his coffin was found in the reign of Henry II. **542 A.D.**

The Kings of the Heptarchy were at constant war among themselves, and the bounds of the seven states were always changing. The King who for the time had the ascendency was called Bretwalda, a word meaning 'powerful king.'

Christianity, which had been forgotten in these wars, now began to revive, and Pope Gregory became ambitious of bringing the Saxons under the rule of the Roman see. Purchasing some English youths in the slave-market at Rome, he attempted to train them for the work of missionaries; but soon abandoning this project, he sent Augustine, with forty monks, to preach the cross in Britain. The conduct of these emissaries of Pope Gregory was such as cannot in many things be justified; yet God overruled all for good, and the heathenism of the Saxons gradually fell before the power of Christianity. Ethelbert, King of Kent, influenced by his wife Bertha, a professed Christian, was the first royal convert; and the chief church was built at Canterbury, which has ever since continued to be the ecclesiastical capital of England. Sebert, King of Essex, was also converted. He destroyed the temple of Apollo at Westminster, and built a church in honour of St. Peter, where the abbey now stands. The temple of Diana fell too, and on its site was raised a church to St. Paul. Edwin was a famous Bretwalda of this period, who subdued Anglesea and Man. His dominion extended over nearly the whole country from the Forth to the Thames. On the southern shore of the Forth he founded a city, still bearing his name,—Edwin's burgh or Edinburgh. On becoming a Christian himself, he convoked the National Assembly, and explained the reasons of his change of faith. His chiefs, following his example, solemnly renounced the worship of the ancient gods; and Coifi the high priest was the first to give a signal for destruction by hurling his lance at the idol in the pagan temple. Thirty-three years previous to the mission of Augustine, Columba had landed in Scotland with twelve companions, and established a Christian seminary in the island of Iona. His followers were called Culdees (worshippers of God). They founded institutions in many parts of Scotland, and penetrated into England. Oswald, successor to Edwin of Northumbria, had, during an exile among the Scots, wandered to Iona, and received the lessons of Christianity. On his return he founded a monastery on Lindisfarne, thence called Holy Isle. In their principles and practice the Culdees offered a vigorous opposition to many of the errors and corruptions of the Romish Church.

A.D. 596

The followers of Augustine set themselves to arrest their progress, and bring the whole of Britain under the spiritual supremacy of the Pope. All who struggled for the independence of the early British Church were pursued with unrelenting hostility; and ultimately the policy of Rome triumphed. Many words connected with the Christian worship were brought into use by the Roman monks, such as minster, for *monasterium;* candle, for *candela;* preach, for *prædicare*.

The seven kingdoms were at last reduced to three, Northumbria, Mercia, and Wessex. Northumbria soon fell before the prowess of the Mercian Kings. One of these, called Offa the Terrible, is worthy of notice. He conquered the Welsh, and confined them to their mountains by Offa's Dyke, a ditch and rampart stretching from the mouth of the Dee to the channel of Bristol. He also subdued a great part of Wessex. He did much good to the church, although not a pious man. His palaces, coins, and medals, prove him to have been a man of some refinement.

Wessex was the last surviving kingdom of the Heptarchy. When Offa died, Beortric, a usurper, held the throne. He had married Offa's daughter, Eadburga, and was upheld by the influence of the Mercian King. Soon after her father's death, Eadburga poisoned her husband and fled to France; but, being driven from that country, she fell into great want, and died a beggar on the streets of an Italian town. Egbert, the true King, who had been living for fourteen years at the court of Charlemagne, returned to England on his rival's death, and received the crown of Wessex. He defeated the Britons of Devon and Cornwall; overthrew Bernwulf, usurper of Mercia, who was killed in the battle; added Mercia to his kingdom of Wessex; and soon united under his sway all the territories south of the Tweed. 827 A.D.

The kingdom thus formed was called England, or the land of the Angli, from the most powerful of the three invading tribes.

CHAPTER II.

EARLY SAXON KINGS.

827 A.D. to 1017 A.D.—190 years.—15 Kings.

9TH CENTURY.

	A.D.
EGBERT—began to rule	827
ETHELWULF (son)	836
ETHELBALD (son)	857
ETHELBERT (brother)	860
ETHELRED I. (brother)	866
ALFRED (brother)	871

	A.D.
EDMUND I. (brother)	941
EDRED (brother)	946
EDWY (nephew)	955
EDGAR (brother)	959
EDWARD the Martyr (son)	975
ETHELRED II., the Unready (half-brother)	978

10TH CENTURY.

	A.D.
EDWARD the Elder (son)	901
ATHELSTAN (son)	925

11TH CENTURY.

	A.D.
EDMUND II., Ironside (son)	1017

Leading Features: LAW AND ORDER SLOWLY IMPROVING; THE DANES A CONSTANT SOURCE OF TROUBLE.

The Danes.	Ethandune.	The Five Burghs.
Peter's Pence.	Landing of Hastings.	Dunstan.
Alfred the first Earl.	Improvements in Education.	Dane-geld.
Alfred King.		Massacre of Danes.
War with the Danes.	Law and Justice.	Sweyn.
Chippenham.	Bible translated into Anglo-Saxon.	Triumph of Canute.
Alfred's Hiding-place.		

EGBERT was crowned at Winchester, then the chief city. His achievements prove him to have been a man of fortitude, valour, and decision. He was called Egbert (Bright-eye), according to the custom of half-civilized nations, whose names are often derived from personal appearance. The Danes began to be troublesome in this reign. They came, like the Saxons, originally from the forests of Germany; but, being worsted in war with Charlemagne, they removed to the country we call Denmark. Akin to the Saxons—for they were both from the Scandinavian stock—they hated these with no common hatred, as renegades from the faith of Woden and Thor Their first descent on the island was

787 A.D.

at Teignmouth. They continued their ravages till Egbert defeated them at Hengsdown Hill in Cornwall. Egbert died in the following year. **835 A.D.**

Ethelwulf, eldest son of Egbert, succeeded. He had been a monk. By his first wife, Osberga, daughter of Oslac his cup-bearer, he had four sons; all of whom in turn held the throne. In his latter days, he made a pilgrimage to Rome with Alfred, his youngest son, who had been there before. His second wife was Judith, daughter of Charles the Bald, King of France. She was probably not more than twelve years old when the marriage took place. In this reign a tax called 'Peter's pence' was levied by the Pope, to maintain an English college at Rome. Tithes were also granted to the clergy, and every Wednesday was set apart for prayer against the Danes. Ethelwulf died at Stambridge in Essex, and was buried at Steyning in Sussex.

Ethelbald married his step-mother, Judith; but was induced by the Bishop of Winchester to give her up. She retired to the court of her father, by whom she was imprisoned; but, escaping, she eloped with Baldwin, forester of France, on whom was afterwards conferred the earldom of Flanders. She was the ancestress of the Conqueror's wife.

Ethelbert's reign is noted only for a descent of the Danes upon Thanet. It closed in 866 A.D.

Ethelred I. was hardly pressed by the Danes, and fought many battles with them. Aston and Merton were the chief. In the latter he was mortally wounded. His brother Alfred, who was by him created an Earl, was the first to bear that title in England. During this reign there was a great famine, followed by a pestilence upon men and cattle. Edmund, Prince of East Anglia, was murdered by the Danes, near the town called on that account Bury St. Edmunds.

Alfred, surnamed the Great, now became King. He was not the heir, for his brother's infant son, Ethelwald, was living; but the nobles of Wessex, it being a time of peril, transferred the crown to one better able to guard its rights. He was in his twenty-second year, and had been for some time married to Alswitha, daughter of a Mercian noble. Though the victim of an internal disease which left him few painless hours during twenty-four **871 A.D.**

years, his energies never drooped through all the changes of a toilsome life. It is said that a love of literature was first stirred in his breast by his mother, Osberga, who promised a richly bound and illuminated volume of Saxon poems, greatly admired by her sons, to him who should first learn to read them. Alfred won the prize, and from that time a great love of study distinguished him.

The ravages of the Danes grew more formidable every day. A battle was fought at Wilton, in Wiltshire, in which Alfred was defeated. He then entered into negotiations with the Danes, who withdrew from Wessex on payment of a large sum. Their ravages were afterwards directed to Mercia and Northumbria, where they burned and butchered without mercy.

For many years Alfred held possession of the country south of the Thames. During this time he equipped a fleet that did signal service against the Danes. After a period of prosperity, misfortune overtook the King once more. Guthrum, a Danish leader, who had taken post at Gloucester, made a night-march on Chippenham, a royal villa upon the Avon, where Alfred was then residing. The King fled in disguise, and sought refuge with a swine-herd, while his adherents were scattered by the Danes. The chroniclers of his life tell a story of his retirement, which has formed a subject for picture and for poem. The wife of his humble host set him to watch cakes; but, in his absence of mind, he let them burn. She scolded him soundly—some say struck him—saying that, lazy as he was in turning them, he would be active enough in eating them. His hiding-place was Athelney, a marshy island formed by the meeting of the rivers Parret and Tone; and here he lay for some months, visited at times by his nobles, who were gradually and secretly gathering strength for a fierce struggle.

878 A.D.

Hearing that the Danes under Ubba had been surprised and beaten by the Earl of Devon, Alfred resolved to strike the blow at once. In the disguise of a harper he visited the Danish camp, and, by the beauty of his music, won his way to Guthrum's tent, where he was feasted for some days. He saw the carelessness of the Danes, heard their plans discussed, and then, stealing from the camp, called his friends together in Selwood Forest. The summons was joyfully received. The Saxons and the Danes met at the foot of Ethandune, a hill in Somersetshire, and the victory was Alfred's. He laid siege to the Danish camp, and in fourteen days forced Guthrum to capitulate. This chief with many of his followers having consented to be baptized as Christians, received a strip of the eastern coast from the Thames to the Tweed. This tract was hence called the Danelagh. **878 A.D.**

Once more the Danes, in 330 ships, under Hastings, landed on the Kentish shore, and ravaged the south of the island for three years; but the genius of Alfred met every difficulty, and again he was the victor. The rest of his reign was peace. **893 A.D.**

During his latter years he was engaged in carrying out those plans for his people's welfare which he had conceived amid the storms of his earlier life. He built strong castles, both inland and on the shore, where an enemy could be best withstood. A militia system was organized by him, according to which all men capable of bearing arms were divided into three sets. One body occupied the towns as garrisons, while the other two were by turns engaged in military service and the cultivation of the land. He encouraged learning, both by his example and his laws. His court was the home of many distinguished scholars; and we owe to the King himself several works, among which are Saxon translations of 'Æsop's Fables' and of 'Bede's History of the Saxon Church.' He founded the University of Oxford, and passed a law enforcing on the nobles the education of their children. His day was divided into three parts: one devoted to business of state; a second, to prayer and study; a third, to sleep, meals, and recreation: and these periods he measured by candles, burning one inch in twenty minutes.

But perhaps Alfred's strongest claim to the name 'Great' is founded on his political institutions. He framed a code of laws, in which the chief enactments of Ethelbert and Offa had place; and these he executed with such stern impartiality that crime became rare. We can trace to his wisdom many principles of modern British law. Among such, trial by jury, the great safeguard of our personal rights, stands pre-eminent. The division of the land into counties, hundreds, and tithings or tenths, enabled him to hold all parts under strict control; and the terror of his name was so great, that it became a common saying, that golden ornaments might be hung up by the road-side, and no robber would dare to touch them.

901 A.D. He died at Farringdon, in Berkshire, and was buried at Winchester.

Edward, surnamed the Elder, Alfred's son, succeeded. He was the first to assume the title 'King of England.' Even Alfred, in his will, called himself 'Alfred, of the West Saxons King.' His cousin Ethelwald made a desperate attempt to seize the crown, but was defeated by Edward, and slain. This monarch is the reputed founder of the University of Cambridge, although a school had been established there by Sebert of East Anglia nearly three centuries before. He left behind him many sons and daughters.

925 A.D. Athelstan, illegitimate son of Edward, succeeded. The leading event of his reign is the overthrow of a league formed by the Scots and the Danes. He placed in every church a copy of the Anglo-Saxon Bible, which had been translated by his order; and he encouraged commerce by granting the title 'Thane' to those merchants who made three voyages in their own ships. He died at Gloucester.

941 A.D. Edmund, son of Edward the Elder, succeeded. He married Elgiva, and left two sons, Edwy and Edgar, who afterwards reigned, though at first passed over as too young. He routed the Danes, driving them from *the Five Burghs*—Derby, Leicester, Nottingham, Stamford, and Lincoln—which they had long held. In the height of his success he was stabbed, while sitting at supper in Pucklechurch, Gloucestershire. Leolf, whom he had banished for robbery, six years before, was the assassin.

947 A.D. Edred, brother of Edmund, was now elected by the great Council or Witenagemot. He suffered from a painful disease, which weakened both mind and body; and for this reason public affairs were managed by his ministers. Turketul, at first Chancellor, and afterwards Abbot of Croyland, and Dunstan, abbot of Glastonbury, were his chief favourites. He died at Winchester.

Edwy, surnamed the Fair, eldest son of Edmund, succeeded. He was a prince addicted to low vices, and regardless of his kingly dignity. He incurred the hatred of Dunstan, because he resisted the efforts of that prelate to make the church supreme in the government of the country. A quarrel arose about Elgiva the Queen, and Dunstan was banished. Elgiva, who had been sent to Ireland to separate her from the King, having returned, was cruelly murdered by Odo, Archbishop of Canterbury. The Mercians and Northumbrians rose in revolt, and made Edgar, brother of the King, their ruler. Edwy was forced to content himself with the counties south of the Thames, and soon died, it is said, of grief at the loss of his territory. **955 A.D.**

The Witan then made Edgar King. He was called the Peaceable; for during his reign no foe, foreign or domestic, vexed the land. His form was small and spare, but his mind was full of vigour. All Albion and the isles owned his sway. It was his yearly custom to make a progress through the land; and, on one occasion, eight princes rowed his barge on the Dee at Chester. He favoured the clergy, especially Dunstan, whom he had, when King of Mercia, recalled from exile, and whom he now created Archbishop of Canterbury. He has been blamed for favouring the Danes of Northumbria. It is true that he allowed them to choose their own laws; but he reduced their power, by dividing the earldom between two of his courtiers. He permitted the Welsh to pay every year, instead of their money tribute, three hundred wolves' heads; a plan which, in four years, cleared their forests of these animals. By his order, all weights and measures used in England were reduced to a standard. He left two sons; Edward by his first wife, Elfleda; Ethelred by his second, Elfrida. **959 A.D.**

Upon Edgar's death the succession was disputed; but Dunstan's influence secured the crown for Edward. His elevation to the throne cost him his life; for, in less than four years, he was stabbed while drinking a cup of mead on horseback at Corfe Castle in Dorsetshire, the residence of his step-mother, Elfrida, who desired the crown for her son. This sad fate procured for him the surname of 'Martyr.' **975 A.D.**

The murder of Edward gained for Ethelred the throne, but not the hearts of the people. Famine and plague cast a gloom over the land, which grew deeper when the Danes renewed their ravages. The King, who was surnamed 'Unready,' attempted to buy them off; and for this purpose levied a tax, called Dane-geld, amounting to twelve pence in the year upon each hide of land for all classes except the clergy; but this foolish policy had no other effect than to bring the pirates in larger swarms on the English shores. This was the first direct and annual tax imposed on the English nation. Ethelred's difficulties increased; and, in his folly, he devised the mad scheme of a general massacre of Danes. The bloody day was the festival of St. Brice. Burning with rage, Sweyn, King of Denmark, whose sister Gunhilda was among the slain, burst upon the coasts; and, returning again and again, took a terrible revenge. At last Oxford and Winchester fell before the invaders. Sweyn was proclaimed King at Bath, and soon after at London. Ethelred fled to the Isle of Wight, and thence to Normandy, the native place of Emma, his second wife. Sweyn died in three weeks after, at Gainsborough in Lincolnshire, leaving his conquests to his son Canute. But the Saxons, having recalled Ethelred, supported him so vigorously that Canute was forced in turn to abandon the island. When leaving, he took a barbarous revenge, by cutting off the noses, ears, and hands of the Saxon hostages whom he held. Ethelred, now triumphant, provoked renewed incursions by repeated murders of his Danish subjects; and his untiring foe, Canute, returning, landed at Sandwich, then the chief port. The Dane was pushing towards the capital, leaving a track of blood and ashes behind him, when the death of Ethelred transferred the crown to his eldest son, Edmund. Ethelred was twice married; first to Elfleda, whose sons, Edmund, Edwy, and Athelstan, survived; secondly to Emma, daughter of Richard, Duke of Normandy, by whom he left two sons, Edward and Alfred.

Edmund, surnamed Ironside, struggled bravely for the throne of his father for seven months; during which London

978 A.D.

Nov. 14, 1002 A.D.

1013 A.D.

was assaulted twice, without success, by the Danes under Canute. But, at last, after a meeting in Olney, an island in the Severn,—where, some writers say, a duel was fought between the rivals,—they agreed to a division of the kingdom; the Saxon holding the counties south, the Danes those north of the Thames. The Dane-geld was to be levied off both districts alike, but was to be applied to the support of the Danish fleet. In a month after this agreement Edmund died, leaving Canute sole monarch. The cause of his death is uncertain. He left two sons, Edward and Edmund.

CONTEMPORARY SOVEREIGNS.

FRANCE.

	A.D.		A.D
CHARLEMAGNE, sole king,	770	RAOUL,	923
LOUIS I. (le Debonnaire),	814	LOUIS D'OUTREMER (IV.),	936
CHARLES the Bald,	840	LOTHAIRE,	954
LOUIS II.,	877	LOUIS V.,	986
LOUIS III.,	879	HUGH CAPET,	987
CHARLES the Fat,	884	ROBERT I.,	996
CHARLES the Simple,	898		

CHAPTER III.

TIME OF DANISH RULE.

1017 A.D. to 1041 A.D.—24 years.—3 Kings.

CANUTE (son of Sweyn), ...1017
HAROLD (son), ...1036
HARDICANUTE (half-brother), ...1039–1041

Leading Feature: **ENGLAND DIVIDED BETWEEN THE SAXONS AND THE DANES.**

Canute secures his power.	Claims to the title of 'Great.'	Sons of Ethelred in England.
Dismissal of Danish troops.	Religious acts.	Hardicanute.
	Harold.	Earl Godwin's present.

CANUTE now received the crown of England. His first care was to remove all rivals. The surviving sons of Ethelred were Edwy, Edward, and Alfred. Edwy he caused to be murdered; Edward and Alfred took refuge in Normandy; while their mother, Emma, married the King. The infant sons of Edmund Ironside were conveyed to Sweden, and thence to Hungary; where Edmund died in youth. Canute at first divided his English dominions into four parts, reserving Wessex for himself; but, fearing treachery on the part of his lieutenants, he reunited all under his own sway.

Anxious to reconcile the Saxons to his usurpation, he dismissed the Danish soldiers to their own country; but not without first rewarding them with large sums. He retained a body-guard of 3000 men, whom he ruled with the strictest discipline. Having on one occasion killed a soldier in a fit of anger, he, in presence of this band, laid aside his crown and sceptre, and demanded that they should pronounce sentence on him. All were silent, and Canute imposed upon himself a fine nine times greater than the lawful sum. Again, at Southampton, he rebuked the flattery of his courtiers, by setting his chair upon the shore and commanding the waves to retire. While the tide was flowing round his feet, he sternly blamed the presumption of those who compared a weak earthly King to the Great Ruler of the Universe. By such acts as these he won the title 'Great.'

Besides England, he ruled over Norway, Sweden, and Denmark, and is said to have exacted homage from Malcolm of Scotland. In his latter days he became religious in life, after the fashion of the time. He endowed monasteries, built churches, gave money for masses to be sung for the souls of those whom he had slain, and went, staff in hand, clad in pilgrim's gown, to Rome; where he obtained from the Pope that English pilgrims should be freed from the heavy dues then levied upon travellers. He also introduced the Christian faith into Denmark. He died at Shaftesbury, and was buried at Winchester. By his first wife he had two sons, Sweyn and Harold. His second wife, Emma, widow of Ethelred, bore him a son and a daughter,—the former named Hardicanute. To Sweyn was allotted Norway, Harold seized England, while Hardicanute was forced to content himself with Denmark.

By Canute's desire, the crown of England was to have devolved on Hardicanute; but Harold, surnamed Harefoot, seized it without delay. The Witan, meeting at Oxford, divided the country between the rival princes; assigning to Harold London and the counties north of the Thames; to Hardicanute the district south of that river. The latter, however, trifled away his time in Denmark, and left the support of his claims to his mother Emma, and Godwin, Earl of Wessex. About this time, Edward, son of Ethelred, landed at Southampton, to assert his right to the throne; but, being menaced by a formidable force, he abandoned the enterprise. His brother Alfred, who was soon afterwards enticed over from Normandy by a letter from Emma, met a cruel death at Ely, where his eyes were torn out by the officers of Harold. Emma in alarm fled to the court of Baldwin, count of Flanders. Harold died at Oxford, and was buried at Winchester. **1036 A.D.**

Hardicanute (Canute the Hardy) was on his way to England with a large fleet, when he heard of Harold's death. On his arrival he was at once acknowledged King; but great discontent was at first excited by the oppressive taxes he imposed. He **1039 A.D.**

wreaked a poor revenge on Harold's dead body; which was by his order dug up, beheaded, and flung into the Thames. Suspicion of being a party to Alfred's murder fell upon Earl Godwin, and he lost favour with the King; but, his peers having sworn to his innocence, he was reinstated. As a peace-offering, he presented to Hardicanute a ship, of which the stern was plated with gold, and which bore eighty warriors glittering with decorations of gold and silver. No striking event marked the reign of the last Dane that held the English throne. He died suddenly at Lambeth, while engaged in celebrating the marriage of a Danish noble, and was buried at Winchester.

CONTEMPORARY SOVEREIGNS.

SCOTLAND.	FRANCE.
A.D	A.D.
DUNCAN I. began to rule 1034	HENRY I.,..........................1031
MACBETH, ...1040	

CHAPTER IV.

SAXON LINE RESTORED.

1041 A.D. to 1066 A.D.—25 years.—2 Kings.

	A.D.
EDWARD the Confessor (son of Ethelred),	1041
HAROLD II. (son of Earl Godwin),	1066

Leading Feature: BEGINNING OF FRENCH INFLUENCE.

Opening of Edward's reign.	Visit of William of Normandy.	Benefits of Edward.
Favour shown to Normans.	Godwin's death.	Harold King.
Revolt of the English.	Power of Harold. [cessor.	Battle of Stamford Bridge.
	Arrangements for a suc-	Battle of Hastings.

EDWARD, son of Ethelred and half-brother of Hardicanute, being then in England, received the crown, chiefly through the influence of Godwin. The surviving son of Edmund Ironside had a prior claim to the throne; but this was forgotten in the joy with which the people hailed the restoration of the Saxon line. So great was the favour with which Edward was received, that he was permitted to take back all grants that had been made by his predecessors,—an act rendered necessary by the poverty of the throne. His resources were further increased by the confiscation of treasure amassed by his unnatural mother, Emma. The King was about forty on his accession, and had spent twenty-seven years at the Norman court. It is not surprising, therefore, that he regarded with peculiar favour the friends of his youth, and bestowed upon Normans some of the chief offices of state. The French language and fashions were adopted at the English court. Lawyers wrote their deeds and clergymen their sermons in Norman French.

This displeased the English nobles, and Godwin was foremost in revolt. Edward had married Edith, Godwin's daughter, and had advanced his sons to stations of honour; but the haughty Earl snapped all ties of family union and personal gratitude by boldly refusing to acknowledge the

King's authority. A bloody fray had taken place at Dover, a town under Godwin's protection, between the burghers and the retainers of Eustace, a Norman Count, who had married the King's sister. Edward commanded Godwin to punish the insolent citizens; but the Earl took the field rather than submit. However, a delay took place, until the Great Council should decide the points in dispute; and in the meantime Godwin's army deserted him. He was forced to seek refuge in Flanders. The Queen was deprived of her lands, and placed in custody of Edward's sister, the Abbess of Wherwell, in Hampshire.

As soon as this revolt began, Edward asked aid from William, Duke of Normandy; but, when the fleet of that prince appeared off the English shore, all need for help had passed away. However, the Norman landed with his knights, and was hospitably entertained by Edward, who, it is related, appointed him heir to the crown. William heard French spoken on all sides; saw Dover, Canterbury, and the leading towns defended by Norman garrisons; and noted many other signs of Norman influence.

1052 A.D. Next year Godwin returned; and Edward, by the advice of Stigand, an artful and ambitious priest, became reconciled to him. The Earl died soon after, leaving to his son Harold his title and his territory.

Edward, afraid of this new rival's growing power, gave to Alfgar the earldom of East Anglia, previously held by Harold. This led to war. Alfgar was driven to Wales, but in the end he recovered his dignities. The appointment of Tostig, Harold's brother, to the earldom of Northumberland, and Harold's own successes against the Welsh, greatly extended his influence. He so far reduced the Welsh spirit, that they submitted to a law dooming every Welshman found east of Offa's Dyke to the loss of his right hand.

The horrors of a disputed succession now seemed impending; and to remove this danger Edward, by the advice of the Witenagemot, sent for Edward, son of Edmund Ironside, then an exile in Hungary. He came with his wife, Agatha, and three children, Edgar, Margaret, and Christina; but died immediately on his arrival. About this time Harold, suffering shipwreck on the Norman coast, was seized by

William, and made to swear a most sacred oath to favour his pretensions to the English throne.

Edward died at the age of sixty-five, and was buried in Westminster Abbey, which had been erected by himself on the site of the old church to St. Peter. About a century after his death his name was ranked among the saints of the Romish Church; and, from his religious character, he gained the name 'Confessor.' The chief benefits he conferred upon his people were, the compilation of a code of laws, embracing all that was good in former legislation; and the repeal of the tax Dane-geld in a time of sore distress from failing crops and dying cattle.

Harold, son of Godwin, was at once chosen King by the Witan, Edgar Atheling being too young to wear a crown in times so stormy. But to compensate the Saxon prince for this injustice, the earldom of Oxford was conferred on him. It was not the fate of Harold to wear his crown in peace; for, from the day of his accession, the dread of a Norman invasion haunted him. William resolved to stake on the issue of a battle the crown, which he claimed as his own by the bequest of the Confessor; and all Normandy resounded with preparation. 1066 A.D.

Meanwhile, unexpected foes descended on the shores of England. Hardrada, King of Norway, and Tostig, the outlawed brother of Harold, sailing up the Humber, captured York, the capital of Northumbria. Harold pushed northward, and was met by the invaders at Stamford Bridge on the Derwent. There the Norwegian spearmen formed a glittering circle, their royal banner floating above them. Again and again the English cavalry dashed upon the serried ring, but without avail, until the hot Norway blood led some to break their ranks in pursuit. Instantly Harold poured his troops through the gap, and cleft the circle like a wedge. Hardrada fell shot through the neck, and Tostig soon lay dead beside him. 1066 A.D.

This battle was fought on the 25th of September, and on the 29th William of Normandy landed on the coast of Sussex, near Pevensey, and at once pressed on to Hastings. Harold was sitting at a banquet in York when the news came. Marching night and day, he reached the hill Senlac, nine miles from Hastings, on the 13th October; and here he marshalled his men, all on foot, armed with heavy battle-axes. Early on the 14th the Normans advanced to the attack, led by the consecrated banner of the Pope, archers in the van, mail-clad infantry following; while the main strength of a Norman army, lines of knights, sheathed man and horse in steel, brought up the rear. The battle began. The English battle-axes did fearful execution, and the Norman lines gave way. A panic, increased by the report of William's death, was spreading fast, when the Duke rode bareheaded to the front and restored their sinking courage. However, it was not till the wily Norman, detaching bodies of horsemen as if in flight, drew the English from their ranks, that the invaders gained any decisive advantage. Even then the islanders met the shock of their steel-clad foes with the courage of despair; nor was it until sunset, when their King fell pierced in the left eye by an arrow, that they broke and fled into the woods. Harold's mother offered for the body of her son its weight in gold; but the Conqueror refused to grant her request, and ordered the dead King to be buried on the beach. However, the remains were afterwards removed to Waltham Church. The ruins of Battle Abbey, built by William, still commemorate this fatal day, on which the crown of England passed to a race of French Kings, who wore it during more than three centuries.

CONTEMPORARY SOVEREIGNS.

SCOTLAND.	FRANCE.
A.D.	A.D.
MACBETH began to rule...1040	HENRY I.,..................1031
MALCOLM (Canmore),.......1056	PHILIP I.,....................1060

CHAPTER V.

SCOTLAND AND IRELAND DURING THE SAXON PERIOD.

| Early Scottish tribes. | Duncan and Macbeth. | Patrick. |
| Fusion of Picts and Scots. | State of Ireland. | Brian Boru. |

SCOTTISH history does not begin until the reign of Malcolm Canmore, the contemporary of Edward the Confessor and William the Conqueror. Earlier events are wrapped in fable. We know that the Romans traversed North Britain, or Caledonia, as they called it, more than once. We know that a region called Strathclyde, consisting chiefly of the basin of the Clyde, was inhabited by Britons akin to those of Wales. We find the tribes of North Britain called Picts and Scots at the close of the Roman Period; and we learn that the Scots had crossed from Ulster, and had gradually spread over the mountain districts. Such names as Galloway and Arran, in the south-west of Scotland, show a connection between that part of Britain and the west of Ireland, where lie Galway and the Isles of Arran. About 563 A.D., Columba, crossing from Ireland, blessed the land with the knowledge of Christ. The Culdees, as his followers were named, continued the good work. Under the influence of the Gospel and kindred causes, the Picts and Scots were blended into the Scottish nation about 843 A.D., when Kenneth Macalpin ruled the whole land north of the Forth; and, some hundred years later, the country was first called Scotland. But it must be remembered that the Border line ran at this time from the shore of the Forth west of Edinburgh to the mouth of the Solway. The story of Duncan's murder and Macbeth's usurpation, as drawn by Shakspere, is highly coloured, for the sake of dramatic effect. The facts are these, so far as we can now judge: Duncan ascended the throne in 1034. Six years after, he was slain near Elgin, in open daylight, by Macbeth, whose claim appears to have been stronger. His son, Malcolm Canmore, escaped to the English court; and returning thence in 1056, defeated and slew Macbeth, and was crowned King of Scotland.

IRELAND.

Ireland was in these early times much more civilized than either England or Scotland. While Britons and Romans, Picts and Scots, Saxons and Danes, were struggling for the sovereignty of the larger island, the Celts of Ireland lived in comparative peace. Druidism decayed before the divine power of the Gospel, first preached in Ireland by Patrick. His native place seems to have been Kilpatrick, near the mouth of the Clyde. In his youth he spent six years as a slave in Ireland, and then formed the resolve of preaching the Gospel in that land. Obtaining his release, he went to study for a while in France; and at the age of forty he landed in Ireland, 432 A.D. Ere long he was preaching to the Druids in their great temple at Tara, then the capital of Ireland. With Christianity the Irish people received the knowledge of letters, and learning began to flourish so much among the clergy, that students from the Continent flocked to the Irish schools. There are still existing manuscript chronicles and other works in the Irish Celtic of very ancient date. But the ravages of the Danes destroyed the peace of Ireland. Ashes and blood filled the land. The great deliverer of the island from these savage pirates was a King named Brian Boru. He defeated them in twenty-five battles. The last and most glorious was fought on the shore of Clontarf near Dublin. After the battle, the King was in his tent thanking God for his victory, when he was discovered and slain by some of the fugitive Danes—1014 A.D.

CHAPTER VI.

SOCIAL CONDITION OF THE ANGLO-SAXONS.

King and Queen.	Crime and its punishment.	Coins.
Freemen of different ranks.	Ordeals.	Early Idolatry.
Slaves.	Anglo-Saxon houses.	Occupations of the monks.
The Great Council.	Daily life.	Language.

AT the head of the Anglo-Saxon nation stood the Cyning, or King (from cunnan, 'to know.') He was elected by the Great Council from among the relatives of the late King; and was generally chosen on account of his fitness for the office. The name 'Queen,' and the honours of royalty, were conferred on the wife of the King, until Eadburga, Queen of Wessex, forfeited all distinctions by poisoning her husband. From that time the Anglo-Saxon Queens bore no title but 'the lady;' and none except Judith, wife of Ethelwulf, received the crown, or sat on the throne beside her husband. Indeed, in style and position, the wife of the Anglo-Saxon monarchs resembled the lady rather than the Queen of our day. The monk Ingulf tells us that, when he was a boy, Edith, wife of Edward the Confessor, would often stop him as he came from school, make him repeat his grammar lesson; and, if he did well, would give him a piece of silver and send him to the pantry.

Next to the King were the Eldermen, or Earls. Governing in the name of their sovereign districts called shires, they led to battle the men under their rule, presided with the Bishop over the courts of justice, and received one-third of the fines and royal rents paid within their counties. The inferior nobles were called Thanes (from thegnian, 'to serve,') and consisted of those who possessed at least five hides of land. The lowest class of freemen were the Ceorls (hence churl) or husbandmen; with whom we may rank the Burghers, or inhabitants of towns. The latter were engaged in trade, and were in most respects freemen.

Two-thirds of the Anglo-Saxon nation were in a state of slavery. The largest class consisted of those who lived on the land of their lord, close to his castle (Norman, *ville;*

Saxon *tun*, whence our word town); and were called by the Normans 'Villains.' Besides those born in bondage, all captives in war and persons arrested for debt or crime became slaves. Sad and humiliating was the ceremony of degradation. Before a crowd of witnesses, the hapless man laid down the sword and the spear which he had borne as a freeman, and, whilst in a kneeling posture he placed his head beneath his•master's hand, took up the bill and the goad. Many slaves were released by the bounty of their masters; others, engaging in trade and handicraft, made money enough to buy their freedom. Sale and purchase of slaves were quite common, the usual price being four times that of an ox. Foreign slaves were often imported; and although all export was forbidden by law, the Anglo-Saxons of the coast carried on a profitable trade in men and women. Bristol was long notorious for its slave-market.

The great council of the Anglo-Saxons was called Witenagemot, or 'the assembly of the wise,' and was formed of the higher clergy and the nobles. They met regularly at Christmas, Easter, and Whitsuntide, but were often summoned on special occasions. They were the advisers of the King, the judges of state criminals, and had the general superintendence of the courts of justice. One important branch of their power has been already noticed—in their hands lay the appointment of a new King.

Throughout the land justice was administered in various courts; in which also, before magistrates and witnesses, all bargains of purchase and sale beyond the value of twenty pennies were concluded. The execution of the laws was vested in officers called Reeves; of whom the chief in each county was called Shire-reeve, and was the original of our Sheriff. The morality of the Anglo-Saxons was very far from being pure. The characters of even their best Kings were stained with drunkenness and worse vices. The chief crimes were murder and theft; and for these certain fines were inflicted. On the life of every Anglo-Saxon freeman, according to his rank, was set a price, called 'were,' ranging from two to six thousand shillings. If a man was killed, the murderer, on conviction, paid 'were' to the widow or heir of his victim: the transgressor of the law forfeited his 'were' instead of his life to the King. Slaves were imprisoned or whipped; but the meanest freeman was exempt from this disgrace. Theft became so common in the time of the later Anglo-Saxon Kings, that it was punished by death. This was abolished by Canute, who substituted mutilation, condemning a thief, three times convicted, to the loss of his eyes, nose, ears, and upper lip.

There were two methods by which a man accused of crime could clear himself. The first was by swearing publicly to his innocence, and bringing a number of his neighbours—from four to seventy-two, in proportion to the offence—to confirm his oath. If this plan failed, recourse was had to the ordeal. Those most used were by hot water, and by fire. For the former, a caldron of boiling water was set in the church, and a piece of stone or iron placed in it. Before witnesses, the accused plunged his bare arm into the water and took out the weight. The priest wrapping the scalded limb in clean linen, set on it the seal of the church. It was opened on the third day, and, if the wound was perfectly healed, the accused was pronounced innocent. In the ordeal by fire, a bar of red-hot iron was placed on a small pillar, and the prisoner, grasping it, made three steps with it in his hand, and then threw it down. Innocence or guilt was decided in the same manner as in the ordeal by water.

The houses of the Anglo-Saxons improved very much during the six centuries of this period. At first they were nothing better than thatched huts with holes in the walls to admit the light. Even the cathedrals and the houses of the Kings were built of wood, not very well jointed; for we read of Alfred making lanterns to protect his candles from the draughts that swept through the chinks in his palace-walls. The dwellings of the lower and middle classes continued to be built of wood; but about the seventh century masonry was used for the chief buildings. The few still existing specimens of architecture ascribed to the Anglo-Saxons are built of small rough stones, in a rude and massive style. But the evidence that these are Anglo-Saxon rests on very uncertain ground.

The daily life of even the noblest Anglo-Saxons was that of a half-savage people. The war and turbulence, which were the chief characteristics of at least four centuries of this period, were not favourable to the cultivation of the domestic virtues. When not engaged in war, the nobles amused themselves in hunting and hawking; and when the sports of the day were over, all—master and servant—met in the great hall. At the upper end of this, on a dais or raised part, was placed a rude table, canopied with hangings of cloth, to serve as a protection from draughts of air, and from the rain, which often leaked through the roof; and round this sat the lord, his family, and his guests. This table was served by slaves, who knelt as they offered to each huge joints on the spit; from which the chiefs cut slices with their daggers. The principal article of food was swine's flesh; besides this, game and fish of various kinds, coarse cakes, and green pulse were used. The favourite drink was mead, a liquor fermented from honey and water. Wine, beef, mutton, and wheaten bread were delicacies found only at the tables of the highest. The chief servants took their meal next, and in turn passed the joints to the lower end of the hall, where slaves, hounds, and hawks squabbled over the fragments of the feast. The meal over, drinking began, and continued till all, even the clergy, were intoxicated. To beguile the time, the Saxon harp of five strings was passed round; and each took his turn in singing verses to its music. This general practice of the musical art is almost the only redeeming trait in a picture of coarse sensuality; but the tones of the harp were soon drowned in wild shouts of drunkenness, and often in the clashing of brawlers' swords, nor did the riot cease till sleep brought silence. They slept where they had feasted, lying on straw or rushes, and covered with their clothes. The ladies spent their time more peacefully, and to more purpose, in the use of the needle and the distaff. The linen and the woollen cloths, of which the long cloaks and close tunics of their lords were made, were the produce of their industry; and some specimens of their skill in embroidery still exist, the principal one being the celebrated Bayeux tapestry, on which are depicted in exquisite needle-work the scenes of the Norman Conquest.

We know very little about the coinage of the Anglo-Saxons. They had none but foreign gold; the coin most used was the Byzant, equivalent to £15 sterling of our money. Their silver coins were the penny, halfpenny, and farthing; which seem to have resembled in size and value our florin, shilling, and sixpence. Their only copper coin, called 'styca,' was value for one-fourth of their farthing, or a little more than our penny.

When the Anglo-Saxons settled in Britain, they were the slaves of a gross and absurd idolatry, which prevailed among all the northern tribes of Europe. They dedicated each day of the week to a particular deity; and we still name the days after their fashion. Sun daeg (Sunday), and Moon daeg (Monday) were set apart for the worship of the great lights of heaven; Tuiscaes daeg (Tuesday), Wodenes daeg (Wednesday), Thores daeg (Thursday), and Freyaes daeg (Friday) were sacred to Tuisca, Woden, Thor, and Freya; while Saturnes daeg (Saturday) was devoted to the service of Saturn, a god borrowed from the Roman mythology. Though Christianity had been introduced into Britain before the time of Augustine, it was not till he and his followers landed in Kent that the heathenism of the Anglo-Saxons was overthrown. The Anglo-Saxon priests spent their leisure in the practice of many arts. Painting on glass and working in metals were favourite employments of even the highest ecclesiastics; and not a few churches owed their bells and their coloured windows to the Dunstans of this age. The monasteries were now, as they continued to be for many centuries, almost the only seats of learning; and from their quiet cells issued the scanty pages of our Anglo-Saxon literature.

It must not be forgotten that the great body of the pure English tongue, as we read it in the Bible and the Pilgrim's Progress, as we speak it in our streets and by our firesides, had its origin in the Anglo-Saxon period. The Danes introduced some slight changes of construction, and left a few geographical names, such as those ending in 'by,' the Danish for town; but their rule in the island made no permanent impression on the language, which has continued, through all changes of the nation, to be in spirit and in structure essentially Saxon.

LEADING AUTHORS OF THE ANGLO-SAXON PERIOD.

GILDAS,..............................The first British historian—died 570 A.D.
ALDHELM,.........................A famous Latin scholar—died 709 A.D.
BEDE,................................Called 'Venerable'—born at Sunderland—chief work, 'The History of the Church of the Angles'—died 735 A.D.
ALCUIN,............................Born at York—pupil of Bede—teacher of Charlemagne—wrote poetry, theology, and elementary science—died 804 A.D.
JOHN SCOTUS ERIGENA,...A native of Ireland—flourished about middle of 9th century—lived chiefly in France—said to have been 'the only learned layman of the Dark Ages.'
CAEDMON,........................A monk of Whitby—the earliest writer in Anglo-Saxon—wrote religious poetry on the Creation, &c.—lived in the 8th century.
ALFRED,...........................King of England—translated the Psalms, Bede's History, Æsop's Fables, &c., into Anglo-Saxon—died 901 A.D.
ASSER,..............................A Welshman—writer of Alfred's life—died 909 A.D.
ÆLFRIC,...........................Called the 'Grammarian,' from a Latin Grammar he wrote—Archbishop of Canterbury in close of 10th century—composer of eighty sermons in Anglo-Saxon.

LEADING DATES—ANGLO-SAXON PERIOD.

GENERAL EVENTS.	A.D.		A.D.
Landing of the Jutes,	449	Massacre of Danes,	1002
Heptarchy established,	582		
Landing of Augustine,	596	**BATTLES.**	
Cambridge University founded by Sebert,	644	Hengsdown Hill,	835
First landing of Danes,	787	Merton,	871
Egbert crowned,	827	Ethandune,	878
Alfred made King,	871	Stamford Bridge,	1066
Oxford University founded by Alfred,	886	Hastings,	1066

GENEALOGICAL TREES

CONNECTING THE ANGLO-SAXON AND NORMAN PERIODS.

SAXON LINE.

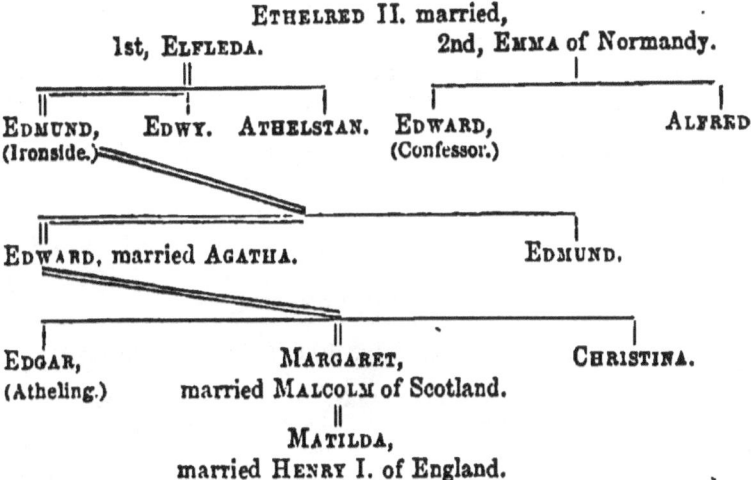

NORMAN LINE.

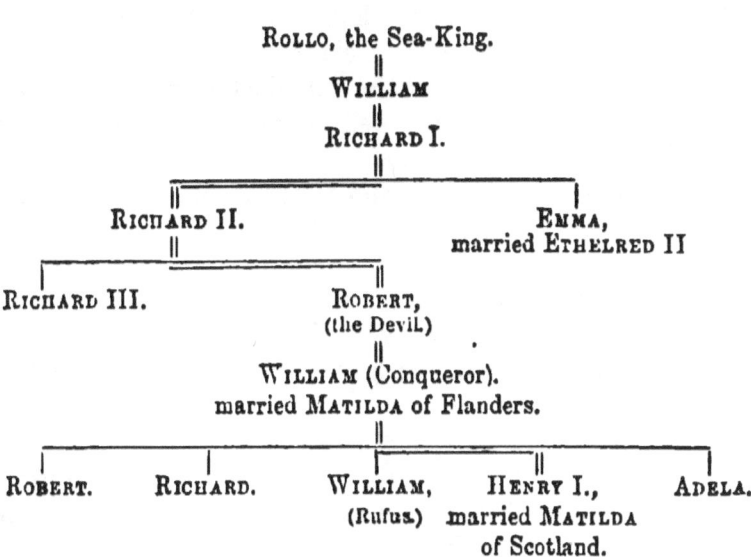

EARLY NORMAN KINGS.

From 1066 A.D. to 1154 A.D.—88 years.—4 Kings.

A.D.

WILLIAM I. (The Conqueror),......began to reign 1066.
WILLIAM II. (Rufus), Son,................................1087.
HENRY I. (Beauclerc), Brother,........................1100.
STEPHEN (Count of Blois), Nephew,..................1135 to 1154.

Leading Feature: **ESTABLISHMENT OF THE FEUDAL SYSTEM.**

CHAPTER I.

WILLIAM I. THE CONQUEROR.

Born 1027 A.D.—Began to Reign 1066 A.D.—Died 1087 A.D.

Edgar elected King.	Visits Normandy.	Domesday-Book, curfew,
William's coronation.	Revolt in west and north.	forest-laws.
He secures his conquest.	Treatment of Saxons.	Death. [qualities.
	Troubles of latter life.	Character and personal

THE Conqueror was the illegitimate son of Robert, fifth Duke of Normandy. His wife was Matilda, daughter of Baldwin V., Earl of Flanders.

After the battle of Hastings he pushed on to Dover, which surrendered. Here he stayed eight days, until reinforced from Normandy; and then he marched towards London. There the Witan had appointed Edgar Atheling King; his chief ministers being Stigand, Archbishop of Canterbury, and two Saxon Earls, Edwin and Morcar. William fixed his camp at Berkhampstead, to cut off communication with the north. But disunion crept in among the adherents of the Saxon. Stigand was among the first to desert, and Edgar's hopes of a throne faded fast. Soon a message reached William, offering the crown; which he accepted amid the applause of the Normans.

He was crowned at Westminster on Christmas-day; but not without tumult. Aldred, Archbishop of York, during the ceremony asked the Saxons if they received William as their King. They assented with shouts. At once, as if on a given signal, the Normans round the Abbey, setting fire to the houses, began to plunder. All rushed from the church. William and the prelates stood alone by the altar. In haste the oath was taken and the ceremony ended. This event imbittered the feeling of the Saxons toward their conquerors.

William began his reign well. He retained the Saxon laws, granted a new charter to the citizens of London, and received Edgar among his nearest friends. But this did not last long. He felt that the sword must guard what the sword had won; and, to retain the Norman lords in his service, he rewarded them with the lands of the conquered race. The widows and heiresses of those rich nobles who had fallen on the field of Senlac were married to Normans. The churches of Normandy were decorated with the spoils of England; and among other precious gifts from William to the Pope was the golden banner of Harold. He built a fortress, where the Tower of London now stands; and strengthened his position in Winchester—then the capital—by erecting a similar stronghold.

Having thus spent six months, he passed over to Normandy, carrying in his train the flower of England's nobility. His friend Fitzosbern and his half-brother Odo were appointed Regents; and they ruled with a rod of iron. The Saxons rose; and, when the Regents strove to trample out the flame of insurrection, it broke forth with greater violence than ever. After eight months William returned; and, though the spirit of revolt seemed to die in his terrible presence, it still lingered in the west and north. The fall of Exeter reduced the west to peace; and Edwin and Morcar, who had raised the standard of rebellion in the north, were surprised and forced to yield: York opened its gates, and even Malcolm of Scotland for a time owned the supremacy of the Norman.

Twice the sons of Harold, who had taken refuge in Ireland, landed in England, once near Bristol, and once near Plymouth; but they were driven to their ships with great loss.

Again the English of the north rose, massacred a body of Norman horse at Durham, and laid siege to York. They were joined by Edgar, who, having set out with his mother and sisters for Hungary, was driven northward by a storm, and had been for some time the guest of Malcolm at Dunfermline. But William obliged them to raise the siege; and, having plundered the city, returned to the south. A Danish squadron arrived with timely help, and York was re-captured by the English. The King again marched northward, the English rising everywhere as he passed. Turning upon these, he defeated them, and then carried the northern capital at the sword's point. Here he kept his Christmas court, having sent to Winchester for his crown. With fire and sword he now traversed York and Durham, taking a revenge so terrible, that from the Ouse to the Tyne there stretched for almost a century a vast wilderness, studded with blackened ruins, its soil unbroken by the plough. On his southward march he left behind him many strong castles, garrisoned by Norman soldiers.

1069 A.D.

No dignity, no power, very little land were now permitted to remain with the Saxons. Even the monasteries, which were the banks of that time, afforded no safety from the royal officers, who without remorse rifled the sacred treasuries. The Saxon prelates, too, were obliged to resign their cathedrals to Norman strangers. Of the latter, the most distinguished was Lanfranc, appointed Archbishop of Canterbury in the room of Stigand. Many of the Saxon landholders, when driven from their estates, fled into the woods, and kept up an incursive warfare. Hereward the Saxon was the most noted. He built a wooden fort in the Isle of Ely, where, surrounded by marshes, he long bade defiance to William. Malcolm of Scotland, who had married Margaret, sister of Edgar Atheling, now felt himself forced to be on a friendly footing with the Conqueror, though he refused to deliver up the Saxon refugees who had fled to the north.

1072 A.D.

William's latter days were imbittered by many woes. A plot to seize the kingdom was formed by some Normans, dissatisfied with their rewards. They were defeated, and every prisoner lost his right foot. His half-brother Odo, too, incurred his anger by aiming at the Popedom, and was imprisoned in Normandy during the King's life. But his chief troubles arose from his own children. Robert, the eldest, surnamed Curt-hose from his short legs, was nominal Duke of Normandy. His brothers, William and Henry, jealous of his power, insulted him by throwing a pitcher of water from a balcony on him in the street of the small French town L'Aigle. He rushed with drawn sword to take vengeance on them; but, on his father's interference, he withdrew, and left the town that evening. For five years he wandered in neighbouring countries, secretly supported by his mother, Matilda. At length he fixed his quarters in the Castle of Gerberoi, which William besieged, and before which the father and son met unwittingly in single combat, when Robert wounded his father in the hand. **1077 A.D.**

William's chief acts were the compilation of 'Domesday Book,' the institution of the curfew-bell, and the enactment of the forest-laws. The first was a register of English land, which occupied six years in completion, and which still remains in two vellum manuscripts, one folio, the other quarto, recording the size of each estate, its division into arable, pasture, meadow, and woodland, the name of the owner, and other details. **1080 to 1086 A.D.** The curfew-bell (from *couvre feu*, 'cover fire') was rung at eight o'clock in the evening, as a signal for putting out all fires and candles; and, though long looked on as a tyrannical measure, may have been wisely intended to preserve the wooden houses from being burned. The forest-laws—the origin of our game-laws—inflicted upon the man who killed a deer, a wild boar, or other beast of chase, the terrible punishment of having his eyes torn out. The land between Winchester and the sea was converted into an immense hunting-park by the King, who burned cottages and churches to clear the ground for his plantation. This still remains, under the name of the New Forest. Justices of the Peace, the Courts of Chancery, Exchequer, and Common Pleas had origin in this reign. The Cinque Ports—Dover, Hastings, Romney, Hythe, and Sandwich—were now fortified. To these have since been added Winchelsea and Rye. The Channel Islands were first annexed to England at the Conquest.

The revival of the Dane-geld, forfeitures, royal rents, and tolls could not satisfy the King's avarice, although they raised his revenue to more than £1000 a-day. His reign was to the Saxons one scene of misery; beginning in bloodshed and spoliation, it ended in famine and pestilence, caused by the rains and storms of 1086.

The French King sneered at William's corpulence when old; and from this trifling cause a war began. The English King, besieging Mante, rode out to view the burning town; and the plunging of his horse, which trod on some hot ashes, bruised him severely against the high pommel of his saddle. The bruise inflamed; and, after six weeks, the Conqueror died near Rouen. His corpse, deserted by all his minions, who fled with the plunder of the palace, lay for three hours naked on the ground, and owed its burial to the charity of a French knight, who conveyed it to Caen.

The character and appearance of the Conqueror are sketched in the Saxon Cronicle. Stern and ambitious; avaricious in his latter days, and brooking no interference with his will; of short stature and corpulent; of a fierce countenance, and devoted to the sport of hunting: he owed the terror of his name both to the force of his passions and to his immense bodily strength; which, we are told, was so great that he could bend on horseback a bow which no other could draw on foot.

CONTEMPORARY SOVEREIGNS.

SCOTLAND.	A.D.	EMPEROR.	A.D.
MALCOLM III.		HENRY IV.	
FRANCE.			
PHILIP I.			
		POPES.	
SPAIN.		ALEXANDER II., died	1073
SANCHO II., died,	1073	GREGORY VII., died	1085
ALPHONSO VI.		VICTOR III., died	1087

CHAPTER II.

WILLIAM II.—RUFUS.

Born 1057 A.D.—Began to reign 1087 A.D.—Died 1100 A.D.

William seizes the crown. Odo's plot. Designs upon Normandy.	Scotland and Wales. Revolt of Mowbray. William's extortion.	Normandy pledged by Death of Rufus. [Robert. Character and works.

WILLIAM, surnamed Rufus from his red complexion, was third son of the Conqueror. Robert was, in accordance with his father's will, acknowledged Duke of Normandy; but, while he was enjoying the new dignity of his coronet at Rouen, his more active and ambitious brother had crossed to England, and, within three weeks after the Conqueror's death, had secured the crown, chiefly by the influence of Lanfranc.

A deep-laid plot to set Robert on the throne, of which the leading spirit was Odo, Bishop of Bayeux, and Earl of Kent, shook the newly founded dominion of William. But the English, conciliated by some temporary concessions, and still remembering the cruel regency of Odo, supported Rufus; and at their head, the King, storming the Castle of Rochester, drove into exile the rebellious prelate, who sailed for Normandy, followed by the deep curses of the Saxons.

The duchy of Normandy, feebly ruled by the indolent though brave Robert, had great attractions for Rufus; who, by the skilful use of the treasures hoarded by his father, soon made himself master of all the fortresses on the right bank of the Seine, and prepared to follow up his fraud by force. But the Norman barons and the French King reconciled the brothers, who agreed that the survivor should hold the united dominions. **1091 A.D.**

No longer occupied with Norman affairs, William led an army against Malcolm of Scotland. Peace was made between the two countries; but next year Malcolm, enraged at the settlement of an English colony at Carlisle, which he considered a Scottish town, invaded Northumberland. Here he died before Alnwick Castle, some historians say pierced in the eye by Roger de Mowbray, who was handing him the keys of the castle on the point of a lance, and who afterwards bore the name Pierce-eye, or Percy. Wales, too, was traversed by Rufus, but with little success; and he was forced to content himself with the old plan of erecting a chain of forts round the mountain-land.

Robert Mowbray, the strongest of the Norman barons, rebelled, and within Bamborough Castle defied the attack of William. Being decoyed, however, from this stronghold, he was made prisoner, and was brought before the castle walls, where Matilda, his wife, still held out. She refused to yield until she saw an executioner preparing to tear out her husband's eyes; then, to save him, she gave up the keys. For thirty years he lingered in the dungeons of Windsor Castle.

1095 A.D.

The extravagance of Rufus knew no bounds. The chief instrument of his extortion was Ralph, surnamed Flambard, or the Torch, a dissolute Romish priest. Among other means of raising money, this minister devised the plan of keeping abbeys and bishoprics vacant, that the King might receive their revenues; and of demanding, from those who received appointments, large sums as the price of the benefices. One of the chief sufferers by this system was Anselm, successor of Lanfranc. He had been forced by the King to accept the office, and yet the persecutions he endured from William and Ralph obliged him to leave England.

William had agreed to repay Robert for the lost castles; but the promise was never kept, for falsehood was a part of William's character; and again the sword was drawn by the brothers. Just then came an offer from Robert to transfer the government of Normandy and Maine to the English King for five years, on receipt of 10,000 merks (the merk was 13s. 4d.) The wars of the Cross had begun. The appeal of Pope Urban II. and the fierce war-cry of Peter the Hermit had stirred all Europe from Sicily to Norway, and the knights of the first Crusade were on the march to rescue from the infidels the sepulchre of our Saviour. Robert burned to join their ranks, and hence his offer. William at once agreed to the terms; and the merks, wrung from the hapless English, carried Robert and his vassals to Palestine. Edgar Atheling, too, followed the red-cross banner of France.

1096 A.D.

Rufus died by violence. He was at Malwood, a hunting-lodge in the New Forest, on the fatal day. Disturbed by feverish dreams during the previous night, he had given up the idea of hunting; but the wine he drank at dinner—then a forenoon meal—scattered his fears, and he rode into the forest. His train gradually left him in the heat of the chase, and at sunset they found him lying dead, a broken shaft sticking in his breast. A cart bore the corpse to Winchester, where it was buried within the cathedral, but with no religious service. Whose hand sped the shaft none can tell. The common story fastens the guilt on Walter Tyrrel. Some say that Tyrrel's arrow, aimed at a stag, glanced from a tree and pierced the King's heart; while a dark whisper of the time pointed to his brother Henry as the murderer.

1100 A.D.

Rapacious, prodigal, debauched, and cruel, the character of Rufus bears no redeeming feature. In person he was short and corpulent, with flaxen hair and red face; and he stammered in his speech. A wall round the Tower, a bridge over the Thames, and the Hall of Westminster were the chief public works of a King who did little else for his people.

CONTEMPORARY SOVEREIGNS.

SCOTLAND.
A.D.
MALCOLM III., died............1093
DONALD BAIN, deposed......1094
DUNCAN, died...................1095
DONALD BAIN, died...........1097
EDGAR.

FRANCE.
PHILIP I.

SPAIN.
A.D.
ALPHONSO VI.

EMPEROR.
HENRY IV.

POPES.
URBAN II., died...................1099
PASCHAL II.

CHAPTER III.

HENRY I.—BEAUCLERC.

Born 1070 A.D.—Began to reign 1100 A.D.—Died 1135 A.D.

Henry seizes the crown.	Disputes with the Church.	Henry's death and character.
His early acts and first marriage.	Prince William drowned.	Improvements.
He gains Normandy.	The Queens. Maud.	Learning and literature.

HENRY, youngest son of the Conqueror, immediately on his brother's death, rode to Winchester and seized the royal treasures. These being secured, he hastened to Westminster, and was there crowned on the following Sunday by Maurice, Bishop of London. Robert, whose the crown was by right, still lingered in Italy on his homeward journey. The early acts of Henry, like those of most usurpers, were intended to please the people. He published a charter of liberties, promising to abolish the Curfew and the Dane-geld, to restore the laws of the Confessor, and to redress the grievances under which the nation had groaned since the Conquest. His marriage with Matilda, daughter of Malcolm, the Scottish King, and niece of Edgar Atheling, united the Norman and Saxon royal lines, and thus began that blending of the races from which arose the true English nation.

Flambard, the minister of Rufus, had been imprisoned in the Tower by the new King, to please the English; but, a friend having conveyed to him a rope hidden in a jar of wine, he escaped by a window, and reached Normandy. Robert had just arrived with his Italian wife, and was easily induced to invade England. He was marching on Winchester, when Henry overtook him. The princes met in conference between the armies, and a few minutes decided the treaty. Robert agreed to give up his claim on England in return for a yearly pension of 3000 merks. This allowance, however, he was afterwards forced to resign as ransom to Henry, in whose power he had unsuspiciously placed himself. The disputes between the brothers grew worse daily, and ended in open war. The first campaign decided nothing; in the second Robert lost his coronet and his freedom at the battle of Tenchebrai. He was brought to England, and, after thirty years in

1106 A.D.

prison, died at Cardiff Castle, a year before his brother. Some writers say that his eyes were burned out; and indeed the character of Henry seems to justify the charge. The war lingered for many years, during which the claims of William, Robert's son, were supported by Louis of France; but Henry triumphed at the battle of Brenville, and his son received the dukedom.

During these wars Henry had been involved in a dispute with the Church. The contested points were Henry's claims that the clergy should do homage for their lands, and that he should be permitted to use the right of his predecessors, who were accustomed in great state to invest new abbots and prelates with the ring and crosier of their office. Anselm, who sided with the Pope, was a second time banished; but in the end Henry gave up his claims,—a concession which, after all, did not affect the substance of his power.

The King and his son, William, now aged eighteen, crossed to Normandy, to receive the homage of the barons; but on the voyage back the prince was drowned. When about to embark with his father, a sailor, named Fitzstephen, whose father had steered the Conqueror's ship to England, offered to the prince the use of 'The White Ship,' manned by fifty skilful rowers. The other vessels left the shore early in the day; but the White Ship delayed till sunset, the crew drinking and feasting on deck. They set out by moonlight, and were rowing vigorously along to overtake the King's ship, when the vessel struck on a rock in the Race of Alderney and went to pieces. William might have been saved, for he had secured a boat; but, melted by a sister's shrieks, he returned, and the boat sank beneath the crowds that leapt from the ship's side. None lived to tell the sad story but a poor butcher of Rouen, who floated ashore on a broken mast. The news was kept from Henry for some days, when a page, flinging himself in tears at the monarch's feet, told all. It is said that Henry never smiled again. This event revived the hopes of Robert's son, who had meanwhile received the earldom of Flanders; but his death of a wound, inflicted at the gates of Alost, left Henry without a rival for the Norman coronet.

More than two years before Prince William's death,

1120 A.D.

Henry lost his wife Matilda. They had been estranged for twelve years, which the Queen had spent in devotion and quiet benevolence, music and poetry forming her chief amusements. The first stone bridge in England was built over the Lea by her orders. She left two children; William, who was drowned; and Maud, who married Henry V., Emperor of Germany, and was left a widow after six months. Henry's second wife was a French princess, Adelais, daughter of the Duke of Louvain. She had no children.

Thus left without a son to inherit his throne, Henry exacted from the prelates and nobles an oath to support Maud's claim. At the same time, to strengthen his connections in France, he caused her to marry Geoffrey Plantagenet, Count of Anjou, a boy of sixteen,—an alliance which pleased neither English nor Normans. The marriage was not a happy one, and the broils between Maud and her husband disturbed the latter years of Henry's reign.

The King died at St. Denis in Normandy, after seven days' illness, brought on by eating to excess of lampreys.

He was, like Rufus, cruel, faithless, and debauched; but was more accomplished and refined. He gained his surname, Beauclerc or 'Fine Scholar,' by translating 'Æsop's Fables.' Several attempts on his life made him suspicious. He frequently changed his bed-room, and kept sword and shield near his pillow. His great aim was to extend his power on the Continent; for he despised his English subjects, and looked on them as fit only to supply money for his schemes of pleasure and ambition.

Henry was the first English King who delivered a formal speech from the throne. During his reign silver half-pence and farthings, which had previously been formed by clipping the penny into halves and quarters, were made round; the coinage, which had been debased, was renewed, and severe laws were made against false coiners; rents were paid in money instead of in kind; a standard of weights and measures was established, the ell being fixed at the length of the King's arm; and the woollen manufacture was introduced by some Flemings, who settled first on the Tweed, and afterwards at Haverfordwest in Pembroke, and Worsted in Norfolk.

Himself a scholar, Beauclerc encouraged learning. English students might be found in Spain studying among the Moors medicine and mathematics; others remaining at home drew the truths of science from the pages of Latin writers. A curious account is given of the teaching at Cambridge at this time. At first the students met in a large barn, but in the second year each teacher had a separate room. Very early in the morning one master taught the rules of grammar; at six, a second lectured on the logic of Aristotle; at nine, Cicero and Quintilian were construed and expounded; and before twelve, a theological class received an explanation of difficult passages in the Scriptures. Romances—so called from being written in a corrupted form of the ancient Roman tongue—now took the place of the Saxon poems. They described the adventures of some great warrior;—Alexander, Arthur, and Charlemagne were the favourites. These were dressed up as feudal knights, and made the heroes of wild adventures,—slaying dragons and giants, storming enchanted castles, setting free beautiful ladies, and doing other wondrous deeds.

1110 A.D.

CONTEMPORARY SOVEREIGNS.

SCOTLAND.	A.D.	EMPERORS.	A.D.
EDGAR, died	1106	HENRY IV., died	1106
ALEXANDER I., died..,	1124	HENRY V., died	1125
DAVID I.		LOTHAIRE II.	

FRANCE.			
PHILIP I., died	1108	POPES.	
LOUIS VI.		PASCHAL II., died	1118
SPAIN.		GELASIUS II., died	1119
ALPHONSO VI., died	1109	CALIXTUS II., died	1124
ALPHONSO VII., died	1133	HONORIUS II., died	1130
ALPHONSO VIII.		INNOCENT II.	

CHAPTER IV.

STEPHEN, EARL OF BLOIS.

Born 1105 A.D.—Began to reign 1135 A.D.—Died 1154 A.D.

| Stephen made King. Battle of the Standard. | War between Maud and Stephen. Henry acknowledged heir. | Death and character of Stephen. |

STEPHEN, third son of Adela, the Conqueror's daughter, who had married the Earl of Blois, claimed the vacant throne in opposition to Maud. He was first prince of the blood royal, and had in his favour the feeling of feudal times, that it was disgraceful for men to submit to a woman's rule. His brother Henry, Bishop of Winchester, gained for him the leading clergy, and he was joyfully received by the citizens of the capital and of London. The embalmed body of Henry was escorted to Reading Abbey by Stephen, who helped to bear the coffin. After the burial, at a meeting of Prelates and Barons held in Oxford, the Earl, already crowned King, swore to abolish the Dane-geld, to preserve the rights of the clergy, and to allow the barons the privilege of hunting in their own forests, and of building new castles on their estates. These concessions gained a strong party for Stephen; but the immediate result of the last was, that there arose throughout England one hundred and twenty-six new castles, which, with those built before, long continued to be the strongholds of lawless robber nobles, who lived by plunder, and often headed their vassals against the King himself.

David of Scotland was the first to draw the sword for Maud. Thrice in one year he ravaged with pitiless cruelty Northumberland, which he claimed as his own. In his third invasion he reached Yorkshire; but was there met at Northallerton by the northern Barons and their vassals, who had been roused to action by the aged Thurstan, Archbishop of York. There was fought the battle of the Standard. Above the English forces rose the mast of a ship, adorned with the ancient banners of three Saxon saints, and surmounted by a cross and a silver box containing the sacramental wafer; the whole being bound to a rude car. Hand in hand the

1138 A.D.

Aug. 22.

English chiefs swore to conquer or die, then knelt in prayer, and rose to battle. The Scots rushed to the onset with shouts, and bore back the English van. The flanks, too, yielded; but round the Standard the English spears formed an unbroken front. For two hours the Scottish swordsmen strove, amid unceasing showers of Saxon arrows, to hew their way to victory; but they spent their strength in vain, and the dragon-flag of Scotland was hurried from the field, blood-stained, torn, and drooping, like the flying relics of that gallant army which had marched at sunrise beneath its brilliant folds. More than 12,000 Scots lay dead. David collected his scattered forces at Carlisle, where he was joined on the third day by his son Henry, who had escaped into the woods by following the pursuit as an English knight. The energies of the Scottish King were not yet exhausted; but early in the next year peace was made. All Northumberland, except Bamborough and Newcastle, was conferred on Prince Henry of Scotland; and five Scottish nobles were given as hostages to Stephen.

Maud soon landed on the southern coast with 140 knights. At first she occupied Arundel Castle in Sussex; but, with a generosity more chivalrous than politic, Stephen permitted her to reach Bristol, the chief stronghold of her half-brother, Robert, Earl of Gloucester. Civil war began. **1139 A.D. Sept. 30.** The Barons, who lived like independent Kings within their strong castles, watched its progress without joining much in its operations; the people were mercilessly robbed, imprisoned, and tortured by them; trade and tillage were neglected; and a man might have ridden for a whole day in some districts without seeing a cultivated field or an inhabited dwelling. Maud's cause was at first successful. At the battle of Lincoln, Stephen, whose sword and battle-axe had been shivered in his grasp, was brought to the ground **1141 A.D.** by a stone, and made prisoner. Heavily fettered, he was cast into the dungeons of Bristol Castle; while his wife, Matilda of Boulogne, withdrew to Kent. Maud was now acknowledged Queen by the clergy; but her scornful arrogance soon estranged her warmest supporters. The men of Kent, rising in Stephen's cause, entered London; and Maud, alarmed at the pealing of bells and the shouts of the citizens, fled on horseback to Oxford. The failure of an attack on Winchester, in which her brother Robert was taken prisoner, ruined her cause; and Stephen, exchanged for the Earl of Gloucester, sat once more on the throne. Maud still held Oxford, and was there besieged by the King. She sustained the siege far into the winter, in hopes that Stephen would yield to the severity of the weather; but famine forced her to leave the castle. With three knights clad in white, in order to escape the eye of Stephen's sentinels, she fled over the snow, crossed the Thames on the ice, and reached Wallingford. She remained for four years longer in England, holding Gloucester as the centre of her sway, which was acknowledged in the western half of the kingdom. Then, having lost by death her chief supporters, Milo of Hereford and Robert of Gloucester, she retired to Normandy.

1142 A.D.

Her son Henry had been meanwhile growing up. He had been knighted at Carlisle by his uncle David; had succeeded, on his father's death, to Normandy and Anjou; and had gained Aquitaine by his marriage with Eleanor of Poitou, the divorced wife of the French King. Thus powerful in France, he invaded England, to wrest from Stephen the crown of his grandfather; but the sudden death of Stephen's eldest son, Eustace, hindered the war, and a treaty was made at Winchester, by which Henry was acknowledged heir to the English throne, while William, surviving son of Stephen, inherited the earldom of Boulogne and the private domains of his father. Stephen died in less than a year afterwards at Dover, and was buried in the tomb of his wife and son at Faversham Abbey in Kent.

1152 A.D.

1154 A.D.

He seems to have been a man of courage, promptness, and perseverance; generous to friends, forbearing to enemies, and affable to all. But the civil wars, which filled his reign, prevent us from judging of his character as a King. His figure was tall, muscular, and commanding.

CONTEMPORARY SOVEREIGNS.

SCOTLAND.		EMPERORS.	
	A.D.		A.D.
DAVID I., died	1153	LOTHAIRE II., died	1138
MALCOLM IV.		CONRAD III., died	1152
		FREDERIC I.	
FRANCE.		POPES.	
LOUIS VI., died	1137	INNOCENT II., died	1143
LOUIS VII		CELESTIN II., died	1144
		LUCIUS II., died	1145
SPAIN.		EUGENIUS III., died	1153
ALPHONSO VIII.		ANASTASIUS IV.	

CHAPTER V.

SCOTLAND DURING THE NORMAN PERIOD.

From 1056 A.D. to 1153 A.D.—97 years—6 Kings.

	A.D.
MALCOLM III. (son of Duncan) ....began to rule	1056
DONALD BAIN (brother)...	1093
DUNCAN (son of Malcolm III.)	1094
DONALD BAIN again usurps	1095
EDGAR (son of Malcolm III.).......................................	1097
ALEXANDER I. (brother)	1106
DAVID I. (youngest brother)................................	1124-1153

Influence of Saxon Margaret.	Claims of the English Prelates.
Contest for the Throne.	War with England.

MALCOLM III. was surnamed Canmore, or 'Bighead.' Two years after the Normans conquered England, he married the Saxon Margaret, sister of Edgar Atheling. The Queen, Margaret, did much to encourage religion and industry among the Scots; and, through her influence, Malcolm assumed more state than any of his predecessors. Gold and silver plate were to be seen on the royal table.

At this time the Scottish Kings claimed Cumberland and Northumberland. Malcolm perished in attempting to assert this right. He was slain in 1093, while besieging Alnwick Castle.

Four years were occupied in a contest for the crown between Donald Bain, a brother, and Duncan, an illegitimate son of Malcolm Canmore. Donald first seized the throne, but was soon expelled by Duncan. In eighteen months Duncan was murdered, and Donald again became King; but in 1097 the old usurper was dethroned by an army from England.

Edgar, son of Malcolm Canmore, succeeded, and reigned peacefully for nine years.

His brother, Alexander I., then came to the throne. The chief event of this reign was a contest between the King and the English prelates, who claimed the right of consecrating the Bishop of St. Andrews. The King firmly maintained the independence of the Scottish clergy. He died in 1124.

David I., the youngest of Malcolm Canmore's sons, succeeded. It was he who fought the battle of the Standard in defence of Maud Plantagenet; but this was his only war. He was a pious and peaceful prince, and during his reign the Scottish nation advanced much in agriculture, commerce, and manufactures. He was found dead in bed, with hands clasped as if in prayer. This occurred in 1153.

Thus, while the early Norman Kings held the English throne, Saxons sat upon the throne of Scotland. The Scottish court was the grand refuge of Saxon nobles who disdained to bow to the Norman yoke; and from it came the Saxon princess, daughter of Malcolm Canmore, whose marriage with Henry I. of England united the rival races.

CHAPTER VI.

SOCIAL CONDITION OF THE NORMANS.

Feudal System.	Manner of living.
Chivalry.	Dress.
The Joust or tournament.	Coins.
Norman castles.	Language.

THE Normans brought with them into England the Feudal System, which continued to hold great power over English society, until after the last Norman King fell on Bosworth field. It is true there were some traces of a similar plan among the Saxons; but the system was fully developed on the Continent, and chiefly among the Normans. It derived its name from *feod*, or *feud*, a piece of land; and its leading feature was, that all land was under military tenure; an expression which means that a tenant, instead of paying his whole rent in corn, or cattle, or money, gave only a small portion of these, and for the rest was obliged to fight under his lord's banner without any pay, when called to arms. The King owned all land; he allotted large districts to the nobles; they subdivided these among the gentry (the Saxon *thanes*, called by the Normans *franklins*); these again sublet their land to their vassals,—in every case the higher requiring from the lower service in war. When the King needed an army, he summoned his barons; they called to arms their franklins; these, their vassals and retainers: and thus a large force was gathered round the royal standard. By this system the barons had great power; and under the Norman Kings they often rebelled, and were constantly at war with each other.

Closely interwoven with the Feudal System was chivalry or knighthood. As a knight, the King was on a level with the poorest gentleman, and passed through the same training,—serving first as a page, and then as an esquire, before he received his golden spurs and took the vows of knighthood. The night before this ceremony, the candidate for knightly honours held his *vigil;* when, within some dark chapel aisle, amid the tombs of the fallen brave, he kept a lonely and silent watch over the arms he was about to assume. The knight, when fully equipped, was clad from head to heel in armour, formed of plates rivetted firmly together; below this he wore a dress of soft leather. On his helmet was a crest; on his three-pointed shield a device,—the original of our coat-of-arms. His chief weapon was the lance; but, besides, he wore a two-handed sword, and a poniard called 'the dagger of mercy,' used to kill a fallen foe; and he not unfrequently carried a battle-axe or mace. This last—a club with iron head studded with spikes —was the favourite instrument of war among the Norman clergy, who were often seen on the battle-field with a black cassock over their shining armour; and whose priestly vows, although they forbade the shedding of blood, said not a word about the dashing out of brains. The Templars were a famous order of military monks, founded in 1118. They wore over their armour a long scarlet mantle, with an eight-pointed cross of white sewed on the right shoulder. Their robe of peace was white. The Crusaders also were distinguished by crosses of various colours. The English wore white, the French red, the Flemings green, the Germans black, and the Italians yellow.

The chief sport of chivalry was the tournament or joust. It was held within an enclosed space called the lists. Ladies and nobles sat round in raised galleries, while the lower orders thronged outside the barriers to witness the sport. At each end of the lists tents were pitched for the rival knights. Then arose the clinking of hammers as the rivets were closed by the armourers or smiths, at this time an important and honoured body of craftsmen. With flourish of trumpets the heralds proclaimed the titles of the knights, as they rode into the lists on their pawing chargers; and the cry, ' Largesse, largesse!' with which the proclamation was followed, drew showers of gold and silver coins from the galleries. In the centre of the lists stood the challengers, awaiting their adversaries. These, riding up, touched with their lances the shields of those with whom they chose to contend. If the shield was touched with the sharp end of the lance, the combat was to be at *outrance*,—that is, with sharp weapons as in battle; while touching with lance reversed signified the more peaceful intention of using blunted weapons in a trial of skill. At sound of trumpet the combatants dashed at full gallop from opposite ends of the lists, and met in the centre with a terrible shock. If the knights were equally matched, the lances flew into splinters, and the horses were thrown back on their haunches; but if one struck with stronger and truer aim, whether the helmet or the shield of his rival, the unlucky knight was hurled from the saddle to the ground, stunned, bleeding, and bruised by his heavy armour. This 'gentle and joyous sport,' as the Norman minstrels called it, generally lasted two or three days. The victor in the tilting of the first day, besides winning the horses and armour of those he vanquished, had the privilege of naming some lady, who, as Queen of Love and Beauty, presided over the remaining sports. The second day was often devoted to a *mêlée*, in which the knights fought in bands, till a signal to stop was given by the King or chief noble present casting down his baton. The conqueror in the *mêlée* knelt, with all the stains of the conflict on him, to receive a crown of honour from the hands of the Queen of Love and Beauty. After the tilting, the lower classes held sports, the favourite being archery, bull-baiting, and playing at quarter-staff. The last was a kind of cudgel-playing; the staff was a pole about six feet long, which the combatants grasped in the middle, striking, parrying, and thrusting, with both ends. Very similar to the tournament was the trial by combat; which, like the ordeal of the Saxons, was the Norman appeal to the justice of Heaven.

The castles of the Normans were built for strength and safety in turbulent days; and their grey ruins, still rising in solid grandeur here and there through the land, teach us how it was that the feudal Barons were able so often and so successfully to bid defiance to the King. Their distinctive feature is the rounded arch, as opposed to the pointed arch and lancet-shaped window of the later Gothic style. Encircled by the parapet and turrets of a wall about twelve feet high, stood the keep. This was a square tower of five stories, with walls ten feet thick. The lowest story contained dungeons, the second was filled with stores, the third held the garrison, while the upper two were occupied by the

Baron and his family. The entrance to the keep was in the third story, and was reached by a winding stair in the wall. In the middle of this stair was a strong gate; at the top was a drawbridge; while before the door, a portcullis, dropping from above with iron teeth, effectually barred the entrance against all foes. Round the whole castle ran a moat, or deep ditch filled with water; over which was thrown a drawbridge, defended at its outer edge by a tower, called the barbican. Close to the castle the shops and houses of those employed by the Baron and his vassals clustered together. Smiths, carpenters, workers in leather, bakers, butchers, tailors, and numerous other craftsmen lived there, having built their huts side by side for the safety that lies in numbers; and thus the feudal castle was often the nucleus of a feudal town.

In their manner of life the Normans were more temperate and delicate than the Saxons. They only had two regular meals; dinner, taken by the higher classes at nine in the morning; and supper, about four or five in the afternoon. But a meal was often taken in private before going to rest. The Normans introduced the general use of the chief flesh meats found on our tables;—a change which is curiously illustrated in our language, where we find the words denoting the living animal, *ox, sheep, calf, pig*, to be Saxon; while the words applied to the flesh used as food, *beef, mutton, veal, pork*, are Norman or French in their origin. The banquets of this period were served with much state by attendants called sewers, who were under the direction of higher domestics carrying white rods of office. The table was covered with varieties of meat, game, and pastry; and with cakes called by different names, such as wastle-cakes and simnel-bread. The higher Normans drank foreign wines, and closed their revelry with a draught called the grace-cup. The lower classes cheered their hearts with home-brewed ale. A fixed etiquette was now observed at table, and much ridicule fell on those who neglected its rules. Thus we read of a Saxon who was laughed at by the Normans, because he dried his hands on a napkin, instead of waving them in the air until the moisture had evaporated. The sleeping rooms of the great contained rude wooden beds with coarse coverlets; but the mass of the people were obliged to content themselves with straw and sheepskins.

In dress, as in food, the Normans introduced many novelties. The gallant of this time, closely shaven, with long hair curling on the shoulders, wore a loose doublet reaching half-way down the leg, girt with a gold-embroidered belt. Over this was a short cloak, richly furred and laced with gold. The shoes were the strangest article of dress. They had very long toes, pointed and twisted like the horns of a ram; and the fashion grew to so absurd a length that the toes were fastened by chains of gold or silver to the knees. A bonnet of velvet, and long hoes fastened to the doublet by very many strings called *points*, completed the costume. Many curious characters, illustrative of the social history of the time, might have been seen among the Normans:—the minstrel, with his harp slung on his shoulder, a plate of silver on his arm, and a chain round his neck bearing the *wrest* or tuning key; the fool or jester, with his cap and bells, his dress of motley, and his stockings, one red and one yellow; the palmer, or pilgrim from the Holy Land, his hat bordered with cockle or scallop shells, sandals on his bare feet, carrying a staff shod with iron with a palm-branch on the top; the Saxon serf, clad in untanned hide, with sandals of boar-skin and leathern bandage rolled half-way up the leg, wearing round his neck a collar of brass, engraved with his master's name; and the Jew, with yellow cap high and square, whose nation, reaching England during the Conqueror's reign, though abhorred, scouted, and plundered by all, continued to drive their trade in money-lending until the days of the first Edward. The Norman ladies wore a kirtle or under-gown of silk, over which hung a loose wide-sleeved robe reaching the ground. The clergy, whose professional mark of distinction was a heavy gold signet ring, often vied with the gallants of the day in the splendour and fashion of their dress.

The Saxon coinage was little changed. Some new foreign coins came into use, of which the chief were the merk, worth 13s. 4d.; and the zechin or sequin, an Italian coin, worth about 9s. 5d., brought into use by the Crusades.

The Norman tongue—rich in words relating to war,

chivalry, law, and the sports of the field—being the language of the court, speedily became that of the church, the halls of justice, and the schools, where, we are told, the boys construed their Latin lesson into French. There arose also at this time a mixed tongue, *lingua Franca*, in which the Normans addressed their Saxon servants and tenants. The language of the Saxons, like the race that spoke it, made little progress during these days of bondage; and, from its intermixture with the French tongue, gets the name Semi-Saxon, until the reign of John. Ever since the Conquest, a struggle for predominance had been going on between the Saxon and the Norman languages. About the time of Magna Charta a reaction began, which ended in the triumph of the former tongue. Three-fifths of our modern English may be traced to the Anglo-Saxon.

Surnames were brought into general use by the Normans. They were derived from various sources, of which the most fruitful were personal qualities, as Armstrong, Whitehead, Swift; and occupations or trades, as Smith, Falconer, Taylor, Miller. Many were formed from Christian names by adding the Saxon *son*, as Wilson; the Celtic *Mac* or *O*, as Macdonald, O'Connell; or the Norman *Fitz*, as Fitzgerald.

LEADING AUTHORS UNDER THE EARLY NORMAN KINGS.

THE SAXON CHRONICLE,..........This work was compiled from the registers kept in the monasteries—passing events from Alfred's time to the year 1154 are noticed.

INGULF,.................................1030 to 1109—Abbot of Croyland—chronicler.

GEOFFREY OF MONMOUTH,......Died 1130—wrote Chronicles in Latin.

WILLIAM OF MALMESBURY,...1067 to 1143—wrote Latin Chronicles.

HENRY OF HUNTINGDON,.........Died 1168—chronicler.

LEADING DATES—EARLY NORMAN KINGS.

GENERAL EVENTS.	BATTLES, SIEGES.
A.D.	A.D.
Court held at York, 1069. Wm. I.	Siege of Gerberoi,...1077. Wm. I.
Malcolm III. pays homage,...............1072. —	Battle of Tenchebrai,...............1106. Hen. I
Domesday-book compiled,..........1080–1086. —	— of Brenville,......1119. —
Mowbray rebels,....1095. Wm. II.	— of the Standard,1138. Steph.
First Crusade,........1096. —	— of Lincoln,........1141. —
P. William drowned,1120. Hen. I.	Siege of Oxford,......1142. —
Maud lands,..........1139. Steph.	
P. Henry lands,.....1152. —	

GENEALOGICAL TREE

CONNECTING THE EARLY NORMAN KINGS WITH THE PLANTAGENETS

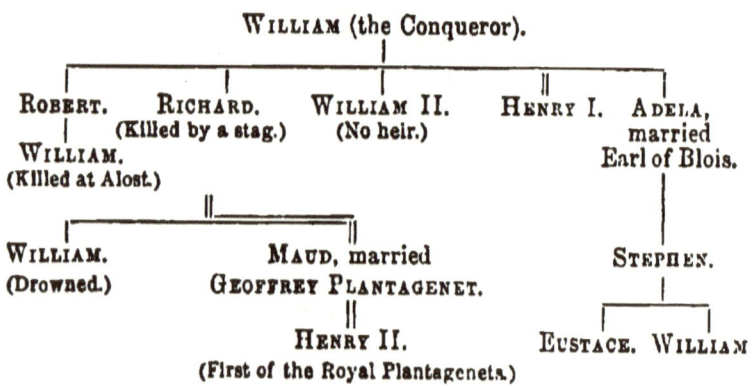

PLANTAGENET LINE.

1154 A.D. to 1485 A.D.—331 years.—14 Kings.

Leading Feature: **THE FEUDAL SYSTEM IN ITS PRIME AND ITS DECAY.**

PLANTAGENETS PROPER.

	A.D.		A.D.
HENRY II. began to rule,	1154	EDWARD I. (son),	1272
RICHARD I. (son),	1189	EDWARD II. (son),	1307
JOHN (brother),	1199	EDWARD III. (son),	1327
HENRY III. (son),	1216	RICHARD II. (grandson),	1377

CHAPTER I.

HENRY II.—CURTMANTLE.

Born 1133 A.D.—Began to reign 1154 A.D.—Died 1189 A.D.

The name Plantagenet. Henry's power and early Becket's rise. [policy. His magnificence. His quarrel with Henry.	His escape and murder. State of Ireland. Story of Dermot. Conquest of Ireland. Henry's penance.	Capture of the Scottish King. Henry's death and character. Changes in his reign.

THE heads of the Plantagenet line were Geoffrey of Anjou and Maud, daughter of Henry I. of England. The name is derived from *Planta Genista*, the Latin term for the shrub we call broom; which, as an emblem of humility, was worn by the first Earl of Anjou when a pilgrim to the Holy Land. From this his successors took their crest and their surname.

Young Henry had a brilliant prospect before him. In France he held some of the fairest provinces, all the western coasts owning his sway. With his Queen, Eleanor, he received the crown of England at Westminster. During several years he was engaged in redressing the evils which had sprung from the turbulence of Stephen's reign. He issued new coins; drove from England the foreign hirelings, who had swarmed into the

Dec.
1154
A.D.

land during the civil war; and—hardest task of all—set himself to destroy the castles of the robber-barons.

The story of Thomas à Becket fills more than one half of the reign. Tradition tells us that Gilbert Becket was imprisoned in Palestine; that he was set free by a Saracen girl who loved him; and that she, feeling wretched after his escape, followed him to England. She knew only two English words, *London* and *Gilbert:* the first gained for her a passage in an English-bound ship; and by crying the second in the streets of London, she at length found her lover. They were married, and Thomas à Becket was their son. He was educated for the Church, and was soon made Archdeacon of Canterbury, a post then worth £100 a-year. By the advice of the aged Theobald, Archbishop of Canterbury, Henry appointed him Chancellor, and tutor to his son, and he speedily became chief favourite.

He outshone the King by his magnificence, had in his train thousands of knights, and lived in the height of the luxury which the times afforded. His table was free to all: the uninvited guests were often so many that there were not seats for all, and numbers sat on the floor upon clean straw or rushes. On the death of Theobald, Becket became Archbishop of Canterbury, then, as it is now, the highest dignity in the Church. At once he changed his conduct. He resigned his chancellorship, became as frugal in his style of living as he had been dissolute and luxurious, and exchanged his gay train of knights for the society of a few monks.

From this time he began to lose the favour of the King. Dislike deepened into hatred; hatred burst into open quarrel. The rights of the clergy formed the immediate cause of contention. Becket was an Englishman by birth, and the first of Saxon race who had obtained the primacy under the Normans. He therefore enlisted the sympathy of all his countrymen in his struggle against the royal power. Henry required that priests accused of crime should be tried by the royal judges. Becket opposed him, maintaining the right of priests to answer for their conduct only to the courts of the Church. A council held at Clarendon in Wilts decided in Henry's favour. Becket

1164 A.D.

yielded at first; but the struggle was resumed, and he fled to France to escape ruin. After six years he was reconciled to Henry, by Pope Alexander III. and Louis of France. Returning to England, he found the domains of his see forfeited. Henry seemed unwilling to restore them, and this renewed the quarrel. Becket then excommunicated all who held lands belonging to the see of Canterbury. The King, who was in Normandy when the news reached him, happened to say, 'Is there none of the cowards eating my bread who will free me from this turbulent priest?' Four knights, who heard him, took an oath to slay Becket; and, travelling to England, burst into the Cathedral at Canterbury, where they cruelly murdered the prelate, scattering his brains on the steps of the altar. **1170 A.D.** The scene of the murder, and the saintly reputation of the victim, deepened the horror with which the people looked upon this crime.

The great event of this reign was the annexation of Ireland. The island was then divided into six provinces,— Leinster, Desmond or South Munster, Thomond or North Munster, Connaught, Ulster, and Meath; the last being specially attached to the dignity of *Ard-riagh*, or supreme monarch, which was then claimed by the O'Connors, Kings of Connaught. The ports were in the hands of Ostmen, or Eastmen, descended from the Danish pirates; and were very prosperous, the commerce of Dublin rivalling that of London. But the mass of the people fed cattle. Their clothing was spun from raw wool. Their houses were built of wood, and wicker-work. They had forgotten the art by which their ancestors raised those strange round towers that still puzzle the antiquarian. Like the Welsh, they excelled in the music of the harp.

A feud arose between Dermot, King of Leinster, and O'Ruarc, Prince of Breffni or Leitrim. Dermot had carried off O'Ruarc's wife; but she had been recovered by the aid of O'Connor, the Ard-riagh. War ensued, and Dermot was driven from the island. From Henry he obtained leave to enlist soldiers in England. Richard le Clare, Earl of Pembroke, surnamed Strongbow; Robert Fitzstephen; and Maurice Fitzgerald, accepted his terms.

Fitzstephen landed at Bannow Bay with 140 knights, and 300 archers, and Wexford fell before him. Fitzgerald followed. Then came Strongbow with 1200 men. Waterford and Dublin were carried by storm, and no efforts of the Irish could dislodge the invaders from the fortresses with which they rapidly secured their conquests. Henry now crossed by the usual route, from Milford Haven to Waterford; and at Dublin received the homage of the chieftains. The princes of Ulster alone disdained submission. On his return to England Henry appointed Prince John, a boy of twelve, to the lordship of the island. The foolish boy and his Norman train mocked the Irish chieftains, as they came to pay homage, and insulted them by plucking their beards. Such treatment estranged the natives, and their revolts became fiercer and more frequent. These events are called the conquest of Ireland, but its final subdual was of much later date.

1172 A.D.

Four years after Becket's murder, Henry did penance at his tomb. Walking barefoot through the city, he threw himself on the pavement before the shrine, and was there scourged with knotted cords.

Immediately afterwards he received news of the capture of William, King of Scotland, who had been surprised in a mist near Alnwick Castle by Glanville. This Henry exultingly ascribed to the mercy of reconciled Heaven, deeming it, according to the notions of his Church, the direct fruit of his penance. William was not released until he acknowledged his kingdom a fief, and himself a vassal of the English crown,—a forced submission which it is important to remember, for on it Edward I. founded his claims to the lordship of Scotland.

Henry's sons, urged on by their mother and the French King, often defied his power; and the shock of finding his favourite son, John, mentioned in a list of rebels, whom he was asked to pardon, threw him into a fever, of which he died at Chinon. The church of Fontevraud received his remains, over which his son Richard wept bitter but useless tears of remorse. Of his five sons—William, Henry, Geoffrey, Richard, and John—only the last two survived him. One of his daughters, Maud, married Henry, Duke of Saxony, and thus became the ancestress of the noble family now holding the English throne.

In character Henry was the type of his race. His pride was great. Equally great was his ambition, but tempered by caution. His passion has been called the fury of a savage beast. His faithlessness was concealed by his winning tongue and pleasant manners. In person he resembled his ancestor, the Conqueror.

During this reign commerce was much extended. The Crusades had introduced the merchandise of the East, and gold, spices, gems, and rich cloths adorned the stalls of London. The Continent received from England flesh, herrings and oysters, lead and tin, skins and cloths. Glass was first used for the windows of private houses 1180 A.D. Six circuits of justice were fixed, and three judges appointed to each. London now became the capital, the civil wars of Stephen's reign having laid Winchester almost in ruins.

CONTEMPORARY SOVEREIGNS.

SCOTLAND.	EMPEROR.
A.D.	A.D.
MALCOLM IV., ...died 1165	FREDERIC I.
WILLIAM.	
	POPES.
FRANCE.	ANASTASIUS IV.,........died 1154
LOUIS VII., ...1180	ADRIAN IV. (the only English Pope; true name, Nicholas Breakspear),...........1159
PHILIP AUGUSTUS.	
	ALEXANDER III.,..............1181
SPAIN.	LUCIUS III.,........................1185
ALPHONSO VIII., ...1157	URBAN III.,........................1187
SANCHO III., ...1158	GREGORY VIII.,..................1187
ALPHONSO IX.	CLEMENT III.

CHAPTER II.

RICHARD I.—CŒUR DE LION, OR THE LION-HEARTED.
Born 1157 A.D.—Began to reign, 1189 A.D.—Died, 1199 A.D.

Money raised for a Crusade.	The Crusade.	His death.
Sufferings of the Jews.	Richard in prison.	Character.
	His return to England.	Effects of the Crusades.

CROSSING without delay to England, Richard received his father's crown at Westminster. But to rule England was not his ambition. He burned to win glory on the plains of Palestine, and his earliest measures were undertaken to raise money for a Crusade. To this he devoted the hoards of his father; for this purpose he sold the honours and offices in his gift; and gave up for 10,000 merks the homage wrested by his father from the Scottish King.

The Jews now suffered terrible woes. They were the bankers and usurers of the age, and their money-chests were an irresistible temptation. From France their nation had been driven with the scourge and the axe; and, dreading like treatment in England, they approached the Abbey on Richard's coronation-day with splendid offerings. Their presence roused the mob, and the cry spread that the King had proclaimed a massacre. Every Jewish dwelling was soon in a blaze, and the streets were slippery with Jewish blood. But York Castle was the scene of a darker tragedy. Five hundred Jews had there taken refuge with their wives and children, and were besieged by the citizens. They offered money, but in vain; and, to baulk those who thirsted for their blood, they hurled their treasures into the flames, slew their dear ones, and then stabbed one another. A few cried for mercy, and opened the gates; but the rabble rushing in put them to the sword. Lynn, Norwich, Stamford, Edmondsbury, Lincoln also echoed the dying groans of God's ancient people. The butchers received slight punishment; while Richard, although no doubt sharing the plunder, declared by proclamation that he took the Jews under his protection.

Richard of England and Philip Augustus of France then mustered their soldiers on the plains of Vezelai in Burgundy. It was the third Crusade. The united armies numbered 100,000 men. At Lyons the Kings parted, to meet at Messina in Sicily. During the winter they passed in Sicily Richard forced the King, Tancred, to restore 40,000 ounces of gold—the dowry of his sister Joan. Here, too, many petty jealousies arose between Richard and Philip. Another delay took place at Cyprus, where Richard was married to Berengaria of Navarre. He stayed to conquer the island; and, having captured the King, Isaac, cast him into prison, loaded with fetters of silver. Nearly twelve months had passed before the English King reached Acre, then the centre of the war. The graves of 200,000 soldiers, slain before the walls, attested the fury of the strife. Saladin, the infidel Soldan, watched every movement of the besieging force from the mountains that encircled the city. Philip had been for some time in the camp before the walls, but the presence of the Lion-heart alone could strike terror into the defenders. Very soon after Richard's arrival, the gates were thrown open. The jealousy, which began in Sicily and had since been increasing, now caused Philip, on pretence of ill-health, to return to France. Before his departure he swore not to invade the dominions of Richard. From Acre Richard led the Crusaders to Jaffa, inflicting upon Saladin, who strove to impede the march, a severe defeat. At last the walls of the still fair Jerusalem rose before the soldiers of the Cross; but their ranks were so thinned by war, hunger, and disease, and their energies so weakened by disunion and national jealousy, that Richard, even with the prize, for which he had neglected his duty as a King, glittering before him, was forced to turn away. The Crusade was over, and the monarch of England soon took leave of the sacred shore, with outstretched arms commending it to the mercy of Heaven.

July 1, **1190** A.D.

Oct. 9, **1192** A.D.

·Wrecked upon the northern shore of the Gulf of Venice, Richard resolved to cross the Continent in the dress of a pilgrim, under the name of Hugh the merchant. He reached Vienna in safety: but there the imprudence of his page, who, going into the town to buy provisions, wore gloves—then a mark of the highest rank—betrayed him into the hands of Leopold, Duke of Austria, whom he had beaten with his own hands in the town of Acre. At first he was confined in the Castle of Tyernsteign, but the Emperor Henry VI., who purchased the chained Lion for £60,000, flung him into a castle in the Tyrol. There is a legend that a French minstrel, named Blondel, discovered the place of Richard's captivity. Wandering through the land, he happened near a grated window to strike his harp to an air of Richard's own composing. The strain was answered from within, and he knew it was the King of England who sang. After much debate, a ransom was fixed; 100,000 merks were wrung from the English people; and Richard was free.

1194
A.D.

As yet the King had spent only four months in England. He now spent little more than two. When he recovered his freedom, he found his crown of England and his French coronets equally in danger. His brother John, having driven into exile the Regent, William of Longchamp, aimed at the one: Philip of France desired the others; and this, perhaps, was the true cause of his desertion at Acre. John's party melted away before his brother's presence, and he humbly sought for pardon; which was granted at the intercession of his mother.

The rest of Richard's reign was occupied by wars in France, carried on at the expense of his English subjects. In two years he drew from this country £1,100,000. In France he received his death-wound in a mean quarrel. A treasure had been found on the estate of his vassal, Vidomar. Richard received part, but demanded all. Being refused, he besieged the Castle of Chaluz, from the walls of which an arrow struck him in the shoulder. The head was extracted by an unskilful surgeon, and mortification set in. The castle being taken, the archer, Gourdon, was brought a captive to the monarch's dying bed; but Richard pardoned him. In spite of this, the unhappy youth was flayed alive by Richard's general. The dead King was buried at the feet of his father in Fontevraud: his heart was bequeathed to the citizens of Rouen.

The daring valour and muscular strength of this prince; his bright blue eyes and curling chestnut hair; his skill in music, and his accomplishments in the poetry of the Troubadours, have made him a favourite hero of historians and novelists. He was, indeed, the very model of a feudal knight; but the King of England, who spent six months among his people during a reign of ten years, and whose brightest victories brought poverty and hunger to English homes, cannot but be deemed unworthy of the name.

The famous Robin Hood lived now. Heavy taxes stirred up a riot in London, headed by Fitzosbert, or Longbeard, who was hanged. The three lions still seen in the royal shield were adopted by Richard. The social effects of the Crusades began to be felt. They excited a somewhat kindlier feeling among the nations leagued in a common cause; they opened up the East to commerce, and poured its riches into England; they drained the country of those restless spirits, whose broils convulsed society unceasingly; lastly, and of most importance, by weakening the power of the nobles, whose estates began to pass into the hands of the wealthy commoners, they elevated the standing of the middle classes, and laid the foundation of those changes by which was afterwards established our House of Commons.

CONTEMPORARY SOVEREIGNS.

SCOTLAND.	EMPERORS.	A.D.
WILLIAM.	FREDERIC I.	died 1190
	HENRY VI.	1197
FRANCE.	PHILIP.	
PHILIP AUGUSTUS.		
	POPES.	
SPAIN.	CLEMENT III.	1191
ALPHONSO IX	CELESTIN III.	1198
	INNOCENT III.	

CHAPTER III.

JOHN—SANSTERRE, OR LACKLAND.

Born 1166 A.D.—Began to reign 1199 A.D.—Died 1216 A.D.

John not the heir.	Magna Charta.
Loss of French provinces.	Broken oaths.
	Death.
Quarrel with the Pope.	Character.
Philip in Flanders.	Notes.

RICHARD, who left no heir, bequeathed his throne to his brother John, Duke of Mortaigne. A council held at Northampton confirmed the choice, and John was crowned at Westminster. He was not the lineal heir, for his elder brother, Geoffrey, had left a son,—Arthur, Duke of Bretagne, now aged twelve years. This boy's claim was supported by the French King; but at the Castle of Mirabeau, in Poitou, he fell into the hands of John, who cast him into the dungeons of Rouen. Here all trace of him was lost. There were some who said that John slew him with his own hand. Arthur's sister, Eleanor, called the Maid of Bretagne, another rival, was imprisoned within Bristol Castle till her death.

John, having divorced Joanna, married Isabella of Angouleme, the affianced wife of the Earl of Marche; and this seduction, coupled with the murder of Arthur, roused against him enemies, who soon stripped him of Normandy, Anjou, and Maine.

The see of Canterbury having fallen vacant, the monks nominated John de Gray, Bishop of Norwich; the Pope, Innocent III., elected Stephen Langton. The monks yielded to the Pope; but John, defying the Pontiff, drove them from their abbeys and seized their treasures, because they had deserted his minister and favourite, De Gray. This conduct drew upon the country the terrors of an interdict. For six

1208 A.D. TO 1214 A.D.

years there was no worship in the land; the churches were closed; their silent bells rusted in the steeples; the dead were cast without prayer into unhallowed graves; the statues of the saints were shrouded in black. The people groaned under the curse; but the King, unmoved, visited Scotland, Ireland, and

Wales, exacting homage and imposing tribute. The Pope at last called upon Philip of France to dethrone the impious monarch; and then John yielded. Sensible that of the 60,000 warriors who marched under his banner he could trust not one, he took an oath of fealty to the Pope, agreeing to pay to the Roman coffers 1000 merks as yearly rent for his kingdoms of England and Ireland.

Philip, who was at Boulogne, ready to invade England, proposed to cross the Strait notwithstanding John's submission to the Pope. Ferrand, Earl of Flanders, objected; and the enraged monarch ravaged Flanders to the walls of Ghent. His fleet, however, was scattered by William Longsword, Earl of Salisbury, who commanded the navy of England. John, in the flush of this success, sailed to Poitou; but his hopes of victory were blasted by the defeat of his allies, the Emperor Otho and Ferrand, at Bouvines. He then sought and obtained a truce for five years.

1214 A.D.

A number of men from Anjou and Poitou, who had been allied with King John, sought an asylum in England. Adroit and insinuating, and better fitted to please a King than the Normans settled in the country, they were received with favour at the Court, and speedily supplanted the old aristocracy in the good graces of the King. He distributed among them all the offices and fiefs at his disposal; and, under various pretexts, deprived several rich Normans of their posts in favour of these new comers. He married them to the rich heiresses under his wardship, according to the feudal law, and made them guardians of rich orphans under age. The new courtiers, by their exactions, soon rendered themselves as odious to the Saxon citizens as they were to the nobles of Norman origin; and thus the two races of men who inhabited England were, for the first time, brought together by a common feeling. Here we may date the birth of a new national spirit, common to all born on English soil.

The Barons of England, roused by the dishonour and loss which the tyrant had heaped upon their noblest families, swore to suffer no longer. When John heard their demands, he cried, 'As well may they ask my crown!' But he had to deal with stern and resolute men; and though he shifted and delayed while he could, yet the loss of London, which the Barons seized one Sunday when the people were in the churches, forced him to compliance. At Runnymead, between Staines and Windsor, he signed Magna Charta, a document still preserved in the British Museum. The most important provision of this Charter was, that no 'freeman should be arrested, imprisoned, outlawed, or dispossessed of land, except by the lawful judgment of his peers.' Besides, it confirmed the ancient charters of London and other cities, and granted to foreign merchants leave to reside in England or depart from it without exaction. Thus does God's mercy turn evil into good. To a reign among the blackest in our annals we can trace much of the peace which cherishes our freedom and brightens our homes.

June 15,
1215
A.D.

John was bound by solemn oaths to keep the Charter; but oaths were nothing to him. He was all courtesy and kindness at Runnymead; but, when the Barons had departed, he raved like a madman, and cursed the day he was born. The first tidings the Barons heard were, that the tyrant, having raised an army of mercenaries, was laying waste the land. The sky was red with the blaze of burning towns and corn-fields: the people fled to the forests and hills. In despair, the Barons called Louis of France, who had married the niece of John, to take the crown; and then was England in peril. On the one hand were the horrors of a second conquest and a new French dynasty; on the other, the fury of a savage, who, if successful, would stop at no revenge, however terrible. The hand of God interposed. Louis had landed at Sandwich, and John was marching to meet him; but on the shores of the Wash he saw his money, his jewels, and the records of the kingdom, swept away by the rising tide; and his agitation brought on a fever. Some writers say that he died by poison; others, that a surfeit of peaches and new ale laid him on his death-bed. He died at Newark Castle, and was buried at Worcester.

Oct. 19,
1216
A.D.

Of John we know nothing good. He was a mean coward, a shameless liar, the most profligate in a profligate age, the most faithless of a faithless race. In person he was tall, though corpulent; and his face was a true picture of his degraded mind.

By his last wife, Isabella, he left three sons—Henry, Richard, and Edmund; and three daughters—Joan, Eleanor, and Isabella.

During this reign London Bridge was finished; letters of credit were first used in England; and the custom of annually electing a Lord Mayor and two Sheriffs of London was begun, Henry Fitzalwyn being the first *Lord* Mayor. The fisheries were now very profitable,—the salmon of the Dee, and the herrings of the Sandwich shore being especially prized.

CONTEMPORARY SOVEREIGNS.

SCOTLAND.	A.D
WILLIAM	died 1214
ALEXANDER II.	

FRANCE.
PHILIP AUGUSTUS.

SPAIN.
HENRY I.

EMPERORS.	A.D.
PHILIP	died 1208
OTHO IV.	

POPES.	
INNOCENT III.	1216
HONORIUS III.	

CHAPTER IV.

HENRY III.—WINCHESTER.

Born 1207 A.D.—Began to reign 1216 A.D.—Died 1272 A.D.

Henry crowned.	Scotland and Wales.	Battle of Evesham.
Defeat of Louis.	Discontent of the Barons.	Henry dies.
De Burgh and De Roches.	The Mad Parliament.	His character.
Fall of De Burgh.	Battle of Lewes. [tuted.	Notes.
War with France.	House of Commons Insti-	

LOUIS held London and the southern counties; but the Barons, whose feeling had changed on the death of John, rallied round young Henry, who was at once crowned at Gloucester with a plain golden circlet, for the crown had been lost in the waves of the Wash. All true Englishmen were at the same time commanded to wear round the head for a month a white fillet, in honour of the coronation. The King being only ten years old, the Earl of Pembroke was appointed Regent. The first act of the new reign was to confirm the Great Charter, its sixty-one chapters having been reduced to forty-two.

Louis did not leave the island without a struggle for the crown, which had been almost in his grasp; but he was forced to abandon the enterprise by a complete defeat sustained at Lincoln. At the same time his fleet was destroyed at Calais by Hubert de Burgh, who, causing powdered quicklime to be flung into the air, so that the wind bore it into the eyes of the French, took advantage of the disorder to cut their rigging.

May 19, 1217 A.D.

Pembroke having died in the third year of his regency, the power was divided between Hubert de Burgh and Peter de Roches, Bishop of Winchester, a Poictevin. They did not agree, and Pandulph, the legate, had much trouble in preventing an open quarrel. However, when Henry was declared of age at seventeen, De Burgh became chief favourite; and De Roches, feeling his cause grew weak, took the pilgrim's staff for the Holy Land.

1223 A.D.

At a great council, one-fifteenth of all movables was

granted for an expedition to France, on condition that Henry should ratify the Charter for the third time. Sir Edward Coke tells us that it has been ratified in all thirty-two times. The expedition failed to recover Poitou and Guienne, which Louis had seized; and Henry incurred the charge of having wasted his own time and the people's money in idle revelry. He cast the blame on De Burgh, who speedily fell into disgrace. An account of money received during his time of office was demanded: he could not give it, and fled to the altar of Boisars Church; whence he was carried, half naked and tied on a horse, to London. The King, fearing that this violation of a sanctuary would rouse the anger of the priests, sent him back, but ordered the Sheriff to blockade the building. A moat was dug, palisades were raised round the church, and in forty days hunger forced Hubert to yield. Transferred from prison to prison, he at length escaped to Wales, and after some time made his peace with the King.

1225 A.D.

Besides the expedition already noticed, Henry, at the urgent entreaty of his mother, who had married her old lover, the Count of Marche, engaged in a second war with Louis. The battles of Taillebourg and Saintes, though not decisive, inclined the balance in favour of the French King; and truces, often broken, often renewed, led to a peace, by which Henry received Limousin, Perigord, and Querci, as an equivalent for Normandy, Maine, Anjou, and Poitou, still held by Louis.

1242 A.D.

With Scotland the sword was never drawn during this long reign, although there were many disputes about the three northern English counties. Two royal alliances united the sister kingdoms: Joan, Henry's eldest sister, was married to Alexander II.; and, at a later date, Margaret, the daughter of Henry, to Alexander III. The armies of the English King often traversed Wales; but the Welsh princes still held their mountain thrones unconquered.

Henry's fondness for the Poictevins, who swarmed around the restored De Roches, and the Provençals, who had flocked into England when their countrywoman, Eleanor, became its queen, roused the spirit of the nation. The Barons revolted under Simon de Montfort, Earl of Leicester, the husband of Eleanor, the King's sister. His desertion of his royal brother-in-law, together with the departure for Germany of Richard, Henry's younger brother, who had won laurels in the fourth Crusade, and had just been created King of the Romans, shook the throne, and raised the hopes of those who desired its overthrow.

At Westminster the Barons came to the council in full armour; and, when they again assembled at Oxford, 1258 A.D. in what is called 'the Mad Parliament,' they appointed a committee of twenty-four to reform the state. This committee enacted—1. That four knights should come to Parliament to represent the freeholders of every county; 2. That sheriffs should be chosen annually by vote; 3. That accounts of the public money should be given every year; 4. That Parliament should meet three times a year—in February, June, and October. But reform was delayed by disunion among the Barons; and the King of France, being chosen umpire, gave decision in Henry's favour. This kindled the civil war. Leicester held London; and, when the great bell of St. Paul's rang out, the citizens flocked round his banner with riot, the pillage of foreign merchants, and the murder of unhappy Jews. At May 14, 1264 A.D. Lewes, in Sussex, Henry was defeated and taken prisoner. Prince Edward gave himself up next day. A treaty, called 'the Mise of Lewes,' was made for the liberation of the King, but was never fulfilled. Henry and his two sons remained in close custody.

Early in the following year a Parliament was called by Leicester; to which he summoned, along with the 1265 A.D. prelates, barons, and knights of the shire, representatives from cities and boroughs. This was the first outline of our modern Parliament, the first two classes corresponding to the House of Lords, the last two to the House of Commons.

Prince Edward, having escaped from his guards, met Leicester at Evesham in Worcestershire. The 1265 A.D. battle raged long and bloodily. The captive King, who had been forced into the field by Leicester, fell slightly wounded, and would have been killed if he had not cried out, 'I am Henry of Winchester, the King.' Edward knew his voice, and rushed to his aid. The body of Leicester, who died fighting over his dead son, was mutilated by the victors.

The crown sat firmly now on the monarch's head, and, the civil war being over, the martial Edward joined the Crusade of St. Louis. During his son's absence Henry died, worn out by the troubles of a reign,—the longest in our annals except that of George III.

In character weak and credulous, Henry has been blamed for cowardice and indolence; but his lot was cast in stormy days, when it would have needed a strong hand to hold the helm of the state. In private life he was gentle and affectionate. He was of middle size, and a droop of the left eyelid gave an odd expression to his face.

The introduction of the linen manufacture by some Flemings, the use of leaden water-pipes, and of candles instead of wooden torches, were among the improvements of this reign. A license to dig coal, a mineral, whose abundance in Britain has so much advanced our national wealth, was now first granted to the people of Newcastle. We may also trace to this reign our gold coinage. Science was much benefited by the researches of Roger Bacon, a monk, whose magnifying glasses and magic lanterns gained for him the reputation of a wizard. On the Continent, Paulus, a Venetian, is said to have invented the mariner's compass, the needle being placed between floating straws.

CONTEMPORARY SOVEREIGNS.

SCOTLAND.	A.D.	EMPERORS.	A.D.
ALEXANDER II.,	died 1249	OTHO IV.,	died 1218
ALEXANDER III.		FREDERIC II.,	1250
		INTERREGNUM, 22 years..	1272
FRANCE.			
PHILIP AUGUSTUS,	1223	**POPES.**	
LOUIS VIII.,	1226	HONORIUS III.,	1227
LOUIS IX.,	1270	CELESTIN IV.,	1241
PHILIP III.		GREGORY IX.,	1241
		INNOCENT IV.,	1254
SPAIN.		ALEXANDER IV.,	1261
HENRY I.,	1217	URBAN IV.,	1264
FREDERIC III.,	1252	CLEMÉNT IV.,	1268
ALPHONSO X.		GREGORY X.	

CHAPTER V.

EDWARD I.—LONGSHANKS.

Born 1239 A.D.—Began to reign 1272 A.D.—Died 1307 A.D.

Edward's return.	French war.	Character.
Coronation.	Balliol deposed.	Constitutional changes.
Conquest of Wales.	Death of Edward.	Notes.
Scottish succession.		

WHILE in the Holy Land, Edward was stabbed with a poisoned dagger, by an infidel. Tradition ascribes his recovery to the affection of his wife, Eleanor of Castile, who sucked the poison from the wound. His crusading exploits were few and insignificant, and he left Palestine after a stay of eighteen months. In Sicily he heard of his father's death, but his homeward journey was delayed by a disturbance in Guienne. Here a tournament, between Edward and the Count of Chalons, ended in a serious affray, in which the English knights were victors. Before passing into England, Edward arranged with the Countess of Flanders a quarrel, which had long interrupted the trade in English wool,—a commodity highly prized by the Flemish cloth-merchants.

The King and Queen were crowned at Westminster two years after Henry's death. Alexander of Scotland was present, and received £5 a-day for the expenses of his journey. The great aim of Edward's ambition was to conquer Wales and Scotland, and thus unite under his sway the whole island.

Many English princes had tried to subdue Wales, but without success. Among the crags and forests of Snowdon and Plynlimmon, the mountain race baffled the Norman spears and defied pursuit. Merlin had prophesied that, when money was made round, a prince of Wales should be crowned in London. The time had come; a brave prince held Arthur's throne; and Welsh hopes were high. When Edward demanded homage, Llewellyn refused with disdain. But it was the pride that goes before a fall. For five years the English King traversed the land with foreign troops, skilled in mountain warfare; Llewellyn held out bravely;

but his death while defending the passage of the Wye, sealed the doom of Welsh independence. In mockery of his hopes, his head was sent to London; where, crowned with ivy, it was fixed upon the Tower-gate. His brother David held out for a while; but, being delivered up by his own countrymen, he was hanged by order of the conqueror. Edward is charged with a massacre of the Welsh bards at Conway, lest their songs should preserve the spirit of ancient freedom among the people. Upon this story, whether it is true or false, our poet Gray founded his celebrated Ode. The title 'Prince of Wales, borne by the eldest son of the British sovereign, was first given to the young Edward, who was born at Caernarvon.

1282 A.D.

The death of Margaret, 'the Maid of Norway,' confused the succession to the Scottish crown. Thirteen competitors appeared; but the claims of two, John Baliol and Robert Bruce, were superior. These were descendants of David, a younger brother of William the Lion, Baliol being the grandson of the eldest daughter, Bruce the son of the second. Edward claimed a right to interfere, on the ground that William the Lion, when the captive of Henry II., had acknowledged himself a vassal of the English crown, and that Richard I. had no right to sell the deed of vassalage, since it was not his property, but that of all English sovereigns. On this pretence to meddle with the affairs of Scotland, Edward appointed Baliol King.

1292 A.D.

Soon after these events, a naval war arose between France and England. It sprang from a quarrel among sailors at Bayonne. An Englishman having slain a Norman, the Normans seized an English ship and dragged out of it a passenger, whom in revenge they hanged topmast high. The sailors of the Cinque Ports joined in the quarrel; privateers swarmed in the Channel and the Bay of Biscay; and engagements, in which the English were generally victorious, frequently occurred. Edward, as Duke of Aquitaine, was summoned to France; but he refused to appear, and prepared for war. His supplies were derived partly from the plunder of the Jews, and partly from heavy taxes. He raised the wool tax from half a merk to five on every sack, and twice he seized and sold all the hides and wool in the stores of the London merchants. The fleet lay at Portsmouth, but the King, when about to embark, was forced to turn by a Welsh rebellion; and, that being crushed, a Scottish revolt claimed his presence.

Baliol, called repeatedly to London to answer for his conduct, found his vassalage so irksome that he rose in arms. But his feeble resistance was soon subdued: he was dethroned, and was after some time allowed to retire to Normandy. Edward marched through Scotland to Elgin, exacting homage; and, on his departure, left the Earl of Surrey guardian of the land. War soon broke out again; but the story belongs to Scottish history. Its heroes were Wallace, and Bruce the grandson of Baliol's rival;

1306 A.D. and it resulted in the independence of Scotland.

Three years before this event Edward recovered by treaty the province of Guienne, of which he had been cheated by the French King.

The news that Bruce had been crowned at Scone roused the old warrior of England, and the last effort of his life was to reach Scotland. He lay long at Carlisle on a bed of sickness, and died at Burgh on Sands.

July 7, 1307 A.D. His last wish was, that his bones should be carried at the head of the army as it marched onward.

His first wife, Eleanor of Castile, who died in 1290, left four sons, of whom the eldest was afterwards Edward II.; his second, Margaret of France, bore him a daughter and two sons, Edmund and Thomas.

Edward possessed many good qualities. He was a brave soldier, a sagacious and successful statesman. But cruelty, revenge, and excessive ambition seem to have been inseparable from the character of the early Plantagenets. His person was tall and majestic.

The chief constitutional changes of this reign were,— 1. That no aid or tax was to be levied by the Sovereign without the consent of Parliament; 2. That the Commons began to couple with their grants of money petitions for the redress of their grievances,—a practice which gradually changed into the power of proposing new laws.

The Jews, having drunk the cup of suffering to its bitterest dregs, were banished from the kingdom in 1290. Goldsmiths from Lombardy, who came to take their place as money-lenders and bankers, gave a name to Lombard Street, which has ever since been the favourite resort of money-dealers. Windmills and spectacles, paper from the East, and looking-glasses from Venice, were now introduced; while the use of coal was forbidden, from the public annoyance caused by the smoke. The regalia of Scotland and the ancient coronation chair were brought to England by Edward, who at the same time destroyed all Scottish records which might keep alive the spirit of that nation. The chair, and a stone on which, the legend says, Jacob laid his head at Bethel, were placed in the Abbey of Westminster, completed by Edward in 1285.

CONTEMPORARY SOVEREIGNS.

SCOTLAND.	EMPERORS.
A.D.	A.D.
ALEXANDER III., ... died 1286	RODOLPH, ... died 1292
MARGARET, ... 1290	ADOLPHUS, ... 1298
Interregnum ends, ... 1292	ALBERT.
BALIOL, ... 1296	
Interregnum ends, ... 1306	POPES.
ROBERT I.	GREGORY X., ... 1276
	INNOCENT V., ... 1276
	ADRIAN V., ... 1276
FRANCE.	JOHN XXI., ... 1277
PHILIP III., ... 1285	NICHOLAS III., ... 1280
PHILIP IV.	MARTIN IV., ... 1285
	HONORIUS IV., ... 1287
	NICHOLAS IV., ... 1292
SPAIN.	CELESTIN V., ... 1294
ALPHONSO X., ... 1284	BONIFACE VIII., ... 1303
SANCHO IV., ... 1294	BENEDICT XI., ... 1304
FERDINAND IV.	CLEMENT V.

CHAPTER VI.

EDWARD II.—CAERNARVON.

Born 1284 A.D.—Began to reign 1307 A.D.—Died 1327 A.D.

Rule of Gaveston.	Quarrel of the King and Queen.
The Ordainers.	Edward dethroned.
Bannockburn.	His murder.
Famine and plague.	His character.
The Spensers.	Notes.

THE bones of Edward I. were buried at Westminster. The Scottish war was abandoned. So much for the wishes of a dead King. Piers Gaveston, a Gascon, the vicious companion of young Edward's boyhood, was recalled from exile; and to him was committed the regency of the kingdom, while Edward sailed to Boulogne to marry Isabella, the beautiful daughter of Philip, King of France. The splendour of Gaveston excited the jealousy of the Barons; the nicknames which he showered on them roused their anger. Twice the weak King banished him; twice he was recalled to his honours; but the confederate nobles, headed by the Earl of Lancaster, seized him at Scarborough Castle, and caused his head to be struck off at Blacklow-hill, near War-

1310 A.D. wick. Before the death of the favourite, a Parliament, sitting sword in hand, appointed a council of twenty-one peers to manage the King's household and to reform the Government. These peers were called *Ordainers.*

Linlithgow, Roxburgh, Edinburgh, and Perth had been taken by Bruce, when, to save Stirling, which was sorely beset, Edward marched northward. Bruce, with

June 24, 1314 A.D. 30,000 picked men, met and routed the chivalry of England on the field of Bannockburn. Five years after, the English King besieged Berwick, 'the key of Scotland;' but again he failed, and a truce was made. About the same time Edward Bruce, brother of the Scottish King, landed in Ireland, and at Car-

1318 A.D. rickfergus was crowned King. He held Ulster for two years, when his death in battle at Fagher near Dundalk restored the English ascendency.

The years 1314 and 1315 were darkened by the miseries of famine. Even the royal table was scantily supplied with bread. The poor fed on roots, horses, and dogs. The breweries were stopped, to prevent the waste of grain. Plague followed the famine. The nobles dismissed crowds of their retainers: these had no resource but robbery. Ruin, pillage, and bloodshed filled the land.

Edward's new favourites were the Spensers, son and father; who, acting the same part as Gaveston, met a similar fate. It would be useless to detail the story. The elder was gibbeted at Bristol; the younger at Hereford.

The execution of Lancaster, who was beheaded at Pontefract, had already shown that Gaveston's death rankled in the King's breast. But the Lancastrian party still survived, and new events stirred it to more vigorous life. There was an open quarrel between Edward and his Queen. She fled to France; her son followed; Lord Mortimer, an adherent of Lancaster, joined them; and it was not long until the Queen landed on the Suffolk coast with a foreign army. The King escaped into Wales; but soon surrendering, it was declared in Parliament that he reigned no longer, and that his son held the sceptre in his stead. From castle to castle the dethroned monarch was removed, until within the walls of Berkeley keep he died by violence. Nothing more is known than that fearful shrieks broke the stillness of one awful night, and on the next morning the citizens of Bristol were called to look on the distorted face of him who had once been King of England. The corpse was privately buried at Gloucester. His children were Edward, his successor; John, who died young; Jane, married to David II. of Scotland; and Eleanor.

Jan. 18, 1327 A.D.

Edward was fickle and indolent. His days were spent in hunting, his nights in revelry, while the government of his kingdom was left to favourites. His figure resembled that of his warlike father.

During this reign earthenware came into use. The interest of money was 45 per cent. Bills of exchange were introduced, and the first commercial treaty was made between England and Venice. Other events were the suppression of the Templars and the foundation of Dublin University. It was in 1308 that Tell achieved the independence of Switzerland.

CONTEMPORARY SOVEREIGNS.

SCOTLAND. A.D.
ROBERT I.

FRANCE.
PHILIP IV.,..............died 1314
LOUIS X., ...1316
PHILIP V., ...1322
CHARLES IV.

SPAIN.
FERDINAND IV.,............1312
ALPHONSO XI.

EMPERORS. A.D.
ALBERT..................died 1308
HENRY VII......................1313
LOUIS IV.

POPES.
CLEMENT V.,..................1314
JOHN XXII.

CHAPTER VII.

EDWARD III.—WINDSOR.

Born 1313 A.D.—Began to reign 1327 A.D.—Died 1377 A.D.

Invasion of the Scots.	Nevil's Cross.	Death of the Black Prince
Fall of Mortimer.	Calais.	and the King.
Scottish war.	The Plague.	Character.
War with France.	Battle of Poictiers.	Constitutional changes.
Battle of Creçy.	Captive Kings.	Notes.

THE young Edward and the council of regency were but the instruments of Isabella and Mortimer, who held all power.

A Scottish army invaded the northern counties. It was difficult to follow their rapid movements, for they were all cavalry, carrying no food except a bag of oatmeal at every saddle-bow. Edward offered knighthood, with £100 a-year for life, to him who should discover their route. Thomas Rokeby won the prize, and led the English King to the Wear, on the opposite bank of which lay the foe. But no battle followed. In the dead of the fifth night the Scots retreated towards the Border, and a peace was soon made, in which Edward, by the advice of Mortimer, acknowledged Scotland to be a distinct and independent kingdom. The treaty was cemented by the marriage of Jane, the King's sister, to the Scottish Prince, David.

The odium of this peace; the execution of the Earl of Kent, uncle of the King; and the growing manhood of Edward, now eighteen, overthrew the power of Isabella and her favourite. He was seized in Nottingham Castle, and hanged upon the elms of Tyburn: she dragged out the remaining twenty-seven years of her life in her mansion of Risings, where the King paid her a formal visit once a-year.

The great Bruce was dead, and his son David was yet a child. Edward Baliol, making a bold push for the throne, which his craven-spirited father had held as a vassal of England, laid siege to Berwick. The Regent moved to save a fortress so important, and was met at Halidon-hill by the English King, who supported Baliol. There was fought a battle so disastrous to the Scots,

July 19, **1333** A.D.

that Baliol gained the crown, and the eastern lowland counties south of the Forth were for a time under the sway of Edward.

To unite in his person the crowns of France and of England was the greatest effort of Edward's policy. The three sons of Philip IV. had died heirless; and Edward of England and Philip of Valois were rivals for the vacant throne. Edward's mother was a daughter of Philip IV.: Philip was the nephew of that monarch. The Salic law, which enacted that no female could inherit the throne, stood in Edward's way, and Philip was elected. The English King seized all the wool and tin in his kingdom, pawned his crown and his jewels, quartered on his royal shield the golden lilies of France, and sailed to the Continent to assert his rights on the battle-field. Two campaigns were indecisive. A naval victory at Sluys, on the Flemish coast, was gained by the English; but they were beaten back from the walls of Tournay, and a truce for a year was made. Again the war was renewed; again it failed. But in the seventh year an English army entered Guienne. Edward landed in Normandy with another, and bent his march towards Calais. He passed the Seine and the Somme in the face of French soldiers; and the way to Calais was opened by the victory of Crecy.

1338 A.D.

1340 A.D.

The morning of the battle broke with storm and rain, lightning and thunder,—a fitting prelude for a day of blood. It was not until five in the afternoon that the cavalry of France under Count Alençon, with a band of Genoese cross-bow men, advanced to attack the English lines. They were met by clouds of cloth-yard shafts from bows of English yew, and their ranks wavered. Still the shower poured on; horses and men rolled on the earth, and the cavalry retired in confusion. The men-at-arms now engaged; the second lines advanced,—France and England were locked in a deadly struggle. Edward, who watched the fight from a windmill, felt so sure of victory that he refused to send aid to the Prince of Wales, a lad of fifteen, who was sorely pressed in the front of the battle. 'No!' said he; 'let the boy win his spurs: his shall be the glory

Aug. 26, 1346 A.D.

of the day.' In vain the French King tried to pierce the phalanx of archers who stood between him and his routed horsemen; his bravest knights fell fast around him; the horse he rode was killed;—there was no hope but in flight. Eleven princes, twelve hundred knights, and thirty thousand common soldiers are said to have fallen in the battle and the carnage of the next day. John, the blind King of Bohemia, was among the slain. He was led into the battle by four attendant knights, whose bridles were interlaced with his. His crest and motto—three ostrich feathers with the words *Ich dien*, 'I serve'—have ever since been borne by the Prince of Wales. We are told that cannon of a rude sort were first used at Crecy.

In the same year, but two months later, was fought the battle of Nevil's Cross. David of Scotland, having regained his throne, invaded England as the ally of France; but he was defeated and made prisoner by Philippa of Hainault, a Queen worthy of her warlike husband.   Oct. 17.

The conqueror at Creçy at once invested Calais. He raised no mounds, directed no engines against the city, but for twelve months he ground the garrison with the slow torture of famine, and thus forced them to open their gates. He placed a colony of his own subjects in the city, which, for more than two centuries afterwards, was a flourishing mart for the exports of England.

But the strife of men was now hushed before the breath of the Destroying Angel; for a terrible sickness called the Black Plague, which had swept over Asia and the south of Europe, broke out in France and England. The London church-yards were soon filled; throughout the country the dead cattle lay rotting and poisoning the air; labour and trade stood still; the lower classes fell by hundreds in the day; the rich shut themselves in their solitary castles;—wailing and desolation filled every city. Many evils followed the pestilence. Nearly all the artisans and labourers had perished, for plague is always heaviest on the poor; those who had escaped left the country. The crops were often allowed to moulder away for want of money to pay the exorbitant wages of the harvestmen, and the price of food rose fourfold. A common feeling ascribed this disaster to the long toe-points and curled beards of the men, and to the masculine dress assumed by the belles of the day; and laws to curb extravagance in dress were enacted. A set of enthusiasts, too, called Flagellants, came from Hungary, and passed through the country, lashing themselves till the blood ran down their shoulders, that the plague might be stayed. There can be no doubt that the plagues, which from time to time visited England, were rendered more virulent and lasting by the want of cleanliness in the houses, the streets, and the persons of the people. Good ventilation, proper sewerage, wholesome food, and the abundant use of water, have banished from our shores the terrible plague, which still lurks in some close and filthy cities of the East, and have much lessened the violence of those epidemic diseases with which God is pleased still to smite the nation.

Philip of France had died, and his son John ruled. The war was renewed in 1355, chiefly under the conduct of the Prince of Wales, called the Black Prince from the colour of his armour. The first campaign was occupied in wasting the provinces round Bordeaux; the second was signalized by the battle of Poictiers. The Prince had pierced too far into the centre of France, and on his return found an army, seven times as large as his own, between him and Bordeaux. A brave fight was his only resource. Fortunately for him the battle-ground was among vineyards, which impeded the French cavalry. As at Creçy, the English archers won the day. Protected by the hedges, they poured upon the French ranks shafts which no armour could resist. The first and second divisions of the French fell back; the King on foot led on the third, but was beaten to the ground and made prisoner with his young son. Father and son were led to England by the triumphant Edward.

Sept. 18, 1356 A.D.

There were thus two royal captives in England,—David of Scotland, ransomed in 1357, the eleventh year of his imprisonment; and John of France. The latter was freed by the *treaty of Bretigny*, called 'The great peace,' by which Edward renounced all claim to the French crown, retaining, instead of his ancestral

1360 A.D.

dominions, Poitou, Guienne, and the town of Calais. Three millions of golden crowns were to be paid as the ransom of John; but, failing to raise this sum, he returned to his captivity, and died at the Savoy, a palace on the Strand, then a fashionable country suburb of London.

The Black Prince ruled in Guienne, but an expedition into Spain, in support of Pedro the Cruel, loaded him with debt and shattered his health. He was soon obliged to visit England, where he wasted and died. He had married his cousin Joan of Kent, and left a son named Richard. From the time that he left the French shores, the English cause grew weak. One by one the provinces won at Creçy and Poietiers fell from the now enfeebled grasp of Edward, until, of his once mighty French possessions, Calais, Bordeaux, and Bayonne alone were his. His latter days were sad. The murmurs of an unruly Parliament and the death of his son weighed heavily on his soul: his once proud mind was degraded beneath the rule of Alice Perrers, a woman of wit and beauty, but of bad reputation. The tree still stood, but its blossoms and its leaves had fallen. He died, a year after his son, at Shene, near Richmond, and was buried in Westminster Abbey. His family was large, but only four of his children survived him. The Black Prince, Lionel of Clarence, John of Lancaster—born at Ghent, and Edmund of York were his most distinguished sons.

The character of Edward was good. He was brave, wise, and merciful; and we can pardon him if his ambition to wear the French crown carried him too far. Under his rule the hatred which had long severed Saxon, Norman, and Briton, began to disappear; and from the blended races rose the true British nation. Norman knight, Saxon bowman, and Welsh lancer fought side by side at Creçy and Poietiers, where a common danger and a common glory united them. Then, too, the use of Norman-French in the courts of law, in the schools, and in the proceedings of Parliament, began to die out, and the simple manly English tongue to take its place.

In this reign the Lords and the Commons were distinctly defined, and began to sit in separate chambers. The Commons occupied St. Stephen's Chapel, were presided over by a Speaker, and held the power of granting supplies; in return for which they gained from the King many beneficial laws. A check was given to the great evil of *purveyance*, by which the King's officers seized corn, cattle, forage, horses, carriages, and all necessaries for him and his train, as he journeyed. Edward III. extended this system to the seizure of the lower orders for soldiers and sailors, and of merchant vessels for use in war. This was the origin of the press-gang of later days.

The abolition of *first-fruits*, a tax by which the Popes received the first year's income from all clergy obtaining new appointments, shook the Papal power in England. To this reign are ascribed the institution of the Order of the Garter, and the revival in England of the title 'Duke,' the Black Prince being styled Duke of Cornwall. The invention of gunpowder by Schwartz, a monk of Cologne, and the use of fire-arms and cannon, produced a great change in the art of war.

CONTEMPORARY SOVEREIGNS.

SCOTLAND. A.D.
ROBERT I., ...died 1329
DAVID II., ...1370
ROBERT II.

FRANCE.
CHARLES IV., ...1328
PHILIP VI., ...1350
JOHN, ...1364
CHARLES V.

SPAIN.
ALPHONSO XI., ...1350
PEDRO, ...1368
HENRY II.

EMPERORS. A.D.
LOUIS IV., ...died 1347
CHARLES IV.

POPES.
JOHN XXII., ...1324
BENEDICT XII., ...1342
CLEMENT VI., ...1352
INNOCENT VI., ...1362
URBAN V., ...1370
GREGORY XI.

CHAPTER VIII.

RICHARD II.—BORDEAUX.

Born 1367 A.D.—Began to reign 1377 A.D.—Dethroned 1399 A.D.

Richard crowned.	The rise of Lollardism.
Tiler's rebellion.	Fall and death of Richard.
Scottish war.	Character.
The Wonderful Parliament.	Notes.

RICHARD, son of the Black Prince, was crowned in his eleventh year. In honour of the event, London was gay with banners and arches: the merchants of Cheapside erected in the market-place a fountain running wine. During the King's minority, the power was vested in twelve councillors, his uncles being excluded.

The first memorable event of the reign was a rising, excited by a poll-tax of one shilling on every person above fifteen. It burst forth in Essex and Kent; but spread westward to Winchester, and northward to Scarborough. The leaders were Wat Tiler, and Jack Straw, a priest. In this insurrection we discover traces of the old hostility of the two races,—the Saxons and the Normans,—though the old English cry, 'Down with the Normans!' no longer resounds in history. Instead of it, the enmity of the two races appears in the form of a struggle between the rich and the poor,—the motto of the English peasants being

'When Adam delved and Eve span,
Who was then a gentleman?'

Swarming in immense numbers to London, they sacked the private dwellings, burned the prisons, and slew many of the honest Flemish clothiers. Richard met them at Mile-end, and granted their demands, which were,—1. That slavery should be abolished; 2. That the rent of land should be fourpence an acre; 3. That all might have liberty to buy and sell in fairs or markets; 4. That all past offences should be pardoned. The charter was no sooner sealed than the riots began again, and several murders were committed. Next day the King held a conference in Smithfield with Tiler, who was followed by 20,000 men. The rebel leader, happening to lay his hand on his dagger, was stabbed in the throat by Walworth, the Lord Mayor, and as he lay on the ground was killed by one of the King's esquires. Richard, regardless of the frowns and bended bows of the rebels, galloped up to them, crying, 'Tiler was a traitor: I myself will be your leader!' This boldness had a great effect on the crowd: their numbers melted away, and the rebellion was over. But the promise of pardon was recalled, and fifteen hundred perished on the gibbet.

France and Scotland in alliance attempted an invasion of England, but met with little success. Richard, in **1385 A.D.** return, penetrated the latter kingdom as far as Aberdeen, reducing to ashes Edinburgh, Dunfermline, Perth, and Dundee. But in 1388 the battle of Otterbourne, between the Douglases and the Percies, ended in the defeat of the English. This battle, better known as Chevy Chase, is celebrated in old English ballads.

Richard, young and inexperienced, trusted much to favourite ministers. But the jealousy of his uncles often interfered with the government; and ultimately one of them, the Duke of Gloucester, was elected head of the **1388 A.D.** council. The Parliament, called both 'wonderful' and 'merciless,' put two of the favourites to death, and confiscated the property of the rest. Richard, watching his opportunity, at twenty-two shook himself free from the trammels of guardianship, and for some years ruled with justice and mercy; but he had not the iron will necessary to cope with the fierce and turbulent spirits that surrounded his throne.

The death of Anne of Bohemia in 1394 led to the King's second marriage with Isabella of France, then only eight years old. But an event much more important was the rise of the Lollards. They were the followers of John Wycliffe, who, in the latter years of Edward III., began to attack the corruptions of the Romish Church. He translated the Bible into English, and by his works sowed the first seeds of the Reformation in this land. Protected by John of Ghent, he died in peace; but the wrath of Rome was beginning to burn against his disciples. The name Lollards (from old German *lollen* or *lullen*, 'to sing') arose from their practice of singing hymns.

The removal of Gloucester, who was murdered mysteriously in the prison of Calais; the repeal of all acts passed by the 'wonderful Parliament;' and the grant of a life tax on wool made Richard in his last year an absolute King. But his fall was at hand. A quarrel arising between the Duke of Norfolk and the Duke of Hereford, son of John of Ghent, the King banished both, Norfolk for life, Hereford for ten years. Norfolk never returned, but Hereford came, as he said, to demand the estates of his dead father, which Richard had seized. He landed at Ravenspur in Yorkshire with only twenty followers; but, when he reached London, 60,000 men marched under his banner. Richard, who was in Ireland, was delayed for three weeks by bad weather; and, when he arrived at Milford-haven, he found that the crown had fallen from his head. At Flint he became the prisoner of Hereford, and was led with mock respect to London. The two Houses met in Westminster Hall, where stood the empty throne covered with cloth of gold. Solemnly Richard was deposed, and the same shouts which greeted his downfall hailed Hereford as King Henry IV. of England. Before the second month of 1400, the dethroned King had died in the dungeons of Pontefract, either by starvation or by the axe of an assassin. A legend of Scottish history says that Richard fled to Scotland, lived long on the royal bounty, and died at Stirling. He left no heir.

Sept. 30, 1399 A.D.

The second Richard and the second Edward were much alike in their character, their policy, and their mysterious fate. Richard's ruling passion was the love of display. His dress was stiff with gold and gems; his attendants numbered ten thousand. His last two years betrayed a spirit of reckless revenge and a thirst for absolute power, which cost him his life. He was handsome, but feminine. His manner was abrupt; his speech impeded.

In this reign bills of exchange were first used; the Order of the Bath was instituted; and Windsor Castle was completed, the workmen being obliged, by the odious system of purveyance, to give their services for nothing. Peers were now first created by letters patent; and, for the first time, at the King's coronation a knight cast down his glove, daring any one to dispute the monarch's claim. This chivalrous ceremony, which then had meaning, still lingers, and is duly performed by the royal champion.

CONTEMPORARY SOVEREIGNS.

SCOTLAND.	A.D.	EMPERORS.	A.D.
ROBERT II.,	died 1390	CHARLES IV.,	died 1378
ROBERT III.		WINCESLAS.	

FRANCE.		POPES.	
CHARLES V.,	1380	GREGORY XI.,	1378
CHARLES VI.		URBAN VI.,	1389
		BONIFACE IX.	

SPAIN.	
HENRY II.,	1379
JOHN I.,	1390
HENRY III.	

CHAPTER IX.

SCOTLAND AND IRELAND DURING THE FIRST SEVEN PLANTAGENET REIGNS.

From 1153 to 1370.—217 years.—8 Scottish Sovereigns

A.D.
MALCOLM IV. (grandson of David I.), began to rule 1153
WILLIAM I. (brother), ... 1165
ALEXANDER II. (son), ... 1214
ALEXANDER III. (son), ... 1249
MARGARET (grand-daughter), ... 1286
JOHN BALIOL (descendant of David I.), ... 1292
SIR WILLIAM WALLACE (Guardian).
ROBERT BRUCE (descendant of David I.), ... 1306
DAVID II. (son), ... 1329 to 1370

Cession of northern counties.	Bannockburn.
William the Lion.	Nevil's Cross.
Disputed succession.	Confusion in Ireland.
William Wallace.	Edward Bruce.
His betrayal and death.	The Anglo-Irish.

MALCOLM IV., grandson of David I., succeeded. His father was that Prince Henry who so narrowly escaped from the field of Northallerton. This King was called "the Maiden," either from his girlish features or his timid nature. Influenced by Henry II., he yielded to England all right over Northumberland and Cumberland. He died at Jedburgh, 1165 A.D.

William I., Malcolm's brother, then ascended the throne. He received the name of Lion, perhaps because he was the first to assume the lion rampant on the royal shield of Scotland. While attempting to recover the lost territories of Northumberland and Cumberland, he was made prisoner at Alnwick by English troops. To obtain his freedom, he took an oath of allegiance to Henry II., and agreed to hold Scotland as a fief of the English crown. This claim to the lordship of Scotland was sold for 10,000 merks by Richard Cœur de Lion. William I. died in 1214, having reigned forty-nine years. His was the longest reign in Scottish history.

Alexander II., son of William, was the next King. He

was chiefly occupied in quelling insurrections among the Danes of Caithness, the Highland Celts, and the wild Scots of Galloway.

Alexander III. succeeded his father. He was then a child of eight; and at that tender age was married at York to Margaret, daughter of Henry III. of England. The leading event of his reign was his successful resistance of a great Norwegian invasion. The Norsemen, under Haco their King, conquered Bute and Arran, and landed on the shore at Largs; but, a great storm having shattered their fleet, they were driven by the Scots into the sea. Haco reached the Orkneys only to die of grief. By this victory the Western Isles were united to the Scottish crown. Some time after, Margaret, daughter of Alexander, was married to Eric, King of Norway. Alexander III. was the Alfred of Scotland. By limiting the number of their retainers, he repressed the power of his nobles; and, to secure the pure administration of justice, he divided his kingdom into four districts, through which he passed every year. In the prime of life, while riding along the shore on a dark night, he fell over a rock near Kinghorn, and was taken up dead. This happened in 1286.

The succession now rested in Margaret—daughter of Eric, King of Norway, and the Scottish Princess, Margaret. Edward I., who had lately revived the claim of his ancestor Henry II. to the lordship of Scotland, proposed a marriage between his son, afterwards Edward II., and the Maiden of Norway, as young Margaret was called; but, in 1290, she died at Orkney, on her way to Scotland, aged only eight.

Then began that struggle for the crown which laid Scotland for many years under the English yoke. Robert Bruce and John Baliol were the rivals, and both traced descent from William the Lion. Bruce was the son of Isabella, second daughter of David, Earl of Huntingdon, brother to William the Lion. Baliol was grandson of Margaret, eldest daughter of the same noble. Edward I. decided in favour of Baliol, who was placed on the throne as a vassal of England. But so many indignities were heaped on the vassal King by his lord paramount, that the timid man was goaded to revolt. Edward wished for nothing more. He dethroned Baliol and ravaged Scotland from south to north. The Earl of Surrey was appointed Guardian; Hugh de Cressingham, Treasurer; and William Ormesby, Justiciary of the kingless land.

But a deliverer was at hand. For eight years (1297 to 1305) Sir William Wallace nobly maintained the cause of Scotland. He was the second son of Sir Malcolm Wallace of Ellerslie, near Paisley. Having slain a young Englishman, who insulted him at Dundee, this giant in size and courage betook himself to the woods. Here a band of his countrymen gathered round him, and he began, with great success, to storm the castles held by English garrisons. Surrey and Cressingham moved with a large force to crush the daring Scot. Wallace took post near Stirling, where a narrow wooden bridge spanned the Forth. His troops lined the north bank of the river; but the rising grounds concealed their full number. When Surrey saw the bridge he halted; but at length, overcome by the jeers of Wallace and the reproaches of Cressingham, he gave the order to cross. When half the English army had crossed the bridge, Wallace charged their scattered ranks, and a complete victory rewarded his generalship. In a few months not a Scottish fortress was in the hands of the English. **1297 A.D.**

Edward, hurrying from Flanders, raised a force exceeding 100,000 men, and marched to Scotland. He found the southern counties all laid waste, and was about to lead his starving forces back over the Border, when, by the treachery of two Scottish lords, he heard that Wallace lay in Falkirk Wood. Here the armies met, and the English archers won the day. For some years longer Wallace held out among the mountains of his native land; but in 1305, basely betrayed by a false friend, Sir John Menteith, he was sent in irons to London, where he was hanged, beheaded, and quartered. **1298 A.D.**

And now arose the second bright star in Scotland's history. Robert Bruce, Earl of Carrick, and grandson of that Bruce who had contended with Baliol, claimed the crown. His rival was the Red Comyn of Badenoch. They met and quarrelled in the chapel of the Minorite Friars, at Dumfries, where Bruce stabbed Comyn. This crime injured the cause of Bruce; but after some time he was crowned at Scone

(1306). The death of Edward I. saved Scotland's freedom. The war lingered for seven years, without any decisive success,—Bruce still holding the crown.

But Edward II. resolved to crush the Scottish monarchy at a blow. With 100,000 men he crossed the Border. Bruce could muster only 30,000 troops. The armies met at Bannockburn, near Stirling. On the evening before the great day, Bruce, mounted on a small pony, and armed only with a battle-axe, slew an English knight, Henry de Bohun, who attacked him in front of the lines. Before the battle began, the Scots knelt to pray. On thundered the English cavalry, sure of victory; but they soon retreated in wild dismay, for the ground was full of pits, armed with sharp stakes and covered with sods. Then poured in a close and deadly flight of arrows from 50,000 English bows. No instant was to be lost, for the Scots were falling fast. Bruce, with his light cavalry, drove the archers back; and, with a rapid charge of the men of Argyle and the Isles, shook the English ranks. Just then, a body of 20,000 men rushed down from the hill close by. To the fearful eyes of the English, this was a new Scottish army; but it was only a band of camp-followers, eager to seize the plunder of the vanquished host. The English were in headlong rout, and the victory of Bruce was decisive. On that day Bannockburn became one of Scotland's proudest names.

June 24, 1314 A.D.

Two more feeble attempts of Edward II. to regain his footing in Scotland,—two more invasions of England by the Scots,—and we find the independence of Scotland and the rights of her King acknowledged by an English Parliament, held at York in 1328. One year later, King Robert Bruce died, leaving a solemn charge with Lord Douglas to bury his heart in Jerusalem. Douglas, faithful to his promise, sailed for the Holy Land; but on the Spanish plains he died in battle with the Moors. When he saw that death was certain, he flung the silver casket, enclosing the heart of Bruce, far into the Moorish ranks, and cried, 'Forward, gallant heart, as thou wert wont; Douglas will follow thee or die!' He was found dead, with the casket clasped to his breast. The heart of Bruce was carried back to Scotland, and buried in Melrose Abbey.

David II. was only six years old when his father died. His minority was spent chiefly in France. Randolph and Murray held the regency in succession. The leading event of the minority was an attempt of the English King to seat Edward Baliol on the Scottish throne. This injury long rankled in the heart of David; and, when Edward was in France in 1346, he led an army into England. But he was defeated at Nevil's Cross, near Durham, and made prisoner. He obtained his freedom after a captivity of eleven years. But Scotland had little reason to rejoice at his release, for he was the unworthy son of a great sire. His vicious indulgences, and his quarrels with all around his throne, filled up the measure of a reign unmarked by any good event.

IRELAND.

The Danish invasions left traces upon Ireland which were felt for centuries. The land, so famous for beauty and fertility that it has been called the Emerald Isle, was reduced to a state of confusion resembling the condition of England under the Saxon Heptarchy. Descendants of the Danes, who had settled on the coasts, received the name of Ostmen, or Eastmen. These gradually blended with the general population. Above the host of petty chiefs six Kings seem to have been distinguished. They ruled over Ulster, Leinster, Connaught, North Munster, South Munster, and Meath. Occasionally there was a slight union, but war was the general rule. Such was Ireland in 1172, when its conquest was begun.

The government of Ireland under the Plantagenets was marked with cruelty and spoliation of the worst kind. Rebellions were frequent. The south-eastern part of the island, where the English settlers lived, was called the English Pale. The Barons within this Pale held the first Irish Parliament in 1295.

A striking episode in Irish history is the attempt of Edward Bruce to make himself King of the island. Aided by his brother Robert, he crossed to Ulster with 6000 men. He was crowned at Carrickfergus, and held the northern province for two years. But in 1318 he was killed in battle with the English at Fagher, near Dundalk.

The English in Ireland split into two hostile factions about the reign of Edward III. The descendants of the first invaders looked with contempt on the colonists of a later date. Many of the former had intermingled with the native Celts, adopting their dress, language, and laws. The feeling in England was so strong against these Anglo-Irish, that imprisonment and heavy fines were denounced by law against any Englishman who wore an Irish dress, or even learned the Irish language, while it was declared high treason to submit to the Brehon laws of Ireland.

CHAPTER X.

SOCIAL CONDITION OF THE PEOPLE UNDER THE PLANTAGENETS PROPER.

Houses and furniture.	Sports.
Merchants, soldiers, labourers.	Education.
Dress.	Language.

The Feudal System was in its prime when Cœur de Lion reigned: its decay may be dated from the time that the Commons first sat in Parliament: the Wars of the Roses laid its crumbling frame-work in ruins.

Gradually the higher classes became more refined. The use of spices in cookery gave new relish to their food: glass windows, earthen vessels, coal fires, and candle-light, added to the comfort of their homes. The use of tiles instead of thatch improved their dwellings. The style of architecture belonging to this period has been called the decorated Gothic. Pointed arches and profuse ornament are the distinctive features of the style. But furniture was still scanty. A decent farm-house could boast of little more than one or two beds, a few seats, a set of fire-irons, a brass pot, with a dish and a cup of the same metal.

The leading merchants dealt in wool. Even the Kings did not disdain to trade in fleeces. The Conqueror at Crecy, one of the bravest and best of them, was called, in derision, by his French rival, 'The royal wool-merchant.' The army was composed of four classes: 1. The men-at-arms, comprising knights, esquires, and their followers. These were heavy cavalry. 2. The hoblers, who were light cavalry, mounted on inferior horses, and were chiefly engaged in the Scottish wars. 3. The archers, whose skill gained some of the greatest victories of the period. Their bows were of two kinds,—long-bows to discharge shafts, and cross-bows for bolts or quarrels. 4. The footmen, armed with spears, and wearing skull-caps, quilted coats, and iron gloves. Some idea of the value of money in these days may be gathered from the rate of wages. Haymakers got a penny a-day; labourers, threehalfpence; carpenters, twopence; and masons, threepence. None were allowed to work out of their own neighbourhood, except the men of Staffordshire, Derbyshire, Lancashire, and those from the marches of Scotland and Wales, who helped to reap the English harvest. Agriculture was a favourite employment of the clergy: we read of even Becket and his monks tossing hay, and binding sheaves in the fields. Many of the improvements of the time in gardening were owing to the monks.

The dress of Edward of Windsor's court may be taken as a specimen of the fashion prevailing during the period. The exquisites wore a coat, half blue, half white, with deep sleeves; trousers reaching scarcely to the knee; stockings of different colours; and shoes with toes so long that they were fastened by golden chains to the girdle. Their beards were long and curled; their hair was tied in a tail behind; while a close hood of silk, embroidered with strange figures of animals and buttoned under the chin, enclosed the head. The most striking part of the ladies' dress at this time was a towering head-dress like a mitre, some two feet high, from which floated a whole rainbow of gay ribbons. Their trains were long; their tunics of many colours. They wore two daggers in a golden belt, and rode to the tournament and the forest on steeds of fiery spirit. Anne of Bohemia, the Queen of Richard II., introduced the use of the side-saddle.

The tournament was still the first of sports: but there were also tilting at the ring, when knights strove at full horse-speed to carry off on the point of a levelled lance a suspended ring; and tilting at a wooden figure, called a Quintain, which, swinging on a pivot, bore with outstretched arm a wooden sword. He who struck fairly in the centre was untouched; but if the lance struck too much on one side, the awkward tilter caught a sound blow from the wooden sword as he rode past the whirling image. Horse-racing and bull-baiting were sports in which high and low took equal interest: but the great pastime of the lower classes was archery, which they were bound by royal proclamation to practise on Sundays and holidays after Divine service; upon which occasions other sports, such as quoits, cock-fighting, foot-ball, hand-ball, were forbidden.

In an age when 'might was the only right,' and the qualities most prized were personal strength and skill in arms, it is not strange that education, according to our notions of it, was neglected. War and woodcraft were all the great cared to know. They neither read nor wrote; or, if they did read, it was, as has been humorously said, by spelling all the small words and skipping all the large ones. The clergy alone were learned; but their knowledge was confined within a narrow circle. Theology was their favourite study; but glimmerings of other sciences began to appear in the cloisters. They represented all the peaceful professions. They were the lawyers, the physicians, and the teachers of the day. Every monastery had its *scriptorium*, or writing-room, where manuscripts, of which every page was bordered with a beautiful design in gold and bright colours, were copied by the patient monks. The books thus produced were very costly, as much as £40 being paid for a copy of the Bible.

The Anglo-Saxon tongue, modified by the changes of the Conquest, became Semi-Saxon, a form which lasted till the time of Henry III. From Henry III. to Edward III. was the Period of Old English. The great law which governs all such transitions of an old form of speech into a newer one, is,—' As the language advances, its grammatical terminations drop off, and their place is supplied by auxiliary words.' As the language grows with the nation, with the nation also it gradually changes. Their history is inseparable. It was not until the time of Edward III. that England began to recover from the shock of the Norman Conquest. Then the English mind awoke from the lethargy of bondage, and our literature had its birth. English prose and English poetry alike sprang to life. Inspired by Italian song, Geoffrey Chaucer wrote his 'Canterbury Tales;' about the same time appeared the works of John Wycliffe, who, as Chaucer is called the father of English verse, may justly be styled the father of English prose. These writers inaugurated the Period of Middle English, which lasted till the reign of Elizabeth began.

LEADING AUTHORS OF THE PERIOD—(1154-1399).

SEMI-SAXON.

LAYAMON,..................................A priest of Areley Regis in Worcestershire—wrote a rhyming Chronicle of Britain about 1200.

OLD ENGLISH.

ROBERT OF GLOUCESTER,...(1230-1285)—wrote a rhyming History of England.
ROBERT MANNING,................Of Brunne or Bourne—chronicler.
BASTON,......................................A Carmelite monk—poet—brought by Edward II. to Scotland to celebrate his victories—taken by the Scots, and made to sing the victory of Bannockburn.

MIDDLE ENGLISH.

JOHN GOWER,..........................(1320-1402)—wrote moral poetry.
GEOFFREY CHAUCER,............(1328-1400)—first great English poet—lived at the courts of Edward III. and Richard II.—chief work, 'The Canterbury Tales.'
JOHN MANDEVILLE,...............(1301-1372)—wrote Travels in the East in English, French, and Latin.
JOHN WYCLIFFE,....................Died 1384—a native of Yorkshire—Professor of Divinity, Baliol College, Oxford—translator of Bible—earliest English Reformer.
JOHN BARBOUR,.....................Archdeacon of Aberdeen—wrote about 1371 a rhyming Chronicle of Robert Bruce.

LEADING DATES OF THE PERIOD—(1154-1399).

GENERAL EVENTS.	A.D.	CONSTITUTIONAL CHANGES.	A.D.
Becket murdered,	1170...Hen. II.	Council of Clarendon,	1164...Hen. II.
Interdict,	1208-1214...John.	Magna Charta,	1215...John.
Baliol King of Scotland,	1292...Ed. I.	Mad Parliament,	1258...Hen. III.
Robert Bruce crowned,	1306... —	House of Commons founded,	1265... —
		Ordainers,	1310...Ed. II.
		Wonderful Parliament,	1388...Rich. II.

PLANTAGENET DATES.

WARS, BATTLES, TREATIES.	CHANGES OF DOMINION.
A.D.	A.D.
Third Crusade 1190-92...Rich. I.	Ireland conquered 1172...Hen. II.
Battle of Bouvines 1214...John.	Wales conquered...1282...Ed. I.
— Lincoln..........1217...Hen. III.	Calais taken..........1347...Ed. III.
— Lewes............1264... —	Poitou and Guienne acquired......1360... —
— Evesham........1265... —	These provinces lost..................1375... —
— Bannockburn 1314...Ed. II.	
— Halidon-hill..1333...Ed. III.	
French war begins 1338... —	
Battle of Creçy......1346... —	
— Nevil's Cross — ... —	
— Poictiers.........1356... —	
Treaty of Bretigny 1360... —	
Tiler's rebellion....1381...Rich. II.	
Battle of Otterbourne..............1388... —	

GENEALOGICAL TREE

CONNECTING THE PLANTAGENETS PROPER WITH THE HOUSES OF YORK AND LANCASTER.

EDWARD III., married PHILIPPA.

```
├── EDWARD (Black Prince).
│       └── RICHARD II.
├── LIONEL, Duke of Clarence.
│       └── PHILIPPA, married to EDMUND MORTIMER.
│               └── ROGER, Earl of March.
│                       ├── EDMUND, Earl of March, Died in 1424.
│                       └── ANNE, married Earl of Cambridge.
├── JOHN of Ghent, Duke of Lancaster.
│       ═ HENRY IV., married MARY BOHUN.
│               ═ HENRY V., married Catherine of France.
│                       ═ HENRY VI., married MARGARET of Anjou.
│                               ═ PRINCE EDWARD, married ANNE NEVILLE.
└── EDMUND, Duke of York.
        └── RICHARD of Cambridge, married ANNE, daughter of ROGER, Earl of March.
                └── EDWARD of York.
                        └── RICHARD, Duke of York, married CECILY NEVILLE.
                                ├── EDWARD IV., married ELIZABETH WOODVILLE.
                                │       ├── ELIZABETH of York.
                                │       ├── EDWARD V.
                                │       └── RICHARD.
                                ├── GEORGE of Clarence.
                                └── RICHARD III.
                                        └── EDWARD, Prince of Wales, died 1484.
```

The double line marks the direct descent of the House of Lancaster; the dotted line that of the House of York.

HOUSE OF LANCASTER.

	A.D.
HENRY IV. (son of John of Ghent),	1399
HENRY V. (son),	1413
HENRY VI. (son),	1422–1461.

CHAPTER I.

HENRY IV.—BOLINGBROKE.

Born 1367 A.D.—Began to reign 1399 A.D.—Died 1413 A.D.

Henry succeeds.	The Prince of Wales.
Scottish war.	Death of Henry.
Plots.	Character.
Glendower.	Power of the Commons.
The Percies.	Notes.
France.	

THE representative of the House of Lancaster now sat on the throne. He detained in close custody the young Edmund, Earl of March, who, being descended from an elder branch of the royal Plantagenets, was, according to our law of inheritance, King by right. It was not, however, until a later period that the law of primogeniture became the leading principle of succession to the English throne.

A successful Scottish war was the first great undertaking of the new King. The old hostility of the Border Lords, Douglas and Percy, flamed out anew. On Nesbit Moor and at Homildon Hill the Scots suffered severe defeats. **1402 A.D.**

Several insurrections shook the power of Henry. There was a common report that Richard was living and in Scotland. The Earl of March, too, lived; and the King's title was defective. Upon grounds like these, plots were built up; but none succeeded.

Throughout the entire reign a Welshman named Owen Glendower maintained his independence among the hills. He had been educated in the law-schools of London, and had served as an esquire at the court of Richard II.; but on his return to Wales, where his superior learning gained for him the reputation of a wizard, a part of his estate was seized by Lord Grey of Ruthyn, a near friend of the King; and his anger drove him to revolt.

But Henry's greatest enemies were the Percies, father and son. The father was Earl of Northumberland; the son, from his dashing and fiery spirit, was named Hotspur. It is uncertain why they drew the sword against the monarch whom they had helped to place on the throne. Perhaps the cause may be found in Henry's refusal to ransom from the Welsh Sir Edmund Mortimer, a kinsman of Hotspur. Glendower and the Scots joined the Percies. The King met them at Shrewsbury. The battle was long and bloody, but was decided in favour of Henry by the death of Hotspur. Northumberland, who had been detained from the field by illness, submitted at once, and was pardoned; but, revolting again, he led a wandering life for many years in Scotland and Wales, and was at last slain near Tadcaster in Yorkshire.

1403 A.D.

With France a dispute arose about the jewels and the dowry of the widowed Isabella; which, according to agreement, should have been returned on her husband's death. The English King met the demand by a counter-claim for the ransom of John, who was captured at Poictiers. For some time there was no open declaration of war; but the French nobles were allowed to hurl insulting challenges at Henry, and even to ravage his coasts in their privateers. Two events, however, gave Henry the ascendency in Scotland and in France. James, the eldest surviving son of the Scottish King, when on his way to the schools of France, was driven by a storm on the English coast, and captured, and was imprisoned at Pevensey. The murder of the Duke of Orleans kindled in France a civil war between the adherents of the houses of Orleans and Burgundy, called respectively the Armagnacs and Bourguignons. Henry, becoming in turn the ally of each, regained the sovereignty of Aquitaine, Poitou, and Angouleme.

Henry's declining years were vexed by the vicious conduct of his eldest son; who, however, sometimes showed gleams of a better nature. Once, when Chief-Justice Gascoigne had sentenced to imprisonment a riotous companion of the Prince, the royal youth drew his sword on the judge; who, nothing daunted, sent him too to the King's Bench; thus vindicating the power of the laws even over the royal line. The Prince submitted with a good grace, and bore no malice against Gascoigne, whom he afterwards treated with much kindness. Again: hearing that some unguarded words had excited a suspicion that he aimed at the crown, he entered his father's closet, and, casting himself at the royal feet, held out a dagger, demanding death rather than disgrace.

Fits of epilepsy wore out the strength of Henry at a comparatively early age. The last seized him at Westminster, and he was buried at Canterbury. He was married twice: first to Mary Bohun, daughter of the Earl of Hereford; then to Jane of Navarre. Jane had no children; Mary's were Henry—afterwards King, Thomas Duke of Clarence, John Duke of Bedford, Humphrey Duke of Gloucester, Blanche, and Philippa.

Henry IV. was daring, watchful, active. He well understood the temper of the nation and the Parliament. Some idea of his difficult position may be gathered from the fact, that in the first Parliament of his reign forty gauntlets of defiance were cast on the floor, while 'liar' and 'traitor' were common words of debate. He was of middle size, and in his last years his face was disfigured by an eruption, which the superstition of the time ascribed to the judgment of Heaven for the execution of Scroop, Archbishop of York, an adherent of the rebel Percies.

Step by step the Commons extended their power. They confirmed the privilege by which they and their servants were free from arrest or imprisonment. They secured the right of presenting their petitions by word of mouth, instead of writing them. The addresses from the Speaker's chair took a bolder tone. They established their claim to vote supplies of money, to determine the particular object of the sums voted, and to inquire into the expenditure.

During this reign occurred the first execution for religious opinions. The victim was the Rev. William Sautre, Chaplain of St. Oswith's in London. Holding with unshaken faith the opinions of Wycliffe, he was accused of heresy, and burned in public, A.D. 1401.

The earliest mention of cannon in England occurs in the narrative of the siege of Berwick by Henry in 1405; in which we are told that a shot from a great gun shattered one of the towers so much that the gates were thrown open by the alarmed garrison.

CONTEMPORARY SOVEREIGNS.

SCOTLAND.	A.D.	EMPERORS.	A.D.
ROBERT III.,	died 1405	WINCESLAUS,	died 1400
JAMES I.		ROBERT,	1410
		SIGISMUND.	

FRANCE.		POPES.	
CHARLES VI.		BONIFACE IX.,	1404
		INNOCENT VII.,	1406
		GREGORY XII.,	1409
SPAIN.		ALEXANDER V.,	1410
HENRY III.		JOHN XXIII.	

CHAPTER II.

HENRY V.—MONMOUTH.

Born 1388 A.D.—Began to reign 1413 A.D.—Died 1422 A.D.

Henry reforms.	Glorious position.
Sir John Oldcastle.	Death.
A French war.	Character.
Battle of Agincourt.	The Commons.
Henry Regent of France.	Notes.

The riotous Prince Hal was suddenly transformed into the brave and spirited King Henry V. His earliest act was to discard his old companions, and to call around him the wisest of the land, conspicuous among whom was Sir William Gascoigne. He set free the Earl of March. He restored the Percy estates to the exiled son of Hotspur.

Early in his reign the sect of the Lollards, by their efforts for religious reform, drew upon themselves the royal anger. Chief among them was Sir John Oldcastle, or the Lord of Cobham. He had been one of the Prince's former intimates, and some have considered him the original of Shakspere's Falstaff; but repenting of his follies, he amended his life, and made his castle of Cowling the central mission-station of Lollardism. Hence he was borne to the dungeons of the Tower by the soldiers of Henry; who, seeking to please the clergy, proclaimed the heresy, as it was called, a crime of the blackest dye. Escaping, he called his followers together in St. Giles' Fields; but the vigilance of the King, who burst upon their meeting at the dead of night, scattered the Lollards. The leader fled, but many of those who were taken were doomed to death; and, three years afterwards, Oldcastle, who had left his hiding-place to join the invading Scots, was burned as a felon and a heretic.

The title 'King of France' was claimed until lately by our monarchs; but Henry of Monmouth was the only English sovereign who really deserved the name. Taking advantage of the civil war which still convulsed France, he revived the claim of Edward III., and demanded that the treaty of Bretigny should be fulfilled. For answer there came a load of tennis-balls,—a gentle hint from the Dauphin that the English King was fitter for such sports than for war. Stung by the insult, Henry prepared for battle. The Duke of Bedford was appointed Regent; the royal jewels were pawned; loans were exacted; and the Barons were called to arms. But delay arose from the discovery of a plot in favour of the Earl of March. The King's nearest friends, Lord Scroop, who shared his bed, and his cousin Richard of Cambridge, suffered death for the treason.

A fleet now bore Henry with 30,000 soldiers from Southampton to the mouth of the Seine. He took Harfleur, a strong fortress on the right bank of the river, in five weeks; and then, with an army reduced to one-half its former number by wounds and sickness, he formed the daring resolve of reaching Calais by the same route as that by which the troops of Edward III. had marched to victory. He found the bridges of the Somme broken down, and the fords defended by lines of sharp stakes; but, after a delay of some days, an unguarded point was discovered high up the stream. Crossing rapidly, he moved straight upon Calais, while the Constable of France awaited his approach before the village of Agincourt. It was a dark and rainy night, when the wearied English saw before them the red light of the French watch-fires.

One hundred thousand French lay there. The odds were seven to one. But Crecy was not far distant, and the memory of former glory stirred in every English heart. The invincible archers led the way in the early morning. With a cheer they rushed on, bearing with their usual weapons long sharp stakes. These they fixed obliquely before them, so that a wall of wooden pikes met the French charge; and, thus protected, they poured in their close and deadly arrows. Then slinging their bows behind them, they burst with the men-at-arms upon the breaking ranks; and the first, the second, and the third divisions gave way in succession. Henry fought in the thickest of the battle; and, though mace and sabre were levelled at his life more than once, he escaped unhurt. The confusion caused by the tactics of the English

Oct. 25, 1415 A.D.

King, who had secretly sent a body of troops to set fire to the houses of Agincourt in the French rear, completed the rout. The Constable, the flower of the French nobility, and eight thousand knights and esquires, fell on this fatal day: the victors lost only sixteen hundred men. Without following up this terrible blow, Henry crossed to Dover. No welcome seemed too warm for him. The people rushed into the sea to meet his ship; his journey to London was through shouting crowds and beneath waving banners. The Parliament, unasked, voted him large sums, and granted to him for life a tax on wool and leather.

The war was renewed in 1417. Slowly but surely the King of England extended his conquests, until the fall of Rouen, after a siege of six months, laid Normandy at his feet. His path to the French throne was opened by an unforeseen occurrence. The Duke of Burgundy was foully murdered; and his faction, thirsting for revenge, threw their whole weight on Henry's side. He was thus enabled to dictate terms of peace to the French monarch, and the treaty of Troyes was framed. Its leading conditions were three:—1. That Henry should receive in marriage the French princess Catherine; 2. That he should be Regent during the life of the imbecile Charles; 3. That he should succeed to the French throne on the death of that prince.

1419 A.D.

1420 A.D.

A short visit to England with his bride was suddenly clouded by sad news, which recalled him to France. The Dauphin, re-enforced by a large body of Scots, routed the English troops at Beaujé, and slew the Duke of Clarence, Henry's brother. In hopes that the Scots would not fight against their own King, the English sovereign led into battle the captive James. The hope was vain; but, ever invincible, Henry drove his foe into Bourges, and paralyzed all hostile efforts by the capture of Meaux, a stronghold near Paris.

He had now climbed the highest steeps of his ambition. He was master of Northern France to the banks of the Loire; no leaf had fallen from the laurels won at Agincourt and Rouen; a son had been lately born to inherit his honours and his name; when Paris was gay at Whitsuntide, the splendour of the Louvre, where the Regent held his court, far outshone the petty pomp of the real King. But in the very noon of his glory he died. His disease has been variously named; one thing is sure, that the debaucheries of his early life sowed the seeds of his early death. In gorgeous state his remains were borne to England, and were there laid in the vaults of Westminster. He left one son, afterwards Henry VI. His widow, Catherine, married Owen Tudor, a gentleman of Wales; and thus was founded the line of royal Tudors.

Henry was a warrior and a statesman. His arrogance often wounded, but his even justice atoned with his people for many faults. He was the darling of the soldiers whom he led so often to victory. In figure he was tall and slight.

The Commons gained during this reign an important point,—that no law should have force unless it had received their assent. At no time were supplies of money more freely given; for the King had so dazzled his people by the lustre of his victories that they never denied his requests. Taxes were granted for life, and on the security of these he was allowed to raise heavy loans. The yearly revenue was nearly £56,000, but the expenditure often passed that sum. Calais alone is said to have cost close upon £20,000 a-year. The foundation of the British navy may be ascribed to this reign; for Henry caused a ship of considerable size to be built for him at Bayonne. The fleets already spoken of were either merchant vessels or ships hired from foreign states. Richard Whittington, a merchant of London, was during this reign three times Lord Mayor. He made a great fortune by the voyages of a ship called the *Cat*,—a name which has given rise to the well-known nursery tale.

CONTEMPORARY SOVEREIGNS.

SCOTLAND.	A.D.	EMPEROR.	A.D.
JAMES I.		**SIGISMUND.**	
FRANCE.			
CHARLES VI.			
SPAIN.		POPES.	
HENRY III.,	died 1406	**JOHN XXIII.,**	died 1415
JOHN II.		**MARTIN V.**	

CHAPTER III.

HENRY VI.—WINDSOR.

Born 1421 A.D.—Began to reign 1422 A.D.—Dethroned 1461 A.D.

The Regency.	Richard of York.	Margaret in the field.
Bedford in France.	Death of Suffolk.	Henry deposed.
Siege of Orleans.	Cade's rebellion.	Power of Parliament.
Joan of Arc.	Wars of the Roses begin.	The revenue.
Loss of French dominions.	The compromise.	Notes.

THE successor to the throne was an infant nine months old. A council of twenty managed the affairs of the kingdom. The Duke of Bedford was made Regent of France, while Humphrey of Gloucester bore the title, "Protector of the Realm of England."

After the death of the French King, which followed close upon that of Henry V., the Dauphin assumed the title, Charles VII. The Loire now separated the English provinces from the French. Bedford nobly maintained the honour of England in the battles of Crevant (1423), and Verneuil (1424). But Gloucester having married Jacqueline of Bavaria, claimed a large part of the Netherlands as her inheritance. The Duke of Brabant, also claiming to be the husband of this princess, opposed the demand of Gloucester, and was supported by his cousin, the great Duke of Burgundy, who thus became estranged from the English alliance. At home, too, Gloucester quarrelled with Beaufort, Bishop of Winchester, a haughty and powerful prelate. So Bedford's hands grew weak.

In 1428 it was resolved in council, contrary, we are told, to the will of the Regent, that the English army should cross the Loire, and ravage the provinces which owned the sway of Charles. As a preparatory step, Orleans was besieged. While the English troops lay before the walls, a skirmish took place which has received a strange name,— 'The battle of herrings.' At Roverai an English knight beat back a body of French cavalry, who attacked him as he was escorting a train of provision-cars to the camp of the besiegers. Salted herrings formed a large part of the stores, and hence arose the name. This success, and the energy with which the English carried on the siege, dispirited the French, who now looked upon Orleans as lost.

But suddenly there came a change. Joan of Arc, the servant in a village inn, sought the presence of the French King, and there proclaimed that she had a mission from Heaven to drive the English from Orleans and to lead Charles to Rheims. Either believing her story or desirous to work upon the superstition of his soldiers, the monarch paid her every honour. Clad in armour, she rode on a gray steed to the rescue of Orleans. She entered the city; stormed the fortress before the gate; and drove the English from before the walls; thus winning her name,—'The Maid of Orleans.' In two months more Charles was crowned at Rheims, and her mission was fulfilled. But soon began a reaction. In a sortie from the city of Compeigne, she was pulled from her horse by an archer, and made prisoner. She was sold to the English Regent; and, after twelve months' imprisonment, was burned as a witch in the marketplace of Rouen.

1429 A.D.

1431 A.D.

The young Henry was now crowned at Westminster and at Paris,—a step considered necessary after the coronation of Charles at Rheims. But the crowning at Paris was an empty form. A congress was held at Arras in 1435, at which the clergy strove in vain to bring about peace. Then two great blows shook the English power in France : The great Bedford died; and the Duke of Burgundy made peace and alliance with France. The loss of Paris speedily followed; and in 1444 the English were glad to make a truce for two years. In the following year Henry married the beautiful and high-spirited Margaret, daughter of René, Duke of Anjou and Maine. These provinces were now, by a reversal of the ordinary custom, restored to the father of the bride. They were called the keys of Normandy, and deep murmurs resounded through England when they were severed from the crown. French troops poured across the Loire; and soon Rouen and all Normandy submitted. From the north of France, Charles turned to the south. Gate after gate of the Gascon cities opened to his triumphant march, until, in 1451, the banner of England waved nowhere, from the Straits of Dover to the Pyrenees, except on the citadel of Calais. Thus ended the dream of an English empire in France.

Early in this reign (1423) James of Scotland was released, and returned to his own country. He brought with him to Scotland, to share his throne, an English wife, Jane Beaufort, daughter of the Earl of Somerset.

The great pillars of the House of Lancaster were the Duke of Gloucester, and his uncle, Cardinal Beaufort. Though rivals for political fame, they united in upholding the throne of Henry; who, as he grew to manhood, gave every day clearer signs of a weak intellect. But they died within six weeks of each other; and then visions of a throne began to rise before the mind of Richard, Duke of York, sprung by his mother from the second son, by his father from the youngest son, of Edward III.

The removal of a faithful minister from Henry's councils gave new colour to the hopes of York. The loss of the French provinces had excited great discontent throughout England; and the Duke of Suffolk, by whose advice Anjou and Maine had been restored to René, was marked as an object of special hatred. He was impeached, was banished, and had left the English shores with the hope of being allowed to land at Calais. But a fleet of war-ships bore down upon his frail craft, and he was summoned on board 'the Nicholas of the Tower;' where the captain received him with the words, 'Welcome, traitor!' Two days after, a boat reached the side, carrying a headsman, a block, and a rusty sword; and on this strange scaffold Suffolk died.

This was a heavy blow to Henry. The rumour of preparations for a terrible revenge reached the men of Kent, who had furnished the ships to seize Suffolk. They were the descendants of those who had followed Tiler to Smithfield. They rose in arms under Jack Cade, who took the name of Mortimer a cousin of York. The King's troops were defeated at Sevenoaks, and their leader was slain. Cade, arraying himself in the armour of the fallen knight, marched to London; upon which Henry withdrew to Kenilworth. Unresisted the rebels entered the city, Cade cutting the ropes of the drawbridge with his sword as he passed. For two days they held the city, but on the third the pillage of some houses roused the Londoners, who seized the bridge and held it gallantly for six hours, when a short truce was made. The Bishop of Winchester took advantage of this interval to offer a free pardon to all who should return to their homes at once; and Cade was left with scarcely a follower. A second time he tried to raise a force, but failed; and fleeing, he was discovered in a garden, near Lewes in Sussex, by Iden, an esquire, who slew him, and received 1000 merks as the price of his head. There is a strong probability that York was at the bottom of this plot; and that, if successful, the rebels would have placed him on the throne.

A cloud, at first no bigger than a man's hand, had long been darkening round the throne of the Lancasters. It now burst in civil war. The Duke of York had matured his plans, and the time was ripe for action. It was true, a son had been born to Henry amid general rejoicings; but the anger of the people had been excited by the bestowal of the King's favour on Somerset, whom they blamed for the loss of Normandy, and by the miserable failure of an attempt to recover Guienne. At this critical point the King was seized with a fit of insanity, and the reins of government were thrown into the hands of York with the title of Protector. This, however, did not last long; for the recovery of Henry deprived York of his office. But the Duke having

1455
A.D.

tasted the sweets of power, took up arms. The famous Wars of the Roses began. They were so called from the badges of the rival armies: the ensign of the House of York was a white, that of the House of Lancaster a red rose. The chief supporters of York were the Earl of Salisbury, and his son the Earl of Warwick.

During the remaining years of Henry's reign, six battles were fought. The question of right to the throne was not confined to the armies in the field, but was fiercely discussed at every fireside in the kingdom; and all England was divided into two great parties. At St. Albans in 1455 the Lancastrians were defeated, and the King was made prisoner. He was, however, soon released, and a pretended reconciliation followed. But, the war being renewed, the Yorkists were again victorious, at Bloreheath in Staffordshire (1459). Henry was a second time made captive, at Northampton, by the Yorkists under Warwick (1460). Now, for the first time, York publicly laid claim to the throne, as the representative of the eldest surviving branch of the royal family. The question was debated in Parliament, and an arrangement was made that Henry should reign during his life, and that the crown should then pass to York and his heirs.

This roused a mother's heart. Margaret of Anjou, burning with anger that her son Edward, Prince of Wales, should be thus shut out from the throne, called the Lancastrian lords to her side, and routed the Yorkists at Wakefield Green in Yorkshire; where, for the first time, the Red Rose triumphed (1460). Here the Duke of York was slain; and, according to the barbarous fashion of the time, his head, adorned with a paper crown, was fixed upon the walls of York. This loss, instead of dispiriting, roused the Yorkists to madness. Edward, Earl of March, the son of the fallen Duke, succeeded to the title and the claims of his father. He was a brave and handsome youth of nineteen, and the hearts of the people leaned to him. At Mortimer's Cross he swept the royalist troops before him (1461). A few days later, Margaret, defeating Warwick in the second battle of St. Albans (1461), released the King from confinement. But when Edward marched to London, he was received by the citizens with shouts of joy. A great council having declared that Henry had forfeited the throne when he joined the army of the Queen, the young Duke was at once proclaimed King, with the title of Edward IV. **March 4, 1461 A.D.**

Henry of Windsor was weak in body and in mind. His long minority formed in him the habit of trusting much to his councillors; and their faults were often visited upon him. But in his private character he was meek and inoffensive, more ready to forgive than to punish, and easily led, for the sake of peace, to betray his own interest.

The House of Lords still formed the governing body, and by their advice the King was ruled in all great transactions.

They appointed Regents; and it was by their vote that Henry was dethroned.

The Commons gave assent, not advice. They granted the supplies, however; and in this lay their real strength. They were not very regular in their attendance on the Parliaments; and it seems that the pay they received from those whom they represented, and the freedom from arrest or punishment which their office conferred, were the strongest motives to the discharge of their public duty. In this reign the franchise, or right of voting, was limited to those owning a freehold worth, at the least, forty shillings a-year.

The revenue of the crown had lately very much decreased. Henry IV. drew from France a great part of his income. Henry VI. found his French dominions narrowed to a single town, and his direct income fallen so low as £5000 a-year. Owing to the immense expense of the French wars, and other causes, the debts of Henry were far above £300,000.

In this reign Eton College, and King's College, Cambridge, were founded (1440); and the establishment of Glasgow University followed in 1454. Halley's comet was first observed in 1456, and the manufacture of glass in England was begun in 1457;—two facts which show that Science and Art were progressing, though slowly, amid the storms of civil war. On the Continent might be seen the gradual development of an art destined to possess an influence such as no art had ever yet possessed. In 1442 Faust printed from wooden blocks. In 1444 Guttenberg cut types from metal. In 1450 the roller press was invented. In 1452 the types of Schoeffer, cast in hollow moulds, came into use.

CONTEMPORARY SOVEREIGNS.

SCOTLAND.	A.D.	EMPERORS.	A.D.
JAMES I.,	died 1437	SIGISMUND,	died 1437
JAMES II.,	1460	ALBERT II.,	1439
JAMES III.		FREDERIC IV.	
FRANCE.		POPES.	
CHARLES VI.,	1422	MARTIN V.,	1431
CHARLES VII.		EUGENIUS IV.,	1447
SPAIN.		NICHOLAS V.,	1455
JOHN II.,	1454	CALIXTUS III.,	1458
HENRY IV.		PIUS II.	

HOUSE OF YORK.

A D.
EDWARD IV. (son of Richard of York),....began to rule 1461.
EDWARD V. (son),..1483.
RICHARD III. (uncle),..1483–1485.

CHAPTER I.

EDWARD IV.

Born 1443 A.D.—Began to reign 1461 A.D.—Died 1483 A.D.

Wars of the Roses continued.	Edward flees.	Death of Clarence.
Edward's quarrel with Warwick.	Battle of Barnet.	Death of Edward.
Exile of Warwick.	War with France.	Character.
	Treaty of Pecquigny.	Notes.
	The King's revenue.	

THE Wars of the Roses were not yet euded. The north remained faithful to Henry; London and the south had declared for Edward. But a victory, won at Towton in Yorkshire, amid falling snow (1461), established the kingdom of Edward. Margaret sailed to France in hope of aid. Again the shattered ranks of the Lancastrians were arrayed; but at Hedgeley Moor and Hexham (1464) they were again broken. Henry fled from the field of Hexham to the wilds of Lancashire, where for more than a year he eluded pursuit; but, taken at last, he was thrown into the Tower of London.

In 1464 Edward married privately the Lady Elizabeth Grey, daughter of a knight named Woodville. When she was crowned as Queen, her brothers and sisters received in marriage the richest and noblest wards of the court. This incensed the nobles, especially the haughty Nevils, of which family the Earl of Warwick was head. Warwick, known in history as the 'King-maker,' was minister-in-chief, and governor of Calais, then the richest office in the King's gift, and could not tamely brook the loss of his influence with Edward. The breach, growing daily wider, ended in an open quarrel. Warwick, aided by the Duke of Clarence, brother of the King, raised an insurrection among the men of York and Lincoln. But the Earl and the Duke were forced to flee to the court of Louis XI., where they met Margaret of Anjou. Warwick and Margaret had now a common cause, and they united to dethrone Edward. The union was cemented by the marriage of Prince Edward, Margaret's son, to Anne, daughter of Warwick.

After an absence of five months, the King-maker landed without resistance in the south of England. The hopes of the Lancastrians revived, when 6000 men cast the white roses from their bonnets and cried, 'God bless King Harry!' Edward fled to Holland, and Henry was brought from his cell to wear the crown once more.

The Duke of Burgundy was married to a sister of Edward: and from him the exiled Prince received men, money, and ships, and landed in a few months at Ravenspur in Yorkshire. When Edward reached Nottingham, 60,000 men wore the white rose. His brother Clarence, long an adherent of Warwick, rejoined the Yorkist ranks, and the army was soon within the walls of London. The decisive battle was fought on Easter Sunday, 1471, at Barnet, where every petal of the Red Rose was scattered from the stem. Warwick, his brother Montague, every leader of the Lancastrians died on the bloody field. On that very day Margaret and her son landed at Plymouth. Three weeks later, their army was cut to pieces, and they were made prisoners at Tewkesbury in Gloucestershire. They were brought before the victor, and the queenly heart of Margaret, which had borne her bravely through so many perils and disasters, now sank beneath the heaviest blow of all, when she saw the face of her darling son bruised by the iron glove of Edward, and his young life-blood streaming on the daggers of Clarence and Gloucester. Ransomed by Louis of France, she survived that fatal day eleven years. Henry died by violence in the Tower on the day of Edward's triumphal entry into London.

A fierce dispute arose between the brothers of the King. Clarence, as the husband of Warwick's eldest daughter, claimed the estates of the King-maker; Gloucester, who now sought out Anne, another daughter, the widow of the murdered Prince Edward, and married her, demanded a share. With difficulty both were satisfied, a division being made, by which the aged Countess was left penniless.

Edward then formed the project of a French war, reviving the old claim to the French crown. He had strong motives to such a war. He was kinsman by marriage to the Duke of Burgundy, a deadly foe of France. He wished to employ in foreign war those who might be inclined to plot against his government, or to stir up the embers of the civil strife. In addition to the supplies voted by Parliament, he invented a new and most elastic method of raising money. Calling rich subjects before him, he demanded presents of money, which they dared not refuse. These sums he called *benevolences*. After much delay he invaded France, but found his allies unable to give him any aid. In the midst of his uncertainty, there came a welcome message from Louis proposing peace and alliance. At Pecquigny a bridge was thrown across the Somme. Midway the monarchs met, and, shaking hands through a wooden grating, swore to observe the terms of the treaty. The chief conditions were:— 1. That Louis should pay 75,000 crowns at once, and an annuity of 50,000 to Edward during his life; 2. That a truce and free trade should exist between the countries for seven years; 3. That the Dauphin should marry Elizabeth, Edward's eldest daughter. French gold, lavishly scattered among the English courtiers, bought this treaty of Pecquigny, and many nobles were not ashamed openly to avow themselves the pensioners of Louis.

1475 A.D.

The people of England murmured loudly at the disgraceful end of a war for which they had been heavily taxed, and a slight breath would have kindled an insurrection. Edward had the sense to see this, and his future policy was directed to the support of his throne without drawing from the purses of his people. By levying the customs more rigorously, by extorting tenths from the clergy, by taking back lately bestowed grants, by exacting all feudal fines, and by trading in his own name to the Mediterranean ports, he was able, not only to meet all expenses, but to grow rich amid a tolerably contented people.

The death of the Duke of Clarence left a dark stain on the memory of Edward. The brothers had been long estranged, chiefly because Edward prevented the marriage of Clarence with Mary, the rich heiress of Burgundy; and when Thomas Burdett, a friend of the Duke, was executed on a charge of practising 'the black art,' Clarence loudly blamed the King. In revenge, Edward summoned him before the House of Lords. He received sentence, and in ten days he died within the Tower. A common report said that he was drowned in a butt of Malmsey, a wine of which he was fond.

It was a strange feature of Edward's foreign policy that he endeavoured to make marriages for his children from the day of their birth; but none of his schemes succeeded. His favourite project, the marriage agreed upon at Pecquigny, was frustrated shortly before his death by the marriage of the Dauphin to Margaret of Burgundy. Some days later, a slight illness working on his frame, which was worn out by debauchery, suddenly assumed a fatal character. He died in his forty-first year, and was buried at Windsor. His children were Edward, now aged twelve; Richard, Duke of York; and five daughters, of whom the eldest, Elizabeth, was afterwards married to Henry VII.

The love of vicious pleasures was the chief quality of Edward's character. His lustful passions brought shame on many an honest household. Gorgeous dresses, rich meats, costly wines were among his highest enjoyments. He waded to a throne in blood, and he maintained it by a spy system, so perfect that nothing could happen around his court or in the most distant county without his knowledge. He was handsome and accomplished; but his sensual indulgences rendered him, in his later life, bloated and unwieldy.

The petitions of the Parliament were now framed into what we still call 'Acts of Parliament,'—a plan intended to prevent the King from making any change in the law, before he gave his assent to its passing.

The reign of Edward IV. is distinguished by the introduction of Printing into England. William Caxton, who learned the art in Holland, translated a French work, called 'The Recuyell of the Histories of Troye,' and printed it at Ghent in 1471. This was the first specimen of printing in the English language. In 1473 he set up a press at Westminster, and in 1474 issued from it the first book printed on English ground,—'The Game and Playe of Chesse.' Scotland received this boon in 1508, Ireland in 1551. Posts were now first used in England on the road from London to Scotland. Horsemen were placed twenty miles apart, and the despatches were thus passed on at the rate of one hundred miles a day.

CONTEMPORARY SOVEREIGNS.

SCOTLAND.	A.D.	EMPEROR.	A.D.
JAMES III.		FREDERIC III.	
FRANCE.			
CHARLES VII.,	died 1461		
LOUIS XI.		**POPES.**	
SPAIN.		PIUS II.,	died 1464
HENRY IV.,	1474	PAUL II.,	1471
FERDINAND and ISABELLA.		SIXTUS IV.	

CHAPTER II.

EDWARD V.

Born 1471 A.D.—Began to reign April 9.—Dethroned June 25, 1483.

Edward and his brother.
Hastings and Rivers.
Richard of Gloucester King.

EDWARD V., the eldest son of the late King, reigned only eleven weeks. During that time Richard Duke of Gloucester, who assumed the title of Protector, and pretended the purest loyalty towards his royal nephew, was engaged in clearing his own way to the throne. The boy-King was seized at Stony Stratford near Northampton, led with the mockery of public honours to London, and cast into the Tower. The Queen-mother was forced to part also with her second son, who was committed to the same prison; and there the two boys, busied with their sports, lived all unconscious of the dark web which was slowly infolding them.

Gloucester's next step was to remove those nobles who were faithful to the cause of the young Edward. Lord Hastings, arrested in the council-room on a charge of sorcery, was at once beheaded on a block of wood in the chapel-yard of the Tower. On the same day Lord Rivers, maternal uncle of the King, and the patron of Caxton, was executed with three others at Pontefract Castle, into which he had been thrown when Edward was made captive. When this was done, the Duke of Buckingham, a prince of royal blood, met the citizens of London at Guildhall, and in an earnest speech declared Richard of Gloucester the true heir to the throne. The citizens kept silence, but a few hirelings cried out 'Long live King Richard;' and on the next day Buckingham, in the name of the English people, presented a petition entreating Gloucester to wear the crown. With feigned reluctance the Protector consented, and Edward's reign was at an end.

CHAPTER III.

RICHARD III.—CROOKBACK.

Born 1452 A.D.—Began to reign 1483 A.D.—Died 1485 A.D.

Richard's progress.	Buckingham in rebellion.
Story of the young Princes.	Bosworth-field.
Henry of Richmond.	Character.

A FORTNIGHT later, at Westminster Richard was crowned with his wife Anne, the daughter of the King-maker. By raising the rank of many nobles, and by lavish distribution of the dead King's hoards, he gathered round his throne a band of adherents. Then making a progress through the country, for the purpose, as he said, of securing the peace of England and the pure administration of justice, he was crowned again at York.

But before he reached York a terrible crime is said to have been committed. Sir Thomas More tells us that James Tyrrel, Richard's master of the horse, was sent from Warwick to London with a royal letter charging Brackenbury, the governor of the Tower, to give up the keys of the fortress for twenty-four hours. The dethroned Edward and his brother were confined there; and in the dead of night Forrest and Dighton, hired assassins, smothered the sleeping boys with the bed-clothes, showed the corpses to Tyrrel, and then buried them at the foot of the staircase. This story rests on the confession of the murderers. It is right to say, however, that strong, though not conclusive, arguments have been advanced to clear the memory of Richard from this foul blot, and the story must ever remain a disputed point in English history.

A strong party against Richard had always existed, and now that the sons of Edward IV. had disappeared, they proposed a union of the Houses of York and Lancaster, by a marriage between Henry, Earl of Richmond, and Elizabeth of York. Henry was the great-grandson of John of Ghent through his mother, Margaret Beaufort; Elizabeth was the eldest daughter of Edward IV.

Dangers grew thick around the usurper. Buckingham, changed at once into a deadly foe, declared in favour of Henry. A rising took place (October 18, 1483). But a storm beat back the Earl of Richmond from the shores of Devon as he was about to land. Buckingham, who had drawn sword at Brecknock, was hindered by a flood in the Severn from joining his confederates, and his army of Welshmen melted away. Fleeing in disguise to the house of a retainer named Bannister, he was betrayed—some say by his host—and was beheaded in the market-place of Salisbury.

The marriage of Henry and Elizabeth was dreaded by the King, and he sought to unite the Princess to his own son; but the scheme was thwarted by the sudden death of the destined bridegroom. He had then some idea of marrying his niece himself; and incurred the suspicion of having poisoned his wife, Anne, for this purpose. But Ratcliffe and Catesby, his chief councillors, dissuaded him from the unnatural union, and there was no resource left him but to await the result of that struggle which was fast approaching. He did so with a troubled heart. His gold had long been spent, and now that his power seemed tottering, the fidelity of his adherents began to fail. Lord Stanley, whose estates were the richest in Lancashire and Cheshire, was the object of his greatest suspicion. His nights were sleepless, and we are told that he often started from his bed with wild cries of horror. Soon came the news that Henry with 3000 troops was at the mouth of the Seine. Richard took his station at Nottingham, as the centre of the kingdom. Horsemen were in the saddle on all the chief roads, to bring the earliest tidings of his rival's approach. On the first of August Henry landed at Milford-Haven: in a fortnight the armies met at Bosworth, Richard's weakened by repeated desertions. There was fought a battle, —the last between the rival Roses,—in which Richard, who had cut down the standard-bearer of the Lancasters, was slain in the act of aiming a deadly blow at Richmond. The crown, which he had worn on the battle-field, was found in a hawthorn-bush close by, and was placed by Lord Stanley on the victor's head. The

1485
A.D.

body of Richard, carried to Leicester on a horse, was there buried in the church of the Greyfriars.

The character of the last of the Plantagenets has been painted by historian and by dramatist in the darkest colours. He is represented as a man cruel and treacherous, lured on by the demon of unbridled ambition to commit crimes most terrible and unnatural. Though he cannot have been a good man, yet it is due to his character to remember that the picture of Richard III. familiar to our minds was drawn under the Tudor sovereigns; and that, on this account, some allowance should be made for the rancour of a hostile feeling. He was of meagre and stunted body, with a withered arm and a deformity of the shoulders, from which he took his name of Crook-back.

CONTEMPORARY SOVEREIGNS.

SCOTLAND.	A.D	EMPEROR.	A.D.
JAMES III.		FREDERIC III.	
FRANCE.			
LOUIS XI., ... died 1483			
CHARLES VIII.		**POPES.**	
SPAIN.		SIXTUS IV., ... died 1484	
FERDINAND and ISABELLA.		INNOCENT VIII.	

CHAPTER IV.

SOCIAL CONDITION OF THE PEOPLE UNDER THE HOUSES OF YORK AND LANCASTER.

Civil War.	Houses and meals.
Villenage abolished.	Miracle and moral plays.
Government.	Books.

During the Wars of the Roses social improvement stood still. Men whose lives were uncertain cared little for education. Present safety was their great object; and the use of arms was therefore of chief importance. The high and the low suffered alike. Whole families of the great were swept away, massive castles were thrown down, and villages were by hundreds laid in ashes.

The great social feature of the period was the extinction of Villenage, or Slavery. From the earliest Saxon times this evil had prevailed in England. The Norman Conquest had changed the masters without freeing the slaves. But about the reign of Henry II. the good work began. During three centuries it went on slowly, yet surely,—so slowly, indeed, that it was remarked by scarcely any writers of the time. When it was a disgrace to be called an Englishman, Nicholas Breakspear, an Englishman, was made Pope. About the same time Thomas à Becket, an Englishman, dared to oppose the Norman King of England. Among the priests of Rome there were soon found many who had sympathy for the enslaved race; and it became a custom, when a slaveholder was dying, to persuade him, by all the authority of the Church, to set free his slaves. The civil war, by breaking the power of the ruling race, aided this great movement, and the opening of the Tudor Period saw Villenage abolished in England for ever.

The government of the country was then, as it is now, a limited monarchy. It was of a class which sprang up in Europe during the middle ages; and of this class the English Constitution was the best example. The office of King had become strictly hereditary. He possessed the chief power and was feudal lord of the whole soil. But three great principles, existing from the earliest times, limited his power: 1. He could make no law without the consent of Parliament. 2. He could lay on the people no tax without the same consent. 3. He must govern by the laws; and if he broke them, his agents and advisers were responsible.

Instead of the Norman castles already described, the nobles now began to build large manor-houses of wood, decorated with carving and painting. Their rooms were hung with tapestry. In towns, the upper stories jutted out over the lower, so that in narrow streets the fronts of opposite houses were only a few feet apart. This style may still be noticed in old towns like Chester. The people had not yet learned the value of clear light and fresh air to both mind and body. The higher classes took four meals in the day. They rose about five; took breakfast at seven; dined at ten; supped at four; and at nine had the 'livery'—a slight repast of cakes and spiced wine—served in their bed-chambers. The working classes dined at noon. This is nearly the same hour as at present; for, while the leisure of the great permits them to change the hours of their meals, the labouring classes are compelled by their daily toil to keep the same hours in all ages.

Dramatic performances now took a regular shape. They were acted first in the churches, chiefly by the clergy, and were then called Miracle Plays, or Mysteries. Although intended to teach the lower classes the history of the Bible, they seem to have been very profane. In the reign of Henry IV. a miracle play, performed in Smithfield, lasted for eight days. It began with the creation, and took in almost all the sacred history. About the time of Henry VI. Moral Plays came into fashion. These were a great improvement on the Miracles: the actors were laymen, and scriptural characters were not assumed. They have been called Allegories, since the performers personated Mercy, Justice, Truth, and such qualities. Then followed, in the Tudor Period, the introduction of actual characters from history and social life.

In all modern history, no event has had wider or more lasting consequences than the invention of Printing. It formed a mighty instrument in spreading the Reformation.

It was a true saying, 'Let the Pope abolish printing, or printing will abolish him.' A complete change took place in book-making. The black-letter manuscript gave place to the printed volume. The latter, however, had as yet no title-page, no capital letters, and no points except the colon and the period. The words were spelled without attention to anything but their sounds. Hence every writer had his own style of spelling, and very often there were two or three different forms of the same word in a single page. The language of the period was Middle English,—slightly different from that used in Chaucer's 'Canterbury Tales.'

LEADING AUTHORS OF THE PERIOD—(1399-1485.)

MIDDLE ENGLISH.

JAMES I.,.....................King of Scotland—a prisoner in England for nineteen years—studied Chaucer—wrote poems—only remaining work, 'The King's Quhair,' or Book.

JOHN LYDGATE,................(Flourished about 1420)—a monk and poet —kept a school of poetry—chief works, 'History of Thebes,' and 'Siege of Troy.'

WALSINGHAM,....................A monk—wrote Chronicles (about 1440).

SIR JOHN FORTESCUE,...(Flourished about 1450)—Chief Justice—chief work, on the English Constitution.

WILLIAM CAXTON,..............(1410-1491)—first English printer—wrote or translated about sixty works.

LEADING DATES OF THE PERIOD—(1399-1485.)

GENERAL EVENTS.	WARS, BATTLES, TREATIES.
A.D.	A.D.
Martyrdom of Sautre,.............1401...Hen. IV.	Bat. Nesbit Moor, 1402...Hen. IV.
James I. of Scotland released,...1423...Hen. VI.	— Homildon Hill,1402... —
	— Shrewsbury,...1403... —
Joan of Arc burned 1431... —	— Agincourt,......1415...Hen. V.
First book printed in England,......1474...Ed. IV.	Siege of Rouen,....1419... —
	Treaty of Troyes, 1420... —
	Bat. Crevant,......1423...Hen. VI
CHANGE OF DOMINION.	— Verneuil,........1424... —
All French possessions except Calais lost,............1451...Hen. VI.	Cade's rebellion,--1450— —
	Treaty of Pecquigny,............1475...Ed. IV.

WARS OF THE ROSES.

From 1455 A.D. to 1485.—30 years.—Twelve battles.

		A.D.	VICTOR.
HENRY VI.	First battle, St. Albans,	1455	York.
	Bloreheath,	1459	—
	Northampton,	1460	—
	Wakefield,	1460	Lancaster.
	Mortimer's Cross,	1461	York.
	Second Battle, St. Albans,	1461	Lancaster.
EDWARD IV.	Towton,	1461	York.
	Hedgeley Moor,	1464	—
	Hexham,	1464	—
	Barnet,	1471	—
	Tewkesbury,	1471	—
RICHARD III.	Bosworth,	1485	Lancaster.

GENEALOGICAL TREE

CONNECTING THE PLANTAGENETS WITH THE TUDOR LINE.

EDWARD III.
|
JOHN, Duke of Lancaster (third son), had by CATHERINE SWYNFORD,
|
JOHN BEAUFORT,   CATHERINE, widow
Earl of Somerset.   of HENRY V., married OWEN TUDOR.
|
MARGARET BEAUFORT married EDMUND, Earl of Richmond.
|
HENRY, Earl of Richmond, afterwards HENRY VII.

TUDOR PERIOD.

From 1485 A.D. to 1603 A.D.—118 years.—5 Sovereigns.

                                                                          A.D.

HENRY VII., ...began to reign 1485
HENRY VIII. (son),............................1509
EDWARD VI. (son), ...1547
MARY (half-sister), ...1553
ELIZABETH (half-sister), ...1558 to 1603

Leading Features:—THE RISE OF PROTESTANTISM,
                        THE REVIVAL OF LITERATURE,
                        THE EXTENSION OF COMMERCE.

CHAPTER I.

HENRY VII.

Born 1455 A.D.—Began to reign 1485 A.D.—Died 1509 A.D.

The rivals of Henry.	War in France.	Henry's extortion.
Early disturbances.	Perkin Warbeck.	Death and character.
Lambert Simnel.	Lands in Cornwall.	Power of the nobles lessened.
Rise of the Star-Chamber.	Surrender and death.	
	Marriage projects.	Discovery of America.

TRUE English history begins with the reign of Henry VII. As storm clears the air, so had the civil war swept from the land the relics of the decaying Feudal System, and a new and better order of things arose. Knowledge, long pent within the monasteries, now began to be diffused in printed books among the homes of the people. Men began to read and think for themselves, instead of taking their opinions from the priests of Rome. We have hitherto seen French Kings triumphing with English armies on French soil. We have seen the nobles of England little better than robbers, the peasantry of England little better than slaves. We shall now see British Sovereigns on the throne, the slaves set free, and a middle class of farmers and merchants arise. During the Tudor Period we shall see the commerce, the literature, and the Protestantism of England in their splendid dawn; still later, we shall see the Constitution of Britain, which had been growing for centuries, receive the key-stone of its topmost arch; and, passing to the time of the illustrious dynasty now wielding the sceptre, we shall behold the nation, enriched with all the elements of national health and life, reposing in peace and freedom beneath the shadow of that august temple.

Henry was not without rivals. There was living at Sheriff-hutton in Yorkshire a boy of fifteen, Edward, Earl of Warwick, son of the Duke of Clarence. John de la Pole, Earl of Lincoln, the son of Elizabeth, eldest sister of Edward IV., had been appointed heir by Richard III. Warwick was at once, by Henry's order, transferred to the Tower of London. Lincoln, having paid homage to the new King, remained at liberty.

The King's public entry into London and his coronation were delayed from August 22d until October 30th, by a plague, called, from its strongest symptom, 'The sweating sickness.' When these ceremonies were over, he called a Parliament to confirm his title. He claimed the throne by right of inheritance and of conquest; but to secure his seat, and at the same time to lull for ever the hostility of the rival Roses, he married Elizabeth of York, the daughter of Edward IV. He obtained, besides, from Pope Innocent VIII., a bull threatening with excommunication all who should disturb him or his heirs in the possession of the throne. His chief confidence was given to John Morton and Richard Fox, two priests who had been faithful to him in his exile. He made Morton Archbishop of Canterbury, and Fox Bishop of Winchester.

Notwithstanding these precautions, his throne was, during the first fifteen years of his reign, a seat of much danger. Plot after plot rose to disturb his tranquillity. He was at Lincoln, on a progress through the north, when news reached him of a rising in Yorkshire under Lord Lovel, and near Worcester under the Staffords. But it was soon suppressed. The elder Stafford was hanged, and Lord Lovel escaped to the court of Margaret, Duchess-dowager of Burgundy. She was the sister of Edward IV., and her court appears more than once in this reign as the asylum of pretenders to the English throne. The royal progress was soon resumed. In York the King spent three weeks conferring honours and reforming abuses. Thence he passed to Bristol, escorted through each county by the nobles and the sheriffs. In Bristol he did much good by encouraging the citizens to build ships and to renew their trade, which had greatly fallen off during the civil war.

This reign was the age of imposture. It has been already stated that an heir to the throne was imprisoned in the Tower in the person of the young Earl of Warwick. Strange to say, although this was well known to all, there appeared in Dublin an Oxford priest named Simon with a boy whom he called Edward Earl of Warwick, but who was really a baker's son, by name Lambert Simnel. Richard, Duke of York, had governed Ireland under Henry VI.; the Duke of Clarence had also been Lieutenant; and the white rose was the favourite in that island. The Earl of Kildare, a keen Yorkist, was now Lord-Deputy; and by him the boy was received with all honours, as a prince of Yorkist blood. The Butlers, four bishops, and the city of Waterford remained faithful to Henry; the rest of the island followed Kildare; and the pretender was proclaimed King with the title of Edward VI. Henry, in alarm, called the peers and prelates round him; and by their advice granted a general pardon to his opponents of former days, led the real Warwick in view of the citizens from the Tower to St. Paul's and thence to the Palace of Shene;—and, what cannot well be explained, arrested the Queen-dowager, Elizabeth, and imprisoned her in the Convent of Bermondsey.

1486 A.D.

A new source of alarm was the desertion of the Earl of Lincoln, who had, ever since the death of Richard, appeared devoted to Henry's cause. He fled to his aunt, the Duchess of Burgundy, and soon with 2000 troops joined Simnel at Dublin. The impostor was now crowned, and a Parliament was called in his name. While Henry was at Kenilworth, the residence of his Queen, he heard that Lincoln and Simnel had landed near Furness in Lancashire, and were marching to surprise him. In haste the royalists mustered and moved towards Newark; but so bad were the paths and roadways that the King's army lost their way between Nottingham and Newark. The rebels came upon them at Stoke, and attacked the royal vanguard. With firm bravery Henry's soldiers met the onset and repulsed it. His heavy cavalry poured in and completed the rout of the invaders. Lincoln died on the field. Lovel, who had joined the enterprise, was never heard of from that day. Simon and Simnel surrendered. The former died in prison; the latter was employed in the royal kitchen as a scullion, but was afterwards raised to the post of falconer.

The Queen, of whose better title Henry seemed to be jealous, and who had hitherto been kept in the back-ground, was now crowned with great pomp. This may be looked upon as the work of the people; for they felt and spoke so strongly on the subject that the King dared not refuse the honours of royalty to his wife. About the same time a court, known as the Star-Chamber from the decorations of the room in which it sat, received the authority of Parliament. It consisted of the chancellor, the treasurer, the keeper of the privy seal, one bishop, one temporal peer, and the chief judges. The principal work it had now to do was the abolition of 'maintenance,'—a system by which the nobles retained around them a band of lawless men wearing their livery and bound by oath to fight in their quarrels.

The ruling principle of Henry's foreign policy was to maintain peace, and only once was he led into a foreign war. Of all the great fiefs of France, Bretagne alone remained free; the rest had been gradually attached to the crown. Duke Francis of Bretagne now died, leaving his coronet to his daughter Anne, a girl of twelve. The French King claimed the dukedom. Henry, who had spent a great part of his exile in Bretagne, was forced to send an army to aid the defenceless princess; but his help was burdened with the condition that she should give up two forts as security for the money spent in her cause, and that she should not marry without his consent. The raising of taxes to equip this army excited a revolt in the north of England. But the Earl of Surrey soon dispersed the insurgents; and John à Chambre, one leader, suffered death at York; while Sir John Egremont, the other, fled to the Duchess of Burgundy. Anne of Bretagne was betrothed to Maximilian, King of the Romans, with the consent of Henry. Charles of France, however, forced the princess into a marriage with him, and the King of England resolved on a French war. This was pleasing to the English people. Henry had long been talking of war, and had often received supplies and extorted benevolences for a purpose never yet fulfilled. Still he invented causes of delay, and it was not until October 1492 that he landed in France and laid siege to Boulogne. But the French King knew that the love of money was Henry's master-passion, and by promising to pay a large sum he secured a treaty. The voice of England was loud in murmurs; for many knights and nobles had almost ruined themselves, by borrowing money and selling their estates, that they might take a part in the expected conquest of France.

The great impostor had just appeared. This was Perkin Warbeck, a native of Tournay, who called himself Richard Plantagenet, Duke of York and second son of Edward IV. Though there is strong evidence that the prince thus personated was murdered in the Tower, yet the affair is wrapped in mystery so dark that many in Warbeck's day believed his story, and ingenious arguments have been advanced in his favour by modern writers. Appearing first in Ireland, he was soon invited to Paris; but, when peace was made with Henry, he was forced to leave that court. Margaret of Burgundy, the untiring friend of Henry's foes, received him as her nephew, gave him a body-guard and all honours of a prince, and named him the "White Rose of England." A Yorkist plot was at once set on foot. Sir Robert Clifford was the agent in Burgundy, and he had several meetings with Warbeck, whom he declared, in his letters to England, to be without doubt the Duke of York. But Henry was on the watch. His well-paid spies were everywhere. Clifford turned traitor, and within the same hour the chiefs of the plot in England were seized. Their letters to Flanders were produced as evidence against them, and Simon Mountford, Robert Ratcliff, William Daubeney, and Lord Fitzwalter were executed. Sir William Stanley, too, who had saved the King's life at Bosworth, and whose brother, Lord Stanley, had crowned Henry on the field, being charged with a share in the plot, confessed his guilt and was beheaded. As Stanley was one of the richest men in England, his execution added much to Henry's wealth.

The spirit of Warbeck's faction grew faint under these losses. The pretender, therefore, resolved on action. Three years after his first appearance, he approached Deal with a few followers, and sent a small body ashore to stir up the people in his favour. But the gentlemen and yeomen of Kent beat back the invaders, and took 150 prisoners. Warbeck returned to Flanders. In anger at the shelter afforded to Warbeck in Flanders, Henry had removed the English cloth-market from Antwerp to Calais, had banished from England the merchants of Flanders, and had ordered his own subjects to leave the Low Countries. This put a stop for a time to the traffic between the English and the Flemings; but, the latter growing restless under their losses, a new treaty of commerce was made, and Warbeck again lost an asylum.

He sailed thence to Cork; but the English rule was too firmly founded there to leave any hope of a revolt. This was chiefly owing to Poynings' Law, called after Sir Edward Poynings, by which it was enacted that all former English laws should have force in Ireland, and that no bill should be brought into the Irish Parliament until it had received the assent of the English Houses. Perkin then passed to James IV. of Scotland, by whom he was royally entertained. There was then a close alliance between the courts of France and Scotland, and as Perkin had been recommended to James by the French King, he was made welcome. The fine figure, agreeable manners, and romantic story of the young man, won the heart of the Scottish King. The adventurer won at the same time another and more faithful heart. An affection sprang up between him and a lady of royal blood, Catherine Gordon, the daughter of the Earl of Huntly. The marriage took place with the full consent of the King. But James did more. He coined his plate to raise an army, and crossed the Border with Warbeck in the 1496
depth of winter. The English people, however, had A.D.

learned from dearly bought experience the value of peace, and none joined the invaders. The pillage of the Scots rather excited their anger. This, and the tidings that an army was on the march to attack him, caused the Scottish King to return to his own land.

The taxes levied by Henry to repel this invasion excited discontent in Cornwall. The Cornish men, complaining that they were burdened with taxes, not for their own good, but to benefit the northern counties, took arms under Flammock an attorney, and Joseph a farrier. They were joined by Lord Audley at Wells, and marched through Salisbury and Winchester to Blackheath, from which they could see the roofs of London. Henry led the army raised to oppose the Scots against the rebels, who, being armed only with axes, bows, and scythes, could not long withstand his attack. Their leaders were captured and executed.

The failure of a second expedition into England, during which James besieged Norham Castle without success, induced that monarch to think of peace. The mediator was the ambassador from Spain,—a country which was during the Tudor Period a leading power in Europe. A treaty was concluded which made it impossible for Perkin to remain in Scotland. With his wife and a very few followers he crossed to Ireland, and lurked for some time in the wilds of that island. But the rebellious spirit still alive in Cornwall encouraged him to invade England once more. He landed at Whitsand Bay on the Cornish shore, and unfurled his standard as Richard IV. at Bodmin. He headed 6000 men before he reached Exeter. This city he besieged; but the want of artillery and the resolution of the citizens, who kept the rebels at bay by kindling a great fire in the gateway while they intrenched their position, caused him to retreat without success. His next move was on Taunton. The royal army was near,—a battle seemed certain; but his heart failed him. Secretly he left the men whom he had drawn from their homes, and fled to the sanctuary of Beaulieu in Hampshire. The rebels submitted; a few were hanged; the rest were sent home. Warbeck's wife fell into the King's hands, and was appointed to an honourable post as attendant on the Queen. She was called in the English court the White Rose,—a name once borne by her husband. Being induced to throw himself on the King's mercy, he was brought amid gazing crowds to London, and there examined. A full confession of the imposture was made, and was published, that the people might be satisfied. Perkin was then placed in close custody; but in six months he contrived to escape, was retaken, and condemned to sit in the stocks for two days. There he was obliged to read aloud the published confession of his true parentage and his pretensions. He was then committed to the Tower, where lay the unfortunate Earl of Warwick. The prisoners became friends, and formed a plan of escape; but they were detected and executed. Warbeck died on the gallows at Tyburn, confessing his fraud and asking pardon of the King. The unhappy Warwick, whose whole life had been spent in prison, and whose only crime was being the last male heir of the Plantagenet line, suffered on a pretended charge of exciting insurrection. Ralph Wilford, a shoemaker's son, had lately come forward in Kent claiming to be the Earl of Warwick. A priest named Patrick first announced the secret in a sermon. Wilford died by the law; Patrick died in prison. Upon this attempt Henry founded the charge on which Warwick was condemned. The execution of this prince is the greatest stain on Henry's character.

The King was now settled on the throne. Henceforward he devoted his attention to the advancement of his foreign influence by marriages, and to the amassing of money. The old enmity between England and Scotland, which was fiercest in the Border counties, was set at rest by a marriage between the Scottish King, James IV., and Margaret, Henry's eldest daughter. This marriage must be carefully remembered, for it was the source of the union of the English and Scottish crowns in 1603. Further to increase his influence, Henry married his eldest son, Arthur (so called from the ancient British prince), to Catherine of Arragon, daughter of Ferdinand and Isabella. The bridegroom, a gentle and learned prince, lived only six months after the union; and his brother Henry, afterwards King, was by a Papal bull permitted to marry the young widow. The Queen died in

1503, and the King set himself to secure a rich second wife; but all his schemes were unavailing.

Richard III. had bequeathed the crown to the house of Suffolk. Edmund, a brother of John de la Pole who was killed at Stoke, claimed the estates of the fallen Earl. Henry refused, and Edmund fled to his aunt, the Duchess of Burgundy. Henry, in alarm, seized several members of the family; but Suffolk, left in poverty by his aunt's death, was delivered up by the Archduke Philip, and imprisoned in the Tower.

Through all these events infamous extortion was going on. Richard Empson and Edmund Dudley were the chief agents of Henry's rapacity. They were both lawyers, and Dudley was chosen Speaker of the Commons. A single occurrence will show the nature of these extortions. Henry visited a favourite general, the Earl of Oxford. When leaving the mansion, the King passed through two lines of fine-looking men, splendidly equipped. 'My lord,' said he to the Earl, 'these are of course your servants?' The Earl smiled and said, 'No, your majesty, I am too poor for that; these are my retainers, assembled to do you honour.' The King started and said, 'I thank you, my lord, for your good cheer; but I cannot have my laws broken in my sight.' He referred to a law abolishing 'maintenance'; and Oxford was fined £10,000 for his anxiety to do honour to royalty!

Henry died in the spring of 1509. His health gave way under repeated attacks of gout, and consumption at length set in. In his dying hours he ordered that those whom he had injured should be recompensed. He was married once. His eldest son, Arthur, died before him; his second son was Henry VIII.; his daughters married monarchs, Margaret being the wife of James of Scotland, and Mary the wife of Louis XII. of France. The last named princess, when left a widow, married Brandon, Duke of Suffolk.

Lord Macaulay has given three points as the general character of the Tudors: They were more arbitrary than the Plantagenets; they well knew the temper of the nation they governed; and they all had courage and a strong will. Henry VII. was, besides, a man suspicious and reserved. His great vice was avarice; but during his reign many useful laws were passed, peace was preserved, and the foundation of our great commerce was laid.

Of the laws passed by Henry, the most important was one allowing the nobles to sell their estates, regardless of the entail. This term 'entail' means the fixing of the estate to some particular line of heirs, none of whom has the power to sell or to bequeath it. Henry's object in passing this law was to lessen the power of the nobles, whom he feared. But it also exalted the commons; for those who had made money bought the estates which the nobles, loaded with debt, were only too glad to sell. Many noble houses had been destroyed during the civil war. In 1451 fifty-three temporal lords answered the call of Henry VI.; in 1485 only twenty-nine assembled, and many of these were newly created. A new aristocracy, composed of the leading commoners, thus sprang up.

By Henry's order the Great Harry, a war-ship of two decks, was built. It cost £14,000, and was of one thousand tons burden. But what gives to this reign its deepest interest is that during it the New World was discovered. On the 12th of October 1492 Columbus discovered the Bahama Islands. At first, baffled in Spain, he had sent his brother Bartholomew to England, to seek ships from Henry. Bartholomew, who brought with him maps, then first seen in our island, was on his way back to invite Christopher to the English court, when he was seized by pirates. Meanwhile Christopher had obtained Spanish ships and had begun his perilous voyage. However, the credit of discovering the mainland of America is due to English enterprise. Sebastian Cabot, a Venetian, sent by Henry from Bristol, touched at Labrador in 1497, and sailed southward to Florida. In the same year Vasco di Gama, a native of Portugal, doubled the Cape of Good Hope, thus opening a watery path to India. Compared with these, all other events of European history during this reign shrink to insignificance. And ever since, while rich and useful products of distant lands have been borne on every tide into our harbours, from the British Islands as a centre there have been flowing towards the rising and the setting sun our arts, our sciences, our literature and language; and, best of all, the faith in Jesus, which we prize as the chief blessing of our nation.

CONTEMPORARY SOVEREIGNS.

SCOTLAND.
A.D.
JAMES III.................died 1488
JAMES IV.

FRANCE.
CHARLES VIII...................1498
LOUIS XII.

SPAIN.
ISABELLA, } 1504
FERDINAND.

EMPERORS.
A.D.
FREDERIC IV..............died 1493
MAXIMILIAN I.

POPES.
INNOCENT VIII................1492
ALEXANDER VI................1503
PIUS III.

CHAPTER II.

HENRY VIII.

Born 1491 A.D.—Began to reign 1509 A.D.—Died 1547 A.D.

Early conduct.	Want of money.	Bible translated.
French war.	French alliance.	Pilgrimage of Grace.
Battle of spurs.	The divorce.	The Bloody Statute.
Cardinal Wolsey.	Wolsey's fall.	Fall of Cromwell.
Foreign policy.	Cranmer and Cromwell.	Catherine Howard.
Field of the Cloth of Gold.	Papal power overthrown.	Catherine Parr.
The Reformation in Germany.	Suppression of monasteries.	The last victim.
	Union of Wales.	Death.
Defender of the Faith.	Anne Boleyn.	Character.

HENRY VIII. became King when eighteen. A Lancastrian by his father, a Yorkist by his mother, he united in himself the claims of the rival houses. The nation, ground by the avarice of the late King, gladly welcomed to the throne a prince seemingly gallant and generous. One of his earliest acts was the execution of Dudley and Empson; and the people, thus appeased, settled into a tranquillity unknown during five reigns. As often happens, the miser father had a spendthrift son. Encouraged by the Earl of Surrey, now chief minister, the young King plunged into a whirl of costly pleasures. Tournaments, dances, pageants, revels followed in quick succession; and if Henry stole a quiet hour now and then, it was given to music and literature. In the first year of his reign he married Catherine of Arragon, the widow of his brother Arthur.

The Kings of France had long been desirous of subduing Italy, and Louis XII. now seemed likely to achieve the conquest. The Pope, Julius II., formed a league with Ferdinand of Spain and the Venetians to oppose the French armies; and, by sending to Henry a rose perfumed with musk and anointed with oil, invited his aid. The vanity of the young Englishman was pleased. He joined the league. His first Parliament readily granted supplies. An English army was sent into Spain to invade France on the south. But Ferdinand having used the troops in his private schemes against Navarre, their leader in disgust brought them back to England without attempting the invasion of Guienne. Indirectly, however, this first campaign fell heavily upon Louis. His troops being drawn from Italy to France, his splendid conquests in the plain of Lombardy yielded, all but a few garrisons, to the Swiss pikemen of the Pope.

The Parliament of 1513 having granted a poll-tax and other supplies, Henry sailed with his troops to Calais. He was there joined by the Emperor Maximilian, who came to serve under the English flag. Terouenne, a town of Picardy, was invested. The garrison held out for two months; during which Henry gained the battle of Guinegaste, known as the 'battle of spurs,' from the rapid flight of the French cavalry. Tournay was then taken, and Henry returned in triumph to England. Meanwhile James IV., prompted by the strong alliance then existing between France and Scotland, had invaded England; but on Flodden field, near the Till, his army was routed, and himself and many of his nobles were slain, by the English under Lord Surrey.

Aug. 18, 1513 A.D.

Thomas, Cardinal Wolsey, was a prominent figure during the first twenty-one years of this reign. Born at Ipswich in 1471, he was only fourteen when he graduated at Oxford. The Boy Bachelor, as he was called, soon received from the Marquis of Dorset, whose sons had been his pupils, the rectory of Limington in Somersetshire. His next step was the chaplaincy of Calais, where he was noticed by Fox, Bishop of Winchester, and by that prelate recommended to Henry VII. The deanery of Lincoln and the post of King's almoner rewarded him for his zeal in the royal service; and under the gay young Henry VIII., who was pleased to find that a priest so able to conduct the business of the state scrupled not to drink and dance and sing in the wild court-revels, he rose to be Archbishop of York and Chancellor of England. The splendour of the prelate now rivalled that of the King. His train numbered eight hundred; his silken robes sparkled with gold; he permitted his Cardinal's hat to be laid nowhere in the royal chapel but on the high altar; and, when in 1518 he was created Papal Legate, he caused the first nobles of England to serve him on feast-days with towel and water. By this glitter and pride he pleased the people, from whose ranks he had risen. His fostering care of learning and literature gained for him the applause of the wise.

Francis I. now sat upon the French throne. He had inherited the desire of conquering Italy, and he therefore sought to live at peace with England. To secure this, he courted the favour of Wolsey by presents and flattery; and obtained, as the first-fruits of his intriguing, the restoration of Tournay. In 1519 Maximilian died, and Charles V. was chosen Emperor. Charles, Francis, and Henry were then the leading powers of Europe; and the foreign policy of each was closely interwoven with that of the others. Charles ruled Spain, Austria, Naples, and the Netherlands. His, too, was the New World with its mines of gold and silver. Francis, holding a compact and prosperous kingdom almost in the centre of the Emperor's scattered dominions, was a formidable rival. Henry, close at hand yet securely guarded by the waves of the Channel and the North Sea, could in a week pour his troops upon the shores of either realm. The English King was, therefore, courted by both Charles and Francis. He was invited by Francis to a meeting near Calais. He was visited in England by Charles. To be Pope was Wolsey's highest ambition; and Charles, by promising to use all his influence in favour of that desire, won the friendship of the Cardinal.

Henry at once crossed to Calais, and met Francis between Guisnes and Ardres. The interview has been called, from the splendour of the monarchs and their retinues, 'The Field of the Cloth of Gold.' Three weeks were spent in empty visits of state, tournaments, and feasts; but nothing of importance was done. At Gravelines, a town on the shore a little north from Calais, Henry and Charles met immediately afterwards; and any feeling in favour of Francis which may have grown up in Henry's mind was completely swept away.

<small>May 30, 1520 A.D.</small>

The execution of Edward Stafford, Duke of Buckingham, took place upon Henry's return to England. Misled by astrology and the pride of his royal blood, he had let fall unguarded words hinting that, if the King should die without children, he would seek the throne. With him died the office of Constable of England.

The Reformation—the greatest series of events in modern history—was now in progress. The magnificent temple of St. Peter had for many years been rising on the banks of the Tiber. To raise funds for the building, Leo X. had sent out monks to sell indulgences. These were pardons from the Pope of even the grossest sins. They were first invented by Urban II., in the days of the Crusades. The misguided people thought that the money paid for these pieces of paper or parchment would buy for them the righteousness of saints, and would free their souls from purgatory. But God inspired Martin Luther, an Augustine monk of Saxony, to oppose the impious falsehood. In his ninety-five propositions fixed on the door of the church in Wittenberg he defended the great truth of *justification by faith in Christ alone.* In the palace-hall of Leipsic, before the great and the wise of Northern Germany, he maintained the authority of the *Bible as the only rule of religious faith,* and claimed for every man the right to read and interpret the sacred book for himself. At the gate of Wittenberg Castle he severed the last tie which bound him to the Church of Rome, by casting into a bonfire the Papal bull denouncing against him the once terrible doom of excommunication. The news of these things was heard joyfully in England by many who remembered with reverence the doctrines of John Wycliffe. But Henry was as yet a strict Papist. He wrote a book in Latin defending the seven sacraments of the Romish Church, and sent a copy of it to the Pope. Leo, glad to receive aid so illustrious, conferred on him the title Defender of the Faith. Our sovereigns still bear the title, which has now a deeper and truer meaning: the letters F. D., for *Fidei Defensor,* may be seen on all our coins. Luther replied to Henry forcibly and fearlessly. The eyes of Europe turned on the controversy. The good work prospered, and every day added to the ranks of the Reformers.

In the war which arose between Charles V. and Francis I. Henry at first sided with the Emperor. Twice English troops invaded France, but without success, although on the

Margin dates: 1517 A.D.; June, 1519 A.D.; Dec. 10, 1520 A.D.; 1521 A.D.

second occasion the army reached a town eleven leagues from Paris. Want of money was one cause of these failures. The immense hoards of the late King were long since exhausted; and, to fill his empty treasury, Henry was forced in 1523 to call a Parliament. There had been no meeting of the Houses for seven years, and so little did their conduct now please the King, that for seven years more they were not once called together. The benevolence was during these years the most fruitful source of Henry's income. When the Commons assembled, Wolsey entered the hall to demand £800,000 for the King. He was seconded by the Speaker, Sir Thomas More; but the House would grant only half the sum; and, when the haughty priest still pressed his claim with arguments, he was told that members of the Commons alone were allowed to debate on questions there.

But the foreign policy of Henry, or rather of Wolsey, soon changed. Two Popes had died,—Leo X. in 1521, and Adrian in 1523,—and twice Wolsey was defeated in the dearest wish of his ambitious heart. The double disappointment rapidly cooled his friendship for the Emperor, for whose promised aid and influence he had long been working. Francis, too, was now an object of pity. At the battle of Pavia (February 25, 1525) he had lost, as he said himself, all but honour, and was now the prisoner of Charles. He was not released for more than a year, when by the treaty of Madrid he agreed to give the fair province of Burgundy to the Emperor as his ransom,—a promise, however, never kept. Two years later, when Rome was sacked by the Emperor's troops, under Bourbon a French refugee, and the Pope was cast into prison, Henry and Francis united in a firm league to release the unhappy Pontiff, and to carry war into the Emperor's dominions.

After nearly twenty years of married life the King pretended to have doubts about the legality of his marriage with Queen Catherine, who had been previously his brother's wife. She was a beautiful and virtuous woman. The truth seems to be that Henry was tired of her, and had taken a violent fancy for one of her maids of honour, Anne Boleyn, grand-daughter of the first Duke of Norfolk. A divorce then became the great object of Henry's life. There were many difficulties in the way. Catherine was the aunt of Charles V.; she was, besides, a zealous Romanist, and in high favour with the Pope. But a divorce Henry would have; and so he told Wolsey, who knelt for four hours at his feet, seeking vainly to change his purpose.

Wolsey did not know what to do. The Pope, awed by the Emperor, dared not grant the demand of Henry; and Wolsey dared not oppose the Pope. To his own ruin the Cardinal acted a double part. Openly he seemed to urge on the divorce; secretly he delayed it in obedience to the Pope. At length a court was opened in London to try the case. Wolsey and Campeggio an Italian Cardinal sat as judges. On the first day a touching scene took place. When the Queen's name was called, instead of answering she flung herself with tears at her husband's feet, pleading for mercy as a stranger in England and his faithful wife of twenty years. Then, refusing to submit to the court, she left the hall. Unmoved, Henry pressed his suit. But no decision was made; and, after the court had sat for almost two months, an order from the Pope transferred it to Rome. This delay roused Henry's anger against Wolsey. The great seal, the badge of the Chancellor's office, was taken from him and given to Sir Thomas More. His palace—York Place, afterwards Whitehall—was seized with all its rich plate and furniture. Compelled to retire to Yorkshire, he survived his disgrace about a year. Then, being arrested by the Earl of Northumberland for high treason, he was on his way to a scaffold in London, when dysentery seized him, and he died at Leicester Abbey. His last words are full of solemn warning,—'Had I but served God as diligently as I have served the King, he would not have given me over in my grey hairs. But this is my just reward.'

Henry's mind was gradually turning, from political, not religious causes, to look favourably on the Reformers, who had assumed the name of Protestants at the Diet of Spires. Thomas Cranmer and Thomas Cromwell were now his chief advisers. Cranmer, a Fellow of Cambridge, had, some time before Wolsey's death, suggested that the divorce case should

May 31, 1529 A.D.

be referred to the universities. The King, hearing of this, exclaimed, in his rough style, that Cranmer had got the right sow by the ear, and acted on the hint. The case was laid before all the universities in Europe, and a decision was given in Henry's favour. This made the fortune of Cranmer. Cromwell, too, gained the royal favour by a single suggestion. His was a chequered life. A factory clerk at Antwerp, a soldier in the sack of Rome, again a clerk at Venice, then a lawyer in England, he became at last Wolsey's solicitor. By his advice the King resolved to deny the supremacy of the Pope, and to make himself head of the English Church.

And now the chain, which had so long bound England to Rome, was breaking link by link. The Parliament of 1531 owned Henry as head of the Church. The Parliament of 1532 forbade the payment of first-fruits, by which the Pope had received the first year's income of vacant bishoprics. The Parliament of 1533 forbade appeals to Rome. In the same year Anne Boleyn was declared Queen. Catherine, formally divorced, retired from the court, and died three years afterwards in Huntingdonshire, leaving a daughter, Mary. When these things were heard at Rome, the Pope laid Henry under a terrible curse, unless Queen Catherine was restored; but no curses could bend the stubborn King of England.

The dispute, when the divorce was thus settled, centred in the question, 'Who was to be head of the Church in England,—the King or the Pope?' The point was decided by the Parliament of 1534 conferring the title with its privileges on Henry. About the same time appeared the Holy Maid of Kent, a half-witted girl, subject to hysterical fits, who raved against the new doctrines, and denounced woe on the King for his treatment of Queen Catherine. Her true name was Elizabeth Barton, and she was only a tool in the hands of some artful monks, many of whom suffered with her for the imposture. More distinguished victims of Henry's wrath were John Fisher, Bishop of Rochester; and Sir Thomas More, famed as the author of 'Utopia.' They were beheaded in 1535 on a charge of denying the King's supremacy in the Church. This was the final breach

1535
A.D.

with Rome. Henceforth the Church of England had a separate existence. Paul III., now Pope, hurled the thunders of excommunication at Henry; but the English King cared not.

The suppression of monasteries was then resolved on by the King; and Cromwell, to whom was given complete control of the Church with the title of Vicar-General, proceeded to the work. There were good grounds for this step, for the monks generally led most dissolute lives, and many of the monasteries were dens of the vilest sin. But Henry's motive was not hatred of evil; he rather desired to deal a terrible blow at the Papal power, and at the same time to fill his coffers with the riches of the monks. His obedient Parliament, now in its sixth session, passed a bill to suppress those monasteries which possessed revenues below £200 a-year. Three years later, the greater monasteries were destroyed. In all, 3219 religious houses were laid in ruins, and the King was enriched with their yearly income of £161,000. Six new bishoprics were then established.

1536 A.D.

The worst evils of the Feudal System still lingered in Wales. The marchers or great lords, claiming independent rule in their own districts, were at constant war with one another: pillage and murder occurred every day. But now these lords were deprived of separate jurisdiction, and the English laws were everywhere enforced. Henceforth Wales sent twenty-four members to the English Parliament. This was the real union of Wales with England.

1536 A.D.

The 6th day of January 1536 saw Catherine of Arragon die. On the 19th of May in the same year, her rival, Anne Boleyn, was beheaded. While the divorce remained unsettled, Henry's passion for her had been violent; when his wish was gained, he grew careless, then cold. A new face, that of the lovely Jane Seymour, caught his changeful fancy. Anne's enemies plied him with evil stories; of her friends, Cranmer alone dared to raise his voice in her favour. She was tried on a charge of unfaithfulness to her royal husband, and condemned to die. She met her doom calmly, and on the scaffold prayed for the King. She left a daughter, afterwards Queen Elizabeth. On the next day Jane Seymour became Queen.

During this reign the Bible took its fitting place as the sole standard of Christian faith. A century and a half had passed since John Wycliffe translated the Scriptures into English; but the version used in England during the earlier years of Henry's reign was that of William Tyndale, a young scholar of Oxford, who published the New Testament in 1526, and the Old Testament four years later. In 1535 he suffered death by fire in Flanders. In the same year Miles Coverdale of Cambridge published the whole Bible in the English tongue. These were translations from the Latin version called the Vulgate. By a royal order a copy of Coverdale's translation was chained to a pillar or desk in every parish church, so that all who chose might read. In 1539 appeared a translation called the Great Bible, prepared under the superintendence of Cranmer, who was now Archbishop of Canterbury. The people received these gifts of God with joy; families clubbed their savings to buy a copy of the sacred volume, still a costly purchase; and those who could read were often seen surrounded by a crowd of listeners, earnestly hearkening to the words which tell of life eternal.

The abolition of the monasteries caused much discontent, especially in the northern counties. North of the Trent 40,000 men rose in arms under a gentleman named Aske. Their avowed object being to restore the Romish Church, they called their insurrection the Pilgrimage of Grace. Priests marched before them; while their banners bore the crucifix and the chalice. They held York and Hull for a while; but the promise of a general pardon, and the heavy rains of winter induced them to return to their homes. A renewal of the revolt early in the next spring came to nothing. Aske and other leaders were executed.

The birth of a son, baptized Edward, added to Henry's triumph; and even the death of his Queen, Jane Seymour, which occurred a few days after the prince was born, was almost disregarded in his great joy. **Oct. 12, 1537 A.D.**

Though the King had broken with Rome, he was no friend

to Luther. He retained many of the old doctrines, especially transubstantiation, by which the Romish priests taught that partakers of the Lord's Supper ate, not bread and wine, but the real flesh and blood of Jesus. Standing thus half way between the two Churches, he strove to bend the consciences of both Protestants and Romanists to his own views, and many of both parties were burned for denying what he taught. His opinions were embodied in the Six Articles, of which the first and chief was, that all should on pain of death believe in transubstantiation. From the persecution which followed these enactments, they were called the Bloody Statute. About the same time it was decided by Parliament, that all the proclamations of Henry should have the force of regular laws. This was a measure utterly opposed to the spirit of the English Constitution. In effect it made Henry a monarch as absolute as was ever a Czar of Russia or a Shah of Persia.

1539 A.D.

Henry's fourth wife was Anne of Cleves, the daughter of a Protestant prince. Cromwell, desirous of strengthening the Protestant cause in England, had proposed the union. A picture of the princess was shown to Henry: he was pleased with her face, and she was invited to England. But, when he came to see her, he called her a great Flanders mare. She had neither beauty nor grace, and could speak no language except her own. After some delay the marriage took place; but the King never forgave Cromwell. Three designs filled his mind: revenge on the Vicegerent, a divorce from Anne, and the elevation of a new Queen, Catherine Howard, a Papist, and niece to the Duke of Norfolk. In little more than six months he had gained all these ends. Cromwell, accused of heresy and treason, was brought to the block. Anne, much to her own content, was separated from her husband, and lived in England upon a pension of £3000 a-year until her death. Catherine Howard was raised to the throne amid the rejoicings of the Papists, who hailed her elevation as an omen of good. The last three Queens had favoured the Reformation.

July 28, 1540 A.D.

For about a year and a half the charms of Catherine Howard delighted the King. Then some events of her ear-her life began to be whispered abroad; and of these Cranmer sent a written statement to Henry, who refused at first to believe them. But when she herself confessed, what many witnesses swore, that she had been unchaste before her marriage, the fierce jealousy of Henry blazed forth. Nothing but blood could quench his rage, and she was beheaded on Tower-hill. With her died an accomplice of her guilt, Lady Rochford, who had been chief witness against Anne Boleyn.

In his religious changes, too, the King displayed that fickle nature so evident in his marriages. Not satisfied with the Six Articles, he published in succession two books, each giving a different creed to the nation. The royal permission to read the Bible, formerly given to all, was now confined to gentlemen and merchants.

Wars with Scotland and France occupied his latter years; the details are not of much importance. His sixth wife was Catherine Parr, widow of Lord Latimer. She survived her husband, although her head was once in great danger. The King's temper, naturally fierce, was maddened by his increasing corpulence, and an ulcer which had broken out in his leg. One day, while talking of certain religious doctrines, she opposed his ideas. In high wrath he ordered an impeachment to be drawn up against her. But a friend happening to see the paper, told her; and, when next she saw the King, she spoke so humbly of the foolishness of her sex, and appeared so thankful for what he had taught her, that when the Chancellor came to arrest her, Henry bade him begone.

The last who suffered from this tyrant's wrath was Thomas Howard, Earl of Surrey, famed as the purifier of English poetry, and the writer of our earliest blank verse. He was a cousin of Catherine Howard, and was beheaded on suspicion of aiming at the crown. The fact of his quartering on his shield the arms of Edward the Confessor, long borne by his ancestors, was the chief circumstance advanced in support of this charge. His father, the Duke of Norfolk, who had been seized at the same time, lay in prison awaiting the same fate, when the news came that Henry was dead.

For some days it was well known in the Court that the King was dying, but all feared to tell him so. At length

Sir Antony Denny ventured to warn him of the coming change. He desired to see Cranmer, but was speechless when the Archbishop arrived. When asked by Cranmer to give some sign of his faith in Christ, he squeezed the prelate's hand, and died. He was married six times, and left three children. His will, made nearly a month before he died, bequeathed the throne to Edward, then to Mary, and then to Elizabeth. This arrangement was actually followed.

Henry's vanity was great. He was vain of his learning, and, in earlier days, of his appearance. But his greatest crimes may be traced to his fickleness and his self-will. Few English monarchs were more absolute. At eighteen he was a gay and handsome prince, skilled in music and ready with his pen: at six-and-fifty he was an unwieldy mass of corrupted flesh and evil passions. But God turns evil into good. During this reign was laid the foundation of British Protestantism.

CONTEMPORARY SOVEREIGNS.

SCOTLAND.

	A.D.
JAMES IV.,	died 1513
JAMES V.,	1542
MARY.	

FRANCE.

LOUIS XII.,	1515
FRANCIS I.	

SPAIN

FERDINAND.,	1516
CHARLES I.	

TURKEY.

	A.D.
SELIM I.,	died 1520
SOLYMAN II.	

EMPERORS.

MAXIMILIAN I.,	1519
CHARLES V.	

POPES.

JULIUS II.,	1513
LEO X.,	1522
ADRIAN VI.,	1523
CLEMENT VII.,	1534
PAUL III.	

CHAPTER III.

EDWARD VI.

Born 1537 A.D.—Began to reign 1547 A.D.—Died 1553 A.D.

The Regency.	Plots against Somerset.	Death of Somerset.
War with Scotland	Insurrections.	Succession altered.
Church of England established.	Fall of Somerset.	Death of Edward.
	Reform.	

THE will of Henry VIII. directed that Edward, now only in his tenth year, should come of age at eighteen. In the meantime a council of twenty-eight nobles and clergy were to manage the affairs of the kingdom. This council, however, feeling the want of a leader, chose as Protector the Earl of Hertford, brother of Jane Seymour, and therefore uncle of the King. Many new peers were created; many were advanced to higher rank. Among the latter, the Protector received the title of Duke of Somerset. Archbishop Cranmer was a leading member of the Council of Regency.

It was also enjoined by Henry's will, that a marriage should take place, if possible, between Edward and young Mary of Scotland. But Scottish feeling was strong against the match; and, to force the nation into a consent, Somerset led an army of 18,000 over the Borders. The Regent Arran met him at Pinkie near Musselburgh, but was defeated (Sept. 10, 1547). News of plots against his power soon recalled the Protector to London, and the campaign ended without advantage to the English, while the attempt to extort consent displeased even those Scotchmen who had been in favour of the union. As the Earl of Huntly said, 'He disliked not the match, but he hated the manner of wooing.' The young Queen of Scotland was sent for greater safety to France.

The completion of the English Reformation was the great event of this reign. The Protector was a Protestant, and he took care that all who had access to the young King should be of the Reformed faith. Under this fostering influence the Church of England began to assume her present form,—a work in which Archbishop Cranmer took the largest share. He was ably seconded by Ridley, Bishop of London, and Latimer, Bishop of Worcester. Freer circulation was given to the Bible. To secure purity of doctrine, twelve Homilies or Sermons were published. The statues and pictures of the Romish churches were destroyed. The Latin mass, never understood by the people and seldom by the priests, was abolished, and replaced by the beautiful Liturgy, still read in the Established Church of England. And, lastly, the faith of English Protestants was summed up in Forty-two Articles.

It has been already said that Somerset hastened from Scotland in alarm. There was a plot against his power. His own brother, Admiral Lord Seymour, who had married the widow of Henry VIII., was his most dangerous foe. Though this conspiracy was checked by the execution of Seymour on Tower-hill, yet opposition far more fatal to the Protector was rising. Dudley, Earl of Warwick, was the son of that Dudley who had ministered to the avarice of Henry VII. Created Viscount Lisle by the late King, he was a member of the Council of Regency, in which his restless ambition made him a leading man. Now, as the head of a rival faction, he began to measure his strength with Somerset.

Much more important than the struggles of two ambitious men was the condition of the people at this time. Monasteries, with all their evils, had served some useful ends. The poor man and the traveller found there a shelter for the night. The domains attached were let out at moderate rents to small farmers, who found the monks not only indulgent landlords, but ready purchasers of the farm produce. Discontent and rebellion had therefore followed the suppression of these houses; and the embers of bad feeling were still alive. The working classes had, besides, new grievances. A great demand for wool had turned a large part of England into sheep-walks, and there was little field labour to be done. Wages were low, and were paid in the base coin issued by Henry VIII. to supply his own needs. The price of food rose high. The flames burst out in many shires of England. Exeter was besieged by 10,000 men. Ket, a tanner, sat below an oak-tree, giving law to the gentlemen of Norfolk. In all cases the rebels were soon put down. Ket was hanged at Norwich, after his followers had been scattered by the Earl of Warwick.

While Warwick was thus employed, troops sent from France to aid the Scottish Regent had driven the English garrisons from the castles of Broughty and Haddington. The Protector was then glad to make peace; for his position was daily growing more perilous. After the battle of Pinkie, assuming royal pomp, he had disdained to ask advice from the councillors. Many blamed him for the execution of his brother. Romanists cried out against the man who had pulled down churches, and the houses of bishops, that he might build his palace in the Strand. Warwick artfully used these circumstances to strengthen his own faction. The feeling against Somerset grew so strong that he was forced to resign his Protectorship, and was indicted for usurpation of the King's power. On his knees before the Council he made full confession of all the charges. He was then, by a vote of the Parliament, stripped of all power and condemned to pay a heavy fine. By the mercy of the King, however, he escaped the fine, and soon regained his freedom.

The Council, bent on purifying the Church of England, demanded that all should sign the Articles of Reform. They began with Gardiner; and on his refusal deprived him of his office and committed him to prison. Three other bishops were at the same time forbidden to preach. But in the Princess Mary they found a stubborn Romanist, whom they could not move. Her they let alone, lest they might provoke a war with the Emperor Charles, her cousin.

Warwick's ambition was now gratified with the title, Duke of Northumberland. His rival Somerset, though fallen, was still popular. The time was now ripe to crush that rival for ever. Arrested on a charge of raising rebellion in the north, and of plotting to murder Northumberland and others, the unhappy ex-Protector was tried before the Marquis of Winchester, as High Steward, and a jury of twenty-seven peers. Convicted of felony, he was beheaded on Tower-hill. The people, forgetting all his failings in the sad hour of his death, dipped their

Jan. 22, 1552 A.D.

kerchiefs in his streaming blood, and laid these up among their household treasures.

Northumberland now ruled England; and, as the King's health had been for some time failing, visions of securing the crown for his own family filled his ambitious mind. He persuaded Edward that the Princesses, Mary and Elizabeth, could not wear the crown, since they had been declared illegitimate by an Act of Parliament; that the Queen of Scots was also excluded as a stranger, betrothed to the Dauphin of France; that the succession belonged to the Marchioness of Dorset, daughter of Mary Tudor, who was once Queen of France, and afterwards Duchess of Suffolk; and that the next heir was therefore Lady Jane Grey, the daughter of the Marchioness. He had previously married his fourth son, Lord Guildford Dudley, to the Lady Jane. The King's affection for the Protestant faith inclined him to this settlement of the crown; and, although some of the Council hesitated, the Duke prevailed, and letters patent were issued, transferring the crown to the youngest branch of the Tudor line.

Scarcely was this done when the King grew very ill. The worst symptoms of consumption appeared. Northumberland, constantly by his bedside, placed him under the care of a woman professing great skill. Her medicines made him much worse, and on this rests the suspicion that his death was hastened by poison. He died at Greenwich, aged sixteen years. He was a gentle boy, of very studious habits, and of most promising disposition. A diary from his own pen, giving an account of his reign, is preserved in the British Museum.

CONTEMPORARY SOVEREIGNS.

SCOTLAND.	A.D.	TURKEY.	A.D.
MARY		SOLYMAN I.	
FRANCE.		EMPEROR.	
FRANCIS I............died 1547		CHARLES V.	
HENRY II.			
SPAIN.		POPES.	
CHARLES I.		PAUL III...............died 1550	
		JULIUS III.	

CHAPTER IV.

MARY I.

Born 1516 A.D.—Began to reign 1553 A.D.—Died 1558 A.D

Jane Grey yields to Mary.	Execution of Jane Grey.	Loss of Calais.
Romish worship revived.	Protestants persecuted.	Mary's death.
The Spanish marriage.	Rogers, Ridley, Latimer.	Character.
Insurrection.	Cranmer.	

WHEN Edward died, Lady Jane Grey was at once proclaimed Queen by order of Northumberland. She was only sixteen, accomplished, beautiful, and good. Studying Greek and Latin with the late King, she had learned, like him, to love retirement. The dangers of a throne alarmed her gentle heart, and it was very unwillingly that she yielded to the wishes of her father-in-law. But she was not to be Queen. The feeling of the nation leaned towards Mary, the daughter of Catherine of Arragon, who, writing from Suffolk, summoned around her the leading nobles and gentlemen. Her force increased daily, while Northumberland could muster only 6000 men, and even these were leaving him fast. The councillors and the citizens of London declared for Mary, and she was proclaimed everywhere,—the first Queen regnant of England. Northumberland, Suffolk, Guildford Dudley, and Jane Grey were arrested. Northumberland was executed at once; the others were spared a little longer.

The feeling that she had the best claim was the chief motive of Mary's supporters. She was now in her thirty-seventh year, of a temper soured by her mother's and her own disgrace, and blindly attached to the Romish worship. Her great object was the restoration of that worship in England in all its former pomp and power. One of her earliest acts, therefore, released from prison Romish nobles and prelates. Gardiner and Bonner were restored to their sees. The Duke of Norfolk received his freedom. And, in direct violation of her promise to the men of Suffolk, the religious laws of Edward VI. were repealed: Cranmer, Ridley, Latimer, and other Protestants were sent to prison. All England looked with alarm on these things; but the worst was yet to come.

Another step towards her great end was the Spanish match. In July 1554 she became the wife of Philip, son of the Emperor Charles, and heir of the Spanish crown, which he received during the next year. This alliance with the greatest Romish power in Europe gratified at the same time Mary's ambition and her affections; for she was attached to Philip. But he soon grew tired of a wife, jealous, ill-tempered, and eleven years older than himself; and, since he was no favourite with the English, whom he treated with cold Spanish ceremony, he left this island in less than a year. Except for a few days in 1557 he never saw his wife again.

July, 1554 A.D.

The whole body of the English people disliked this marriage. It was said that England would soon be a province of Spain, and that the terrible Inquisition would soon be at work in London. Rebellion appeared in Devonshire and Kent. The former was easily suppressed; but the men of Kent had seized Southwark and Westminster before they were dispersed. Their leader, Sir Thomas Wyatt, was taken at Temple-bar, and executed. Four hundred of his followers also suffered death. The Duke of Suffolk was concerned in this rising, and his guilt was thought a good excuse for the execution of his daughter, Lady Jane Grey, and her husband. They were beheaded within the Tower walls. Dudley suffered first; and as Jane was on her way to the block she passed his bleeding body. She died calmly, persevering to the end in the true faith. Shortly before her death she sent a Greek Bible to her sister, as a last love-gift. Her father, Suffolk, soon met the same fate.

Then began that terrible persecution of Protestants which has given to the first Queen regnant of England the name of Bloody Mary. Cardinal Pole, the Papal Legate, an Englishman of royal blood, recommended toleration; but Gardiner and Bonner cried out for the stake and the fagot, and the Queen was of their mind. During three years, 288 men, women, and children were burned for their Protestantism, while thousands suffered in a less degree. The chief scene of these tragedies was Smithfield in London. There many of 'the noble army of

1555 A.D.

martyrs,' strong in the remembrance of what their Saviour had borne, died amid the flames of blazing fagots. More than a thousand ministers were driven from their pulpits; and as many of them as escaped fled to the Continent to escape the fury of the tempest. They lived chiefly at Frankfort and Geneva. Among them were John Knox, the Reformer of Scotland; Fox, who wrote the Book of Martyrs; and Coverdale, the translator of the English Bible. Associated during their exile with some of the great spirits of the Continental Reformation, they received truer and purer ideas of the Protestant faith and worship. Returning to these shores, they founded the sect called Puritans, which was destined to do so much in perilous days for England and civilization. This has been the history of Christian martyrdom in all ages. Fierce storms scatter the seeds of the plant far and wide; and, for one, a hundred grow up in new strength and beauty.

John Rogers, Prebendary of St. Paul's, was the first victim of this persecution. Hooper, Bishop of Gloucester, was in torture for three quarters of an hour: one of his hands dropped off, the other still beat his breast, and he prayed till his tongue swelled so that he could not speak. Ridley, Bishop of London, and Latimer, once Bishop of Worcester, suffered together at Oxford. 'Be of good cheer, brother,' cried Latimer, as they bound his aged limbs to the stake; 'we shall this day kindle such a torch in England, as, I trust in God, shall never be extinguished.' He saw with the eye of faith: the torch is now a brilliant sun, blessing with its rays many a once dark land. Bags of gunpowder laid round the martyrs killed Latimer by their explosion, but Ridley's death was very slow.

Early in 1556 Cranmer was led to the stake. Broken down by long imprisonment, and sorely tempted by promises of life and honour, he had agreed to sign a denial of the Protestant faith. But a calmer hour brought repentance; and the strength of God returning to his soul enabled him to die without fear. Of his own accord he held out his right hand in the kindling flames until it was a blackened cinder, while he cried more than once, 'That unworthy hand!' When the fire seized his body, his calm face bore no signs of pain. His heart was found among the ashes, unconsumed.

Though Mary was deeply grieved at the coldness of her husband, now Philip II. of Spain, she joined him in his war with France. An English army, sent into the Netherlands, helped to seize the French fortress of St. Quentin. But this trifling success was followed by a heavy loss. Suddenly in mid-winter the Duke of Guise appeared before Calais. The town, which lay in the midst of marshes, was weakly garrisoned, since it was the custom of the English Government, for the sake of economy, to withdraw most of the troops late in autumn. Assaulted by land and sea, this key of France, held by the English since the time of Edward III., was lost in eight days.

1558 A.D.

Mary's health was failing fast. Dropsy preyed upon her body. Her mind, too, was much disturbed. So deeply did she feel her loss in France, that she said the word 'Calais' would be found after death written on her heart. Her husband neglected her. She knew that her subjects disliked her. She had no children; and her half-sister Elizabeth, whom she hated as a Protestant and the daughter of Anne Boleyn, would wear the crown next. All causes working together produced a lingering fever of which she died.

Sorrow is sent for our good; but Mary's heart was hardened and her disposition soured by the troubles of her early life. Her strongest passion was hatred of the Protestant faith. Instead, however, of branding her with the name of Bloody Mary, we should rather pity the Queen, who in her fierce religious zeal forgot the mercy natural to woman, and who saw, before she died, every aim and hope of her life baffled and broken.

CONTEMPORARY SOVEREIGNS.

SCOTLAND.	A.D.	TURKEY.	A.D
MARY.		SOLYMAN I.	
FRANCE.		EMPEROR.	
HENRY II.		CHARLES V.,	died 1558
		POPES.	
SPAIN.		JULIUS III.,	1555
CHARLES I.,	resigned 1556	MARCELLUS III.,	1555
PHILIP II.		PAUL IV.	

CHAPTER V.

ELIZABETH.

Born 1533 A.D.—Began to reign 1558 A.D.—Died 1603 A.D.

Protestantism restored.	Her execution.	Death of Elizabeth.
Mary Queen of Scots.	Early navigators.	Her character.
The Puritans.	The Armada.	Chief authors.
The Duke of Norfolk.	Its defeat.	The newspaper.
Babington's Plot.	Statesmen of the reign.	Continental events.
Trial of Mary Stuart.	Earl of Essex.	

JOY-BELLS pealed and bonfires blazed when Elizabeth, the daughter of Henry VIII. and Anne Boleyn, was proclaimed Queen. During her sister's reign she had lived chiefly at Hatfield House, nominally free, but really a prisoner. As Queen, one of her first measures was the restoration of Protestantism. This good work was completed in 1562, when the Forty-two Articles of Cranmer were reduced to Thirty-nine, and the Church of England was thus established in her present form. The statesman by whose advice Elizabeth was guided in this change and all the leading transactions of her reign, was William Cecil, afterwards Lord Burleigh.

Scotland, France, Spain, and the Netherlands were the countries with which the foreign policy of Elizabeth was chiefly concerned. The marriage of Mary Queen of Scots with the Dauphin, afterwards Francis II. of France, united the first two lands more closely than ever. Not content with her double crown, Mary claimed that of England, on the ground that Elizabeth had been declared illegitimate and that she was next heir, being descended from Margaret, eldest daughter of Henry VII. This claim Elizabeth never forgave; and when Mary, who left France a widow of nineteen, fled across the Border after seven stormy years in Scotland, the English Queen cast into prison the rival, who came imploring pity. Soon after the departure of Mary from France there began a civil war, which, like most of the great European wars for a century after the Reformation, was a struggle between Protestants and Roman Catholics.

The English Queen sided with the Protestants; and in 1562 the Prince of Condé, leader of the Huguenots, as the French Protestants were called, put Havre into her hands. But the fortress was lost to England in less than a year.

Those Protestants who had fled to the Continent from the flames of Smithfield now returned. For a time they reunited themselves with the Church of England; but being pressed to acknowledge the authority of Elizabeth as Supreme Head of the Church, they separated from that body in a few years. From their desire to establish a purer form of worship, they received the name of Puritans. They objected to the surplice; to the sign of the cross in baptism; to the use of the Liturgy; to the adornment of churches with pictures, statues, or stained windows; and to the government of the Church by bishops. The Act of Supremacy and the Act of Conformity, which were passed soon after Elizabeth came to the throne, were the chief causes of the Puritan secession. The one required all clergymen and those holding offices under Government to take an oath, ascribing to Elizabeth all power both in the Church and State of England, and denying the right of any foreign power to meddle with English affairs. This law was levelled directly at the Pope, who still claimed jurisdiction in England. The other forbade under heavy penalties all worship except in the established form. Many Romanists suffered death by these laws; and the Puritans, who also refused to be bound by them, were fined and imprisoned in great numbers during the rest of this reign. Hence the Puritans are often called Nonconformists.

1566
A.D.

For more than eighteen years Mary Stuart pined in an English prison. In 1568 she fled into England. In the following year the Duke of Norfolk, the first nobleman in England, a strict Romanist, and a man of the best character, offered her his hand in marriage. It was a dangerous step, provoking the anger of Elizabeth. He was at once committed to the Tower, but released upon promise that he would give up his design of marrying Mary. However, two years later, the Duke, tempted to renew his plots for the release of the Scottish Queen, entered into a secret correspondence with the Court of Spain. A servant, whom he intrusted with a bag of gold and a letter for Mary's friends in Scotland, carried both to Lord Burleigh. Treasonable papers were found under the mats and tiles of Norfolk's house. He was arrested, tried, and executed.

1572 A.D.

All attempts, by plot or by treaty, to deliver Mary from her prison failed. The hearts of all the Romanists in England were in her favour, and this made Elizabeth dread her escape exceedingly. A plot to assassinate the Queen and place Mary on the throne brought matters to a crisis. The chief conspirator was Babington, a gentleman of Derbyshire. Letters were conveyed to the Scottish Queen through a chink in the wall of her prison by a brewer who brought ale to the household. These, with her replies, fell by treachery into the hands of Walsingham, Secretary of State. Fourteen conspirators were arrested and executed; and it was resolved to try Mary for her share in the plot.

In Fotheringay Castle, Northamptonshire, the trial took place, before thirty-six royal commissioners. At first Mary refused to be tried, but afterwards consented, lest her refusal might seem to show conscious guilt. The chief charge against her was that she had approved of the plot to assassinate Elizabeth. The chief evidence against her was that of her two secretaries, who had been seized by Elizabeth's order, and who swore that Mary had received from Babington the letters produced on the trial; and that the answers, also produced, had been written by themselves at her command. In her defence she denied the charge, declaring that she was innocent of everything but a natural desire to regain her freedom. She had no advocate to plead for her. Alone but fearless, she stood before her accusers, her famous beauty dimmed by long imprisonment. Clearly and readily she replied to every question, and demanded to be confronted with the witnesses. This was refused, and soon after she was doomed to die.

The warrant for her execution was delayed by the reluctance—pretended or real—of Elizabeth. Meanwhile Henry III. of France pleaded hard for the condemned Queen. James VI. of Scotland, too, made a feeble effort to save his mother. At last, however, Elizabeth signed the warrant, and sent her Secretary, Davison, with it to the Chancellor that it might receive the great seal. Recalling this order next day, she found that she was too late. The seal was affixed, and the warrant was soon on the way to Fotheringay.

1587 A.D. There, in one of the castle halls in the grey light of a February morning Mary Stuart, aged forty-five, was beheaded. Whatever may have been her faults and follies, she received a tenfold punishment in the slow torture of her nineteen years' captivity, and her violent death is a foul stain on the memory of the great Elizabeth.

The naval glory of England dawned in this reign; and a brilliant dawn it was. Spain, Holland, and Portugal had led the way into unknown seas, and England was not backward in following the example. Sir John Hawkins traced the coast of Guinea. Martin Frobisher braved the icebergs of the Arctic Ocean. Sir Francis Drake, doubling Cape Horn, crossed the broad Pacific to the shores of India, and sailed home round the Cape of Good Hope; thus winning the renown of being the first English commander who sailed round the world. Sir Walter Raleigh colonized the American coast, and with a courtier's tact called the settlement Virginia. Amid the blessings thus conferred upon men evils unhappily grew up. These early navigators did not hesitate to commit piracy when a Spanish treasure-ship fell in their way. Then, too, began the African slave-trade.

1588 A.D. Perhaps the greatest event of Elizabeth's reign was the defeat of the Invincible Armada. Ever since that achievement England has been 'Queen of the Seas.' The Armada was a great fleet sent by Philip II. of Spain to conquer England. Philip's grand object was the destruction of Protestantism; but, besides, he was smarting under the loss of many treasure-ships; and it is said that his vanity was wounded by Elizabeth's refusal to marry him. One hundred and thirty large ships left Lisbon, having on board besides their crews nearly 20,000 soldiers and 2630 cannons of brass. At the same time the Duke of Parma, an old and skilful military officer, moved to the coast of Flanders near Dunkirk, ready with 40,000 men to

DEFEAT OF THE ARMADA. 181

second the invasion. The admiral of the Armada was the Duke of Medina Sidonia, who was elected to that post upon the sudden death of the first appointed leader, Santa Croce. The royal navy of England then consisted of only thirty-six sail, and these of small size. But nobles, merchants, citizens, came with their money to the Queen, and equipped vessels at their own expense. A fleet of 140 ships soon rode on the English waters; and, though the vessels were small, the best seamen and the bravest hearts in England were on board. Lord Howard of Effingham was the admiral; and under him served Drake, Hawkins, and Frobisher. The English army, consisting of 70,000 ill-trained soldiers, was divided into three parts: one guarded the southern coast, another was stationed at Tilbury to defend the capital, while the third was reserved to oppose the landing.

Storms delayed the Armada, but at length the English admiral stationed at Plymouth saw them on the horizon, stretching in a crescent form seven miles broad. At once Effingham sailed out to meet them, and, keeping at a distance, lest the Spaniards might board his vessels, poured in his shot with great effect. The Spaniards replied with heavy guns; but from the height of their decks their shot passed clear over the English ships. Slowly the Armada bore up the Channel towards Calais, the English fleet following. Off Calais they anchored, waiting for the Duke of Parma; but eight fire-ships, sent amongst them by the English admiral, caused them to cut their cables in alarm. Effingham was not the man to lose the golden moment. He fell at once upon the disordered fleet, and destroyed twelve ships. The great Armada was now in full flight. They could not return by the Straits of Dover, for the wind was against them, and the English ships lay in the adjacent harbours. The only way to Spain lay through the Pentland Frith, and the storms of those wild seas completed the ruin. The Orkneys, the Hebrides, the coasts of Mayo and Kerry, were strewn with the wrecks of the ill-fated vessels. Fifty-three shattered hulks reached Spain.

During forty years of her reign Elizabeth was guided by the advice of Lord Burleigh, a wise and cool-tempered statesman. He rose to be Lord Treasurer, and by his policy greatly increased the revenue of the kingdom. He died in 1598. Sir Francis Walsingham, too, as Secretary of State, enjoyed much of Elizabeth's favour. The chief favourite of her middle life was the Earl of Leicester, in whose breast her evident fondness kindled the ambitious hope that she meant to marry him. This ambition and its evil effects form the groundwork of Scott's tale of 'Kenilworth,' of which castle Leicester was lord.

But the favourite of her old age deserves a longer notice. This was the rash and daring Earl of Essex. In 1589 he joined an expedition which vainly attempted to seat Antonio on the throne of Portugal. Again in 1597 he led the English soldiers to the capture of Cadiz. The Queen was very fond of him, and forgave him much. Once, disputing with her about the choice of a governor for Ireland, he turned his back upon her with scorn. She promptly gave him a box on the ear; and then, forgetting that she was a woman and a Queen, he laid his hand on his sword, and declared that he would not have taken such usage even from her father. In spite of this he was appointed to command the English forces in Ireland, where Hugh O'Neill, Earl of Tyrone, was in rebellion. Not succeeding, he returned to England without the Queen's leave, was disgraced, and imprisoned. But the fondness of Elizabeth soon gave him liberty again; and then with the Earl of Southampton he strove to raise the Londoners in revolt. For this he was tried and condemned to death. He might still have been pardoned, if a ring given to him by the Queen in some moment of tenderness, to be sent to her when any danger hung over him, had reached her hand. It never came, and he was beheaded in the Tower, aged thirty-four.

1601 A.D.

Some two years later, the Queen was entreated to visit the Countess of Nottingham, who was dying. This lady confessed that Essex had intrusted the ring to her to be carried to Elizabeth; but that she, influenced by her husband, a bitter enemy of the Earl, had not delivered it. Rage and grief seized the Queen; and it is said that she shook the dying Countess in her bed. Never happy since the death of Essex, she sank under this blow. Ten days and nights she lay on cushions on the floor, taking neither food nor medicine; and then, falling into a heavy sleep, she died. She was in her seventieth year.

Firm, resolute, watchful, and self-controlled, Elizabeth as a Queen has had few equals among the sovereigns of England. She was extravagant in nothing but dress, and she thus was able to pay off heavy debts left owing by her predecessors. Her temper was violent, and she desired to be absolute Queen; but she knew her people, and if she found that she had asked too much, she prudently withdrew her demand. Her conduct when the Parliament of 1601 opposed the monopolies, which for forty years she had been granting, serves to show her wisdom. She had granted these unjust patents by scores. Such things as iron, oil, coal, starch, leather, and glass, could be had only from the privileged dealers, who charged immense prices. When the Queen saw the temper of the people, 'she declined the contest, put herself at the head of the reforming party, thanked the Commons in touching and dignified language for their tender care of the general weal, and brought back to herself the hearts of the people.' Vanity was her great fault; and the picture drawn by historians of 'Good Queen Bess,' as she has been called, coquetting in her old age with Raleigh and Essex, and believing all their tender speeches, makes her rather ridiculous in our eyes.

The reign of Elizabeth is one of the brightest periods of our literature. Then Edmund Spenser wrote the 'Faerie Queen' among the woods of Kilcolman; then flourished Philip Sydney, author of a prose romance called 'Arcadia;' then were written the plays of William Shakspere; then the early studies of Francis Bacon laid the foundation of the modern philosophy.

The English newspaper dates from this reign. The Venetians, at war with the Turks in 1536, had printed a sheet called 'Gazetta,' from the small coin for which it was sold. A similar sheet was published in England while the Armada was off our shores in July 1588. It was called the 'English Mercurie,' and is still preserved in the British Museum.

The rise of the Dutch Republic under William of Nassau, Prince of Orange, and the massacre of St. Bartholomew in France (1572), were important continental events during Elizabeth's reign. Both were connected with the Reformation. The alliance of Elizabeth contributed much to the triumph of William. The massacres in France and the cruelties of Alva in the Netherlands drove hundreds of work-people to settle in Britain. Those from France were skilled in silk-weaving; those from Flanders were chiefly dyers and dressers of woollen cloth; and a marked improvement in these two branches of our manufactures may thus be traced to the persecution of the Protestants.

CONTEMPORARY SOVEREIGNS.

SCOTLAND.	A.D.
MARY,............dethroned	1567
JAMES VI.	

FRANCE.	
HENRY II.,............died	1559
FRANCIS II.,	1560
CHARLES IX.,	1574
HENRY III.,	1589
HENRY IV.	

SPAIN.	
PHILIP II.,	1598
PHILIP III.	

TURKEY.	
SOLYMAN I.,	1566
SELIM II.,	1574
AMURATH III.,	1595
MOHAMMED III.	

EMPERORS.	A.D.
FERDINAND I.,............died	1564
MAXIMILIAN II.,	1576
RODOLPH II.	

POPES.	
PAUL IV.,	1559
PIUS IV.,	1566
PIUS V.,	1572
GREGORY XIII.,	1585
SIXTUS V.,	1590
GREGORY XIV.,	1590
GREGORY XV.,	1591
INNOCENT IX.,	1592
CLEMENT VIII.	

CHAPTER VI.

STUART SOVEREIGNS OF SCOTLAND.

From 1370 A.D. to 1603 A.D.—233 years.—9 Sovereigns.

	A.D.
ROBERT II. (grandson of Robert Bruce),	1370
ROBERT III. (son),	1390
JAMES I. (second son),	1406
JAMES II. (only son),	1437
JAMES III. (son),	1460
JAMES IV. (son),	1488
JAMES V. (son),	1513
MARY (daughter),	1542
JAMES VI. and I. of England (son),	1567
Union of the crowns of England and Scotland,	1603

Battle of Chevy-Chase.
Highland combat at Perth.
Battle of Harlaw.
Good laws of James I.
Battle of Sauchie Burn.
Battle of Flodden.

Patrick Hamilton.
George Wishart.
Preaching of Knox.
Mary dethroned.
Gowrie conspiracy.

From the marriage of Marjory Bruce, daughter of the great Robert, with Walter the Steward of Scotland, sprang the line of Stuart monarchs. Their son, Robert II., was the first of the famous but unhappy race. During his reign was fought the battle of Chevy-Chase between **1388** the Percies and the Douglases. The scene of the A.D. battle was Otterbourne, a village of Redesdale near Newcastle. The victory of the Scots was dearly bought by the death of Earl Douglas. Robert II. died in 1390.

His son John then assumed the sceptre under the name of Robert III.; for Baliol had been called John, and the name was ominous of evil. He was a gentle prince, and of delicate health, having been lamed in his youth by the kick of a horse. His brother Albany, therefore, managed the affairs of state. Robert's eldest son, David of Rothesay, a wild and headstrong prince, defied the power of Albany; but the Regent was more than a match for the reckless boy, who was imprisoned in Falkland Castle, and there starved to death. A well-known event of this reign was the combat on the North Inch of Perth between the clans Kay and Chattan. Thirty were selected on each side; but at the hour appointed one of the clan Chattan was missing. Henry Gow, a smith of Perth, offered to fill the vacant place for half a merk. When the fight was over, all the sixty save one lay dead or wounded. The Lowlands were thus relieved from some of their deadliest Highland foes. These events are embodied in Scott's tale, 'The Fair Maid of Perth.' To save his surviving son James from the schemes of Albany, Robert sent him to France; but the vessel was boarded by the sailors of Henry IV., and James, a boy of fourteen, was lodged in the Tower of London. This loss killed the gentle Robert, who died at Rothesay, 1406 A.D.

James remained in England for nineteen years, during thirteen of which Albany was Regent. The chief events were the martyrdom of John Resby at Perth, in 1407, for Lollardism; and the battle of Harlaw in 1411, which decided the superiority of the Scottish Kings over the Lords of the Isles. Albany died in 1419, leaving the Regency to his son Murdoch, under whose weak rule nobles and people fell into the wildest disorder. In this condition James I. found his subjects when in 1424 he returned to his country. His captivity had been of great use to him. He had studied the English laws and constitution, and had acquired great excellence in poetry and music. The worst evil he had now to grapple with was the utter contempt of law, which pervaded all classes. But he resolutely set himself to his toilsome work. Many of the best English laws relating to wages, weights and measures, and police, were enacted in his Parliaments, drawn up in the spoken language of the land. Regular taxes were levied; and large estates, foolishly given away during the late reigns, were reclaimed. This was the most dangerous part of his task; and to enforce obedience he was compelled to put many nobles to death. But the day of his usefulness was soon over. A band of conspirators broke into the Monastery of the Blackfriars at Perth, where he was keeping the Christmas of 1437, and murdered him in a vault below the flooring of his chamber, into which he had leaped for safety.

James II. was only six years old when his father died. During his minority three factions convulsed the land. From one to the other the boy-King was passed by the changes in the strife; but at length the house of Douglas became ascendant, and at one time threatened to overturn the throne of the Stuarts. To break the power of his dreaded foe, James stooped to murder. He invited the Earl to dine with him at Stirling; and, when the meal was over, while they were conversing in an inner room, he slew his guest with his own hand. From this crime sprang a war with England, during which James was killed by the bursting of a cannon at the siege of Roxburgh Castle. Cannon were quite new to the Scots, and were then made of iron bars bound together with hoops.

Once more Scotland was plunged into the horrors of a minority, for James III. was now only eight years of age. The Boyds and the Hamiltons disturbed the peace of the land by their constant feuds. When James grew up, he displayed a feeble and indolent character, and that worst vice of a sovereign,—a desire to abandon all cares of government to unworthy favourites. The nobles saw with anger an architect, a dancing-master, and a tailor, enjoying the confidence of their King. At length they seized Robert Cochrane, whom they scornfully called the 'mason,' and hanged him with five others on the bridge of Lauder. They soon broke out in revolt, headed by the King's eldest son, Prince James, and encouraged by Henry VII. of England. A battle was fought at Sauchie Burn in Stirlingshire, where James was worsted. While galloping from the field, he was thrown from his horse and, while he lay helpless in a cottage close by, he was stabbed to the heart by a straggler from the battle-field.

James IV. now held the throne. The leading events of his history are,—his protection of Perkin Warbeck; his marriage in 1503 with Margaret, eldest daughter of Henry VII.; and the battle of Flodden in 1513.

The immediate cause of the war which ended in the battle of Flodden was an attack by the English upon the ships of Andrew Barton, a Scottish merchant. Barton was killed, and his ship, the Lion, carried as a prize into the Thames. The Earl of Surrey headed the English troops. The armies came face to face on the banks of the Till, a tributary of the Tweed. James was strongly posted on Flodden Hill, a spur of the Cheviot range. It was the 9th of September 1513. The grand mistake committed by James was allowing the English to cross the Till unharmed, when with his artillery he might have torn their battalions to fragments as they were crowding over the narrow bridge. The error was never retrieved. From four in the afternoon till the night fell the battle raged; but the Scots were totally defeated. James and thirteen of his Earls lay dead among heaps of the humbler slain.

A long minority again convulsed unhappy Scotland. Struggles for the Regency among the leading nobles filled up fifteen stormy years. Again the Douglases became keepers of the King; but in 1528 young James stole from Falkland Palace, where he was closely watched, and, fleeing to Stirling Castle, took the government into his own hands.

An event of deeper interest marks the year 1528. The first of those noble men whose names may be read on the Martyrs' Monument of St. Andrews—Patrick Hamilton, Henry Forrest, George Wishart, and Walter Mill—then suffered death by fire in defence of the Protestant faith. The leaven of the Reformation was working fast, and vainly James strove to destroy its rising power. In order to cement his alliance with the Romanists of France, he chose Mary of Guise to be his second wife.

A quarrel with England closed the reign of James V. Henry VIII. strove to persuade the Scottish King to assist him in his schemes against Popery, but met with a refusal. Henry declared war. James was at Fala Moor when his nobles turned against him, and refused to fight. Ten thousand Scots were led to the Esk by Oliver Sinclair; but they fled before three hundred English horsemen. James reached Falkland, and lay down to die of vexation. A low fever wasted him away, and he drew his last breath only a few days after his daughter—the celebrated Mary Queen of Scots—was born.

The most prominent men in Scotland at this time were Cardinal Beaton, the relentless persecutor of the Protestants; and the Earl of Arran, who proved a renegade from the Protestant faith. Both sought the Regency; Arran gained it. But their enmity was laid aside, while they united in the hopeless attempt to restore the power of the Romish Church in Scotland. George Wishart, the last victim of Beaton's bigotry, suffered at St. Andrews in March 1546. Within a few yards of the spot where the ashes of the martyr had lain black, Beaton was slain two months later by James Melville, who with Norman Leslie and others forced their way through the Castle into the Cardinal's chamber.

Henry VIII. desired a marriage between his son Edward and the young Mary; but the Scottish nation withstood his wish. Even their defeat at Pinkie after his death failed to force them into the alliance.

The girl-Queen, sent for safety to her mother's land, married there the Dauphin Francis, afterwards King of France; but his early death compelled her to return to Scotland in 1561. She had been educated as a Romanist, in the gay and frivolous court of France. Her Scottish subjects had begun to look with horror upon tastes and habits which she thought harmless and pleasant. The master-spirit of the nation was John Knox, the pupil of Wishart and the companion of Calvin.

Born in 1505, and educated as a Romish priest, Knox was thirty-eight when he was converted to Protestantism. At St. Andrews he preached his first Protestant sermon. Seized by the Regent and sent to France, he was condemned to the galleys for life; but God had decreed otherwise. After nineteen months his chains were loosed, at the request of Edward VI., in whose court he lived for some time. The persecution of Protestants under Mary I. of England drove him once more to the Continent. Through years of exile and bondage he cherished the hope of again preaching the pure Gospel at St. Andrews, long the fortress of the Romish faith in Scotland. His hope was realized. On the 10th of June 1559 from the cathedral pulpit of that ancient city he poured forth his fiery eloquence against the Romish idolatry. The power of the Gospel struck through the land like an electric shock. Throughout all Fife, and soon throughout all Scotland, images were broken, altars were shivered, mass-books were torn, priestly vestments were rent into shreds. He afterwards boldly denounced the celebration of mass in the chapel-royal of Holyrood.

The gulf between Mary and her people grew wider. Her private life was open to suspicion. By her marriage with Lord Darnley she lost favour with her natural brother, the Earl of Moray, once Prior of St. Andrews, and now leader of the Protestant party. Then followed her fondness for David Rizzio, a musician; which excited the jealousy of Darnley, and thus led to the murder of the Italian in Holyrood. Her son, afterwards King James VI., was born in 1566. In the following February her husband, Darnley, was murdered in the Kirk of Field; the house—a lonely building standing where the College of Edinburgh now rises —being blown up at midnight. Bothwell was strongly suspected of the crime; and yet, two months later, Mary married him. Whether the Queen was guilty or not of the crimes laid to her charge—and that can now be known only to the great Searcher of hearts—these events estranged from her the affections of her people. The nobles took up arms.

1567 A.D. Having surrendered at Carberry Hill, Mary was dethroned, and imprisoned in the Castle of Lochleven. Bothwell fled to Orkney, thence to Denmark; where, ten years later, he died mad and in prison.

Moray became Regent for the infant James. Mary, escaping from her prison by the aid of Willie Douglas, put herself at the head of the Romish nobles, and at Langside near Glasgow made a desperate and final struggle for her crown. In vain. As a last resource she fled to England, and threw herself on the compassion of Elizabeth, in whose reign the rest of her sad story may be read.

For three years Moray, known as the Good Regent, held power. He was shot by Hamilton of Bothwellhaugh, from a window in the main street of Linlithgow (January 23, 1570). The Earls of Lennox, Mar, and Morton, were then Regents in succession. In the latter part of 1572 John Knox died. James VI., educated by the celebrated George Buchanan, grew up a man of learning, but a pedant. He married Anne, daughter of the Danish King. He strove vainly to overthrow Presbyterianism and to establish Prelacy in Scotland. The strange Gowrie conspiracy was the most striking event of the reign. While hunting at Falkland, the King was induced to visit Gowrie House by a false story, that a man carrying a pot of foreign gold had been arrested near Perth. He was well received and entertained by Earl Gowrie; but after dinner, in a small room, he was seized by the Earl's brother, Alexander Ruthven, who strove to tie his hands. James struggled and cried for help. Three of his attendants burst in. Ruthven was slain; and the Earl, who upon hearing the noise rushed in sword in hand, met the same fate. The whole story is wrapped in mystery.

The death of Elizabeth in 1603 made James the unquestioned King of the whole island. Sir Robert Carey rode to Edinburgh with the news. The Queen died at Richmond on Thursday morning at three o'clock, and he reached Holyrood on Saturday evening.

IRELAND FROM 1370 A.D. TO 1603 A.D.

Poynings' law. | Tyrone's rebellion.
Sir John Perrot. | Romanism in Ireland.

Richard II. visited Ireland twice to quell the rebellious natives; but, worn out by constant feuds, they yielded at once. Through all these dark years few merchant ships were to be seen in the fine harbours of the Irish coast. Hides and fish were almost the only exports.

The nobles of Ireland sided chiefly with the House of York in the wars of the Roses. Hence the two impostors, who endeavoured to dethrone Henry VII., chose Ireland as a fitting stage for their first appearance. The Tudors had but little hold over these unruly Barons, until in 1495 Poynings' law was passed. This law, which derived its name from the Lord-Deputy who then governed the island, gave the English sovereign complete control over the Parliament of Ireland. It enacted, 1. That no Irish Parliament could be held without the consent of the English sovereign; 2. That no law should be brought forward in Ireland unless it had been previously submitted to him; 3. That all English laws lately passed should be of force in Ireland.

The feuds of the Fitzgeralds and the Butlers distracted the land in the reign of Henry VIII., by whom in 1541 Ireland was raised from a lordship to a kingdom, many of the chiefs being honoured with the title of Earl.

Under Elizabeth the Protestant religion was established in Ireland. The spirit of the natives was intensely Popish, and strong resistance was made; but she bent the Parliament to her will. Sir John Perrot, made Deputy in 1584, proposed to develop the resources of the island by making roads and building bridges. This true and wise policy was then rejected; but years afterwards the hint was turned to good account.

In 1595, the thirty-seventh year of Elizabeth's reign, the last grand struggle began. Hugh O'Neill, Earl of Tyrone, rose in revolt. Under the cloak of friendship towards England he had long been maturing his plans. In 1599 he won a great battle, which laid Munster at his feet. He looked for help to Spain, the leading Romish power in Europe. The Earl of Essex took the field against him without success. The glory of overthrowing the great rebel, and thus completing the conquest of Ireland, was reserved for Lord Mountjoy. A band of Spaniards landed at Kinsale to aid Tyrone, but were hemmed in by the active Deputy. O'Neill, marching to the rescue, was met and routed, upon which his foreign allies thought best to surrender. The rebellion of Tyrone ended thus in 1602, having lasted for seven years.

Irish history in these days, and indeed up to the opening of the present century, presents a sad picture. To the hatred between Celts and Saxons there was added the discord between Romanists and Protestants. Ireland has been, ever since the Reformation, one of the chief strongholds of Romanism; and the backward condition of the southern and western districts is owing, without doubt, to the ignorance in which that system loves to keep the masses of the people.

CHAPTER VII.

SOCIAL CONDITION OF THE PEOPLE UNDER THE TUDORS.

State of the nation.
Houses and furniture.
Style of living.
Dress.
Out-door sports.

In-door amusements.
Christmas and May-day.
Witchcraft, Astrology, Alchymy.
Commerce.
Learning.

BEFORE the English Reformation crime was fearfully common. In the reign of Henry VIII. about two thousand persons were hanged every year for robbery alone. In the days of Elizabeth the number was reduced to three or four hundred a year. This remarkable change was, without doubt, owing to the diffusion of God's Word among all classes. In the fifth year of Elizabeth the first law to relieve the poor was passed. The population was then under five millions; and the Queen's revenue cannot have exceeded £500,000 a year. The highest legal interest was 10 per cent. Most of the silver coins now current were in use, crowns, half-crowns, and sixpences having been issued by Edward VI.

The Tudor style of architecture was also called Florid, from the profusion of ornament on the buildings. Henry the Seventh's Chapel at Westminster is a good example of the style. Brick and stone were beginning to be used in the houses of the great, and glass windows became common. The poor lived in hovels made of wattles plastered over with clay. The fire was in the middle of the floor, and the smoke escaped through a hole in the blackened roof. This was the case in all houses until the reign of Henry VII., when chimneys began to be built. Erasmus, a Professor of Greek in Oxford under Henry VIII., gives no pleasant description of the floors of the poorer houses. He says: 'The floors are commonly of clay strewed with rushes; under which lies unmolested an ancient collection of beer, grease, fragments, bones, spittal, and everything that is nasty.' To these uncleanly habits were owing the terrible plagues that fell upon the people. In Elizabeth's time, however, houses were built chiefly of oak. Then, too, many changes were made in furniture. Bedding was much improved. In early Tudor reigns a straw pallet, a coarse sheet and rug, and a log of wood for a bolster, were commonly used. The man who lay on a pillow of chaff was thought luxurious. Servants lay on bare straw. Before Elizabeth reigned, all dishes and spoons were wooden, or, as they were called, 'treene.' But, then, pewter platters and silver or tin spoons came into use among farmers and those of the same class. The pewter dishes were at first flat, but were afterwards made deeper and more like basins. About the year 1580 coaches were introduced: before that time ladies rode on a pillion behind their chief servants, whom they held by the belt.

Hops were now first grown in England. Cabbages, cherries, gooseberries, plums, apricots, and grapes might be now seen in English gardens. Wheaten bread was eaten more generally, rye and barley being the food only of the poor. Potatoes were brought by Sir Francis Drake from Santa Fè in America, and were first planted in Lancashire. They were introduced into Ireland by Sir Walter Raleigh. Raleigh also brought tobacco from the West Indian island Tobago, and taught the English its use. Beef and mutton sold in the time of Henry VIII. for a halfpenny per pound; veal and pork for three farthings. But fresh meat was not eaten even by gentlemen, except from Midsummer to Michaelmas. The families of the nobles and gentry still dined in the great hall with all the servants. Halfway down the table stood a large salt-cellar of silver or pewter. Above this sat the master, his family, and guests; below it were retainers and servants of all degrees. The nobles kept up princely style. The Earl of Leicester, who owned Kenilworth Castle, kept there arms for 10,000 men. There in 1576 he entertained Elizabeth for seventeen days with the most splendid feasts and shows. Lord Burleigh, though a self-made noble, had a train of twenty gentlemen, each worth £1000 a year, besides numerous under-servants.

The country folk wore a doublet of russet-brown leather. But the court fashions were, like those of our own day, always changing. The courtiers of Henry VIII. stuffed their clothes as the King grew fat, in order that their figures might resemble his. Queen Catherine Howard introduced pins from France; and, as these were expensive at first, a separate sum for this luxury was granted to the ladies by their husbands. Hence the expression, 'pin-money.' The farthingale was introduced from Spain in Mary's reign. It was a large hooped petticoat. Ruffs of plaited linen were worn by both sexes on the neck and wrists. These were at first held out by pieces of wood or ivory; but in Elizabeth's time they were stiffened with yellow starch. Cloth hose were worn by all, until in the third year of her reign Elizabeth received a pair of black silk stockings. After this she wore no other kind. Three thousand dresses were found in the wardrobe of this Queen after her death! In the travels of Hentzner, a German, Elizabeth is thus described: 'Next came the Queen, in the sixty-fifth year of her age,—very majestic; her face oblong, fair, but wrinkled. She had in her ears two pearls with drops; she wore false hair, and that red; and upon her head she had a small crown. She was dressed in white silk, bordered with pearls the size of beans; and over it a mantle of black silk, shot with silver thread. Her train was very long, and the end of it borne by a marchioness.' The gentlemen wore their hair either short and curled, or set up on end. Their beards were long and pointed. The costume of the yeomen of the Queen's guard, commonly called 'beef-eaters' (a corruption of *buffetiers*), gives a very good idea of the dress worn by men in the Tudor Period. The growth of flax and hemp, and the invention of cotton thread, supplied materials for stocking-weaving and the making of sail-cloth. Rugs, frieze, and baize began to be manufactured largely, and were much improved by the skill of the cloth-dressers who fled from the persecutions of the Continent.

The tournament had now degenerated into a mere sport, for the strength of armies consisted no longer in steel-clad knights. The boat-joust, or tilting on the water, was practised in summer on the Thames and other rivers. Boards were placed across the boats, on which stood men armed with wooden spears and shields; and each, as the boats were rowed swiftly against one another, strove to knock his opponent overboard. Hunting, especially the stag-hunt, has been at all times one of our national sports. During this period the ladies often joined the chase, and shot at the game with arrows. Elizabeth, even in her old age, enjoyed the sport, sometimes every second day. Hawking, though still practised, was now beginning to decline, for the gun was coming into use. There were horse-races for prizes; but the modern system of gambling bets was unknown. Bear-baiting and bull-baiting were favourite sports of the highest in the land. Queen Mary, visiting her sister at Hatfield House, was entertained with a grand bear-baiting. Elizabeth, receiving the Danish ambassador at Greenwich, treated him to a similar sight. The animal was fastened in the middle of an open space, and worried by great English bull-dogs; and, as the dogs were killed or disabled, fresh ones were supplied. The cruel sport of whipping a blinded bear often followed. Even the ladies enjoyed these sports exceedingly; and we cannot, therefore, wonder that the language of the period was very indelicate and coarse. To make the matter worse, the Sabbath afternoon was, until the last years of Elizabeth, the favourite time for these amusements. The principal country sports were archery, foot-races, and various games of ball. Among the last were tennis, club-ball (the origin of cricket), and pall-mall, in which a boxwood ball was struck with a mallet through an iron arch.

Within doors the chief game was shovel-board. It was played on a smooth table with flat metal weights. A line was drawn across the table four inches from the edge, and the skill of the play consisted in shoving the weights so as to cross this line without falling over the edge of the table. Other games were backgammon, then called tables; dice, ruinous in every age; chess, supposed to have come from Asia, and to have been known in this land one hundred years before the Conquest; and cards, invented to relieve the mind of Charles VI., a mad King of France. Dancing and music filled up many hours; but the dance always ceased with night-fall,—a custom very different from that now prevailing. Although the minstrels and joculators (jugglers) of the Norman days were despised in the Tudor Period, music was much cultivated in private life. The fashionable instruments of music were the cittern or lute, a kind of guitar;

and the virginals, a keyed instrument of one string, the original of the harpsichord and the modern piano.

Christmas was the great season of sports. There was then a general license, and all sorts of wild tricks were played. From the Sovereign to the beggar all England went a-mumming in strange dresses and masks. Those who could not get masks rubbed soot on their faces. In every parish a Lord of Misrule was chosen, who, with a troop of idle fellows in green and yellow dresses covered with ribbons, went about shouting and playing drums, sometimes even into the churches during Divine service. These mummers wore masks representing the heads of goats, stags, and bulls, and often dressed themselves in skins to resemble savages. Mummeries on a magnificent scale were got up at the court of Henry VIII. May-day was another festive season in old England. Green branches were pulled immediately after midnight; a Lord and Lady of May were chosen; and dances were kept up round a May-pole crowned with flowers. Connected with these sports was the Morris-dance,—supposed to have been derived from the Moors of Spain. The principal dancer, or foreman of the Morris, was richly dressed; and all had bells attached to their skirts, arms, and knees. Some assumed characters, such as Robin Hood and Maid Marian; and a hobby-horse was always in the band. This was a light wooden frame, representing the head and body of a horse, with trappings that reached the ground and concealed a man inside, who pranced about in imitation of a horse.

Three forms of superstition influenced the minds of the people to a great degree during this period. These were Witchcraft, Astrology, and Alchymy. According to the ignorant, all discoveries in science, all inventions in art were the work of the evil one. Hence Roger Bacon in England and Faust in Germany were believed to have sold themselves to Satan. But poor feeble old women were the most frequent victims of the absurd belief in Witchcraft; and they perished by hundreds. The older and weaker and more withered the object of suspicion, the stronger was the belief that she was a witch. All mischief was ascribed to them. If a child took sick and died, some witch had done it: if a storm arose, the trembling peasants thought they heard the screaming of the witches, who were riding on broomsticks through the midnight skies. This belief kept its hold of the popular mind up to the present century, and is not even yet extinct in some remote country districts. The astrologers, whose art was more than four thousand years old, pretended that they could foretell events by the stars. They were consulted by even the highest and wisest; and were, therefore, honoured and rich. Many of our common words, such as 'consider,' 'disaster,' 'ill-starred,' had, as their derivation shows, at first a purely astrological meaning. Kindred with Astrology was Alchymy, an art which had for its object the discovery of the *philosopher's stone* and the *elixir of life*. The former was an imaginary substance which could change all baser metals into gold; the latter, a liquid which would confer on the person drinking it everlasting life and beauty. In this vain pursuit the time, the health, and the fortune of thousands were wasted, without profit to them. But not without profit to us. From Witchcraft came that knowledge of drugs and plants so useful in medicine and the arts; while from the falsehoods of Astrology and Alchymy sprang the truths of Astronomy and Chemistry,—sciences whose noblest use is to bear witness to the infinite wisdom and power of Him who made the heavens and the earth.

Navigation, geography, and commerce advanced together with rapid strides. Henry VII. laid the foundation of our navy, and, therefore, of our world-wide commerce. English ships were soon ploughing every sea. In Mary's reign the way to Archangel was discovered, and our Russian trade began. It was, however, in the days of Elizabeth that commerce received its mightiest impulse. Wool, lead, and tin had long been exported to the Continent, but in vessels from the Hanse Towns. Elizabeth built large vessels for this trade, and encouraged the English merchants to improve their ships. By granting a charter to the East India Company in 1600, she laid the foundation of our Indian Empire.

A remarkable feature of the period was the revival of learning, especially the study of classics. This was owing chiefly to the Reformation; for the true interpretation of the

Bible depends upon a knowledge of Greek, Hebrew, and Latin; and with the spread of the Bible was diffused a desire to know these languages. They have ever since held a leading place in school and college education. Erasmus, a Dutchman, was Professor of Greek at Oxford in the reign of Henry VIII., and did much for the advancement of classical study. Henry VIII., Edward VI., Jane Grey, and Mary were all good classical scholars; and Elizabeth, even after she became Queen, read, as her tutor old Roger Ascham said, 'more Greek in a day than a clergyman read of Latin in a week.' Westminster School was founded by Edward VI., who, besides, endowed many hospitals and grammar schools. In the same reign Rugby School was founded by Sheriffe. During the reigns of the first four Tudors, the language spoken and written in England was Middle English. In the reign of Elizabeth arose the New or Modern English, which has continued in use ever since. Previous to the regular tragedies and comedies of Marlowe and Shakspere, there appeared short plays, called interludes. The most successful writer of these was John Heywood, who lived at the court of Henry VIII. To ridicule and censure the Romish clergy seems to have been his chief object.

LEADING AUTHORS OF THE TUDOR PERIOD.

MIDDLE ENGLISH.

SIR THOMAS MORE,..........(1480–1535)—prose writer—Lord Chancellor—chief works, 'Utopia,' a fanciful scheme of perfect government, written first in Latin; and the 'History of Edward V. and Richard III.' —beheaded by Henry VIII.

SIR THOMAS WYATT,........(1503–1541)—a lyric poet.

THOMAS HOWARD, ...Earl of Surrey—(1516–1547)—poet—refiner of English verse—introduced the sonnet from Italy—wrote the earliest English blank-verse in some translations from Virgil—beheaded by Henry VIII.

WILLIAM TYNDALE,..........Scholar of Oxford—translated the Bible —burned near Antwerp in 1536.

MILES COVERDALE, ...(1499–1580)—of Cambridge—translated the whole Bible into English.

WILLIAM DUNBAR,............Poet—a Scottish clergyman—flourished about 1500 at the Scottish court—wrote allegorical poems—chief, 'The Dance,' and 'The Union of the Thistle with the Rose.'

GAVIN DOUGLAS,..............Poet—Bishop of Dunkeld—flourished about 1500—wrote 'Palace of Honor'—first translator of Virgil's 'Æneid' into English verse.

NEW OR MODERN ENGLISH.

SIR PHILIP SYDNEY,.........(1554-1586)—wrote a prose romance called 'Arcadia;' also verses—killed at the battle of Zutphen in the Netherlands.

EDMUND SPENSER.............(1553-1598)—second great English poet—secretary to the Lord-Lieutenant of Ireland—lived at Kilcolman, county of Cork—chief work, 'The Faerie Queen,' an allegorical poem, written in a stanza of nine lines, called 'the Spenserian.'

CHRISTOPHER MARLOWE, (1562-1593)—wrote eight plays—chief were 'Faustus' and 'The Jew of Malta.'

WILLIAM SHAKSPERE,.......(1564-1616)—the prince of dramatists—born and died at Stratford-on-Avon—lived chiefly in London—wrote thirty-five plays between 1591 and 1614—wrote also sonnets and tales.

SIR WALTER RALEIGH,......(1552-1618)—wrote verses in earlier years—prose works on politics—spent more than twelve years in prison in the Tower—occupied himself in writing a 'History of the World,' which comes down to about 70 B.C.

FRANCIS BACON,................(1561-1626)—Lord Chancellor and Viscount St. Albans—a great philosopher—wrote ten volumes—chief work, 'The Instauration of the Sciences,' a union of two books, namely, 'The Proficience and Advancement of Learning' (1605), and the 'Novum Organum' (1620).

About 1500 three great painters flourished in Italy,—Leonardo da Vinci, Raphael, and Titian. Albert Durer lived about the same time at Nuremberg. There were no English artists of note. Most of the portraits of the Tudors are from the pencil of Hans Holbein, a German artist.

LEADING DATES OF THE TUDOR PERIOD.

GENERAL EVENTS.

	A.D.	
Discovery of West Indies (Columbus),	1492	Henry VII.
Field of the Cloth of Gold,	1520	Henry VIII.
Wales represented in the English Parliament,	1536	—
Mary I. married Philip of Spain,	1554	Mary I.
Mary Stuart executed,	1587	Elizabeth.
Charter granted to East India Company	1600	—

DOMINION ACQUIRED AND LOST.

Discovery of American mainland by Cabot,	1497	Henry VII.
Loss of Calais,	1558	Mary I.
Havre taken and lost,	1562-63	Elizabeth.

WARS, BATTLES, ETC.

Battle of Stoke,	1487	Henry VII.
— Spurs,	1513	Henry VIII.
— Flodden,	1513	—
— Pinkie,	1547	Edward VI.
Armada defeated,	1588	Elizabeth.

THE REFORMATION.

IN GERMANY,
- Luther publishes the 95 Propositions, ...1517...Henry VIII.
- The Disputation at Leipsic,...1519... —
- Burns the Pope's Bull,...1520... —

IN ENGLAND,
- Henry VIII. made Defender of the Faith,...1521... —
- Final Breach between England and Rome,...1535... —
- Coverdale's Bible published, 1535... —
- Cranmer's Bible (The Great Bible),...1539... —
- The Bloody Statute,...1539... —
- Three years' persecution of Protestants,...begins 1555...Mary I.
- Church of England fully established,...1562...Elizabeth.
- The Puritans separate from the Established Church, ...1566... —

GENEALOGICAL TREE
CONNECTING THE TUDORS AND THE STUARTS.

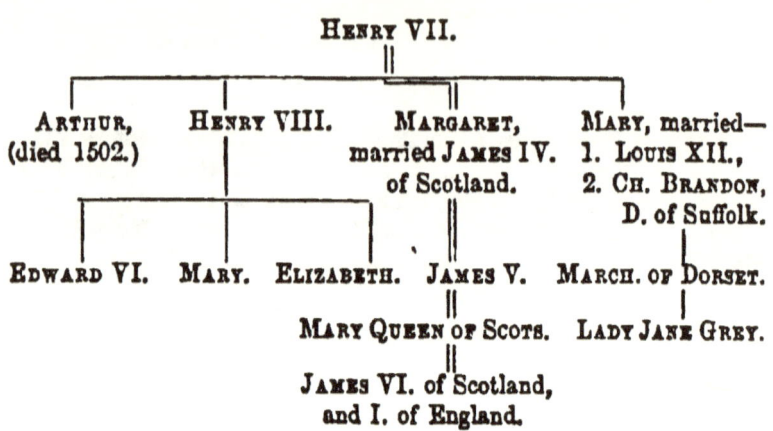

STUART PERIOD.

From 1603 A.D. to 1714 A.D.—111 years.—6 Sovereigns.

	A.D.
JAMES I. (son of Mary Queen of Scots),	1603
CHARLES I. (son),	1625
COMMONWEALTH, during which Cromwell ruled as Protector for five years,	began 1649 ended 1660
CHARLES II. (son of Charles I.),	1660
JAMES II. (brother),	1685
WILLIAM III. (nephew), MARY II. (daughter),	1689
Death of MARY, WILLIAM left sole Ruler,	1694
ANNE (daughter of James II.),	1702-1714

Leading Features :—THE KINGS STRIVING FOR ABSOLUTE POWER.
THE PARLIAMENT RESISTING.
FINAL TRIUMPH OF THE PARLIAMENT.

CHAPTER I.

JAMES I.

Born 1566 A.D.—Began to reign 1603 A.D.—Died 1625 A.D.

Descent of James.	Favourites of James.	The Thirty Years' War.
Three religious parties.	Sir Walter Raleigh.	Death.
Bible translated.	Contest with the Parliament.	Character.
The Gunpowder Plot.		Notes.
Scotland and Ireland.	The Spanish match.	

JAMES VI. of Scotland ascended the English throne as the descendant of Margaret, eldest daughter of Henry VII. To please his new subjects, he created in six weeks more than two hundred knights.

The English nation was then divided into three great parties, the Episcopalians, the Romanists, and the Puritans; and all three were nursing the hope of special favour from James. The Episcopalians trusted to his previous fondness for their church-government. The Romanists thought that the son of Mary Stuart could not but cherish the creed of his mother. The Puritans clung to the hope that a King educated among Presbyterians would not dislike Puritanism. It soon appeared that James was resolved to establish Episcopacy throughout all Great Britain, as the united kingdoms of England and Scotland now began to be called.

The King's liking for the Episcopal form of worship appeared most strongly at a conference held in 1604, at Hampton Court, between the leading men of the two great Protestant parties. James, vain of his theological learning, joined in the discussion, and met all the reasonings of the Puritan ministers with his favourite expression,—*No bishop, no king.* The translation of the Bible, which we now use, was almost the only good fruit of this conference. Forty-seven ministers were engaged in the work for three years (1607 to 1610). It was printed in the Roman character, nearly all the previous copies having been in the type which is called Old English, though Caxton brought it from Germany. The address of the translators to King James I. may be read at the beginning of all our Bibles.

The discontent of the Romanists, when they found that James had no intention of overthrowing the Protestant religion in England, took a terrible shape. They resolved to blow up the King, Lords, and Commons, by gunpowder. Robert Catesby and Everard Digby were the chief conspirators. For eighteen months the preparations went on; and, although many were in the secret, no breath of it seems to have got abroad. A cellar beneath the House of Lords was hired; thirty-six barrels of gunpowder were placed there; coals and sticks were strewed over these; and the doors were then thrown boldly open. Still no detection. Only a few days before the appointed time, Lord Monteagle received an anonymous letter warning him not to attend the opening of Parliament. The mysterious words were,—'The Parliament shall receive a terrible blow, and shall not see from whose hand it comes.' The letter was laid before the Council, and the King was the first to guess that gunpowder was meant. On searching the vaults a Spanish officer, Guy Fawkes, was found preparing the matches for the following morning.

The rest of the conspirators fled into the country, where most of them were cut to pieces while fighting desperately. The 5th of November 1605 was the day fixed for the dreadful crime. Penal laws of the severest kind were the result of this plot. No Roman Catholic was permitted to live in London; none could be a lawyer or a doctor. They were outlawed; at any time their houses might with impunity be broken into and their furniture destroyed.

The great object of James in his government of Scotland was the establishment of Episcopacy. In this he was strenuously opposed by the General Assembly of the Presbyterian Church, and met with little success. In Ireland he did good. Taking almost all Ulster from the rebellious chiefs, he parcelled it out among settlers from Great Britain, and those of the native race who were willing to submit to his rule. The prosperity of the north of Ireland may be traced to these Plantations, as they were called. Ulster has been ever since the centre and stronghold of Irish Protestantism.

James trusted much to favourites. The principal objects of his attachment were Robert Carr, afterwards Earl of Somerset; and George Villiers, the well-known Duke of Buckingham. Carr was a Scotchman, handsome but vicious. He was concerned in a murder, and the odium against him grew so strong that James was forced to dismiss him from the court. Villiers was equally dissolute in his life, but had more prudence. To these even such men as Bacon, the Lord Chancellor, were known to cringe in hope of royal favour.

Sir Walter Raleigh had been committed to the Tower in the first year of this reign, for taking share in a plot to place on the throne Lady Arabella Stuart, a cousin of the King. There he spent more than twelve years, occupying the long days of captivity in writing a 'History of the World.' The work, which is still much admired, he brought up almost to the Christian Era. Growing weary of confinement, he offered, as the price of his freedom, to disclose a gold mine of which he knew in South America. James set him free, and gave him charge of fourteen vessels for the expedition; but, when he reached the South American coast, he found the Spaniards prepared to oppose his landing. Some skir-

1618
A.D.
mishes took place, and the Spanish town of St. Thomas was burned. On Raleigh's return James to please the Court of Spain, caused him to be beheaded on the old charge of conspiracy.

During this reign began that contest with the Parliament which forms the leading feature of the period, and which ended in the dethronement of the ancient Stuart line. The Stuarts were all haunted by an insane desire for absolute power. Their flatterers fed the mischievous feeling; the clergy especially began now to proclaim that the King, by Divine right to the throne, was above all laws. A book was published by Dr. Cowell full of arguments for this strange doctrine. But the Parliament took a high tone, insisting on the suppression of the book; and a royal proclamation was accordingly issued against it. The great abuses complained of by the Commons were the old evil, 'purveyance,' and the sale of monopolies, by which the trade of the entire country was placed in the hands of about two hundred persons. The check exercised by the Commons over the King lay in their power of giving or withholding supplies of money. But, when they applied this check, he strove to invent new ways of filling his purse. The fines of the Star Chamber became heavier and more frequent; titles of nobility were openly sold; and the new title of Baronet was created, of which the price was £1000.

Perhaps the sorest subject of contention was the match, arranged by Buckingham, between Charles, Prince of Wales, and the Princess of Spain. The object of James was by this marriage to secure the influence of Spain in bringing to a close the Thirty Years' War. The voice of the English Parliament and people was loud against the union. Three remonstrances were sent from the Commons to the King, and in each the language grew stronger. The last, in which they claimed freedom of speech as a birthright of which no King could deprive them, was entered on the Journals of the House. James in a rage ordered the book to be brought, and with his own hand removed the entry. He then dissolved the Parliament; which was his favourite plan of meeting their demands.

The match, so hateful to the nation, was never completed.

Charles and Buckingham undertook a journey in disguise, in order that the Prince might see his bride elect. But a quarrel between Buckingham and the Spanish minister, Olivarez, broke off the match. Charles, pretending that his father had recalled him, left Madrid abruptly, and was soon afterwards engaged in marriage to Henrietta Maria of France. The result of these changes was a war with Spain.

The great Thirty Years' War, which lasted from 1618 to 1648, was now convulsing the Continent. Its immediate cause was a contention for the crown of Bohemia between Frederic, Elector Palatine of the Rhine, and Ferdinand of Austria. The leading Protestant powers sided with the Elector; the Romish, with the Emperor. James, whose daughter Elizabeth was married to the Elector Frederic, sent a few troops to help his son-in-law; but his heart was not in the work, and the expedition failed.

In 1625 James died of ague and gout, aged fifty-nine. His eldest son, Henry, had died at nineteen; his second, Charles, succeeded him; his daughter Elizabeth and her German husband were the heads of the princely house of Brunswick, now holding the British throne.

The pedantry, obstinacy, and favouritism of James have been already noticed. His character was full of contrasts. Hunting, cock-fighting, and wine parties occupied much of his leisure; but he found time to write a few books, which gained him some distinction as an author. His appearance was awkward, chiefly from the weakness of his knees; his dress was careless, even slovenly.

In 1614 Napier of Merchiston invented the use of logarithms. The thermometer and the microscope came into use. Early in the next reign, in 1628, Harvey discovered the circulation of the blood.

CONTEMPORARY SOVEREIGNS.

FRANCE. A.D.
HENRY IV.................died 1610
LOUIS XIII.

SPAIN.
PHILIP III.,....................1621
PHILIP IV.

SWEDEN.
CHARLES IX.,.................1611
GUSTAVUS ADOLPHUS.

TURKEY.
MOHAMMED III.,...............1604
ACHMET I.,....................1617
MUSTAPHA I.,..................1618
OTHMAN II.,...................1622
MUSTAPHA II.,.................1623
AMURATH IV.

EMPERORS. A.D.
RODOLPH II.,.............died 1612
MATTHIAS,.....................1619
FERDINAND II.

POPES.
CLEMENT VIII,.................1605
LEO XI.,......................1623
URBAN VIII.

CHAPTER II.

CHARLES I.

Born 1600 A.D.—Began to reign 1625 A.D.—Beheaded 1649 A.D.

First Parliament of Charles.	The National Covenant.	Self-denying Ordinance.
The siege of Rochelle.	The Long Parliament.	Cromwell's army.
The Petition of Rights.	Irish rebellion.	The King a prisoner.
Strafford and Laud.	The two parties.	Pride's Purge.
The three Courts.	The Civil War.	Trial of the King.
Ship-money.	Campaign of 1643.	His execution.
Puritan Emigration.	Oliver Cromwell.	Character.
	Campaign of 1644.	Notes.

CHARLES, the second son of James I., became King in his twenty-fifth year. He married Henrietta Maria, the daughter of Henry IV. of France. The expensive Spanish war, begun in the last reign, still continued. To meet its cost, Charles asked his first Parliament for a supply; but the majority of the Commons were Puritans, and, looking with a jealous eye on the Romish Queen, they granted only £140,000 with tonnage and poundage for one year. Enraged at this want of confidence, and especially at some charges brought against Buckingham, the King dissolved their sitting in three weeks. He then levied taxes by his own authority, revived the old abuse of *benevolences*, and began to quarter his soldiers in private houses. His chief advisers were his Queen and Buckingham. Henrietta, as a Romanist, hated the Puritans; and she had inherited from her father a strong attachment to absolute power. She never ceased, through all her husband's life, to urge him on in that dangerous path towards which his own temper inclined him far too strongly.

The second Parliament, meeting in 1626, prepared to impeach Buckingham; but they had not passed a single Act when a dissolution checked their plans. The same illegal taxation followed. Many who resisted were imprisoned.

To add to the difficulties of Charles, a war with France began. Buckingham was again the cause. He quarrelled with Cardinal Richelieu, the great minister of France, who forbade the Duke ever again to enter French dominions. One of the grand objects of the Cardinal's government was the suppression of the Huguenots; and he was then engaged in besieging their stronghold, La Rochelle on the Bay of Biscay. Foiled in his attempts to take the city on the land side, he built a mole half a mile long across the mouth of the harbour. Twice the English tried to relieve the besieged. Buckingham led the first expedition, but returned, having lost almost half his men. While at Portsmouth, preparing to sail with a second, he was stabbed to the heart by Lieutenant Felton, who had been dismissed from the service. Earl Lindesay led the fleet to Rochelle; but no efforts could pierce the mole, and the city surrendered to Richelieu in 1628.

In the same year Charles called his third Parliament. Before granting any money, the Commons drew up a law—the famous Petition of Rights—requiring the King to levy no taxes without consent of Parliament, to detain no one in prison without trial, and to billet no soldiers in private houses. An assent was wrung from the reluctant Charles; and the Commons, rejoicing in this second great charter of English liberty, gave him five subsidies,—equal to nearly £400,000. But in three weeks it was seen that the King regarded not the solemn promise he had made.

1628 A.D.

The Commons murmured; but the King heeded them not. They set about preparing a remonstrance; he came to interfere. They locked themselves in; he got a blacksmith to break open the doors; but he found that the House had adjourned. Nine members were sent to prison, where one—Sir John Eliot—soon died. The Parliament was at once dissolved by the angry King. Sensible that his domestic policy would need all his energies, he then made peace with Spain and France.

For eleven years (1629 to 1640) no Parliament was called, —a case without parallel in our history. The Earl of Strafford and Archbishop Laud were the principal ministers of Charles during these years. Thomas Wentworth, afterwards Earl of Strafford, had been a leading man among those who forced the King to ratify the Petition of Rights; but the hope of being to Charles what Richelieu was to the French monarch, led him to seek the royal favour. He laid a deep scheme to undermine the power of the Commons, and to secure for Charles absolute power. This plan he called, in his private letters, 'Thorough,'—a name well expressing its nature. A standing army was to be raised, and before it all other power in the State was to be swept away. Appointed Viceroy of Ireland in 1633, he tried the first experiment in that island; and for seven years he had both native Irish and English colonists crouching in terror under his iron rule. William Laud, Archbishop of Canterbury, directed the affairs of the Church. Almost a Papist in his opinions, he hated with no common bitterness the religious services of the Puritans.

And now the nation groaned under the tyranny of three lawless tribunals, directed chiefly by these two ministers. In the Star Chamber men were sentenced to fine, imprisonment, and even mutilation, for resisting the policy of the King. The terrors of the High Commission Court were launched against all who dared to differ in religious opinions from Laud. Besides these, a Council, directed by Wentworth and endowed with absolute control over the northern counties, sat at York.

Of all the illegal taxes levied by Charles, ship-money was the most notorious. In old times the maritime counties and towns had been often called on by the King to equip vessels for the defence of the shore. Finch the Chief-Justice, and Noy the Attorney-General, proposed in 1634 to revive the tax, which dated so far back as the Danish invasion. It was a small thing, but the spirit of the English nation revolted against the injustice. It was a war-tax levied during profound peace; it was laid upon inland counties, as had never before been done; the money was to be applied, not to the equipment of a fleet, but to the support of a standing army; lastly, it was collected by authority of the King alone. For three years there was no open resistance. Then John Hampden, a gentleman of Buckinghamshire, refused to pay the tax of twenty shillings imposed on his estate. The case was tried in the Court of

1637 A.D. Exchequer; and a majority of the judges, who could then be dismissed at any time by the King, gave their decision against Hampden.

Through all these years a great emigration of the Puritans had been draining England of her best blood. Hunted even into their closets by the spies of Laud, dragged causelessly before the High Commission, robbed, tortured, maimed—what wonder is it that, much as they loved England, they chose rather a home in the wild woods of America, where there was none to forbid the evening psalm, or the prayer poured from the full heart? Hampden, Pym, Cromwell himself, were on board, bound for the colony of New England, when a Government order came to stop the sailing of the ship.

Charles followed the policy of his father towards Scotland. During his visit to that country in 1633 he appointed thirteen bishops. Four years later he commanded a semi-popish form of prayer to be read in the churches of Edinburgh; but, when the Dean rose in old St. Giles' to read this new Liturgy, Jenny Geddes flung a stool at his head, and a great riot arose in the church, from which the Bishop and the Dean fled in fear. An order came from Charles to enforce the reception of the new Prayers by the aid of soldiers if necessary. But the spirit of the Scots was roused. Within two months—March and February of 1638—nineteen-twentieths of the nation signed a parchment called the National Covenant, by which they bound themselves to oppose the revival in Scotland of Popish errors, and to unite for the defence of their laws, their freedom, and their King. A General Assembly, held soon afterwards at Glasgow, excommunicated the bishops and abolished Prelacy in Scotland. Thus in thirty days the work of thirty years was undone, and the Church of Scotland was established more firmly than before on the basis of Presbyterianism.

Charles would gladly have crushed this bold opposition, but his want of money entangled him in new difficulties every day. He was forced in 1640 to call his fourth Parliament; but, being met with the same demands as before, he soon dissolved it. He then tried a Council of Lords alone; but they knew the Constitution too well to act apart from the

Commons. Meanwhile, a Scottish army under Leslie had passed the Border and seized Newcastle.

The fifth and last Parliament of this reign, known as the Long Parliament, now began to sit. It existed for more than nineteen years. Its first session was marked by the impeachment of Strafford and the imprisonment of Laud. Pym led the impeachment, and the charge was treason against the liberty of the people. A bill of attainder was brought into the Commons, passed through the Lords, and waited only the signature of the King. Charles hesitated long; but a letter from the condemned Earl, desiring to be left to his fate, decided the matter. The warrant was signed, and Strafford suffered death (May 1641). Laud, detained in prison for four years, was then executed. *Nov., 1640 A.D.*

The effects of 'Thorough' upon Ireland have been already noticed. The reaction now began. A Romish conspiracy spread its deadly roots everywhere through the nation. A day was fixed for the capture of Dublin Castle; but the design was detected. The O'Neills of Ulster were in arms next day. But the darkest event of 1641 was a fearful massacre of Protestants by the Romanists. Forty thousand are said to have perished in the slaughter.

About this time appeared the two great political parties which still divide the nation, assuming the government by turns. The nobles, the gentlemen, and the clergy were in favour of the King. On the other side were a few of the peers, and the great mass of farmers, merchants, and shopkeepers. The King's party received the name 'Cavaliers,' from their gallant bearing and skill in horsemanship: the Opposition were called Roundheads, from the Puritan fashion of wearing closely cropped hair. Although the names afterwards changed into Tory and Whig, and these, still later, into Conservative and Liberal, the principles of the two parties have since remained the same. Order is the watchword of the one; Progress, that of the other. The one, inspired by Memory, seeks to maintain unchanged the old institutions, which have made the country prosperous: Hope leads the other to strive, by well-weighed changes, that prosperity shall become still more prosperous.

On the 22d of November 1641, after a keen contest,—the first pitched battle between these two parties,—it was resolved in the Commons, by a majority of eleven, to draw up a Remonstrance, complaining of the King's previous government. Seeing the stern temper of the House, he made fair promises; but his acts soon belied his words. Early in 1642 he ordered five of his most daring opponents in the Commons to be arrested for high treason. Their names were Pym, Hampden, Hazelrig, Hollis, and Strode. The Commons refused to give them up; he went next day with soldiers to seize them; but they escaped before he entered the House. During all that night the streets of London were filled with armed citizens. There was great excitement against the King, for he had insulted the nation. He left the capital and went to York. The Queen fled to Holland.

For some months messages passed between the King and the Parliament; but there was no desire to yield on either side. At last the Commons demanded that the King should give up the command of the army, one of the most ancient rights of the crown. He refused. The Civil War began. In April 1642 the gates of Hull were shut against the King, who had demanded admission. On the 25th of August 1642 the royal standard was unfurled at Nottingham, and ten thousand men gathered round it.

The soldiers of the King were gentlemen, well mounted, and skilled in the use of arms; but he was badly supplied with artillery and ammunition, and depended for money nearly altogether upon the loyalty of his Cavaliers. The Parliamentary ranks were filled with ploughboys and tradesmen, as yet raw and untrained; but the possession of London and the Thames, along with the power of levying taxes, gave the Commons decided advantage in a continued war. The King in person commanded the Cavaliers: the Earl of Essex was chosen to lead the Roundheads. Prince Rupert, the nephew of Charles, led the Royalist cavalry.

Oct. 23, 1642 A.D. The opening battle was fought at Edge Hill in Warwickshire; but it decided nothing. During the winter Charles established his head-quarters at Oxford, whose ancient university has been at all times distinguished for loyalty. The campaign of 1643 was marked by three events. Bristol, then the second city in the kingdom, was taken by the Royalists. In the flush of this success Charles then laid siege to Gloucester; but, just when success seemed sure, Essex, moving rapidly from London with all the train-bands, raised the siege, and some days later defeated the royal army in the first battle of Newbury. The siege of Gloucester was the turning point of the strife: thenceforward the cause of the Parliament grew strong, although the loss of Hampden, who fell early in the war while skirmishing with Rupert's cavalry, was at first severely felt. Sept., 1643 A.D.

But a greater soldier and statesman than Hampden was already on the scene. At Edge Hill a captain of horse named Oliver Cromwell had fought in the army of the Parliament. He was then above forty years of age, and had long lived a peaceful country life in his native shire of Huntingdon. Among the members of the Long Parliament he was known chiefly by his slovenly dress of Puritan cut and colour, and his strange, rough, rambling speeches. He saw the secret of the King's early success, and resolved that the clownish soldiers of the Parliament should soon be more than a match for the royal Cavaliers. He began with his own regiment; for he was now Colonel Cromwell. Filling its ranks with sober and God-fearing men, he placed them beneath a system of drill and discipline so strict that they soon became celebrated as the Ironsides of Colonel Cromwell.

Under the terms of a Solemn League and Covenant, made between the Parliaments of England and Scotland, 21,000 Scottish troops crossed the Border in the beginning of 1644. Charles drew some trifling aid from Ireland. In the south under Essex the soldiers of the Parliament suffered many defeats; but in the north, on Marston Moor, the Roundheads, aided by the Scots, gained a brilliant victory. On that day Cromwell and his Ironsides swept all before them. Rupert and his cavalry, victors in many a dashing charge, could not withstand the terrible onset of these Puritan dragoons. The immediate result of the victory was the capture of York and Newcastle July 2, 1644 A.D.

by the troops of the Parliament. A second battle of Newbury, fought towards the close of the campaign, ended in the defeat of Charles.

An offshoot from the Puritan party had been for some time taking shape and gathering strength in the nation. These were the Independents, of whom Cromwell was the chief. In religion they held that every Christian congregation formed an independent church of itself, and owed obedience to no synods or assemblies. In politics they desired to see monarchy overthrown and a republic erected. They were called in their own day Root-and-branch men. By their means an Act, called the Self-denying Ordinance, was passed in April 1645: it forbade all members of Parliament to hold command in the army. So Essex and Manchester were removed; Sir Thomas Fairfax was appointed Commander-in-chief; while Cromwell, though a member of Parliament, was soon called, with the rank of Lieutenant-General, to lead the Cavalry, and became in reality, though not in name, the General of the entire army.

And then was organized that strange army, by means of which Oliver achieved all his glories. There were, no doubt, many hypocrites in the ranks; but a spirit of sincere religion pervaded every regiment. Officers and men met regularly in the tents or the barrack-rooms to pray. They neither gambled, drank, nor swore. They often sang hymns as they moved to battle. And when, in later days, they fought the battles of England on the Continent, the finest troops in Europe were scattered in flight before their terrible charge.

June 14, **1645** A.D. The decisive battle of the Civil War was fought at Naseby in Northamptonshire, where the Royalist army was utterly routed. The victories of Montrose, who gained six successive battles in Scotland, and appeared to be complete master of that kingdom, gave the King some hopes of maintaining his cause there; but these hopes soon faded. The unfortunate Charles fled to Oxford, and thence to the Scottish army at Newark.

The Parliament was thus triumphant. But it was no longer a united body. During the war it had slowly resolved itself into two factions; the one Presbyterian, desirous only of limiting the power of the King; the other Independent, bent upon the destruction of the throne. Charles, in the faint hope of regaining his position by the aid of the Presbyterians, had flung himself on the mercy of the Scottish army at Newark. Receiving him loyally, they offered to support him, if he would sign the Solemn League. But this he refused to do; and after some time returned, by his own desire, to his English subjects. When the Scots stipulated for his safety and freedom, the English Parliament expressed great indignation, that they should be even suspected of evil designs on their King. It is due, therefore, to these Scottish Presbyterians to say, that when they gave up King Charles, they had not the faintest suspicion of the dark crime soon to be perpetrated in Whitehall yard.

Rapidly the plot thickened. Cornet Joyce, with a band of horse, acting under secret orders from Cromwell, seized the King at Holmby House. The royal prisoner, passed from castle to castle, found means at last to escape, and reached the Isle of Wight, in hopes of crossing to the Continent; but, being forced to take refuge in Carisbrook Castle, he was there guarded more jealously than ever. The Scots, alarmed at the fast growing power of the Independents, passed the Border under the Duke of Hamilton. About the same time the Royalists of Essex and Kent began to stir. Leaving these to Fairfax, Cromwell pressed northwards by rapid marches, routed Hamilton in Lancashire, and soon established at Edinburgh a government hostile to Charles.

During his absence threatening murmurs rose from the Presbyterians, who still formed the majority in the Parliament. These murmurs Cromwell, on his return to London, met boldly and decisively. Colonel Pride, on the morning of the 6th of December 1648, encircling the House with his troopers, prevented the entrance of about two hundred Presbyterian members. The remainder,—some forty Independents,—voted hearty thanks to Cromwell for his great services. And then the death of the King was resolved on. There are many who charge the blood of Charles on Cromwell's memory; but it may well be doubted whether he could have hindered the crime. It is more charitable to believe, as does our greatest historian of England, that 'on this occasion he sacrificed his own judgment and his own inclinations to the wishes of the army. For the power which he had called into existence was a power which even he could not always control; and, that he might ordinarily command, it was necessary that he should sometimes obey.'

Jan. 20, 1649 A.D. A tribunal, self-created and self-styled the High Court of Justice, met in Westminster Hall for the trial of the King. The Peers had refused to take any part in the proceedings. The members of the court, of whom about seventy sat in judgment, were taken chiefly from the army and the semblance of a Parliament then existing. A lawyer named Bradshaw was the president: Coke acted as the solicitor for the nation. The King, brought from St. James's Palace, was placed within the bar, and there charged with tyranny, especially in waging war against his people. Never did Charles appear to more advantage than at this mockery of a trial. Summoning up all that kingly dignity of which he possessed no small share, he refused to be tried by a tribunal created in defiance of the laws. Where were the Peers, who alone, by an ancient maxim of the Constitution, could sit in judgment on a Peer? But all defence was useless, for the judges had already decided the matter among themselves. The case was spun out for seven days, and then sentence of death was pronounced.

Three days later, on the 30th of January 1649, in front of the Banqueting Hall of Whitehall Palace, Charles Stuart was beheaded. Soldiers, horse and foot, surrounded the black scaffold, on which stood two masked headsmen beside the block. The silent people stood in thousands far off. The King was attended by Bishop Juxon. He died a Protestant of the English Church, declaring that the guilt of the Civil War did not rest with him, for the Parliament had been the first to take up arms; but confessing, at the same time, that he was now suffering a just punishment for the death of Strafford. One blow of the axe, and all was over. A deep groan burst from the assembled multitude, as the executioner raised the dripping head and cried, 'This is the head of a traitor!' Since the Conquest five Kings had fallen by assassination; three had died of injuries received in battle;—once only did a King of England perish on the scaffold, and this page tells the dark and bloody tale.

Charles had three sons and three daughters. The sons were Charles, Prince of Wales, afterwards Charles II.; James, Duke of York, afterwards James II.; and Henry, Duke of Gloucester: the daughters were Mary, married to the Prince of Orange, and thus mother of William III.; Elizabeth, who died in Carisbrook, aged fifteen, a short time after her father's execution; and Henrietta, married to the Duke of Orleans.

The public life and private life of Charles I. present a strange contrast. In politics his leading motives were an attachment to Episcopacy, and that thirst for absolute power which he inherited from his father, and which he bequeathed in even greater intensity to his second son. Double-dealing was his most fatal vice. But in the domestic relations of life he displayed many admirable qualities. A love for his wife and children, and a refined taste in works of art, especially paintings, adorned his character. We know him best from his portraits by Vandyke. A dark-complexioned man, with mild and mournful eyes, lofty brow, long curling hair, moustache, and pointed beard,—this is Vandyke's head of the hapless monarch.

The tax on landed property, and the excise—a duty levied on certain articles of home manufacture—were first imposed by the Parliament, to meet the expense of the Civil War. The Dutch painters Rubens and Vandyke enjoyed the patronage of Charles. Among the improvements of the reign may be noted the invention of the barometer, the first use of coffee in England, and the first rude outline of the General Post.

CONTEMPORARY SOVEREIGNS.

FRANCE.	A.D.	SWEDEN.	A.D.
LOUIS XIII.,	died 1643	GUST. ADOLPHUS,	died 1632
LOUIS XIV.		CHRISTINA.	
SPAIN.		**EMPERORS.**	
PHILIP IV.		FERDINAND II.,	1637
		FERDINAND III.	
TURKEY.		**POPES.**	
AMURATH IV.,	1640	URBAN VIII.,	1644
IBRAHIM.		INNOCENT X.	

CHAPTER III.

THE COMMONWEALTH.
1649 A.D. to 1660 A.D.

OLIVER CROMWELL.

Born 1599 A.D.—Created Lord Protector, 1653 A.D.—Died 1658 A.D.

Revolution.	Expulsion of the Long	Last days and death.
Levellers.	Parliament.	Character.
Conquest of Ireland.	Barebones' Parliament.	Richard Cromwell.
Battle of Dunbar.	Cromwell Protector.	General Monk.
Battle of Worcester.	His foreign policy.	Charles called from
The Dutch War.	His second Parliament.	exile.

ENGLAND, now a Commonwealth, continued so for more than eleven years. A fragment of the Long Parliament still sat. Royalty and the House of Lords were formally abolished. The government was vested in a Council of forty-one members. Of this Council Bradshaw was President; John Milton was Foreign Secretary; Cromwell and Fairfax directed the army; Sir Harry Vane controlled the navy. But Cromwell and his soldiers really ruled the nation. The Duke of Hamilton and two other Royalists shared the fate of their Prince.

Three great difficulties then met Cromwell. A part of the army, calling themselves Levellers, having tasted noble blood, rose in dangerous mutiny, clamouring for more. The vigour and decision of Oliver soon quelled these restless spirits.

The subjugation of Ireland was his next task. Since the massacre of 1641 all had been confusion there. The Marquis of Ormond, leader of the Irish Royalists, now held nearly all the fortresses in the island. Dublin, Derry, and Belfast were the only strongholds of the Parliament. Cromwell, having received his commission as Lord Lieutenant, landed near Dublin with 9000 men. It was a small force, but the soldiers knew not what it was to yield. In six months Oliver completely broke the power of the Royalist party in Ireland. The sack of Drogheda was the chief operation of the war. Garrisons were put to the sword, whole cities were left unpeopled. Everywhere the Romanists fled before their terrible foe. So great was the terror of his name, that even at this day 'The curse of Cromwell on you' is used in the south of Ireland as an imprecation of deadly hatred. When Cromwell left for London, Ireton and Ludlow remained to guard the conquered island.

On his arrival in London Oliver received public thanks for his great services, and was created Lord General of the armies of the Commonwealth. The Scottish nation, loudly condemning the execution of Charles I., had, immediately upon receiving the fatal news, proclaimed his son King. They had taken up arms, they said, not to overturn a throne, but to maintain the Presbyterian worship, so dear to their fathers. They now invited young Charles to Scotland. At first he refused their aid, disliking the idea of turning Presbyterian, and sent the Marquis of Montrose from Holland to attempt a rising independently of the Covenanters. That nobleman was defeated, captured, and executed. There was then no resource for Charles but to place himself in the hands of the Scottish Presbyterians. He agreed to sign the Covenant, and landed at the mouth of the Spey (June 23, 1650). A joyous welcome met him at Edinburgh. Oliver, as was his custom, lost not a day. But, when he reached the Border, he found the whole district from Tweed to Forth laid waste. The Scots under Leslie, a watchful and prudent leader, lay intrenched near Edinburgh. The Ironsides were met by famine, a new and terrible adversary. As Oliver changed his position, he was followed by the cautious Leslie, whose tactics were to avoid a battle and let hunger do its work. At length the Lord General was so hemmed in upon the shore near Dunbar, that he had no choice left but a disgraceful surrender or a hopeless attack on the strong and well-posted Scottish army. Already he had resolved to send away his baggage by sea, and to cut his way through the Scottish host at the head of his horsemen, when, to his great surprise and joy, he saw the enemy leaving the hills and advancing to offer battle on the plain. This movement was made by the rash advice of the clergy in the Scottish camp, and was sorely against the will of Leslie. The Scots were totally routed,

Sept. 3, **1650** A.D.

and thousands fell in the battle and the flight. Edinburgh and Glasgow yielded without delay to the conqueror.

During the following winter King Charles was crowned at Scone on New-Year's-Day, when he signed the Solemn League and Covenant, and thus agreed to maintain unbroken the Presbyterianism of Scotland. Leslie and his Covenanters were at Stirling, still formidable. Cromwell moved to besiege Perth, in order to cut off from them all Highland supplies. Suddenly, with Charles at their head, the Scots marched into England. They had reached Worcester when Cromwell overtook them. A battle followed, which Cromwell was accustomed to call his 'crowning mercy.' The army of Charles was scattered. Among the midland counties he wandered in disguise for more than a month; at one time the guest of humble foresters; at another lying hid for a long September day among the branches of a spreading oak-tree, through whose leafy screen he saw the red-coats of Oliver searching for him everywhere in vain. Through many dangers he at last reached Shoreham in Sussex, where he found a coal-boat, and was landed safely at Fécamp in France. Scotland, thus united to the Commonwealth, was placed under the charge of General Monk.

Sept. 3, 1651 A.D.

A naval war with Holland then began. It was for the empire of the sea. The Dutch admirals were Van Tromp and De Ruyter: to them was opposed the English Blake. Early in 1652 Blake defeated Van Tromp off Portland, and destroyed eleven ships. The Dutch then sought peace; but the Parliament, dreading the ambitious schemes of Oliver, refused to terminate the war; for it was only by keeping up the victorious navy that they could hope to hold the army in check. But Oliver resolved on a decided step. He urged his officers to present a petition for pay still due to them. The Parliament angrily declared that such petitions should henceforward be considered treasonable, and began to prepare a Bill to that effect. Cromwell marched down to the House with 300 musketeers, left these outside, and entering, took his seat. The debate went on; he soon rose to speak. He charged the Parliament with oppression and profanity; and, when some members rose to reply, he strode up and down with his hat on, hurling reproaches at them. 'Get you gone,' cried he, 'and give way to honester men!' He stamped on the floor; the musketeers poured in. 'Take away that bauble!' said he, pointing to the mace which lay on the table. Resistance was use- April 20, less. The hall was speedily cleared, and Oliver, as **1653** he left, locked the door, and carried off the key. A.D. This was the first expulsion of the Long Parliament.

An assembly of about 140 members, selected from the warmest supporters of Oliver, then met instead of a Parliament. It was called Barebones' Parliament, after a leather-seller who took a forward part in its proceedings. But this mockery was soon dissolved amid the jeers of the whole nation. All power then centred in Cromwell.

Elected Lord Protector by his officers, he was presented in Westminster Hall with a sword and a Bible. He sat upon a throne, robed in royal purple. He was declared head of the army and navy. A legal Parliament was called in his name. Freedom of religion was proclaimed. His object seems to have been to rule the empire in the old constitutional way, through his Parliament; but his first House of Commons quarrelled with him on the subject of supplies, and was dissolved in anger before a single Act was passed. Eighteen months elapsed before he called his second Parliament.

The Dutch war continued until April 1654, when a peace favourable to England was concluded. One condition of the treaty was, that the young King Charles should be driven from the Dutch dominions. This triumph was only a part of that foreign policy which made the name of Oliver so famous. The glory of England, which had grown dim during the two preceding reigns, now shone with a lustre brighter than ever. The Barbary pirates, long the pest of the Mediterranean, vanished before the English cruisers. Spain, humbled by land and sea, yielded up in 1655 the rich island of Jamaica. The Protestants of Languedoc and the Alps lived under the shadow of Oliver's favour in peace and safety long unknown to them. Mazarin, the crafty minister of France, sought his friendship; and Dunkirk, a

Flemish fortress taken from the Spaniards by Marshal Turenne, was surrendered by France to England.

At home Oliver met many troubles. He was obeyed only through the fear with which his unconquered army was everywhere regarded. In the flush of his foreign victories he ventured to call a second House of Commons. He attempted at the same time to frame a new House of Lords; but this was his greatest political failure. The peers of England despised him as an upstart; and he was therefore compelled to fill the benches of his Upper House with men of no birth—'lucky draymen and shoemakers,' who had left their craft to follow his banner, and had fought their way up from the ranks. His second House of Commons— opened in September 1656—proposed that he should take the title of King; but Oliver, knowing that he dared not do this, rested content with acquiring the right to name his successor. This, in effect, made his office hereditary; for, of course, he named his son. But when he required this House to acknowledge his newly-created peers, he was met with a distinct refusal. He then dissolved his second Parliament, and during his remaining days he ruled alone.

These last days were dark and cloudy. One plot rose after another to mar his peace. A book called 'Killing no Murder,' in which the author, Colonel Titus, boldly advised his assassination, filled him with ceaseless fears. He carried pistols, and wore a shirt of mail under his clothes. His strength began to waste; the death of a favourite daughter fell heavily on his heart; and he died of ague on the 3d of September 1658, the anniversary of Dunbar and Worcester, and the day which he had always considered the brightest in the year. His wife was Elizabeth Bouchier, daughter of an Essex gentleman. His children were Richard, Henry, and four daughters.

Great decision and energy marked the character of Oliver Cromwell. The secret of his success lay in his splendid military talents, which, dormant for forty years, were stirred to life by the troubles of the Civil War. He was less successful in ruling the English nation than in drilling his great army. He disliked all show and ceremony. In private life he was fond of playing rough practical jokes on his friends.

He was a man of coarse and heavy figure, about the middle size. His eyes were grey and keen; his nose was too large for his face, and of a deep red. His look was harsh and forbidding; his manner, to the last, blunt and clownish. But within this rugged frame there burned a great, and,—let us believe,—a truly religious soul.

His son Richard, a gentle, modest man, quietly succeeded to the station of Protector. But the soldiers, missing their great chief, grew mutinous, and Richard resigned in five months. Retiring to his farms at Cheshunt, he lived the peaceful life of a country gentleman until 1712.

The few Independent members of the Long Parliament, whom Oliver had expelled, were restored by the officers of the army. But disagreement soon arose, and a second expulsion by military force cleared the Parliament Hall. It was a critical hour for England. A day seemed to be coming like that in ancient Rome, when soldiers set up the Empire for auction, and knocked it down to the highest bidder. Cavaliers and Presbyterians forgot their enmity in their fear.

Disunion in the army saved the country. General Monk, a cautious and reserved man, marched from Scotland to London with 7000 troops. The nation waited with trembling anxiety to know his resolve, and great was their joy when he declared for a free Parliament. The Presbyterian members, who had been expelled by Colonel Pride, returned to their seats in the Long Parliament, and that famous body finally dissolved itself.

A new Parliament, composed chiefly of Cavaliers and Presbyterians, was then summoned. It was rather a Convention than a Parliament, since it had not been convoked by the King. It was clearly seen that the hearts of both Parliament and people were leaning towards their exiled Sovereign; and when Monk, one day, announced in the Parliament that a messenger from Charles was waiting for admission, the news was received with joyful shouts. A warm invitation was at once despatched to the King, who gladly returned to his native land.

Among many sects which at this time sprang from the Puritan body, the Quakers deserve notice. Their founder was George Fox of Drayton in Leicestershire, by trade a shoemaker, but occupied chiefly in teaching the Scriptures. He was more than once put in the stocks and imprisoned for preaching. The Quakers, now known as the Society of Friends, are remarkable for their simple manners and industrious lives. They differ from other Protestants in dress, some slight forms of speech, and their mode of public worship.

CONTEMPORARY SOVEREIGNS.

FRANCE.	TURKEY.
A.D.	A.D.
LOUIS XIV.	IBRAHIM.,..................died 1655
	MOHAMMED IV.
SPAIN.	EMPERORS.
PHILIP IV.	FERDINAND III.,................1658
	LEOPOLD I.
SWEDEN.	POPES.
CHRISTINA.,................died 1654	INNOCENT X.,...................1655
CHARLES X.,......................1660	ALEXANDER VII.

CHAPTER IV.

CHARLES II.

Born 1630 A.D.—Began to reign 1649 A.D.—Restored to the Throne 1660 A.D.—Died 1685 A.D.

The Restoration.	Persecution of Scottish Presbyterians.	Exclusion Bill.
Early measures.		Whig and Tory.
Act of Uniformity.	Triple Alliance.	Drumclog.
Standing army.	Treaty of Dover.	Bothwell Bridge.
Dutch war.	The Cabal.	Rye-house Plot.
The Plague.	Closing of the Exchequer.	Death.
The Fire of London.	The Popish Plot.	Character.
General licentiousness.	Statesmen of the reign.	Notes.
Ireland.	Habeas Corpus Act	

EARLY in May 1660 Charles II. was proclaimed King at the gate of Westminster Hall. Within the same month he landed at Dover, and made his public entry into London on his birth-day. Never had there been such joy in England. Flowers strewed the road; bells rang merrily; and old Cavaliers, who had fought at Edge-hill and Naseby, wept for very gladness. On Blackheath stood Oliver's army, sad and angry, but conscious that they were no longer united. No tumult marred the joy of the Restoration, as the great event was called.

May 29, 1660 A.D.

Edward Hyde, afterwards Earl of Clarendon, returned with the King from exile. He was made Lord Chancellor, and soon became closely connected with the royal family by the marriage of his daughter, Anne Hyde, with James, Duke of York.

Among the early acts of Charles were the abolition of the last relic of the Feudal System,—the tenure of lands by knight service, with all its abuses of fines and wardship,—and the disbanding of Cromwell's soldiers, all of whom quietly settled down to their former occupations. The Episcopal Church was restored in England. Few of the men who had been concerned in the regicide of Charles I. suffered death. The Marquis of Argyle, a leader of the Scottish Presbyterians, was executed, although he had placed the crown on the King's head at Scone. The bodies of

Cromwell, Ireton his son-in-law, and Bradshaw were taken from their graves and hanged on gibbets. A general pardon was granted to all who had favoured Oliver's government. Monk was rewarded with the title of Duke of Albemarle.

Religious affairs were in great confusion. The Triers, who had been appointed by Oliver to grant license for preaching, had filled the parish pulpits with Independent and Presbyterian ministers. Charles and Clarendon were bent upon allowing no form of worship but Episcopacy. The Presbyterians were greatly alarmed. They had the handwriting of the King to prove his promise that the Covenant should be respected. But soon faded all hope of favour from him, with whom it was a common saying, that Presbyterianism was no religion for a gentleman. An Act of Uniformity was passed, requiring that all ministers should be ordained by Bishops, and should use the Book of Common Prayer. Two thousand ministers refused to obey, and were turned out of their livings. It was resolved in Parliament that the Covenant should be publicly burned by the hangman. Heavy punishments were inflicted on all Dissenters. About the same time the Corporation Act enjoined all magistrates and officers of corporations to take an oath, that resistance against the King was unlawful under any circumstances.

So great had been the joy of the Restoration, that no care was taken to prevent Charles from seizing absolute power. His first Parliament granted him, for life, taxes amounting to £1,200,000; and a part of this money he devoted to the support of some regiments, then called Gentlemen of the Guard, but now termed Life Guards. These formed the nucleus of a standing army, ever since maintained.

The extravagant habits and dissolute life of the King kept him in constant want of money; and to fill his purse he did many mean things. Marrying for money was one of these. The wife he chose was a Romanist, Catherine of Portugal; and with her he received a dowry of half a million besides two fortresses, Tangier in Morocco, and Bombay in Hindostan. Dunkirk, acquired by the great Oliver, he sold to the French King for a trifling sum. He also plunged into a war with Holland, for which no other cause can be assigned than that he wished to have command of the supplies voted for the purpose.

This Dutch war opened well, but closed ignobly. During the first year a great naval victory was gained off the Suffolk coast, near Lowestoft, by an English fleet under the Duke of York. But the money voted by Parliament for the war was squandered by the King in his wicked pleasures, and ships leaky and badly rigged were sent out to contend with the splendid fleets of Holland. Then came upon England a humiliation such as she had never before,—has never since endured. "The roar of foreign guns was heard for the first and last time by the citizens of London," when a Dutch fleet destroyed Sheerness, burned the ships lying off Chatham, and sailed up the Thames as far as Tilbury Fort. Happily for London the Dutch admiral, retiring with the ebb-tide, rested content with having thus insulted the great Mistress of the Sea.

1665 A.D.

June 10, 1667 A.D.

The summer of 1665 was a deadly season in London. The Plague fell upon the city. The rich fled in terror to their country-houses; but many were stricken down even there. The poor perished in thousands. Grass grew in London streets. The silence of death reigned everywhere, broken only by the rumbling wheels of the dead-cart as it went its rounds. The plague-stricken dwellings were shut up and marked with a cross; the words 'Lord have mercy on us' might often be read there too. Into these none would venture except a few faithful ministers and physicians, who moved and breathed amid the tainted air, as if they bore a charmed life. Plague in a city drives the irreligious into deeper sin. Fearful scenes of riot and drunkenness are too commonly the results of this near approach of death, and London was no exception to the terrible rule. More than one hundred thousand perished. Britain has never since been visited by so heavy a scourge.

In the following year the Great Fire of London broke out, on the night of Sunday the 2nd of September. Though then said to have been the work of malicious Romanists, it is now generally believed to have been quite accidental. It began in the east end of the city. The wind was high, and the flames spread fast among the old wooden houses. The city from the Tower to the Temple was burning for a whole week; and the red glare in the sky is said to have been seen from the Cheviot Hills. Eighty-nine churches, and more than thirteen thousand houses lay in ashes. Old St. Paul's was burned; but on the ruins the distinguished Wren reared that magnificent dome, which rises high above the smoky roofs of London. This great conflagration, like all calamities, was but a blessing in disguise. It purified the city from the plague, still lurking in narrow lanes and filthy rooms; and many spots, dark and close for centuries, were once more blessed with the sweet light and air of heaven. New houses and wider streets sprang up; and, as a natural result, the public health rapidly improved. The Monument,—a tall pillar in the City of London,—still exists to commemorate the Great Fire.

Under the austere Puritan rule of Cromwell sculpture and painting had been almost banished from the land, as savouring of idolatry. Then, too, all public amusements, especially theatrical performances and the cruel sport of bear-baiting, were forbidden; and even the innocent sports round the May pole and by the Christmas fire were sternly put down. The nation, released at the Restoration from such restrictions, plunged wildly into the opposite extreme. The King lived a life of indolence and profligacy, and spent most of his time in the society of beautiful and witty, but very worthless women, whose influence affected the politics of the day to no small extent. Licentiousness spread everywhere. Members of Parliament sold their votes, as a matter of course. The plays written then, in which for the first time female performers took the female parts, are unfit to be read, so disgusting are the thoughts and the language. The power of even the Church was but feebly exerted to stem this torrent of wickedness.

In Ireland the Saxon and the Celt were still at war, and the subject of the strife was now the division of lands. Under Henry Cromwell, brother of the Protector, who had ruled the island as Lord Lieutenant, Puritan colonists had held the lots portioned out to them by the victorious Oliver. Charles resolved to restore to the Romanists part of the territory taken from them, and an Act of Settlement was passed; but this did not mend matters, for some thousands received little or no compensation, and left for France and Spain, crying loudly against the injustice of Charles.

These were dark days for Scotland. The King and the Earl of Clarendon, as before mentioned, had resolved to uproot Presbyterianism and firmly to establish Episcopacy in that land. They found an able and unscrupulous instrument in James Sharp, minister of Crail; who, being sent to London by the Presbyterians to look after their interests, turned traitor, and was rewarded for his apostasy by being made Archbishop of St. Andrews. Nine other Scottish Presbyterians were seduced by similar temptations, and received the mitre. The Earl of Lauderdale, once a Presbyterian like Sharp, and filled with all the bitterness of a renegade, was made Chief Commissioner. Fines, laid upon those who refused to attend the Episcopal worship, were levied by military force, and soldiers were quartered on the unhappy people until the uttermost farthing was paid. A rising took place among the peasantry of Kirkcudbright, and about a thousand men marched to Edinburgh; but they were defeated by General Dalziel at Rullion Green near the Pentland Hills. Many executions followed, and torture became frightfully common. **Nov. 1666 A.D.**
One of the most terrible instruments was the infamous 'boot.' This, which was made of four pieces of board hooped with iron, was placed upon the leg of the victim, and wedges were driven with a heavy mallet between the flesh and the wood, until the whole limb, flesh and bone, was a crushed and bloody mass. Meetings for worship in the open air, called *conventicles*, to which the worshippers came, not with their Bibles alone, but with sword and pistol also, were the consolation of the brave people, whose religious feelings grew deeper and purer, the fiercer blew the hurricane of persecution.

The ambition of Louis XIV. of France, which convulsed Europe so long, now began to be attracted by the Netherlands, to which he professed some shadow of a claim through his wife. To preserve the balance of power, England, Sweden, and Holland formed the Triple Alliance against the

French monarch. In the desire to preserve this balance,—
that is, to prevent any potentate from acquiring by conquest
an ascendency which would be dangerous to other states,—we
find the cause of many wars of which we have yet to speak.
The Triple Alliance pleased the English people mightily, and
Charles became, for once, a great favourite. But little did
the nation dream how basely they had been tricked, and
what foul stains were deepening upon kingly honour. While
Charles openly professed hostility to Louis, he was secretly
in the pay of that monarch, receiving a pension of £200,000
a year. The negotiations between the Courts of England
and France were conducted by a handsome Frenchwoman,
called by the English Madame Carwell, who soon won the
favour of Charles, and was made Duchess of Portsmouth. At Dover was signed a secret treaty, of
which the principal terms were, that Charles
should openly declare himself a Romanist, that he
should fight for Louis against the Dutch Republic,
and that he should support the claims of that monarch upon
Spain. Louis on his part promised plenty of money, and
an army to quell the English if they dared to rebel. The
Earl of Clarendon, who remonstrated earnestly against the
shameless bargain, lost favour on that account, and retired
to the Continent.

May
1670
A.D.

Five men, called the Cabal, because the initials of their
names form that word, then became the chief advisers of the
King. They were Clifford, Arlington, Buckingham, Ashley,
and Lauderdale. So pernicious was their advice, and so
strong the hatred of them entertained by the people, that
the word Cabal has ever since been used to denote a clique
of political schemers.

The Dutch war being renewed in 1672, an English fleet
put to sea, while Louis crossed the Rhine and ravaged the
United Provinces. But the Dutch, acting under the orders
of their heroic leader, William of Orange, broke down their
dikes: the foaming water rushed over the land, and the
French soldiers had to flee for their lives. Hostilities continued until a treaty was made at Nimeguen in 1678.

One of the most disgraceful acts of Charles was the closing
of the Exchequer, or Treasury. About £1,300,000 had been

advanced to the King by the London goldsmiths, and other wealthy merchants, at 8 or 10 per cent. of interest; and for this sum they had the security of the public funds. One day they received a cool message from the King, that their money was not to be repaid, and that they must content themselves with the interest. A general panic ensued. Merchants, unable to meet their engagements, were forced to stop payment. Trade was for the time paralyzed. But all mattered nothing to the dishonest monarch, who rejoiced in possessing new means of gratifying his guilty desires.

Ever since the Fire of London the public feeling against the Romanists had been growing stronger. The Duke of York had openly professed his belief of the Romish doctrines, and there was a general suspicion abroad that the King, too, was at heart devoted to his mother's creed. A sign of the times was the Test Act, by which all persons who held public appointments were compelled to take an oath against transubstantiation. This law excluded all Romanists from office, and the Duke of York was removed from the command of the fleet.

1673 A.D.

Then Titus Oates, a clergyman disgraced for vicious habits, came forward with the story of a Popish Plot to assassinate the King and to massacre all Protestants. Other false witnesses, for so they proved, confirmed his tale. Papers found in the rooms of Edward Coleman, a noted Romanist and secretary to the Duchess of York, seemed to afford additional evidence of a plot. The dead body of Sir Edmondsbury Godfrey, the Justice of Peace before whom Oates had sworn to the conspiracy, was found in a field near London, pierced with his own sword. All England went mad with fear. London was in a state of siege. It was an English Reign of Terror, and the blood of Romanists was shed like water. Titus Oates was rewarded with a pension of £1200 a year, and rooms were assigned to him in Whitehall. Encouraged by his success, new perjurers, such as Bedloe and Dangerfield, poured from the gambling-houses and drinking-dens of London. Execution followed execution. The noblest of the slain Romanists was William Howard, Viscount Stafford, whose grey hairs could not save him from an unmerited death.

After the dissolution of the Cabal, the Earl of Danby became Prime Minister; but the discovery of a letter, in which he craved money from the French King, hastened his downfall. Sir William Temple, a man of much talent, then became the confidant of Charles. His favourite scheme was the appointment of a Council of Thirty to stand between the King and the Parliament. But the plan did not work well. Of those associated with Temple in the direction of affairs, the most distinguished was Viscount Halifax. Belonging to neither extreme of the two great political parties, but standing midway between them in his opinions, he was what the politicians of that day had begun to call a Trimmer, and he thought that the name was no disgrace.

May 26, 1679 A.D. The day upon which the Habeas Corpus Act received the assent of the King, and thus became a law of the land, is memorable in the history of Britain; for this Act is second in importance only to Magna Charta. It secures the liberty of the subject. Former sovereigns had, without restraint, left their enemies to pine and waste for long years in damp, unwholesome prisons. Mary Queen of Scots had lain for nineteen years in English dungeons, when, crippled by rheumatism and bowed by premature old age, she was led to the scaffold. Sir Walter Raleigh lay for more than twelve years, and Archbishop Laud for four in a solitary cell. But, by the Habeas Corpus Act, no sovereign could dare to keep even the meanest subject in prison beyond a certain time without bringing him to a fair trial. This remarkable Act was passed in the first session of Charles' second House of Commons. His first Parliament, which had sat for eighteen years, was dissolved in 1679. At the time that Habeas Corpus was passed, the Press of England received liberty for a short period.

So strongly did the tide of public feeling run against the Duke of York, who, since Charles had no legitimate children, was the heir to the throne, that a Bill to exclude him from the succession was brought into Parliament. It was most angrily contested between the Whigs and the Tories, but passed the House of Commons by a majority of seventy-nine votes. In the House of Lords, however, chiefly by means of the splendid speeches of Halifax, the Bill was thrown out; and Charles and his brother York once more breathed freely.

During these fierce debates the contemptuous nicknames, Whig and Tory, which have since lost their derisive meaning, were for the first time bandied between the rival parties. The Whigs represented the Roundheads; the Tories, the Cavaliers of the last reign. Tory or Toree, meaning 'Give me,' was a name applied to the robbers who infested the woods and bogs of Ireland. The name Whig, meaning, probably, ' whey, or sour milk,' was first given in contempt by dissolute Cavaliers to the sober and grave-faced Presbyterians of Scotland.

The persecutions of the Covenanters still stained Scotland with blood. Lauderdale, now a Duke, presided at the Council-table. A Highland host, numbering 8000 men, were quartered on the Lowland farmers, and permitted, even encouraged, to plunder and oppress without mercy. No man could leave Scotland without special permission from the Council. These and worse grievances were for a long time meekly borne, but at length the suffering people were goaded to madness. One of the first signs of the frenzy was the murder of Archbishop Sharp on Magus Moor, near St. Andrews. A party of twelve, among whom was Balfour of Burleigh, while waiting on the moor for another and meaner foe, saw the coach of Sharp approaching. Taking a sudden and desperate resolve, they dragged him from his seat and slew him before his daughter's eyes. A rising at once ensued, and at Drumclog, near Loudon Hill, Graham of Claverhouse and his dragoons—long the terror of conventicles—were scattered in flight before the stern Covenanters. Four thousand men were soon in arms under a man named Hamilton, and took post at Bothwell Bridge, to defend the passage of the Clyde. The Duke of Monmouth, an illegitimate son of Charles II. by a Welsh girl named Lucy Walters, was sent hastily from London, and advanced to the attack. But there was disunion on religious and political questions in the Covenanting army; and the gallant handful that held the bridge, being left without support, were soon swept away. Three hundred

May 3, **1679** A.D.

Covenanters died on the field; twelve hundred surrendered. Of these some were executed, others drafted off to Barbadoes. The persecution grew fiercer than ever. For no other crime than desiring to worship God as their fathers had done, men were shot down in the fields, and hunted like wild beasts over the moors and mountains. Their loyalty, to which they had clung in the darkest hour, now began to give way. A sect called Cameronians boldly threw off their allegiance, denounced Charles as a bloody tyrant, and solemnly pronounced against him and his ministers a sentence of excommunication. Lauderdale gave place to a bitterer persecutor, James, Duke of York, who often amused his leisure hours by witnessing the infliction of the boot and the thumb-screw. Many yielded an outward obedience, driven by their timid souls to take refuge in a lie; others fled to the American Colonies. In these sufferings the Puritans of England had no small share.

The last remarkable event of the reign was a Whig conspiracy, commonly known as the Rye-house Plot. Young Monmouth, beloved by the people for his handsome face and frank manners, was looked upon by many as the lawful son of Charles and the true heir to the throne. Stories were afloat of a marriage between Charles and Lucy Walters, and of a black box which held the marriage contract. A conspiracy to secure the crown for Monmouth was set on foot. Lord William Russell and Algernon Sidney took a leading share in the plot, which spread its roots far and wide. A set of middle-class men formed, as it seems, without the knowledge of Monmouth or Russell, a design to murder the King on his return from Newmarket races. Their plan was to overturn a cart near the Rye House, a roadside farm, and then to shoot the King during the stoppage of the coach. Thus there was a plot within a plot. All was soon discovered, and the vengeance of the King was let loose. Monmouth fled to the Continent, Russell and Sidney died on the scaffold, and many of lower degree were hanged. During the remainder of his reign Charles ruled as an absolute monarch.

He died after an illness of less than a week, having first declared himself a Romanist, and having received the last rites of the Romish Church from a priest named Huddlestone, who was brought secretly to his bedside. Apoplexy, epilepsy, and even poison were assigned as the causes of his death. He left no lawful children.

Perhaps the only good point about Charles the Second was the gay and buoyant disposition which carried him through so many reverses, and gained for him the name of 'The Merry Monarch.' He was a mean-spirited, treacherous, dissolute man, who, thoroughly vicious himself, scoffed at the idea of virtue or honour in others. Much of his time was passed in worthless company. He was an active tennis-player, an untiring walker, and often amused himself with chemical experiments.

The Royal Society, founded in 1660, did much for the advancement of science. From the tumults and impostures of the reign sprang two words—ever since in common use—Mob and Sham. A penny post was set up in London in spite of great opposition by a citizen named William Dockwray. Newspapers, influenced by the rivalry of Whigs and Tories, began to acquire political importance. 'The London Gazette' and 'The Observator,' edited by Roger Lestrange, were the organs of the Government.

CONTEMPORARY SOVEREIGNS.

FRANCE.	A.D.	TURKEY.	A.D.
LOUIS XIV.		MOHAMMED IV.	
		EMPEROR.	
SPAIN.		LEOPOLD I.	
PHILIP IV.,	died 1665		
CHARLES II.		POPES.	
		ALEXANDER VII.,	died 1667
		CLEMENT IX.,	1670
SWEDEN.		CLEMENT X.,	1676
CHARLES XI.		INNOCENT XI.	

CHAPTER V.

JAMES II.

Born 1633 A.D.—Began to reign 1685 A.D.—Dethroned 1688 A.D. Died 1701 A.D.

Confidence of the nation.	Oxford and Cambridge.	His landing.
Argyle.	Declarations of Indulgence.	Flight of James.
Monmouth.		The Convention.
Battle of Sedgemoor.	Trial of the Bishops.	The Declaration of Rights.
Kirke and Jeffreys.	Lillibulero.	Nature of the Revolution.
Romish Policy of James.	William of Orange.	Character of James.

A QUARTER of an hour after his brother's death, the Duke of York took his seat at the Council as King James II. There he declared his resolve to govern according to the laws, and to uphold the Church of England,—a promise which he repeated in his speech from the throne when he met his Parliament. He was a zealous Romanist, and men might well have grown pale, when they remembered the last Romish sovereign of England. But the confidence of the nation seemed unshaken, and loyal addresses poured in from every side. The King attended a public celebration of the Romish mass, and was soon after crowned in right royal style. The Commons voted him a revenue of £1,900,000, and already he was in the pay of Louis.

April 23, 1685 A.D.

Holland was the refuge of the conspirators who had fled from England on the detection of the Rye-house plot. Monmouth and Argyle were there with many of less note; and a meeting took place at Amsterdam, at which it was resolved that Argyle should descend on Scotland, and that Monmouth should about the same time attempt the invasion of England.

Argyle—known to his clansmen as MacCallum More—landed on Cantire, and sent forth the fiery cross to summon the Campbells to arms. Scarcely two thousand claymores mustered at the call. With these he moved towards Glasgow; but in Dumbartonshire his little army was scattered, and, while attempting to escape in disguise, he was made prisoner. Some days later he suffered death at Edinburgh with Christian patience, and his head was left to moulder on the walls of the Tolbooth Prison.

June was far spent when Monmouth with three ships approached the coast of Dorsetshire, and landed at Lyme. Ploughmen and miners flocked in hundreds to join him; farmers came on their heavy cart-horses to fill the ranks of his rude cavalry; but the nobles and gentlemen made no movement in his favour. His hopes rose when he reached Taunton, a town noted for its woollen manufacture. There he assumed the title of King; green boughs, worn in his honour, were in every hat; and a band of young girls publicly presented him with a Bible and a richly embroidered flag. Bent upon the conquest of Bristol, then the second city in the kingdom, he marched to Bridgewater, and even to the walls of Bath. But the train-bands were gathering fast, and his heart was failing him. He fell back. The royal troops and the rebels exchanged shots at Philip's Norton, but the battle which decided the fate of Monmouth was fought on Sedgemoor, within three miles of Bridgewater.

There lay an army of 3000 men under Feversham, a weak and indolent general. Monmouth, hoping to surprise the royal troops in disorder, advanced from Bridgewater in the dead of night. The moor—the ancient hiding-place of Alfred—was then a partly drained swamp, crossed by trenches full of mud and water, called rhines. Two of these rhines Monmouth and his soldiers had passed in silence, and they were almost upon the foe, when he found a deep, black ditch, the Bussex rhine, of which his guides had not told him, yawning in front of the march. Delay and confusion followed, and a pistol went off by accident. Instantly the royal drums beat to arms; a heavy fire of musketry opened on the rebels from the opposite side of the rhine; the royal cavalry came galloping to the scene of action. Monmouth, conscious that all was lost, took to flight. His foot soldiers fought long and bravely, until, after much delay, the guns of the royal artillery began to play upon their ranks; and then they broke in disorder and fled, leaving a thousand slain. Sedgemoor was the last battle fought on English ground.

July 6, 1685 A.D.

Two days later, Monmouth was found near the New Forest, lurking in a ditch with his pocket half full of raw pease. While on his way to London, he wrote an imploring letter to the King; and, when admitted to the royal presence, he lay upon the floor, and wet the feet of James with his tears. All was useless: he was doomed to immediate execution, and suffered death on Tower-hill.

The task of butchering the unhappy rebels was intrusted at first to Colonel Percy Kirke, who hanged them by scores on the sign-post of the White Hart Inn at Taunton. But the Colonel was outdone in ferocity by Chief-Justice Jeffreys, whose name is a proverb for blasphemy and brutality. This man opened at Winchester that circuit known as the Bloody Assize. The first case for treason was that of Alice Lisle, the widow of one of Cromwell's lords. She was tried for affording food and shelter to two of the flying rebels. Jeffreys cursed and bullied the jury into returning a verdict of 'guilty,' and sentenced her to be burned alive. Through the intercession of noble friends her sentence was altered to beheading; and she died with calm fortitude in the market-place of Winchester. Through the whole western circuit Jeffreys then passed, revelling in blood. More than three hundred perished in this judicial massacre, and crowds who escaped death were doomed to suffer mutilation, imprisonment, or exile.

James, exulting in his triumph, began to unfold his grand design. This design, to which he clung with obstinacy bordering on madness, was the complete restoration of the Romish worship in Great Britain. In defiance of the Test Act, he gave commissions in the army to Romanists. He released all Romanists from penalties, by means of the dispensing power—a privilege which enabled him to pardon all transgressions of the law, and thus, in effect, to destroy the power of the law altogether. He placed the whole Church under the control of a High Commission Court of seven members, at whose head sat Jeffreys, now Lord Chancellor. He prepared to form a great standing army. For the first time since the reign of Mary, a Papal Nuncio was entertained at Whitehall. The Jesuits began anew their dark and terrible plottings in London; and one of their most active men, Father Edward Petre, became the secret and confidential adviser of the King. Scotland was placed under Drummond, Earl of Perth, who had completely won the heart of James by inventing the steel thumb-screw, an instrument of the most exquisite torture. Tyrconnel, a fierce and unscrupulous Romanist—commonly known as Lying Dick Talbot—was made Lord-Deputy of Ireland. Nothing showed the temper of James more clearly than the dismissal of the Hydes, the brothers of his dead wife. Clarendon, the elder, ceased to be Lord-Lieutenant of Ireland; and Rochester, the younger, was forced to resign the white staff he had borne as Lord-Treasurer of England, for no other reason than that they were both stanch Protestants.

James then attacked the Universities of Oxford and Cambridge. A royal letter commanded the Senate of Cambridge to admit Alban Francis, a Benedictine monk, to the degree of M.A. The University refused; for no Romanist could take the oaths. The Vice-Chancellor and eight others, among whom was Isaac Newton, appeared before the High Commission, and the Vice-Chancellor lost his office. Upon Oxford the King made worse inroads. To the vacant presidency of Magdalene College he appointed Antony Farmer, a Romanist. The Fellows chose instead John Hough. In a rage the King went down himself to browbeat the Fellows; but they stoutly refused to obey him. A special commission then installed Parker, Bishop of Oxford,—the new choice of James—while the Fellows were not only driven by royal edict from the University, but the profession of the Church was shut against them. A Romish Bishop was then placed over Magdalene College, and twelve Romish Fellows were appointed in one day. Two years later James felt the bitter truth that this blow, which, as he fondly thought, struck at the root of English Protestantism, had in reality been levelled with suicidal madness at the very prop and pillar of his own throne.

In April 1687 James had published—solely on his own authority, and therefore illegally—a Declaration of Indulgence, permitting all to worship in their own way. Though undoubtedly made for Romanists, it gave liberty of conscience also to Nonconformists or Dissenters. The second and more important Declaration was now proclaimed; and, a week later, it was followed by an Order in Council, commanding all ministers to read it from their pulpits on two successive Sundays. This order the London clergy disobeyed, and the Primate Sancroft, with six Bishops, drew up a petition against the Declaration. James was furious. The seven Bishops were committed to the Tower, where they lay for a week before they were set free on bail. During these exciting events, the news spread that a son was born to James. But few believed that the child was of royal blood. The general opinion was, that by the connivance of Romanists a child had been smuggled into the palace, and was now passed off as the King's son. That child was afterwards James the Pretender.

April 27, 1688 A.D.

The Trial of the Seven Bishops—one of our most important State trials—took place before the Court of King's Bench. They were charged with having published a false, malicious, and seditious libel; and the most talented lawyers of that time were engaged for their defence. All day the trial went on. With much difficulty the lawyers for the Crown proved that the Bishops had drawn up and signed the petition, and had delivered it into the hands of the King. It remained for the jury to decide whether or not that petition was a libel. The four Judges were divided in their opinions, two against two. It was dark when the jury retired: they were locked up all night, and at ten next morning the Court met to hear their verdict. A deep silence prevailed; but, when the words 'Not guilty' left the foreman's lips, cheer after cheer echoed through the hall. The crowd outside took up the joyful sound, and all London was soon filled with shouts and tears of gladness. That night was a blaze of illumination. Rows of seven candles, with a taller one in the centre for the Archbishop, lit up every window; bonfires were in every street; and rockets soared by hundreds from the rejoicing city.

June 29.

Furious at his defeat, James resolved to crush the spirit of the nation by force of arms; and by the advice of Barillon, the French minister, he brought over several regiments of

Irish soldiers. These, as Papists and Celts, were violently hated by the lower orders of the English nation. A doggrel ballad, called from its burden Lillibulero, in which two Irish Romanists congratulate each other on the approaching massacre of Protestants and triumph of Popery, set the whole nation, and especially the army, in a flame against James and his Irish troops. It was sung and whistled everywhere.

On the very day of the Bishops' acquittal, a letter, signed by some of the leading nobles and clergy of England, was sent to William, Prince of Orange Nassau, the nephew and son-in-law of James, entreating him to come with an army and aid them in defending their freedom and their faith. Common wrongs had united for a time the Whigs and the Tories. William, accepting the call, began to make great preparations for the expedition; while James, still holding blindly on in his fatal course, despised the warnings and the offered aid of Louis XIV. Nor did he awake to a sense of his danger till he heard from his minister at the Hague that William, having received the sanction of the States General, had published a Declaration, assigning reasons for the invasion of England. James had no time to lose. In a few hours he yielded almost all the points for which he had been contending so obstinately during three years. He found that he possessed a fleet of 30 sail, an army of 40,000 regular troops. But all was in vain. The hearts of his people were estranged from him, and their eyes looked eagerly over the sea for the sails of William's squadron.

Though delayed for a time by storms, the Prince of Orange landed safely and unopposed at Torbay in Devonshire. Under torrents of rain, along roads deep with mire, he advanced slowly with his force of 15,000 men through Newton Abbot, and in four days reached Exeter, where he was received with joy as the Champion of the Protestant Faith. There, on the following Sunday, he heard his friend Burnet preach from the cathedral pulpit. A week passed without anything to encourage him; but then the Earl of Abingdon entered his camp, and was soon followed by Colonel Lord Cornbury and other officers of James. The King hastened to Salisbury, resolved to stake his kingdom on the issue of a great battle. But

Nov. 5, 1688 A.D.

the policy of William was to avoid bloodshed, and trust rather to time and that English temper which he knew to be thoroughly aroused against James. A few trifling skirmishes took place, but nothing more. The Earl of Bath put Plymouth into William's hands. In rapid succession Lord Churchill, afterwards the great Duke of Marlborough; Prince George of Denmark, married to the King's daughter Anne; and even Anne herself abandoned the falling King. Every day brought new adherents to William, while every day the circle round James grew thinner.

The King then resolved on flight. He sent his wife and son to France; and, when he knew of their safety, he left his palace under cover of darkness, and made his way to Sheerness, where a small vessel, then called a hoy, waited for him. While crossing the Thames he threw the Great Seal into the water, in the childish hope that he would thus confuse all the plans of the new Government. He had scarcely gone on board when some Kentish fishermen, attracted by the hope of plunder, seized him and kept him a close prisoner. Soon released by an order from the Lords, he returned to the capital and passed thence to Rochester. A second attempt to escape succeeded, and the news soon came that James had arrived safely at St. Germains, and had been warmly welcomed by Louis. Meanwhile William passed from Windsor to London, where every citizen wore the orange ribbon in his honour.

Dec. 23, 1688 A.D.

The Prince of Orange then called an assembly, known as the Convention. It differed from a Parliament in nothing but the single fact, that the writs, by which the members were summoned, were issued by one not yet a King. But the Prince and his advisers, careful to shape all their measures according to the ancient English Constitution, avoided the name Parliament, and called their assembly a Convention. The throne was then declared vacant, and great debates ensued on the settlement of affairs. Some proposed a Regency; others that Mary should be Queen, while William held the title of King for her life only. Both plans were pointedly rejected by William, who declared that he would go back to Holland rather than accept a position inferior to his wife. A document, called the Declaration of Rights, was then drawn up and passed. By it William and Mary were declared King and Queen of England, the chief administration resting with him. The crown was settled first on the children of Mary; then on those of her sister Anne; and, these failing, upon the children of William by any other wife. The son of James II. and his posterity were thus shut out entirely from the succession. Halifax took the lead in offering the crown; which William, promising to observe all the laws of the land, accepted for his wife and himself.

The great English Revolution was now complete. Thus terminated the grand struggle between Sovereign and Parliament,—not in the establishment of a wild democracy, but in the adjustment and firm foundation of the three great Estates of the Realm,—the King, the Lords, and the Commons,—upon whose due balance and mutual check the strength of our Constitution mainly depends.

James spent the remaining twelve years of his life at St. Germains near Paris, a pensioner on the bounty of Louis. There he died in 1701. His mad zeal for Romanism, strengthened and sharpened by the thirst for despotic power common to all the Stuarts, cost him a throne. His perversity and petty spite, his childishness and meanness glare out from every page of his history. Even the diligence and punctuality in the despatch of business, for which he was remarkable, cease to excite our admiration, when we remember that these qualities, good in themselves, became in his case instruments of the worst tyranny.

Anne Hyde was his first wife. Her daughters, Mary and Anne, educated as Protestants, both held the throne. After her death he married Mary of Modena, whose son, James the Pretender, made more than one attempt to gain the crown of England.

Besides confirming that great principle of our Constitution which declares that the Sovereign can make or unmake no law, the Revolution released Dissenters from persecution, and caused the Judges, previously liable to be dismissed at the pleasure of the Sovereign, to receive their appointments for life or good conduct.

CONTEMPORARY SOVEREIGNS.

FRANCE.
LOUIS XIV.

SPAIN.
CHARLES II.

SWEDEN.
CHARLES XI.

TURKEY. A.D.
MOHAMMED IV.,........died 1687
SOLYMAN II.

EMPEROR.
LEOPOLD I.

POPE.
INNOCENT XI.

CHAPTER VI.

WILLIAM III. AND MARY II.

William. Born 1650 A.D.—Elected King 1688 A.D.—Died 1702 A.D.
Mary. Born 1661 A.D.—Elected Queen 1688 A.D.—Died 1694 A.D.

Fate of Jeffreys.	Massacre of Glencoe.	The Darien colony.
Revolt in Scotland.	Foreign policy.	William's death.
Siege of Derry.	The National Debt.	His character.
Battle of the Boyne.	The Act of Settlement.	Notes.

WILLIAM and MARY were crowned in Westminster Abbey, where the chief ministers of James stood around the double throne. One there was whose crimes were too black for pardon. Jeffreys lay in the Tower, to which he had been borne amid the roars of a mob thirsting for his blood. He had been found begrimed with coal dust, and in the dress of a common sailor, lurking in a Wapping ale-house. *April 11, 1689 A.D.*

Bloodlessly had the great change been accomplished in England. It was not so in Scotland and Ireland. Although the Scottish Convention, boldly declaring that James had forfeited the crown, had proclaimed William and Mary, yet the whole nation were not of the same mind. The Highland clans, fond of war, and perhaps excited by a desire to uphold the ancient Scottish name of Stuart, took up arms for James, under Graham of Claverhouse, now Viscount Dundee. At the same time, and in the same cause, the Duke of Gordon held out in the Castle of Edinburgh. But the insurrection was short-lived. Edinburgh Castle surrendered in a few months. Dundee, meeting General Mackay in battle at the Pass of Killicrankie in Perthshire, was struck down by a bullet just as his clansmen were sweeping all before them. *July.*
When their leader had fallen, the Highland army soon melted away.

Of greater importance were the events in Ireland; for there James himself, surrounded by the Celtic Irish, who looked upon him as a distinguished martyr in the cause of

Romanism, made his last vain struggle for the crown which had fallen from his head. Louis encouraged the expedition; and Tyrconnel, still Lord-Lieutenant of Ireland, raised a Romanist army. Lord Mountjoy, leader of the Irish Protestants, enticed to Paris by falsehood, was shut up in the Bastile. James landed, and entered Dublin in triumph.

His first great operation was the siege of Londonderry the stronghold of the Ulster Protestants. The citizens, nobly encouraged by the Rev. George Walker, whose monument still rises from the walls, endured the worst miseries of famine for many months; but at last a ship from England broke the beams laid across the River Foyle, and brought food to the starving garrison. The Romanist army, thus baffled, retreated without delay.

Marshal Schomberg then arrived with 16,000 troops; and William, soon landing at Carrickfergus, found himself at the head of 40,000 men. Seventeen days later,

July 1, 1690 A.D.

a great battle was fought on the banks of the Boyne, a few miles above Drogheda. Schomberg, a veteran soldier and an intimate friend of William, was shot as he was crossing the water. James, totally routed, fled to Waterford, and crossed in haste to France. But the war was prolonged for a year by Tyrconnel and St. Ruth. In the battle of Aughrim St. Ruth was killed by a cannon ball. The siege of Limerick, where the fragments of James's army made their last stand,

July 12, 1691 A.D.

ended in a capitulation. On Thomond Bridge, over the Shannon, is still to be seen the stone on which was signed the treaty that made William unquestioned King of Ireland. One million of acres were confiscated to the crown, and their former possessors were driven into exile.

The great stain upon the administration of William was the massacre of Glencoe. To buy over the Highland chiefs, who were still restless, a sum of £16,000 was sent to the Earl of Breadalbane, and at the same time a royal order decreed, that all chieftains of clans should take an oath of allegiance to William before the last day of the year 1691. One refused,—Macdonald of Glencoe, a personal foe of Breadalbane. His motive seems to have been, not so much enmity to William, as a quarrel with Breadalbane about the division of the money. Repenting of his obstinacy in the last days of December, he hastened to Fort William, but found that the governor had no authority to receive his oath, and that he must go to the Sheriff of Argyle. A toilsome journey over snowy hills and across swollen floods threw him a day or two late; but he was permitted to take the oath, and went home well pleased, and, as he thought, safe. In a few weeks Captain Campbell of Glenlyon, with a troop of soldiers, entered Glencoe, a gloomy vale of Argyleshire, in which lay the little settlement of the Macdonalds. They were met with a Highland welcome, and a fortnight went merrily by. The unsuspecting Macdonalds left nothing undone to please and entertain their guests. Hunting and feasting filled the days and the nights, until, when the time seemed ripe, the soldiers rose suddenly in the dead of one terrible night and began the work of blood. The chief, his wife, and thirty-six besides were butchered; the rest fled half naked to the snowy hills, where many died. The earliest beams of the rising sun fell sadly on a mass of smoking ruins, black with fire and red with blood. This foul deed can be traced to the revenge of Breadalbane. William seems to have signed the order without understanding the circumstances; but this does not redeem his memory from the shame, for carelessness can never be considered a palliation of the crimes that too often spring from it.

To humble Louis of France was the great object of William's foreign policy. Louis was the most powerful Romanist Sovereign in Europe. William had long been looked upon as the great Captain of the Protestant armies. Louis, grasping gladly at the dethronement of James as a cause of war, prepared for a mighty invasion of England; but, in an action off La Hogue with the ships of England and Holland, his fleet was so shattered that his plans all fell to the ground. 1692 A.D. Every summer then saw William on the Continent, in spite of his delicate health, engaged in hostilities with Louis, whom, though he could not humble, he kept in constant check,—a matter of the utmost importance to all Europe. The Treaty of Ryswick in 1697 brought the war to a close.

Out of these expensive wars sprang the National Debt, which has since swelled to a sum so enormous. The Parliament, knowing that the chief value of the English crown in William's eyes was the increased weight it gave him in Continental politics, agreed to furnish large supplies of money for his wars with Louis, on condition that he should give up to them the chief share in the domestic government. Though at first reluctant, he soon yielded to the arrangement with a grace and temper which proved his good sense. The influence thus acquired by the Commons has never since been lost.

Queen Mary died of small-pox in the year 1694, leaving William sole ruler. During his eight remaining years the Commons took three remarkable steps in their encroachments on the power of the Crown. These were the Triennial Bill, the arrangement of the Civil List, and the Act of Settlement. The Triennial Bill enacted that no Parliament should sit longer than three years,—an arrangement by which the influence of the King over that body was much lessened. A sum of £700,000 was settled on the King to meet the expenses of the Civil List, while all the remaining revenue was left in the hands of the Commons to support the army and navy, and defray the cost of government. The

1701 A.D. Act of Settlement—a sequel to the Declaration of Rights—provided that the Judges should hold office for life or good conduct, at fixed salaries; that the Sovereigns of Great Britain should be Protestants; that they should not leave their dominions without the consent of Parliament; and that the Princess Sophia of Hanover should be considered next heir to the throne.

A trading company, embodied by an Act of the Scottish Parliament, founded a colony in 1698 on the Isthmus of Darien, as a central position for commerce with both India and America. The sum of £400,000, subscribed in Scotland, which was then a poor country, was embarked in the venture. The merchants of London and Amsterdam took shares to the same amount. But the colony was ruined and the money all lost. The East India Company, looking on the expedition as an invasion of their rights, induced the King to set his face against it. The settlers, badly supported by their countrymen, sank into want. Disease carried them off in scores. The neighbouring British colonies, either through jealousy or acting under orders from home, refused to lend any assistance. And to crown all, the Spaniards, claiming the soil on which their town, New Edinburgh, was built, harassed them with ceaseless attacks. Very few of the unhappy colonists ever saw Scotland again.

William, riding from Kensington to Hampton Court, fell from his horse and broke his collar-bone. This was in itself a slight injury, but, acting on a frame naturally feeble and worn out by long-continued asthma, it brought on a fever, of which he died at Kensington. He left no children. *Mar. 8, 1702 A.D.*

William of Orange was a man prematurely old. Left early an orphan, he had learned in a hard school to be self-reliant and reserved; and at an age when boys are thinking of the cricket-bat and the fishing-rod before all things else, he was deeply learned in politics and skilled in the discipline of armies. For literature and science he had little love. He possessed a courage that was calm amid every species of danger, and never did he rejoice so much as in the day of battle. His most intimate—almost his only—friend was Bentinck, a Dutch gentleman, whom he created Earl of Portland. His frame was feeble, his cheek was pale and thin from long-continued disease; but to his latest day the flashing of his eagle eye and the compression of his firmly-cut lips told at once that bodily anguish had never tamed the iron soul within.

In 1695 the Bank of England, with a capital of £1,200,000, was founded by Paterson, a Scotchman. In the following year an English merchant, named Holland, set up the Bank of Scotland, with little more than £100,000. Paper money then came into use. Chelsea Hospital, for old and disabled soldiers, was founded by William and Mary, who also nobly gave up their palace at Greenwich to the veterans of the navy. It was during this reign that Peter the Great of Russia worked as a ship-carpenter in the dockyard at Deptford.

CONTEMPORARY SOVEREIGNS.

FRANCE.
LOUIS XIV.

SPAIN.
A.D.
CHARLES II., ...died 1700
PHILIP V.

SWEDEN.
CHARLES XI., ...1697
CHARLES XII.

TURKEY.
A.D.
SOLYMAN II., ...died 1691
ACHMET II., ...1695
MUSTAPHA III.

EMPERORS.
LEOPOLD I.

POPES.
INNOCENT XI., ...1689
ALEXANDER VIII., ...1691
INNOCENT XII., ...1700
CLEMENT XI.

CHAPTER VII.

ANNE.

Born 1664 A.D.—Began to rule 1702 A.D.—Died 1714 A.D.

The Spanish Succession.	The Union of England and Scotland.	Fall of the Whigs.
Capture of Gibraltar.		The Treaty of Utrecht.
Victories of Marlborough.	James the Pretender.	Anne's death.
	Abigail Hill.	Her character.
Whigs and Tories.	Trial of Sacheverell.	Notes.

On the death of William, Anne, the second daughter of James II., became Queen. Her husband, Prince George of Denmark, sat in the House of Lords as Duke of Cumberland, but took no further share in the government. The policy of the late reign was followed. The Whigs remained in power, and the French war was continued.

A new cause of war had arisen in a dispute about the Spanish Succession. Louis claimed the crown of Spain for his grandson, who afterwards ruled as Philip V. Britain supported the rival claims of the Archduke Charles. Germany and Holland united with Britain in the Grand Alliance against the ambitious Louis, and Churchill—soon created Duke of Marlborough—led the allied armies. The chief theatres of the war were Spain and the Low Countries, which have well been named "The Battle-field of Modern Europe." In Spain the Earl of Peterborough gained some successes; but the most important achievement of the war was the capture of Gibraltar by Admiral Rooke and Sir Cloudesley Shovel. Aided by a body of Hessian troops, the British, landing on the isthmus which joins the rock to the mainland, carried the works by storm in spite of a heavy fire. July, 1704 A.D.

Marlborough humbled the power of France in four great battles. At Blenheim in Bavaria, in 1704, he defeated Marshal Tallard. At Ramilies in South Brabant, in 1706, he overthrew Villeroi. At Oudenarde in East Flanders, in 1708, the French lost 15,000 men, and more than one hundred banners. The capture of Lisle was a result of this victory. And at Malplaquet, on the north-eastern frontier of

France, in 1709, a bloodier victory still was won by the genius of Marlborough. It was not until 1713 that the peace of Utrecht gave rest to exhausted Europe.

Anne, though at heart a Tory, was long compelled to yield to the guidance of her Whig ministers. Of these the principal were Godolphin, the Lord High Treasurer; Marlborough, the Captain-General of the Forces and the Master of the Ordnance; and Sunderland, the Secretary of State. The strife between Whigs and Tories raged at this time more fiercely than ever around two great questions,—the War and the Church. The Whigs cried out for war; the Tories sought the restoration of peace. The Whigs were Low Church; the Tories, noted for attachment to Episcopacy, bore the name of the High Church party. A measure, called the Occasional Conformity Bill, was brought into Parliament by the Tories. It was levelled against those who attended places of worship not of the Established Church, after they had sworn to the Test Oath and had received public appointments. These Occasional Conformists were to suffer dismissal and heavy fine. The Bill passed the Commons, but was lost in the Lords. It was, nevertheless, a remarkable sign of the growing influence of the Tory party.

Such was the state of politics when a question of much greater importance arose,—the necessity of a union between the Parliaments of England and Scotland. The nations were not on good terms. The Scottish Parliament, still smarting under the disasters at Darien, had passed an Act of Security, which decreed that the successor to the throne of Scotland, on the Queen's death, should not be the person chosen by the English Parliament, unless the commercial privileges enjoyed by England were extended to Scotland also. The Scottish nation then assumed an attitude of war. But commissioners were appointed,—thirty on each side; and by them a Treaty of Union was framed, which, although met by a storm of opposition from the people of Scotland, passed the Scottish Parliament by a majority of one hundred and ten votes. The chief terms of the Union were:—

1707
A.D.

1. That the Electress Sophia of Hanover, and her heirs, if

Protestants, should succeed to the crown of the United Kingdom.

2. That Scotland should be represented in the Imperial Parliament, sitting in London, by sixteen elective Peers and forty-five members of the Commons.

3. That all British ports and colonies should be opened to Scottish traders.

4. That while the laws of public policy should be the same for both countries, those relating to property and private rights should be preserved unaltered, except for the good of the Scottish people.

5. That the Court of Session and other Scottish tribunals should remain unchanged.

6. That the Church of Scotland should be maintained, as already by law established.

To make up for the heavier taxes which were thus laid upon the Scottish people, a grant of £398,000 was made to improve the coinage.

The Union has done incalculable good to Scotland. The strong objections urged at first against the change were the loss of independence and the increased load of taxation; but these were only seeming evils. The commerce, the wealth, and the greatness of Scotland began to advance with rapid strides. Glasgow and Dundee sprang into great and populous cities; fishing villages became thriving seaports. Among the people who, with much difficulty, managed to pinch and scrape together £400,000 to found the Darien colony, we can now point out many a merchant-prince whose single fortune far exceeds that sum.

Louis XIV., taking advantage of the discontent excited in Scotland by the Union, despatched a fleet from Dunkirk to set James the Pretender on the Scottish throne. But timely notice reached England; and the French admiral, finding the Frith of Forth guarded by a squadron under Sir George Byng, returned with the loss of one ship.

Meanwhile Tory influence was growing strong in the Cabinet. The Whigs had retained their ascendency over the Queen chiefly by the aid of Sarah, Duchess of Marlborough, who was on terms of the most intimate friendship with her Majesty. But the favourite grew insolent, and the

Queen became weary of a companion who tried to have the upper-hand in everything. A waiting-woman named Abigail Hill, otherwise known as Mrs. Masham, secretly encouraging their quarrels, at last insinuated herself into the confidence and favour of Anne. Hill was a Tory, and one of the earliest results of her influence was the introduction into the Cabinet of Robert Harley (Earl of Oxford) and Henry St. John (Lord Bolingbroke), the leaders of the Tory party.

Just then occurred events which stirred all England into a flame in favour of the Tories. Dr. Henry Sacheverell, rector of St. Saviour's, Southwark, had preached two sermons—one (August 15) at Derby, another (November 5, 1709) at St. Paul's before the Lord Mayor and Aldermen of London—in which he denounced the Revolution as an unrighteous change, maintained the duty of fierce persecution against all Dissenters, and called on the people to defend their Church, which was in imminent danger. The Commons impeached him for uttering seditious libels; and the case came on before the Lords. The trial lasted three weeks. All the clergy and the common people were for Sacheverell. The Queen attended the trial privately, to give him encouragement. Bishop Atterbury wrote his defence. Every day, as he drove to and from the court, his coach was followed by cheering mobs, whose feelings, not content with this display, found further vent in the destruction of Dissenting houses of worship, and in riots that filled the streets with alarm. He was found guilty, and forbidden to preach for three years. The sermons were burned in front of the Royal Exchange.

Feb. 27, 1710 A.D.

The fall of the Whig ministry was an immediate result of this trial. Godolphin and Sunderland, with their less important colleagues, were dismissed. Harley and St. John came into office. Marlborough, though retained in his command on account of the still raging war, was marked for disgrace; and no sooner did the Tory ministers see their way to the conclusion of peace than the Duke, accused of receiving bribes from a Jew who supplied the army with bread, was compelled to resign his high office. To Blenheim

Park, the nation's gift for one of his greatest victories, he retired, leaving on the pages of our history a character marked with the highest military genius, but sullied by falsehood and base avarice.

The Treaty of Utrecht, already mentioned, was the work of the Tories. The principal terms which concerned Great Britain were, that Louis XIV. should recognise the Sovereigns of the Brunswick line; that he should cease to aid the Pretender; that he should dismantle the batteries of Dunkirk; and that the British should retain Gibraltar and Minorca, Nova Scotia, Newfoundland, and Hudson's Bay. Harley and St. John became Peers; but their union was at an end. Henceforward they were rivals and foes. Anne favoured Bolingbroke. **1713 A.D.**

The question of Patronage, or who should have the appointment of ministers, agitated the Church of Scotland; and several secessions took place about the end of this reign.

Then, too, the Scottish members sitting in the British Parliament began to feel all the petty annoyances at first inseparable from a change of the kind. Their country, their accent, their habits, their appearance, were thought fair marks for the sarcasm of English orators; and so high did their discontent rise, that the question of dissolving the Union was solemnly debated in 1713. Happily for both countries, the measure was lost in the Lords, but only by a narrow majority.

Anne died of apoplexy after two days' illness. She had lost her husband six years before. Not one of her nineteen children was then living. One boy, George, reached the age of eleven years. The rest all died in infancy. **Aug. 1, 1714 A.D.**

She was a woman of little talent and less learning; simple and homely in all her tastes and habits. The expression of her face was heavy,—to the careless eye it might even seem stupid; but it was the dull look of one upon whom sorrow had laid a heavy hand, chilling her motherly affections, and withering, one by one, the gentle household blossoms of her life.

In 1703 the Eddystone lighthouse was swept away by a storm, when Winstanley, the architect, perished. St. Paul's

Cathedral was finished in 1708. It cost about a million, and the building occupied thirty-seven years. The reign of Anne is noted as a brilliant literary period. Addison and Swift were the chief prose writers. Pope was the leading poet.

CONTEMPORARY SOVEREIGNS.

FRANCE.	A.D.	EMPERORS.	A.D.
LOUIS XIV.		**LEOPOLD I.,**	died 1705
		JOSEPH I.,	1711
SPAIN.		**CHARLES VI.**	
PHILIP V.			
		POPE.	
SWEDEN.		**CLEMENT XI.**	
CHARLES XII.			
TURKEY.			
MUSTAPHA III.,	died 1703		
ACHMET III.			

CHAPTER VIII.

SOCIAL CONDITION OF THE PEOPLE UNDER THE STUARTS.

The face of the country.	London.	Health and morals.
Animals.	Country gentlemen.	Dress.
Mineral wealth.	The clergy.	Travelling.
Population.	The yeomen.	The News-letter.
Provincial towns.	The labouring classes.	State of learning.

THOUGH in former periods the face of Britain changed much as years rolled by, yet the change since the Stuarts reigned has perhaps been the most marked of all. Where there are now to be seen green meadows and yellow cornfields; orchards, white with spring blossoms, or golden with autumn fruit; and cosy farm-houses nestling among the sheltering trees, there was then in many places nothing but forest, furze, or marsh.

Through the old woods wandered deer in great troops, a few wild bulls, and, until the peasantry killed them during the Civil War, wild boars, long preserved for royal sport. Badgers, wild cats, immense eagles, huge bustards were common even in the southern and eastern lowlands of England. The sheep and oxen were much smaller than ours. The British horses, now famed all the world over, then sold for fifty shillings each. Spanish jennets for the saddle, and grey Flanders mares for harness were the breeds most prized.

Our mines were still poorly worked. Cornwall yielded tin, and Wales yielded copper, but in quantities far below the present supply. Salt, now a leading export, was then so badly prepared that the physicians blamed it as the cause of many diseases of the skin and lungs. The iron manufacture was checked by the cry which was raised about the waste of wood in the furnaces. The smelters had not yet learned to use coal, which was still only a domestic fuel, burned in the districts where it abounded, and in London, whither it was carried by sea.

The population of England at the close of the seventeenth century was about five millions and a half. The increase of people in the northern counties far exceeded that in the south of the island. The cause of this may be found in the rapid improvement of these counties which followed the union of the Crowns in 1603. Previously, the north had been constantly ravaged by the Border robbers, called Moss-troopers, from whom no house or herd was safe. Gradually these freebooters were hunted down and extirpated. Blood-hounds were kept in many northern parishes to track them to their dens. The paths of the country, long unknown, were opened up; life and property became secure. Coal-beds were discovered. Manufacturing towns began to rise, and were soon filled with a thriving population.

After the capital, Bristol was the greatest English sea-port; and Norwich, the chief manufacturing town under the Stuarts. The Bristol citizens, among whom the sugar-refiners took the lead, were far-famed for wealth and hospitality. The great seats of manufacture were then small and badly-built market towns. Manchester, the modern centre of the cotton trade, contained only 6000 inhabitants, and could boast of neither a printing-press nor a hackney-coach. Leeds, the great woollen mart, had a population of about 7000 persons. Sheffield, whose forges send out the best cutlery in the world, held barely 2000 inhabitants. Birmingham, only rising into notice, was proud of sending her hard-ware so far off as Ireland. There were not more than 200 seamen belonging to the port of Liverpool. Buxton, Bath, and Tunbridge Wells were the fashionable watering-places of the time; but the lodgings were very poor, and the food sold in these places was of the most wretched description. Brighton and Cheltenham are of modern growth.

London, when Charles II. died, had a population of half a million. One old bridge spanned the Thames; and the houses were all built with the upper stories projecting over the shops below. The city was the merchant's home. He did not then, as now, leave his counting-house after business hours for a gay villa in the suburbs. No numbers marked the houses; but, instead of these, the streets were lined with the signs of shops—here the Saracen's Head—there the Golden Key. By these the people described their dwellings, and strangers found their way. The streets, not lighted until the last year of Charles II., and then only during the winter, were infested with robbers, and teemed with other dangers. It was the height of fashion among dissipated young men to parade the foot-way at night, insulting every woman and beating every man they met. From these the feeble tippling watchmen could or would give no protection. The coffee-houses, first set up in Cromwell's time, were the great lounges, where the news and scandal of the day were discussed. In one might be seen the exquisites, with their flowing wigs, their embroidered coats, their fringed gloves, and scented snuff. To another crowded literary men to hear John Dryden talk. There were coffee-houses for every class. Jews flocked together to one; Papists filled another; Puritans met their brethren in a third; and so with men of every rank and opinion.

The country gentlemen, now a polished and an important class, were, at the time of the Revolution, rough and poorly educated. Their lands yielded rents equal to about one-fourth of those now paid. Seldom leaving their native county even for London, they spent their days in field sports or in attending the neighbouring markets, and their evenings in drinking strong beer. Claret and Canary wines were drunk only by the very wealthy. Drunkenness was a common and fashionable vice, and continued to be so more or less until the beginning of the present century. The ladies of the family, whose accomplishments seldom rose above the baking of pastry or the brewing of gooseberry wine, cooked the meals of the household. In the evening they amused themselves by sewing and spinning. The graces of the modern tea-table were quite unknown to the country folk, although that favourite beverage, brought by the Dutch to Europe, was introduced into England by Lords Arlington and Ossory in 1666. It was not till nearly a century later that the middle classes of London and Edinburgh began to use tea daily. In the latter city in the reigns of the Georges tea was taken at four o'clock, and the meal was thence called 'four hours.' But beneath all the roughness of the rural gentry lay qualities which have highly exalted the British character. Reverence for hereditary monarchy and strong attachment to the Protestant faith were their leading principles.

The country clergy stood low in the social scale. The Reformation had humbled the pomp and splendour of the Romish priesthood; and it pleased the great Head of the Church, whose earliest ministers were poor fishermen, to carry on his work at this time with labourers of a humble class. In most mansions there was a chaplain, or, as he was often called, a Levite, who, receiving his board and £10 a year, was no better than an upper servant. His wife was often taken from the kitchen of his patron. Even if he got a parish he lived and worked like a peasant: his sons were ploughmen and his daughters went to service. It must not be forgotten that the London clergy, among whom were Sherlock, Tillotson, and Stillingfleet, formed a class by themselves, and well upheld the character of their Church for zeal, learning, and eloquence.

The yeomen or small farmers, whose income averaged £60 or £70 a year, were numerous and influential. Their chief characteristics were a leaning towards Puritanism and a hatred of Popery. From this class chiefly were drawn the Ironsides of Cromwell.

Of the labouring classes we know little. Four-fifths of them were employed in agriculture. In Devon, Suffolk, and Essex, the highest wages were paid, averaging five shillings a week without food. Those engaged in manufactures earned about six shillings weekly. Children were employed in factories to an immense extent, and were thought fit for work, even by the benevolent, at six years of age. The chief food of the poor was rye, barley, or oats. Rude ballads were their only means of complaint, and in these they poured forth their woes. The poor-rate was the heaviest tax, for the paupers amounted to no less than one-fifth of the community.

Sanitary reform was greatly needed. Even in the streets of the capital open sewers and heaps of filth poisoned the air. The deaths in London in 1685 were more than one in twenty-three; the yearly average now is about one in forty. People of coarse and brutal natures were found in all classes in great numbers. Nor is this wonderful when the training of every-day life is considered. Masters beat their servants; husbands beat their wives, daily. Teachers knew no way of imparting knowledge but by the lash. The mob rejoiced in fights of all kinds, and shouted with glee when an eye was torn out or a finger chopped off in these savage encounters. Executions were favourite public spectacles. The prisons were constantly full, and proved to be most fruitful nurseries of dirt, disease, and crime.

To describe the various costumes and manners of the period would be impossible within the compass of a paragraph. One or two points on this head must suffice here. The Cavalier and the Roundhead present a striking contrast in their dress and habits. Bright colours, profuse ornament, and graceful style marked the costume of the Cavalier. His richly-laced cloak, over which lay an embroidered collar, his broad-leafed hat of beaver with its tall white plume, his silken doublet of the Vandyke pattern, his flowing love-locks, gilt spurs, and slashed boots, made up a figure the most picturesque of any period in our history. The Puritan Roundhead wore a cloak of sad-coloured brown or black, a plain collar of linen laid carelessly down on the plaited cloth, and a hat with a high steeple-shaped crown over his closely clipt, or lank, straight hair. His baptismal name was cast aside, and some strange religious phrase adopted in its stead. His language was full of Scripture texts; and these he delivered through his nose with a peculiar and ridiculous twang. But, for all these solemn freaks, the Puritan character was metal of the true ring and sterling value, and is well deserving of our highest respect. Charles II. introduced the peruke, a long flowing wig which covered even the shoulders. It continued to be the fashion until after the close of the period.

The roads were so bad that travelling was very difficult. In bad weather there was generally only a slight ridge in the centre of the road between two channels of deep mud. Instead of sloping gradually, the roads went right up and down the hills. The stage-waggon and pack-horses carried goods; the former taking passengers also. Rich men travelled in their own coaches, but they were obliged often to have six horses to pull them through the mud. In 1669 a

'Flying Coach' left Oxford at six in the morning, and reached London at seven the same evening,—a feat then considered wonderful and dangerous. From Chester, York, and Exeter, a winter journey to London took six days. We owe the immense improvement of our roads since those days chiefly to the Turnpikes. The inns were good and comfortable,—as indeed they would need to be, when so many nights were spent on the road. Highwaymen, well armed and mounted on fine horses, infested all the great roads; and it is said that many of the innkeepers were paid by them to give information about those travellers who were worth attacking. The post-bags were carried on horseback at the rate of five miles an hour; but in many country places letters were delivered only once a week.

There was nothing at all equal to our modern newspaper. Small single leaves were published twice a week while the Exclusion Bill was discussed; but the only paper afterwards allowed was 'The London Gazette,' a two-paged bi-weekly sheet of very meagre contents. No Parliamentary debates, no State trials were permitted to be reported. An important feature of social life during this age was 'The News-letter.' This was an epistle, despatched to the country generally once a week, giving all the chat of the coffee-houses and the news of the capital. Several families subscribed to pay some Londoner, who gave them the scraps of news gathered during his lounges. 'Our own correspondent' is the modern representative of the system.

There were few printing presses in the country except in London and at the Universities. The only press north of the Trent was at York. Books were therefore scarce and dear, and very few were to be found in the best country houses. In London the booksellers' shops were thronged with readers. Female education was at a very low point, and the most accomplished ladies spelled their letters very badly. At the Universities Greek was little studied; but Latin, in which Governments still conducted their correspondence, was for this reason spoken and written with elegance and ease. But French was rapidly rising to be the language of diplomacy. Astronomy was ably cultivated by Halley and Flamsteed, who was the first astronomer-royal.

Natural Philosophy owed its birth as a science to Isaac Newton. But the favourite and fashionable study of the latter Stuart days was Chemistry. Charles II. had a laboratory in his palace of Whitehall. Even the ladies were smitten with the rage for science, and began to talk learnedly of magnets and microscopes. It was soon discovered that Chemistry—so long a worthless pursuit—might be turned to the improvement of agriculture. Experiments were made on various soils, new fruits and vegetables were grown in the gardens, and farmers began to think that perhaps after all there might be some profit in the study of science.

LEADING AUTHORS OF THE STUART PERIOD.

FRANCIS BEAUMONT,......(1586-1615) }
JOHN FLETCHER,............(1576-1625) } —wrote plays together, fifty-two in all—Fletcher composed the plays; Beaumont fitted them for the public.

BEN JONSON,....................(1574-1637)—dramatic poet—at first a bricklayer—then a soldier—earliest play, 'Every Man in his Humour'—made Poet Laureate in 1619.

PHILIP MASSINGER,........(1584-1640)—dramatic poet—lived chiefly in London—poor and obscure—chief play, 'A New Way to Pay Old Debts.'

ROBERT HERRICK, }
SIR JOHN SUCKLING, } ...Lyric poets in the time of Charles I.

WILLIAM DRUMMOND,.....(1585-1649)—Scottish lyric poet—lived at Hawthornden—wrote sonnets and madrigals.

JEREMY TAYLOR,............(1613-1667)—Bishop of Down and Connor—wrote on theology—chief works, 'Holy Living' and 'Holy Dying.'

JOHN MILTON,................(1608-1674)—greatest epic poet of modern ages—Latin Secretary to Cromwell—finest work, 'Paradise Lost,' an epic in twelve books, on the Fall; written in blindness and poverty, between 1660 and 1667—other works, 'Paradise Regained,' a shorter epic; 'Comus,' a masque; 'Lycidas,' 'Samson Agonistes,' 'L'Allegro' and 'Il Penseroso,' short descriptive poems; and many fine sonnets—wrote also prose, in which he made a vain attempt to introduce into English the order and idioms of Latin.

EDWARD HYDE,..............(1608-1674)—Earl of Clarendon—minister of Charles I.—an exile during the Commonwealth—Lord Chancellor from 1660 to 1667—wrote 'History of the Rebellion,' *i.e.*, of the Civil War—not published till Anne's reign.

SAMUEL BUTLER,............(1612-1680)—a Worcestershire farmer—chief work, 'Hudibras,' a mock-heroic poem, in short couplets, written to caricature the Puritans, and published in the reign of Charles II.

JOHN BUNYAN,...............(1628-1688)—a tinker of Bedford—afterwards a soldier—then a Baptist preacher—imprisoned for preaching—chief work, 'The Pilgrim's Progress,' a prose allegory, describing the life and triumph of a Christian under the figure of a journey.

RICHARD BAXTER,..........(1615-1691)—a celebrated Presbyterian minister—chief works, 'The Saint's Rest' and 'A Call to the Unconverted,'—wrote in all 126 volumes.

JOHN DRYDEN,................(1631-1700)—one of the greatest names in English poetry—chief works, 'Absalom and Achitophel,' a political satire; and 'Alexander's Feast,' an ode—translated Virgil's Æneid into English verse.

JOHN LOCKE,...................(1632-1704)—the great mental philosopher of the period—educated at Oxford—chief work, 'An Essay on the Human Understanding,' published in 1690.

GILBERT BURNET,..........(1643-1715)—a Scotchman—very intimate with William III.—created Bishop of Salisbury—chief works, 'History of my own Times,' and 'History of the Reformation of the Church of England.'

LEADING ARTISTS.

INIGO JONES,	(1572-1652)—native of London—a distinguished architect—designed the Banqueting-house at Whitehall.
RUBENS,	(1577-1640)—a celebrated painter of the Flemish school—a pupil of Titian—patronized by Charles I., for whom he painted the Banqueting-house of Whitehall.
VANDYKE,	(1599-1641)—a Flemish painter—pupil of Rubens—lived for some time at the court of Charles I., whose portrait he painted.
SIR PETER LELY,	(1617-1680)—a painter of Westphalia—patronized by Charles II.—the leading portraits of the court beauties are from his brush.
SIR CHRISTOPHER WREN,	(1632-1723)—the only distinguished English artist in the latter Stuart reigns—a famous architect—chief design, St. Paul's Cathedral.
SIR GODFREY KNELLER,	(1648-1723)—a German portrait-painter—lived at the courts of William III., Anne, and George I.

LEADING DATES OF THE STUART PERIOD.

GENERAL EVENTS.

	A.D.	
Gunpowder Plot,	1605	James I.
Raleigh beheaded,	1618	—
Trial of Hampden,	1637	Charles I.
Charles I. beheaded,	1649	—
The Plague,	1665	Charles II.
The Great Fire,	1666	—
Trial of the Bishops,	1688	James II.
Landing of the Prince of Orange,	—	—
Trial of Sacheverell,	1710	Anne.

CONSTITUTIONAL CHANGES.

Union of English and Scottish crowns,	1603	James I.
Petition of Right,	1628	Charles I.
The Long Parliament begins,	1640	—
Cromwell expels the Long Parliament,	1653	Commonwealth

DATES OF STUART PERIOD.

	A.D.	
The Restoration,	1660	Charles II.
The Test Act,	1673	—
The Habeas Corpus Act,	1679	—
The Second Declaration of Indulgence,	1688	James II.
The Revolution,	—	—
The Declaration of Rights,	—	—
The Act of Settlement,	1701	William III.
The Union of the English and Scottish Parliaments,	1707	Anne.

DOMINION ACQUIRED.

Jamaica taken,	1655	Commonwealth.
Gibraltar taken,	1704	Anne.

WARS, BATTLES, TREATIES.

Thirty Years' War begins,	1618	James I.
Battle of Edge-hill,	1642	Charles I.
First Battle of Newbury,	1643	—
Battle of Marston Moor,	1644	—
Second Battle of Newbury,	—	—
Battle of Naseby,	1645	—
— Dunbar,	1650	Commonwealth.
— Worcester,	1651	—
Secret Treaty of Dover,	1670	Charles II.
Battle of Sedgemoor,	1685	James II.
— Killicrankie,	1689	William III.
— Boyne,	1690	—
— La Hogue,	1692	—
Treaty of Ryswick,	1697	—
Battle of Blenheim,	1704	Anne.
— Ramilies,	1706	—
— Oudenarde,	1708	—
— Malplaquet,	1709	—
Treaty of Utrecht,	1713	—

GENEALOGICAL TREE
CONNECTING THE STUARTS WITH THE GUELPHS.

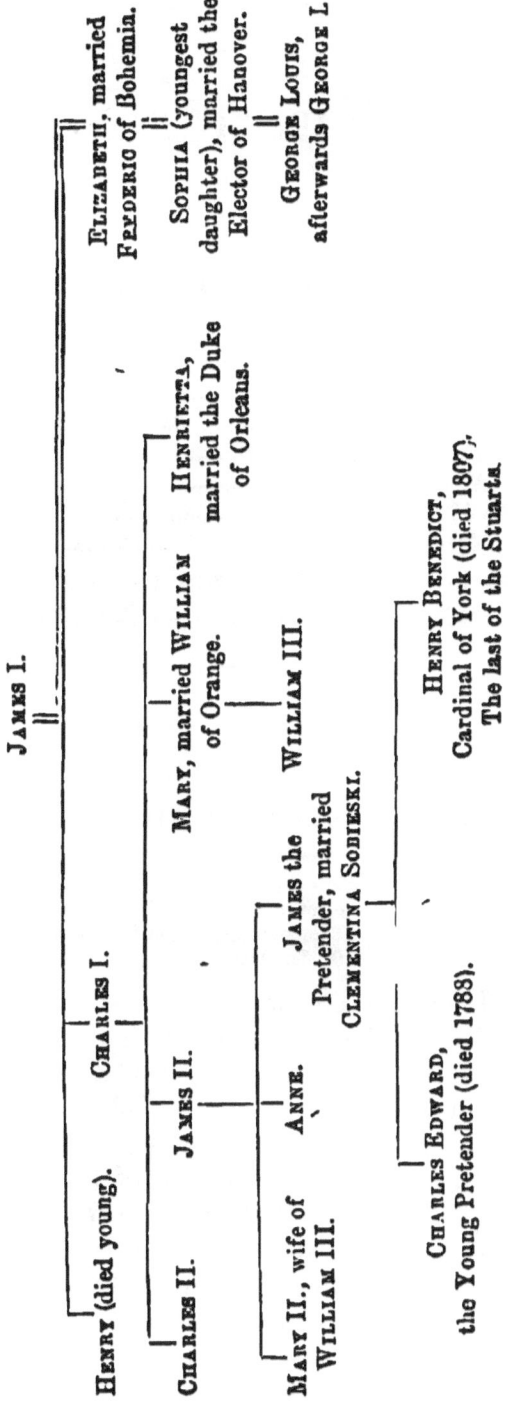

GUELPH LINE;

OR,

HOUSE OF BRUNSWICK.

Opened 1714 A.D.—Has already lasted 144 years.—6 Sovereigns.

                                                                          A.D.

GEORGE I. (great-grandson of James I.),............began to rule 1714
GEORGE II. (son),.. 1727
GEORGE III. (grandson),.. 1760
REGENCY of the Prince of Wales,.. 1811
GEORGE IV. (son),... 1820
WILLIAM IV. (brother),.. 1830
VICTORIA (niece),... 1837

Leading Feature :—THE INFLUENCE OF THE HOUSE OF COMMONS GREATER THAN AT ANY FORMER PERIOD.

CHAPTER I.

GEORGE I.

Born 1660 A.D.—Began to reign 1714 A.D.—Died 1727 A.D.

Hanover united to England.	'The Fifteen.'	The Crash.
Policy of George.	The Septennial Act.	Robert Walpole.
Fall of the Tories.	Sweden and Spain.	Death of the King.
The Riot Act.	The South Sea Scheme.	Character
	Golden dreams.	Notes.

GEORGE I., already Elector of Hanover, became King of the British Empire at the age of fifty-four. His father was Ernest Augustus of Hanover; his mother was Sophia, daughter of Elizabeth, Queen of Bohemia, and therefore grand-daughter of James I. Having spent all his previous life in Germany, he knew but little of England, and to his last day could neither speak nor write the English language well. His wife was Sophia of Brunswick, his own cousin, whom he treated with great cruelty, keeping her for forty years shut up in a castle of Hanover, where not even her own children were allowed to see her. By his accession the crowns of Britain and Hanover were united.

George favoured the Whigs, by whom he had been called to the throne, and took no pains to conceal his dread and dislike of the Tories. His policy is easily understood. It was guided mainly by two principles,—an intense fondness for Hanover, and a constant fear of the Pretender and his partisans. These were now called Jacobites, from *Jacobus*, the Latin name for James.

The fall of the Tory ministry was immediate. A secret committee of the Commons sat to inquire into their conduct with regard to the Treaty of Utrecht. Of that committee the chairman was Robert Walpole, who, born in 1676 and educated at Cambridge, had in 1706 been made Secretary for War, and was now Paymaster of the Forces. The Tory leaders, Oxford, Bolingbroke, and Ormond, against all of whom there were strong suspicions of a secret correspondence with the Pretender, were impeached for high treason. Oxford was sent to the Tower, and his head was saved only by a difference between the Lords and the Commons. Bolingbroke and Ormond fled to the Continent, where they joined the councils of the Pretender.

Great riots then took place, for the feeling of the entire nation ran strongly in favour of the Tories. The coach which conveyed Oxford to the Tower was surrounded by roaring mobs, that afterwards in Smithfield burned William III. in effigy. Bishop Atterbury boldly denounced George as a usurper. The students of Oxford wore the oak leaf on the 29th of May in honour of the Stuart Restoration. The men of Staffordshire assembled in tumultuous crowds to applaud Jacobite speeches. Without delay the Government took strong measures. The Riot Act **1715** was passed, which enacted that any mob of more A.D. than twelve persons refusing to disperse in a given time, should be scattered by military force. A price of £100,000 was set on the head of the Pretender. The army and navy were prepared for war.

The alarm of the King and his ministers was not without foundation. The Pretender was in France, flushed with high hopes of success, and buoyed up by promises of strong support from Louis XIV. But the death of that great monarch blasted all his bright prospects. All hope of

French aid was gone; for the Regent, Duke of Orleans, thought more of repairing the shattered finances of France than of invading England.

Meanwhile the flame of rebellion was actually kindled both in Scotland and in England. The Earl of Mar had gathered 10,000 clansmen around him at Braemar, and held all the Highlands; while the Duke of Argyle, with a royal army strongly posted at Stirling, watched his every movement. The men of Northumberland had been called to arms by the Earl of Derwentwater, and Forster, the member for the county; but few of them had obeyed the summons. They were aided by 1800 Highlanders, a reinforcement from Mar, and were joined by a few lords of the Scottish Border. But the royal troops, forcing Forster into the town of Preston in Lancashire, there compelled him to surrender. On the same day, at Sheriffmuir in the south of Perthshire, Argyle inflicted, not an absolute defeat, but a severe check upon Mar, who after the engagement retreated hastily to Perth.

1715 A.D.

Nov. 13.

The Pretender, who was called on the Continent the Chevalier de St. George, by his English adherents James III., and by his Scottish friends James VIII., resolving to see what his presence in the native land of the Stuarts would do, landed at Peterhead; but with no money, no troops, no warlike stores. He found his party broken and dispirited; and his arrival without the aid from France, so eagerly looked for, cast a deeper gloom over the Stuart cause. At Perth he frivolously wasted many days in preparing for his coronation, while the crown was yet to be won. Amid his dreams of a splendour never to be realized, he heard that Argyle was advancing, and retreated northward towards Montrose, where he and Mar embarked for France, leaving the army to its fate. The Earl of Derwentwater, Lord Kenmuir, and twenty others suffered death; the estates of many were confiscated; and more than a thousand were banished to North America. Thus ended 'The Fifteen.'

Dec. 22.

The most remarkable constitutional change of this reign was the passing of the Septennial Act, by which the maximum length of our Parliaments was fixed at seven years. To the Whigs we owe this wise measure, which has done much to preserve the peace of the nation. **1716 A.D.** In the days of the Triennial Bill the excitement of one general election had hardly time to settle down before the turmoil of another began. Party spirit ran into wild excess. Although the collision of parties, when kept within due bounds, is, like the heaving and sweeping of the ocean, a wholesome influence, tending to keep the nation's life fresh and vigorous, and to prevent the settlement of error and abuse, yet there is no power so destructive when let loose from fit control. Hence the necessity and use of such laws as the Septennial Act.

For the sake of Hanover, George embroiled himself with Sweden and with Spain. He had bought from the King of Denmark the duchies of Bremen and Verden, which Charles of Sweden claimed as his own. A dispute followed, and war seemed certain, when the death of the great Swede at the siege of Fredericshall saved Britain from invasion. The Quadruple Alliance was then formed, by which Germany, England, France, and Holland leagued themselves against Philip of Spain, who had interfered with the Italian interests of the Emperor. Admiral Byng destroyed the Spanish fleet off Cape Passaro in Sicily; and Alberoni, the Spanish minister, in retaliation, sent **1718 A.D.** an expedition to invade Scotland in favour of the Pretender. But, a storm having shattered the fleet, this miniature Armada failed in its object. Philip, worsted by land and sea, sought peace from the four Allies.

In the same year the Convocation of the English clergy, an assembly which, like a Senate of Churchmen, had been used to make ecclesiastical laws, and even to grant money to the King, was dissolved, never to meet again. The political influence of the English Church is now confined chiefly to the Archbishops and Bishops, who have seats among the Lords.

In 1719 the Mississippi Company, a scheme by which paper money was to fill the place of gold and silver, set on foot in Paris by Law, a Scotch banker, ruined thousands by its utter failure. In the year following the South

1720 A.D. Sea Scheme set all Britain crazy. The National Debt then amounted to £53,000,000. The Government were obliged to pay to all those who had lent the money, or, as we say, had invested money in the funds, interest at six per cent., which came to £3,180,000 in the year. This was a heavy burden on a yearly revenue of about £8,000,000; and to remove or lessen the debt became the grand problem, which occupied the financiers of the day. The Bank of England and the South Sea Company both proposed plans to accomplish this object. The offers of the South Sea Company, of which Blunt was a leading director, were accepted by the Government. The Company proposed to buy up all the debts of the nation, and to advance to the Government whatever money they needed at four per cent. They agreed, besides, to pay to the Government, as a bonus, the sum of £7,000,000. This plan would reduce the interest on the debt by one-third every year, and would also give to the Government a large sum of ready money. In return for these advantages the Company received the sole right of trading to the South Seas.

Stories of the endless treasure to be drawn from golden islands in the far-off Pacific found eager listeners everywhere. Hundreds rushed to the offices of the Company to exchange their Government stock for shares in the scheme. Rich men and poor widows, statesmen and errand-boys, jostling each other in the race for gold, paid their money across the counters, and received from the clerks pieces of paper, which they fondly believed would secure to them the possession of twenty-fold riches. The Company promised a dividend of fifty per cent. at least, and the shares rose rapidly. The excitement became a mania, and the mania became a frenzy. Men paid away £1000 for the chance of the profits which £100 might bring from the South Seas. The most ridiculous joint-stock companies were started in imitation of the great scheme,—one for extracting silver from lead, another for making salt water fresh, a third for importing asses from Spain. The South Sea directors, armed with an Act of Parliament, crushed these rival companies; but amid the smaller crashes their own gigantic bubble burst. The eyes of the nation were opened. All ran to sell the South Sea stock: none would buy. The offices were closed, and thousands became ruined bankrupts.

Walpole, who had all along cried out against the huge gambling transaction, now came forward to save the public credit. His plan was to divide the losses, and thus make the pressure on the nation less. Nine millions of South Sea stock were assigned to the Bank of England, nine more to the East India Company, while the Government gave up their bonus of seven millions. But, though the alarm was lessened, and the loss somewhat equalized, penniless crowds cried for vengeance upon the rulers, who had led them into the snare. Sunderland the Premier, and Aislabie the Chancellor of the Exchequer, resigned office. Many a desolate home, many a broken heart, many a suicide's grave remained to mark the traces of the broken bubble.

Robert Walpole, then made Chancellor of the Exchequer, continued for twenty years to direct the Government. His talent lay in financial politics; and England owes much to his measures for the advancement of her commerce and manufactures.

The remaining years of the reign were marked chiefly by the discovery of a Jacobite plot, for connection with which Atterbury, Bishop of Rochester, was banished for life; and by the opening of an unimportant war with Spain and the Emperor, who had founded a rival East India Company at Ostend.

While travelling in Hanover, the King was seized near Osnabruck with apoplexy, and died next day. His children were George, his successor; and Sophia, the Queen of Prussia. **June 11, 1727 A.D.**

George I. was a thorough German in his character and habits,—heavy, cautious, and reserved. He possessed in no small degree the business qualities of industry and punctuality; but his treatment of his wife cannot be defended, and his government of England was sullied by undue partiality to the Whigs, and a tendency in every case to sacrifice British interests to those of Hanover. He was in face and figure plain and solid-looking.

The most note-worthy points of progress during the reign are the invention of Fahrenheit's thermometer; the introduction of silk-throwing machines by Lombe, who brought the plans from Italy; experiments in vaccination, which were tried at first on criminals; and the earliest casting of types in England.

CONTEMPORARY SOVEREIGNS.

FRANCE.	A.D.
LOUIS XIV.,	died 1715
LOUIS XV.	

SPAIN.	
PHILIP V.,	1724
LOUIS,	1725
PHILIP VI.	

SWEDEN.	
CHARLES XII.,	1718
ULRICA LEONORA.	

RUSSIA.	
PETER (the Great),	1725

PRUSSIA.	A.D.
FREDERIC,	died 1700
FREDERIC WILLIAM.	

TURKEY.
ACHMET III.

EMPEROR.
CHARLES VI.

POPES.	
CLEMENT XI.,	1721
INNOCENT XIII.,	1724
BENEDICT XIII.	

LEADING AUTHORS UNDER GEORGE I.

JOSEPH ADDISON,..........(1672-1719)—a prose writer and poet—famous for his beautiful papers in the 'Spectator'—chief poems, 'Cato,' a tragedy, and 'A Letter from Italy'—was made Secretary of State under Anne.

SIR ISAAC NEWTON,......(1642-1727)—native of Lincolnshire—Professor at Cambridge—discovered the Binomial Theorem, and the universal application of the Law of Gravitation—chief work, his 'Principia,' a Latin treatise on Natural Philosophy—wrote also on Daniel and Revelation.

SIR RICHARD STEELE,...(1676-1729)—an Irishman, who in 1709 started the 'Tatler,' the first regular English periodical—in 1711 began the more famous 'Spectator'—wrote many plays also.

CHAPTER II.

GEORGE II.

Born 1683 A.D.—Began to reign 1727 A.D.—Died 1760 A.D.

Sir Robert Walpole.	'The Forty-five.'	The Seven Years' War.
The Excise Bill.	Battle of Prestonpans.	Conquest of Bengal.
Porteous Riots.	March to Derby.	Fall of Quebec.
Spanish War.	Battle of Culloden.	Death of the King.
The Methodists.	Flight of Charles Edward.	His character.
Retirement of Walpole.	His last days.	Notes.
Maria Theresa.	William Pitt.	

GEORGE II., who, as Prince of Wales, had been, like his mother, jealously exiled from the English Court, now became King. He had reached the ripe age of forty-four, and had long been married to Caroline of Anspach, a woman of sense and virtue. The Whigs, or Court Party—as they were called in contrast to the Tories or Country Party—retained their ascendency.

Sir Robert Walpole for fifteen years of the reign held the office of Prime Minister. He was a man of little learning, rough and boisterous in his manners and his life; but he held his great power with a passionate grasp, and preserved it, not very honestly, indeed, but with consummate tact. Bribery was the secret of his long reign as Premier. To some he gave titles of honour, coronets, ribbons, or stars; to others places of profit or of power; and among the general mass of members of the Commons he scattered gold without stint. Thus he had always at his command a majority of votes in the Houses of Parliament.

A new Charter was granted to the East India Company in 1730, for which they paid the sum of £200,000 into the Royal Exchequer. The most noticeable point, however, in Walpole's career was the Excise Bill. The Customs are duties paid upon certain foreign productions, when landed on our shores. The Excise is a tax levied on articles manufactured at home. To check smuggling, which was now practised openly to an immense extent, Walpole proposed to bring wine and tobacco under the law of Excise. The merchants set up a cry of ruin. This cry was loudly echoed by the Opposition, who imagined

1733 A.D.

that they saw in the measure a scheme by which the Premier meant to create a whole army of excisemen, whose votes, always ready at his beck, would carry the day in every election. When the cautious minister saw the violence of the storm, content to lose his point rather than risk his power, he withdrew the Bill altogether. The Opposition, exulting in their success, strove next session to repeal the Septennial Act; but the attempt failed.

In 1736 all Scotland was agitated by the Porteous Riots. The mob of Edinburgh, enraged at the execution of a smuggler named Wilson, who had roused their admiration by helping his fellow-prisoner Robertson to escape, pelted the hangman and the soldiers. Captain Porteous, commander of the City Guard, fired on the crowd, and several were killed. For this he was sentenced to death; but a reprieve came from London, and the rumour spread that a mail or two would bring him a full pardon. It was resolved that he should not escape. On the night of the 17th of September the jail in which he lay was broken open by a mob; he was brought out, and hanged on a dyer's pole. The Government, enraged at this violence, brought in a Bill to demolish the walls and take away the charter of Edinburgh. So spirited, however, was the resistance of the Scottish members that the measure was abandoned, though not until it had excited among all classes in Scotland a feeling of deep rancour and hostility towards England.

The death of Queen Caroline in 1737 deprived Walpole of a warm friend and supporter. The disasters of the Spanish War in 1739 shook his power past retrieving. Besides the ill-will of the King and the hatred of Frederic, Prince of Wales, he had to contend against a brilliant phalanx of literary men, amongst whom were Thomson, Johnson, Swift, and Pope. A section of discontented Whigs, too, who called themselves Patriots, threw their entire weight into the scale of opposition.

The Spanish War was caused by the cruisers of Spain claiming and using the right to search all British vessels, suspected of smuggling on the coasts of Spanish America. Walpole tried negotiation, but in vain; and war was proclaimed. When he heard the

1739
A.D.

London joy-bells ringing for the declaration of the war, he was heard to mutter, 'They may ring their bells now; they will be wringing their hands before long.' The town of Portobello on the Isthmus of Darien was taken; but disasters soon eclipsed this brief success. A great fleet and army under Admiral Vernon and Lord Wentworth failed in an attack upon Carthagena, chiefly through the disagreement of the leaders. The unhealthy climate swept off the British in hundreds; and there naturally arose great discontent at home. Anson was sent with a squadron to relieve Vernon; but, failing in his object, he sailed into the South Seas, plundered Paita, a port of Chili, and, after three years' cruising, took a Spanish treasure-ship bound for Manilla, and laden with £300,000. On his return to England in 1744 with a solitary ship, the people, dazzled by the wealth he brought, received him with joy.

The Methodists—now numerous and influential, especially in England—separated from the Established Church about this time. The founder of the body was John Wesley. When a student at Oxford, he used to hold meetings for prayer in his college-rooms; and, carrying into the world the same spirit of practical piety, he soon became a celebrated preacher. At a time when it was fashionable to sneer at all religion, he drew to his chapel the most brilliant audiences in the land. He was aided in the good work by Whitefield, a yet more distinguished preacher, whose electric eloquence could then be matched by none. To these two men our country owes much, for they led the van in that revival of religion, of which in the present day we are reaping the harvest.

The difficulties of Walpole became so great, that, finding the Opposition in the majority as the result of a general election, he resigned office, and retired with the title of Earl of Orford to his country seat of Houghton. He was succeeded by the Earl of Granville, who held office but a short time. The Pelhams then took the helm of the State; which, partly by aristocratic influence, and partly by dint of wholesale bribery, they contrived to hold for fifteen years.

1742 A.D.

During their administration occurred a Continental War

(1741-1745). Charles VI. of Austria, dying in 1740, left a will called the Pragmatic Sanction, by which he bequeathed all his dominions to his daughter Maria Theresa. Scarcely had she ascended the throne when the Elector of Bavaria demanded the crown of Hungary, Frederic II. of Prussia seized Silesia, and Louis of France denied her right to any part of her inheritance. The British were alarmed at this union between France and Prussia, which under Frederic the Great was fast rising to be one of the leading powers in Europe; and their chivalry was roused at the thought of a young and beautiful Queen surrounded by greedy and treacherous foes, even while she still wore mourning for her dead father. The States of Hungary gathered round their Queen, and a British army crossed the Channel in her defence. George II., leading the British troops in person,—the last occasion upon which a Sovereign of Britain was under the fire of an enemy,—routed a French army near the village of Dettingen on the Maine. Two years later, at Fontenoy in Belgium, his second son, the Duke of Cumberland, was defeated by Marshal Saxe in almost the only victory won by the armies of Louis XV. In the end the cause of the young Queen triumphed; her husband, Francis Stephen, Grand Duke of Tuscany, was chosen Emperor in 1745; and in the same year the peace of Dresden closed the war. This illustrious lady, amongst the most distinguished of the Austrian Sovereigns, held her throne until her death in 1780.

1743 A.D.

The exiled Stuarts, encouraged by France and Spain, now made a bold push for the throne of Britain. Charles Edward Stuart, the young Pretender, the 'bonnie Prince Charlie' of those stirring Jacobite songs which sprang from the burning heart of a revolted nation, landed near Moidart on the coast of Inverness-shire. He came with only seven officers to conquer a great Empire, but at five-and-twenty hope is strong in the human soul. Many Highland chieftains, of whom the most distinguished was Cameron of Lochiel, hastened to his side; and his standard was raised at Glenfinnan. At the head of 700 wild clansmen, whose hearts he had won by donning the kilt and tartans,

July 25, 1745 A.D.

Aug. 19.

he commenced a southward march. Sir John Cope, the royal leader, had incautiously moved to Inverness, and the road was open. At Perth Charles was proclaimed Regent for his father. Thence he passed through Linlithgow to Edinburgh, winning all hearts by his bright smiles and charming courtesy. His little army had swelled to more than 1000 men. The capital was unguarded except by the dragoons of Colonel Gardiner. The magistrates, indeed, were loyal, and the castle held out for the King, but the citizens gladly opened their gates to the young Stuart, who took up his abode in the palace of Holyrood. Sept. 17, **1745** A.D.

Cope, meanwhile, taking ship at Aberdeen, had landed with his troops at Dunbar, and was marching on Edinburgh from the east. Charles, reinforced by 1000 clansmen, moved out to meet him, and the two armies came face to face at Prestonpans. They lay for a night round their watchfires. Before the dawn of the next morning, Sept. 21. Charles and his clansmen, suddenly crossing a marsh that lay between, made a dash at the English lines in true Highland style, first discharging their pistols, and then rushing on with the claymore. The surprise was complete: the royal troops were cut to pieces. Their artillery, stores, and money-chest fell into the hands of the victors. Among the slain was Colonel Gardiner, distinguished for the piety of his latter days.

If Charles had then pressed on to London, the throne of the Guelphs might have fallen. But his ranks were thin, and six weeks passed before he could muster 5000 men. During these six weeks royal troops poured in from Flanders, and the Duke of Cumberland marshalled an army to defend the throne. The young Pretender spared no pains to please the Scottish people. Night after night the ball-rooms of Holyrood were filled with brilliant crowds. All the ladies of Edinburgh were in love with the handsome youth, whose graceful words and kind looks made many a fair cheek blush with pleasure.

Entering England by the western Border, he took Carlisle in three days. But neither there nor in Manchester did the English Jacobites, as he had expected, flock around his banner. On the 4th of December he Nov. 17.

reached Derby; but further he did not go. Bickerings and open quarrels among the Highland chiefs had hampered every movement of the army; but now they united in forcing the Pretender to retreat. He yielded, sorely against his will, and the backward march began.

Dec. 6, 1745 A.D.

With dejected hearts and a hopeless leader the army reached the Highlands, followed by the Duke of Cumberland. A slight success at Falkirk, where he defeated General Hawley, roused the drooping heart of Charles for a time; but, after three months of inaction among the Grampians, he was finally routed by Cumberland on Culloden Moor, nine miles from Inverness. About one in the day the royal guns opened on the rebel ranks. The right wing of the Highlanders answered with a gallant charge, but were met by a storm of grape and musket-shot so terrible that few reached the line of English bayonets. On the left the Macdonalds, who stood gloomily nursing their anger at being deprived of the post of honour on the right, were broken and cut down by scores. In less than an hour the battle was fought and won.

April 16, 1746 A.D.

Charles fled to the mountains. A reward of £30,000 was offered for his head; but none was tempted, even by so great a sum, to betray his hiding-place. For five months he wandered among the Grampians and the Hebrides, often suffering from want, always hunted by his foes; but followed even in his misery by a devoted few, among whom was the fair and courageous Flora Macdonald. And, at length, almost at the very spot where, fourteen months before, fresh from the most brilliant Court in Europe, he had leapt on to the heathery shore with the elastic step of hope, he crept into a hired French boat, a wretched spectre, pale and haggard, with bloodshot eyes and ragged clothes. Though chased by two English cruisers, he landed safely at Morlaix in Bretagne. About eighty suffered death for their devotion to his cause, among whom were the Scottish Lords Kilmarnock and Balmerino. The clansmen were forbidden to wear the Highland dress, the chieftains were stripped of nearly all their ancient power, and the appointment of the sheriffs—long a hereditary office—was vested in the Crown.

Sept. 29.

Charles Edward spent his latter days at Rome, under the title of Duke of Albany. Though the Jacobites long continued the custom of passing their glasses over the water-decanter, as they drank to the 'King over the water,' the Forty-five was the last effort of the exiled family to regain the British throne. The gallant young soldier, of whom so much has been said and sung, sank in later life into a broken-down drunkard. He died of apoplexy in 1788: and nineteen years later died his brother Henry, Cardinal of York, the last male heir of the Stuart line. On a monument by Canova, in St. Peter's at Rome, may still be read three empty titles, not found in the roll of British Kings—James III., Charles III., Henry IX. Beneath the marble the bones of Charles Edward and his brother have long since mouldered into dust.

The war, still lingering on the Continent, was brought to a close by the treaty of Aix-la-Chapelle, by which the rival nations agreed to restore their conquests. When the army was disbanded, a great number of discharged soldiers emigrated to Nova Scotia, where they built the city of Halifax. **1748** A.D.

During these events William Pitt, 'the Great Commoner,' had been fast rising to the head of affairs. His grandfather was that Governor of Madras who had brought from India the celebrated Pitt diamond, still sparkling on the crown of France. William was educated at Oxford, and for a short time served as a cornet in the Life Guards Blue. But, entering the House of Commons in 1735 as member for Old Sarum, he soon became so troublesome to the Ministry that Walpole dismissed him from the army. Thenceforward he devoted himself to politics. He gained the favour of the Prince of Wales, and under the Pelhams became Paymaster of the Forces. As a statesman, he was distinguished for his hatred of bribery and his honest disbursement of the public money. He was a complete master of sarcasm; and often in a few scorching words, delivered with thundering voice and rapid gesture and flashing eye, he withered up the arguments of some unhappy member who had ventured to confront him. He was tormented from his earliest manhood by the gout, and some of his finest speeches were delivered as he leant on crutches with limbs cased in flannel.

The Seven Years' War opened under the administration of the Duke of Newcastle. It was excited by the ambition of Frederic the Great, who still held Silesia. Maria Theresa obtained the aid of France, Russia, and Poland; while Britain formed an alliance with Prussia. Out of the great Seven Years' War grew a Colonial War between Great Britain and France. The boundary lines of their colonies were the subject of dispute. India and America were the theatres of the strife.

1756 A.D.

In the autumn of 1756 Pitt became Secretary of State and leader of the Commons. During the five months of his ministry, Admiral Byng was tried and shot for failing to retake the island of Minorca, which had been seized by the French. Pitt spoke out manfully for the Admiral, but could not save him. When 'the Great Commoner,' who was no favourite with the King, was dismissed, so great a cry of indignation arose that he was at once restored to office; and then began that succession of victories by which Britain became pre-eminent in both hemispheres.

On the peninsula of Hindostan there were trading colonies of British, French, Dutch, and Portuguese. Of these the British settlements were the chief. Dupleix, the Governor of Pondicherry, the central station of the French, formed the gigantic scheme of conquering all India, and resolutely set himself, with the aid of the native princes, to uproot the British settlements. Holding Madras, which had been lately captured by the French, he soon overran the whole Carnatic. But the tide of conquest was turned by Clive, who, entering the Company's service at first as a clerk, had joined the army as an ensign in 1746, and soon distinguished himself by the capture of Arcot. By the seizure of Fort St. David, near Madras, he obtained the complete command of the Carnatic. The conquest of Bengal was his most remarkable achievement. It was Surajah Dowlah, Viceroy of Bengal, who shut up 146 British prisoners for a whole night in the Black Hole of Calcutta,—a den twenty feet by fourteen; from which only 23 came out alive on the next morning. This cruelty was avenged by Clive, who utterly overthrew the Viceroy in the great battle of Plassey, and thus gained for Britain the large and fertile province of Bengal, watered by the noble Ganges and studded with a thousand wealthy cities. **1757 A.D.**

In North America the French held Canada while the British settlers possessed the coast of that territory now called the United States. The natural boundary between the settlements was formed by the St. Lawrence and its Lakes. But the French insisted on building a chain of forts from the Lakes to the Mississippi, thus to shut out the British from the fur-trade with Indian tribes. The New England colonists, naturally resenting this injustice, made several attacks on the French forts, but with little success. However, under the able direction of Pitt, a remarkable change took place. Fort after fort fell, or was abandoned, until the capture of Quebec, before which General Wolfe was mortally wounded, left the British masters of Canada. **Sept. 1759 A.D.**

The year 1759 was also distinguished by a victory over the French at Minden in Germany; and by the total destruction of the Brest fleet by Admiral Hawke, who gained a splendid victory amid the darkness of a stormy night off the rocky shore of Bretagne.

On the morning of the 25th of October 1760 George II. died suddenly of heart-disease. He had in all eight children. His eldest son, Frederic, Prince of Wales, who had married in 1736 Augusta of Saxe-Gotha, was killed in 1751, at the age of forty-four, by the stroke of a cricket-ball, and left nine children. George III. was the eldest son of this prince.

The second George was very like his father in his temper and his attachments. He was fond of the Whigs; and, while he was always niggardly towards his kingdom, he spared neither British blood nor British gold in securing and enlarging his Electorate of Hanover. Science, art, and literature were left by him to thrive as best they could; and he was more than once heard to growl in his German accent, that he saw no good in 'bainting and boetry.' He was of a fair complexion, and of a small but well-shaped figure.

A remarkable change of this reign was the adoption of the Gregorian, or New Style of reckoning time. The time-keeping of the nation had gone, as we say of a clock, too fast; and, to set it right, eleven days were struck out of the year 1752, the 3d of September being reckoned as the 14th of September. Pope Gregory had made the change in Italy in 1582. Hence in our almanacs we have Hallow-eve and Old Hallow-eve, Christmas-day and old Christmas-day. The Russians still reckon time by the Old Style.

In 1731 the 'Gentleman's Magazine' was started by Edward Cave, a bookseller; in 1753 the British Museum was founded; and in 1758 the first canal was made in England.

From the days of Queen Anne until after the accession of George III., the gentlemen wore coats of silk or velvet with broad stiffened skirts, long waistcoats with flaps reaching over the leg half way to the knee, three-cornered cocked hats, knee-breeches, and high-heeled shoes with buckles sometimes sparkling with diamonds, but oftener with stones of paste. Both sexes wore powder in their hair. The most remarkable part of the ladies' costume was the hoop, an article of dress which needs no description in our day. A curious custom was that of spotting the face over with patches of black plaster: in the 'Citizen of the World,' Goldsmith's Chinaman speaks of sending to his friend a map of an English face, patched according to the fashion. The Sedan-chair was the favourite mode of conveyance, and linkboys went before with lighted torches to show the way along the streets, which were lighted only by the feeble glimmer of a few oil lamps. A row of stakes, fixed far from one another, formed the only division between the carriage-road and the foot-way; and in winter every passing coach splashed the black liquid mud far and wide. Every gentleman wore a sword, and duels were of daily occurrence. Gaming was the great vice of the age. Gentlemen gambled in their clubs, ladies in their drawing-rooms; and it was no uncommon thing to lose or win £10,000 in a night at cards or dice. People of fashion dined at three or four, and their evening began at seven. Besides card-drums and balls, there were Assembly Rooms at Ranelagh and Vauxhall, where they met to promenade and dance minuets to the music of a band.

CONTEMPORARY SOVEREIGNS.

FRANCE.	A.D.	PRUSSIA.	A.D.
LOUIS XV.		FREDERIC WILLIAM, I. d.	1740
		FREDERIC II., (the Great).	

SPAIN.		TURKEY.	
PHILIP VI.,	died 1746	ACHMET III.,	1730
FERDINAND VI.,	1759	MOHAMMED V.,	1757
CHARLES III.		ACHMET IV.	

		EMPERORS.	
SWEDEN.		CHARLES VI.,	1740
ULRICA LEONORA,	1751	CHARLES VII.,	1745
ADOLPHUS FREDERIC.		FRANCIS I. and MARIA THERESA.	

RUSSIA.		POPES.	
CATHERINE I.,	1727	BENEDICT XIII.,	1730
PETER II.,	1730	CLEMENT XII.,	1740
IVAN VI.,	1741	BENEDICT XIV.,	1758
ELIZABETH.		CLEMENT XIII.	

LEADING AUTHORS UNDER GEORGE II.

DANIEL DEFOE,..............(1661-1731)—originally a London hosier—a newspaper writer—wrote also prose fiction—chief work, 'Robinson Crusoe,' published in 1719.

ALEXANDER POPE,...........(1688-1744)—the son of a London linen-draper—wrote good verses at twelve—chief works, 'The Rape of the Lock,' a short mock-heroic poem; and a translation of Homer into English verse—lived chiefly at Twickenham on the Thames—deformed, sickly, and peevish.

JONATHAN SWIFT,............(1667-1745)—Dean of St. Patrick's, Dublin—an eminent political writer—chief work, 'Gulliver's Travels'—wrote verses also—very sarcastic—died mad.

JAMES THOMSON,..............(1700-1748)—a poet of Roxburghshire—chief works, 'The Seasons,' in blank verse; and the 'Castle of Indolence,' in the Spenserian stanza—wrote tragedies also.

JOSEPH BUTLER,.................(1692-1752)—born in Berkshire—Bishop of Durham—chief work, 'The Analogy of Religion to Nature,' still a standard work.

ALLAN RAMSAY,.................(1686-1758)—a native of Lanarkshire—chief work, 'The Gentle Shepherd,' a pastoral drama.

LEADING ARTIST.

SIR JAMES THORNHILL,...(1676-1732)—born at Weymouth—the painter of the Dome of St. Paul's and some cartoons in Hampton Court—State-painter to Anne and George I

CHAPTER III.

GEORGE III.

Born 1738 A.D.—Began to reign 1760 A.D.—Died 1820 A.D.

The Family Compact.	The Congress.	Surrender of Cornwallis.
The Peace of Paris.	Bunker's-hill.	The Thirteen States.
John Wilkes.	Invasion of Canada.	Siege of Gibraltar.
The Stamp Act.	The Fourth of July.	Gordon Riots.
Other Taxes on America.	Brandywine River.	Voyages of Cook.
	Surrender of Burgoyne.	Trial of Hastings.
Parliamentary Reports.	Desertion of Arnold.	Indian Conquests.

GEORGE III. ascended a glorious throne. Through the energy and foresight of the Great Commoner Britain had become the first nation in the world.

The Sovereigns of France and Spain, both of the Bourbon line, leagued themselves against Britain by the Family Compact. Pitt knew of this secret treaty, and urged immediate war with Spain. His plans being over-ruled on the ground of an exhausted Treasury, he resigned office in disgust, receiving as rewards of his public service a pension of £3000 a year, and the title of Baroness for his wife. The Earl of Bute, once tutor to the King, became Premier. As Pitt had foretold, Spain declared war. But Spain lost Havannah and Manilla; France was stripped of her finest West Indian islands; and both soon sought for peace. A treaty was signed at Paris, and in the same year the Seven Years' War was closed by the peace of Hubertsburg. **1763 A.D.**

Bute soon gave place to the Hon. George Grenville, whose ministry is remarkable for the prosecution of John Wilkes.

Wilkes, the member for Aylesbury, was the editor of a weekly paper called 'The North Briton.' In No. 45 of this publication he charged the King with uttering a lie in a speech from the throne. Arrested on a general warrant, he was thrown into the Tower. But there was great difficulty about his trial. The Judges declared that no member of Parliament could be imprisoned except for treason, felony, or breach of the peace, and that general warrants, in which no name was given, were illegal. Notwithstanding this, he was found guilty of libel, and was outlawed.

Returning from France in 1768, he was elected for Middlesex by a large majority. But the House of Commons refused to admit him; and, though his sentence of outlawry was reversed, he was sent to prison for two years. There were great riots in his favour: pictures and busts of him were sold everywhere. Four times did the men of Middlesex return him to Parliament, and as often did the House of Commons reject him, accepting in his stead his rival, Colonel Luttrell. But in the end he triumphed, was allowed to take his seat, and became Lord Mayor of London. It was during these stirring times that the famous 'Letters of Junius,' directed chiefly against the Duke of Grafton, appeared in the newspapers.

Meanwhile events had occurred which led to the great American War. Grenville, desirous to meet the cost of the last war, proposed to tax certain papers and parchments used in America; and the Stamp Act was therefore passed. The colonists, most of whom were descendants of those old Puritans who had beheaded Charles I. and reared the Commonwealth, firmly replied, that, since they had no share in the government of the Empire, no members in the British Parliament, they would pay no taxes to Britain and buy no stamped paper.

1765 A.D.

Grenville at once resigned, and, under the brief ministry of the Marquis of Rockingham, the Stamp Act was repealed; but the right to tax the Colonies was still maintained. The Duke of Grafton, and Pitt, now Earl of Chatham, were next called to office; and, in spite of the warnings of the great statesman, new taxes—on tea, lead, glass, paper, and painters' colours—were laid on the Colonies, whose discontent grew hourly greater. In 1768 Chatham gave up the Privy Seal, for his health was failing, and he missed, amid the calm monotony of the Lords, that stirring excitement of debate in which his genius gave forth its finest flashes. Two years later, the Duke of Grafton gave place to Lord North, a Tory Premier, under whom chiefly the American War was conducted.

1770 A.D.

OUTBREAK OF THE AMERICAN WAR.

The public mind was now stirred by a strife between Parliament and the London printers, about the right to publish the debates in the Houses. Woodfall, who had printed the 'Letters of Junius,' took a lead in demanding the right; and, by the support of the magistrates, the printers gained their point. The practice then adopted was, not to report in short-hand as at present, but to take brief notes, and then write out the speeches from memory.

Lord North still sent out taxed tea to America; but the resistance of the States, among which Massachusetts was foremost, yielded not a jot. Some twenty daring spirits, dressed and painted like Indians, boarded the ships which lay in Boston Harbour, and emptied the tea-chests into the sea. The British Government then shut up the port of Boston, and removed the Custom-house to Salem. Meanwhile in London the famous Dr. Franklin, once a printer's boy, strove vainly to bring about a reconciliation.

All the States except Georgia, meeting in a Great Congress at Philadelphia, sent forward an address to the King, in which they asked that the oppressive taxes should be removed. The petition was slighted; but wise men shook their heads. Chatham told the Lords that it was folly to force the taxes in the face of a Continent in arms. Edmund Burke bade the Commons beware lest they severed those ties of similar privilege and kindred blood, which, light as air, though strong as iron, bound the Colonies to the mother-land. The Ministers were deaf to these eloquent warnings, and blind to the gathering storm. British soldiers continued to occupy Boston. **1774 A.D.**

Then, after ten years of wordy strife, actual war began. It continued during eight campaigns.

The first outbreak was at Lexington, where a few American riflemen attacked a detachment of British soldiers, who were marching to seize some warlike stores. Two months later, the armies met in battle on Bunker's-hill,—a height overlooking Boston harbour. It was a drawn battle; but it taught the British troops that the Colonists were not to be despised. George Washington then took the chief com- **April 19, 1775 A.D.** **June 17.**

mand of the American army, whose ranks were filled with raw militia-men and leather-clad hunters; stout and brave, no doubt, and capital shots with the rifle, but undrilled and badly equipped, with few tents, scanty stores, and little money. At Boston, as head-quarters, lay the British army, under General Gage, who was succeeded in October by General Howe. The second remarkable event of this campaign was the fruitless invasion of Canada by the American leaders, Montgomery and Arnold. Montreal fell before General Montgomery. Colonel Arnold, marching through the wild backwoods of Maine, joined him before Quebec. But they were beaten back from that fortress, and Montgomery was slain. Meanwhile 17,000 Hessian troops had been called from Germany to aid the British arms. The royal forces in America now numbered 55,000 men.

1776
A.D.

July 4.

Early in the second campaign, Howe was compelled, by the cannon of the Americans, to evacuate Boston and to sail for Halifax; and then was issued, by the Congress at Philadelphia, that famous and eloquent document called 'The Declaration of Independence.' But the British were well compensated for the disasters of March by the triumphs of August, when General Howe, reinforced by his brother, seized Long Island, drove Washington from New York, and planted the British flag on its batteries.

1777
A.D.

At the opening of the third campaign, aid in men and money came from France to the Americans. Of the French officers, the most distinguished was the young Marquis de La Fayette. A victory at the Brandywine River and the capture of Philadelphia raised hopes in Britain that the subdual of the Colonies was not far distant. But a great humiliation changed all these hopes into fears. General Burgoyne, marching from Canada, was so hemmed in by the American troops at Saratoga, that he was forced to surrender with all his brass cannon, muskets, and military stores. Thenceforward, through five campaigns America had decidedly the best of the war.

During the winter the soldiers of Washington were shoeless and starving in Valley Forge near Philadelphia; but, inspired by the noble patience of their leader, they bore bravely on. The fourth campaign did not open till June. Howe had been succeeded meanwhile by Sir Henry Clinton, who soon abandoned the city of Philadelphia, in which the British army had passed the winter. It was during this year that the venerable Chatham, while thundering in spite of age and illness against the American War, fell in a fit on the floor of the House of Lords, and was carried to a bed whence he never rose. **1778 A.D.**

No event of note marked the fifth campaign, which was conducted chiefly in the southern States.

In the sixth, Sir Henry Clinton took Charleston. Arnold, commander of a fort on the Hudson River, deserted, and became a General in the British service. Major André, who had arranged the affair, being seized by the American sentinels, was hanged as a spy by Washington, in spite of many entreaties. **1780 A.D.**

During the seventh campaign occurred a second great disaster of the British arms. Lord Cornwallis, the conqueror of Gates and La Fayette, was, by the skilful movements of Washington, shut up in Yorktown and compelled to surrender with 7000 men. This was the decisive blow; and, although the war lingered through another campaign, the American Colonies were now completely severed from the British Empire. The independence of the Thirteen United States was after some time formally acknowledged by treaty; and they became a Republic, governed by an elected President. **1781 A.D.**

1783 A.D.

During the latter years of the American War Britain was engaged in a strife nearer home, which taxed her strength to the utmost. France, Spain, and Holland were in arms against her. Russia, Sweden, and Denmark had formed an *Armed Neutrality;* which means, in plain English, that they were ready to pounce upon her when they saw an opportunity fit and safe. But, even against such fearful odds, she triumphed. The chief event of the war was the unsuccessful siege of Gibraltar for three years by the French and Spaniards, (1779-1782.)

In 1780 London was convulsed by the Gordon riots. Two

years earlier some heavy penal laws against Romanists had been repealed. In June 1780 Lord George Gordon, escorted by an immense mob, went to the House of Commons to present a petition against the removal of these laws. The petition was rejected, and a riot began. Romanist chapels were burned. Newgate and other jails were stormed, and the prisoners set free. For a week the mob held London streets, nor did they yield to the sabres and bullets of the soldiers until more than 400 had been killed. Lord George was sent to the Tower, and tried; but he was acquitted. It is said that he afterwards became a Jew.

While civil war, as it may be called, was snapping the ties between Britain and the New England States, the discoveries of Captain James Cook were adding largely to the British Empire in another quarter of the globe. This celebrated sailor, whom we may well call the founder of our great Australian Colonies, was born in Yorkshire in 1728. Between the years 1767 and 1779 he made three voyages round the world, exploring especially the South Seas and the coast of Australia. He was killed in 1779 at Owhyhee, by the spear of a treacherous native.

In 1783 William Pitt the younger, son of the Earl of Chatham, became, at the age of twenty-three, Chancellor of the Exchequer and Prime Minister. There had never been so young a Premier, and few have been so good. He had been already three years in Parliament.

Our Indian Empire was rapidly enlarging. The capture of Pondicherry in 1761 had ruined the French cause in Hindostan. Warren Hastings, who in 1750 had left England, at the age of seventeen, as a clerk in the Company's service, was in 1773 appointed the first Governor-General of India. His chief victories were over the Mahrattas of Central India, and the Mohammedan Rajahs of Mysore—Hyder Ali and his son Tippoo Saib. But the plunder of Benares, a sacred Hindoo city on the Ganges, and the spoliation of the Princesses of Oude, that he might have money to carry on these wars, are dark stains on his administration, and excited so much indignation in England, that on his return he was impeached before the Lords for cruelty and oppression in India.

The trial took place in Westminster Hall. Edmund Burke led the impeachment in a speech, that has seldom been surpassed for stately eloquence. Charles James Fox and Richard Brinsley Sheridan followed on the same side. The culprit was defended by three lawyers, who afterwards worthily wore the ermine of the Bench. For seven years the trial went on at intervals, and ended in the acquittal of Hastings, whom, however, it left nearly penniless. His last days were spent at Daylesford—an old family seat—in the enjoyment of a pension of £4000 from the East India Company.

Feb. 13, **1788** A.D.

Lord Cornwallis, who was made Governor-General in 1786, stripped Tippoo of half his dominions; and under the Marquis of Wellesley in 1799 Seringapatam was taken, Tippoo Saib slain, and the throne of Hyder Ali finally overturned. Four years later, the Mahrattas, who had seized Delhi, were routed on the banks of the Jumna by General Lake, and the Great Mogul became a pensioner of the Company.

CHAPTER IV.

GEORGE III.—(CONTINUED.)

The French Revolution.	Peninsular War.	Escape of Napoleon.
Rise of Napoleon I.	Corunna.	Plans of the Allies.
Mutiny at the Nore.	Walcheren Expedition.	Waterloo.
Irish Rebellion.	The Regency.	The National Debt.
The Nile.	Napoleon in Russia.	Algiers Bombarded.
Union of Ireland.	Vittoria.	Death of the King.
Trafalgar.	War with United States.	Notes.

THE French Revolution, which began in 1789 and ended in 1795, was the greatest event of the eighteenth century. It was excited chiefly by three causes,—the infidel writings of Voltaire and Rousseau, the oppression of the lower orders by insolent nobles, and the want of money consequent on the reckless extravagance of the French Court. During its progress the ancient Bourbon monarchy was overturned; the King and the Queen—Louis XVI. and Marie Antoinette—were guillotined; the Christian faith was trampled under foot, and a goddess of Reason set up for worship; and all France was drenched in blood. The storm spread far and wide over Continental Europe, and beat strongly, though harmlessly, against our island-shores.

The attack of the French mobs upon hereditary monarchy alarmed all the great neighbouring thrones, and, **1793 A.D.** when the blood of Louis stained the scaffold, war was declared against the new French Republic by Britain, Holland, Spain, Austria, Prussia, and five smaller states. The strife, then kindled, continued with little interruption for twenty-two years.

It was soon manifest that the energies of France had been braced rather than exhausted by the hurricane of Revolution. Toulon, a strong fortress of the Mediterranean shore, having surrendered to a British fleet, was retaken by the cannon of the Republic, directed chiefly by a little Corsican officer of artillery called Napoleon Bonaparte, who had been much distinguished for mathematics in the military schools.

Napoleon became conspicuous in France from the day on

which he scattered the National Guard with a volley of grape-shot before the Palace of the Tuileries, and thus saved the French Directory. That day was the 4th of October 1795. In the following year he married Josephine Beauharnois, by whose influence he gained the command of the French army in Italy; and there, in a single campaign, by a series of most brilliant victories, he broke the power of Austria and her Allies.

In the British Parliament Pitt was earnestly urging the prosecution of the war at all risks. Fox, his great opponent, cried eloquently for peace, and pointed to the National Debt, which was now more than four hundred millions.

In 1797 Spain declared war against Britain. Holland had already deserted her alliance. She stood alone among the Powers of Europe. It was a time of great gloom and distress; which grew deeper when the Bank of England stopped cash payments, and a dangerous mutiny broke out in the royal navy. The seamen demanded more pay. At Spithead they were easily pacified; but at the Nore the mutineers seized the ships, and anchored them across the Thames, in order to shut up the mouth of the river. The men did not return to their duty until the ringleaders were arrested and hanged. But two great naval victories relieved the gloom of the year. In February off Cape St. Vincent Admiral Jervis and Commodore Nelson, with twenty-one sail, defeated thirty-two Spanish ships of war. In October the ships of Holland were scattered by Admiral Duncan off the Dutch village of Camperdown.

The following year was noted for the Irish rebellion, and Napoleon's invasion of Egypt.

In no part of Europe did the evil example of the French Revolution bear more bitter fruit than in Ireland. In 1780 the Volunteers, influenced by the success of the American Colonists, banded themselves together to secure the reform of Parliament, and the emancipation of the Irish Romanists from penal laws. They were disbanded by the skilful policy of the Government. In 1791 at Belfast another society, called 'The United Irishmen,' was formed under the same pretence, but with the real purpose of separating Ireland from the British Empire. A secret correspondence was held with France; and, when all seemed ready, a day was fixed for the outbreak of rebellion. But the Government, receiving timely notice of the plot, seized the leaders, among whom was Lord Edward Fitzgerald. Then an aimless and unsuccessful rising took place. In Antrim and Down it was slightly felt; but it raged cruelly and fiercely for about two months in Wicklow and Wexford. In the battle of Vinegar-hill near Enniscorthy in the latter county, General Lake routed the great mass of the rebel army. When all was over, 900 French troops, under Humbert, landed at Killala Bay in Mayo, and marched inland. In less than a month, however, they were forced to surrender at Carrick-on-Shannon.

<small>1798 A.D.</small>

Napoleon spent two campaigns in Egypt and Syria, engaged in a fruitless attempt to open a path to the conquest of India. Sailing from Toulon with a great fleet and army, he took Malta on his way, and landed at Alexandria. Then pressing on to Cairo, he defeated the Mamelukes of Egypt in the battle of the Pyramids. But he had been followed by Admiral Nelson, who annihilated his fleet as it lay in the Bay of Aboukir. The action began at sun-set, and lasted until day-break. Nelson was severely wounded in the head by a splinter of iron. The French flag-ship, Orient, blew up during the battle, with the Admiral and his crew of 1000 men. Never was a naval victory more complete. Of thirteen French men-of-war, nine were taken and two burned; and of four frigates two escaped. By this brilliant victory the army of Napoleon was imprisoned amid the sands of Egypt. But, never inactive, he led his soldiers, early in 1799, across the desert between Egypt and Palestine, took the town of Jaffa by storm, and laid siege to Acre. Thence he was repulsed by British and Turkish troops under Sir Sidney Smith. Alarming news from France caused him to leave his soldiers in Egypt, and hurry to his adopted country. The army, thus abandoned, lost spirit, and was finally routed in 1800 by Sir Ralph Abercromby, who received a mortal wound during the action.

<small>Aug. 1, 1798 A.D.</small>

The rebellion of 1798 showed the necessity of binding Ireland more closely to the Empire. After many debates and much opposition in Ireland, the Union of the Parliaments was accomplished; from which already, even in half a century, Ireland has reaped numberless blessings. Henceforward the people of Ireland were represented in the Imperial Parliament by thirty-two Lords and one hundred Commoners; their traders enjoyed many new and valuable commercial privileges; while the taxes were far less heavy than those paid in Great Britain. For some time after the Union there was considerable discontent in Ireland; and a rising, suppressed, however, in a single night, took place in the streets of Dublin in 1803. The talented but misguided Robert Emmet, who led this attempt at insurrection, suffered death for the crime. Pitt thought that the Union would be more complete and lasting, if the Romanists were emancipated from penal laws. The King did not agree with him on this point. He therefore resigned, and was succeeded by Henry Addington. *Jan. 1, 1801 A.D.*

Russia, under the Czar Paul, now menaced Britain. The Armed Neutrality of the Northern States was revived. But Admiral Nelson, entering the Sound, totally destroyed the Danish fleet at Copenhagen in four hours. A few days earlier the Czar Paul was murdered, and his son Alexander soon made peace with Britain. The Powers of Europe then signed the Treaty of Amiens. But this peace was a mere empty form, and in little more than a year the war was renewed. *Mar. 25, 1802 A.D.*

In 1804 Pitt again became Prime Minister. Napoleon, elected First Consul in 1802, was then Emperor of the French. Surrounding his throne with eighteen Marshals, veterans in war and devoted to his cause, he bent his great genius to the conquest of Europe. Never was the balance of power so seriously threatened, and never was a grasping despot more resolutely met or more utterly overthrown.

The invasion of Britain was a part of the daring scheme, and a flotilla of gun-boats lay at Boulogne, ready to pour a French army on the shores of England; but the watchfulness of Nelson and the terror of his name saved our island from invasion. The army of the French Emperor was then turned to the Danube, on the banks of which Austria was marshalling her legions to oppose his grasping ambition.

At first Spain sided with Napoleon; but Lord Nelson inflicted upon the combined fleets a most decisive defeat off Cape Trafalgar, capturing nineteen ships out of thirty-three.

Oct. 21, 1805 A.D. During the action Nelson was struck by a rifle bullet from the enemy's rigging, as he stood on the quarter-deck of the Victory, and died before the day was past. He was borne to his last resting-place in St. Paul's Cathedral with princely honours amid the tears of a mourning nation.

On the 2d of December 1805 Napoleon crushed the power of Austria in the great battle of Austerlitz; on the 14th of October 1806 Prussia was humbled in one day on the field of Jena. All Europe then lay at his feet except Russia and Britain—the one strong in her snowy steppes and her thick forests of pine; the other safe within her island shores, and securely guarded by her 'wooden walls.'

In 1806 died Pitt and Fox, within a few months of each other, both worked to death by the toils of statesmanship. Pitt was only forty-two; Fox had reached the age of fifty-eight.

Napoleon well knew that in commerce chiefly lay the strength of the British—'that nation of shopkeepers,' as he contemptuously called them. From Berlin he issued Decrees, ordering that the British Islands should be strictly blockaded, and that all the ports of Europe should be shut against British vessels. The British Ministry, in return, decreed that no neutral power should trade with France or her allies. The fleet of Denmark, a neutral state, was then seized by Britain,—an act that can hardly be defended.

Already Napoleon had begun to fill the thrones of Europe with his kinsmen. His brother Louis was King of Holland; his brother-in-law, Murat, sat on the throne of Naples. He now sought to make his brother Joseph King of Spain; and from this act of aggression sprang the Peninsular War, which gave the first decided check to the march of his ambition.

The Spaniards rose in arms, and called upon Britain for help. Sir Arthur Wellesley, already distinguished in Indian wars, was sent to their aid with 10,000 men. Landing at Mondego Bay in Portugal, he defeated Marshal Junot at Vimiera, on the 21st of August.

1808 A.D.

But, through jealousy at home, he was recalled. His successor, Sir Hew Dalrymple, made a treaty called the Convention of Cintra, by which the French were allowed to evacuate Portugal with all their arms and warlike stores. This foolish lenience cost Sir Hew his command, and Sir John Moore took his place. Deceived by promises of aid which the Spanish Junta could not fulfil, Moore led his army into the heart of Leon; but there he received the alarming news that, notwithstanding the gallant defence of Saragossa by the Spaniards, Napoleon was master of Madrid. There was no course open to the British leader but a retreat towards the shore of Galicia. The sufferings of the army during that backward march were past description. It was mid-winter, food was scarcely to be had, and Soult pressed constantly on their rear.

When the British army, famished and rag-clad, reached Corunna, their ships had not yet arrived, and Soult was close upon them. Facing round, they moved to meet him, and won a brilliant and decided victory. Moore, killed by a cannon-ball towards the close of the action, was laid in a soldier's grave on the ramparts of Corunna. Sir Arthur Wellesley then again took the command of the army. Invading Spain, he won a great battle at Talavera on the banks of the Tagus. For this victory he was created Viscount Wellington. But the approaches to Madrid being covered by three French armies, under Soult, Ney, and Mortier, he was then obliged to fall back upon the frontiers of Portugal. Austria during this year made a desperate effort to retrieve the glory of her arms; but on the field of Wagram her power was again shattered by Napoleon, and the eagles of France were borne in triumph into Vienna. George III. having reached the fiftieth year of his reign, the rare event was celebrated in October by a national jubilee. To aid Austria in her struggle against Napoleon, the ill-fated Walcheren expedition was sent to the coast of the Netherlands. One hundred thousand men were placed under the command of the Earl of Chatham, elder brother of Pitt. The great object of the movement was to seize the French batteries on the Scheldt; but in the marshy island of Walcheren disease

Jan. 16, 1809 A.D.

July 28.

swept off the troops in thousands, and only a wreck of the splendid force returned to Britain in December.

Portugal was the scene of the next Peninsular campaign. The armies of France were concentrated upon that **1810** country for the purpose of driving the British to **A.D.** their ships; but in the battle of Busaco Wellington repulsed Massena with heavy loss. Then, retreating to the heights of Torres Vedras, some distance north of Lisbon, he took up a position from which no efforts of the French Marshals could dislodge him. The war in Spain was carried on chiefly by irregular troops called Guerillas.

It was during this year that Napoleon, having divorced Josephine, married Maria Louisa of Austria. An important constitutional question was discussed in the British Parliament. The King's mind, long tottering, gave way; blindness, too, fell upon him. The appointment of a Regent became necessary, and in December it was resolved that the Prince of Wales should rule as Prince Regent, with power little less than royal. On the 5th of February 1811 the Regency began.

1811 Three important victories marked the fourth **A.D.** campaign in the Peninsula. Graham defeated Marshal Victor at Barossa. Massena was routed by the British at Fuentes d'Onoro. More glorious still was the victory of Albuera, where Soult, marching to relieve the frontier fortress of Badajoz, besieged by Beresford, was repulsed with great slaughter. The long war had now begun to tell heavily on the commerce of Britain, and there were many bankruptcies. In the East, Batavia, the capital of the Dutch colonies in Java, surrendered to a British force.

Holding Portugal as a base of operations, on which he could at any time fall back, Wellington invaded **1812** Spain for the third time. Cuidad Rodrigo and **A.D.** Badajoz, great forts which guarded the western frontier of Spain, soon fell before him. The defeat July 22. of Marmont at Salamanca opened the way to Madrid, into which the victor led his troops on the 12th of August amid the rejoicings of all Spain. But the approach of two French armies, marching in hot haste from the south and the east, forced him to retreat upon Portugal.

In the spring of this year the British Premier, Mr. Perceval, was shot in the lobby of the House of Commons by a merchant named Bellingham, whose business had been ruined by the war.

Meanwhile the Empire of Napoleon had received a heavy blow in the defeat of his Russian campaign. With an army of nearly half a million he had penetrated the vast territory of the Czars to its very heart. But the flames of Moscow drove him back; and in all history there is nothing more appalling than the story of his retreat. When the winter snow melted, the bones of 400,000 men lay white from Moscow to the Niemen.

Step by step the French eagles were driven across the Pyrenees. The decisive battle was fought at Vittoria in Biscay. The capture of St. Sebastian and Pampeluna speedily followed; and the victorious Wellington, crossing the Bidassoa into France, scattered the remnant of Soult's army on the 14th of April 1814, in the battle of Toulouse. Ten days earlier, Napoleon, routed in the great battle of Leipsic, and followed even into Paris by a victorious host of Russians, Swedes, Germans, Austrians, and Prussians, had abdicated the throne of France. The Bourbons returned to Paris and Madrid; on the 30th of May 1814 the first Peace of Paris was signed; while the fallen Emperor retired to the island of Elba.

June 21, **1813** A.D.

During these mighty changes Britain had been at war with the United States of America. The British claimed the right of searching American vessels for seamen to serve in the Royal Navy; the Americans resisted; and hence the war arose. It lasted for nearly three years (1812-1814). The Americans made an unsuccessful attack on Canada. British soldiers burned the public buildings of Washington, but were repulsed with loss from New Orleans. Of the many naval engagements between single ships, the chief was that between the frigates Shannon and Chesapeake, in which the British were victorious. The Peace of Ghent, signed in December 1814, put an end to the war, but without deciding the original ground of quarrel.

For his great success in the Peninsula Wellington was made a Duke, was publicly thanked by the Houses of Parliament, and received a grant of £400,000. Towards the close of 1814 a Congress met at Vienna to settle the affairs of Europe, which were all confused after a war so long and costly.

But the news of March 1815 brought their meetings to a sudden close. Napoleon had left Elba, had landed on the 1st of March on the coast of Provence, and was marching rapidly on Paris. His Marshals hastened to his side. The French soldiers, disgusted with the government of the Bourbons, flocked in thousands round his banner. And, in twenty days after his landing, he once more held the capital and the throne of France.

All Europe was alarmed and enraged at his daring disregard of treaties and oaths. The British Parliament voted £110,000,000 for his overthrow. The Duke of Wellington took the command of 80,000 troops. Blucher marshalled 110,000 Prussians for the campaign. Austria and Russia were preparing to invade France on the eastern frontier with enormous armies. All offers of negotiation from Napoleon were unheeded, and his only hope lay in instant action.

Wellington's plan was to join the Prussian army in Belgium, and thence to march on Paris from the north-east. Napoleon, resolving if possible to prevent this union, crossed the French frontier on the 15th of June. The British lay then at Brussels: the Prussians were at Ligny, some miles nearer the frontier. Wellington received the news of the French advance late on the evening of the 15th, in the ball-room of the Duchess of Richmond. A hurried whisper passed round among the officers; and at day-break the British regiments began to pour out of Brussels towards Quatre Bras, an important point sixteen miles off, where two roads crossed. There they were attacked on the 16th by Marshal Ney, who strove without success to force the position. But on the same day Napoleon drove the Prussians from Ligny, and sent Grouchy in pursuit with 35,000 men, to cut them off from a union with the army of Wellington. This defeat of the Prussians obliged Wellington to fall back on the village of Waterloo. Even there Blucher was distant from him nearly a day's march; and Napoleon exulted in the prospect of certain victory, for he had got, as he thought, between the allied armies, and all that now remained was to defeat them in turn.

The battle of Waterloo—called by the French St. Jean—was fought on a Sunday. All night before, the rain had fallen in torrents; and when the troops rose from their cheerless bivouac among the crushed and muddy rye, a drizzling rain still fell. The armies faced each other upon two gentle slopes, near which ran the high road to Brussels. The army of Wellington numbered more than 70,000,—that of Napoleon about 80,000 men. Between, in a slight hollow, lay the farmhouses of Hougomont and La Haye Sainte, round which the bloodiest combats of the day took place. The battle began at ten o'clock. Napoleon knew that he was a ruined man unless he could pierce and break the red masses that lay between him and Brussels. He kept closely to one plan of action,—a storm of shot and shell upon the British ranks, and then a rapid rush of lancers and steel-clad cuirassiers. But the British infantry, formed into solid squares, met every charge like the rocks that encircle their native shore. Again, and again, and again the baffled cavalry of France recoiled with many an empty saddle. This was a terrible game to play; and well might Wellington, when he looked on the squares, growing every moment smaller, as soldier after soldier stept silently into the place of his fallen comrade, pray that either night or Blucher would come. It was seven o'clock in the evening before the distant sound of the Prussian cannon was heard. Blucher had outmarched Grouchy, and was hastening to Waterloo. Napoleon then made the grandest effort of the day. The Old Guard of France, unconquered veterans of Austerlitz and Jena, burst in a furious onset upon the shattered ranks of Britain; but, at one magic word, the British squares dissolved into 'thin red lines,' glittering with bayonets, and, with a cheer that rent the smoke-cloud hovering above the field, swept on to meet the foe. The French columns wavered,—broke,—fled; and Waterloo was won. During the three eventful days 40,000 French, 16,000 Prussians, 13,000 British and Germans were killed. We are told that Wellington wept as he rode over

June 18, **1815** A.D.

the plain by moonlight. But who can tell the thoughts of the fallen despot, as he fled from the field where his mighty sword, stained with the blood and the tears of millions, lay shivered into atoms?

Paris, where he abdicated in favour of his son,—Rochefort, whence he tried to escape to America,—the Roads of Aix, where, on the quarter-deck of the Bellerophon, he cast himself on the mercy of Britain,—the lonely rock of St. Helena, where for six years he dwelt imprisoned by the Atlantic waves,—these are the last scenes in the history of Napoleon I. He died on the 3d of May 1821, and in 1840 his remains were removed to France.

Thus ended a war, during which Britain had made gigantic efforts. The National Debt, which at the end of the Seven Years' War was £130,000,000, and at the end of the American War, £238,000,000, had now reached the incalculable sum of £860,000,000. The sudden change from war to peace caused great distress. Bread was still dear, while wages sank very low. The wheat crop of 1817 failed; and riotous meetings took place, which were not suppressed without much trouble. But fast as our debts grew, still faster grew the wealth of our cotton-mills, where steam-power had come to the aid of the spinning-frame and the power-loom.

In August 1816 Algiers, a nest of pirates, was attacked by a British fleet under Lord Exmouth. After a bombardment of six hours the Dey struck his flag, and agreed to set free all his Christian slaves and to seize no more.

The death of the Princess Charlotte, only child of the Prince Regent, and wife of Prince Leopold, cast a heavy gloom over the nation. A twelvemonth later died Queen Charlotte; and on the 29th of January 1820 George III. closed his long reign at the age of eighty-two. He had twelve children, of whom the four eldest were the Prince Regent, Frederic Duke of York, William Duke of Clarence, and Edward Duke of Kent.

Nov. 6, 1817 A.D.

George III. was a good man and a wise King. Unlike his predecessors of the same name, he made the glory and the good of Britain his highest objects. In his old age nothing pleased him better than to escape from the noise and smoke of London to his quiet farms; and the name

'Farmer George,' by which he was sometimes called, well describes the simple, homely old man, who was known and loved as well in the cottage as in the castle.

In 1781 Robert Raikes of Gloucester opened the first Sunday-school; and about the same time John Howard made his tour of mercy among the prisons of Europe. In 1785 the 'Times' was established, under the name of the 'Daily Universal Register,'—a small sheet of four pages. London streets were first lighted with gas in 1807. In the same year Fulton, an American, launched the first regular steam-boat on the Hudson; and in 1812 Henry Bell of Helensburgh started on the Clyde the first steam-vessel in Europe.

CONTEMPORARY SOVEREIGNS.

FRANCE. A.D.
LOUIS XV.,..................died 1774
LOUIS XVI., dethroned....... 1789
REVOLUTION,..................... 1792
REPUBLIC,......................... 1795
DIRECTORY,....................... 1799
CONSULS,........................... 1802
NAPOLEON, First Consul until............................... 1804
NAPOLEON, EMPEROR,.... 1815
LOUIS XVIII.

SPAIN.
CHARLES III.,.................... 1788
CHARLES IV.,..................... 1808
FERDINAND VII., dethroned........................ —
JOSEPH BONAPARTE, dethroned........................... 1814
FERDINAND VII.

SWEDEN.
ADOLPHUS FREDERIC,..... 1771
GUSTAVUS III.,................. 1792
GUSTAVUS IV.,.................. 1809
CHARLES XIII.,................. 1810
CHARLES JOHN BERNADOTTE.

RUSSIA. A.D.
ELIZABETH,................died 1761
PETER III.,......................... 1762
CATHERINE II.,................. 1796
PAUL I.,.............................. 1801
ALEXANDER.

PRUSSIA.
FREDERIC II.,.................... 1786
FREDERIC WILLIAM II., 1796
FREDERIC WILLIAM III.

TURKEY.
ACHMET IV.,...................... 1789
SELIM III.,......................... 1807
MUSTAPHA IV.,................. 1808
MOHAMMED VI.

EMPERORS.
FRANCIS,........................... 1765
JOSEPH II.,........................ 1790
LEOPOLD II.,..................... 1792
FRANCIS II. (title changed to Emperor of Austria),... 1804

POPES.
CLEMENT XIII.,................. 1769
CLEMENT XIV.,.................. 1775
PIUS VI.,............................ 1800
PIUS VII.

LEADING AUTHORS UNDER GEORGE III.

DAVID HUME,..................(1711-1776)—a Scotchman—librarian to the Edinburgh Advocates—chief work, 'History of England'—held the strange doctrine that we can be sure of nothing—wrote a 'Treatise on Human Nature' and Essays.

SIR WILLIAM BLACKSTONE,...(1723-1780)—an eminent lawyer and Judge of King's Bench—chief work, 'Commentaries on the Laws of England.'

SAMUEL JOHNSON,................(1709-1784)—born at Lichfield—lived generally in London—chief works, 'The Lives of the Poets;' 'Rasselas, an Eastern Tale;' an 'English Dictionary;' and a poem called 'London.'

ADAM SMITH,.....................(1723-1790)—a Scotchman—Professor in Glasgow University—chief work, 'The Wealth of Nations,' by which was founded the science of Political Economy.

WILLIAM ROBERTSON,...........(1721-1793)—a Scottish clergyman—chief works, 'History of Scotland under Mary and James VI.;' 'History of Charles V.;' and 'History of America.'

EDWARD GIBBON,..................(1737-1794)—born in Surrey—chief work, 'The Decline and Fall of the Roman Empire,' in six vols., written in twelve years.

GEORGE CAMPBELL,.............(1719-1796)—Principal of Marischal College, Aberdeen—chief work, 'An Essay on Miracles,' a triumphant reply to the infidel Hume.

ROBERT BURNS,...................(1759-1796)—an Ayrshire farmer—famed for his lyric poems—author of the 'Cottar's Saturday Night' and 'Tam o' Shanter.'

EDMUND BURKE,..................(1730-1797)—born in Dublin—a famous orator—chief works, 'An Essay on the Sublime and Beautiful,' and 'Reflections on the French Revolution.'

LEADING ARTISTS AND INVENTORS. 309

WILLIAM COWPER,.................(1731-1800)—educated as a lawyer—a Christian and moral poet—sometimes deranged—author of the 'Task'—translated Homer.

HUGH BLAIR,........................(1718-1800)—an Edinburgh preacher—chief works, 'Sermons,' and 'Lectures on Belles Lettres.'

WILLIAM PALEY,...................(1743-1805)—Archdeacon of Carlisle—chief works, 'Natural Theology' and 'Evidences of Christianity.'

LEADING ARTISTS.

THOMAS GAINSBOROUGH,.......(1727-1788)—born in Suffolk—a fine painter of English landscapes—lived in Ipswich, Bath, and London.

SIR JOSHUA REYNOLDS ....(1723-1792)—born in Devonshire—the first President of the Royal Academy—a famous portrait and historical painter—published Discourses on Painting—a great friend of Dr. Johnson.

LEADING INVENTORS, ETC.

JAMES BRINDLEY,.................(1716-1772)—native of Tunsted, Derbyshire—engineer of the canal made by Duke of Bridgewater from Worsley to Manchester, and hence the founder of our canal navigation.

SIR RICHARD ARKWRIGHT,...(1732-1792)—born at Preston, Lancashire—originally a hair-dresser—invented the spinning-frame by which hand-labour is saved in the cotton-mills—hence may be called the founder of our great cotton manufacture.

JOSIAH WEDGEWOOD,............(1731-1795)—the great improver of our porcelain manufacture—the son of a Staffordshire potter—inventor of the 'Queen's ware,' made of white Dorsetshire clay mixed with ground flint.

JAMES WATT,........................(1736-1819)—native of Greenock—invented the double-acting condensing steam-engine, and applied it to machinery—lived first in Glasgow, and then in Birmingham.

CHAPTER V.

GEORGE IV.

Born 1762 A.D.—Began to reign 1820 A.D.—Died 1830 A.D.

The Cato Street Gang.	Money Panic.	Death.
Queen Caroline.	Death of Canning.	Character.
Visits of the King.	Navarino.	Notes.
The Burmese War.	The Emancipation Bill.	

The Prince Regent, who had already ruled for nine years, now became King George IV. A few days after his accession, a plot to murder the Ministers, when they were assembled at an official dinner given by Lord Harrowby, was discovered by the police. The leader of the gang was Thistlewood, a broken-down profligate. When the murder was perpetrated, the prisons were to be broken open, London was to be set on fire, and a Revolution accomplished. On the very evening fixed for the crime, the police came suddenly upon them in a hay-loft in Cato Street near the Edgeware Road. A desperate scuffle ensued; a policeman was killed; but the capture was made. Thistlewood and four others were executed; the rest were transported. A slight rising about the same time at Kilsyth in Stirlingshire was soon suppressed.

Nothing showed George IV. in a worse light than his treatment of his wife, Caroline of Brunswick, to whom he was married in 1795. They had never agreed, and had soon separated. Indeed his life was such that no wife could live happily with him. During the Regency she had lived in Italy; but when she heard that her husband was King, she hastened to England to claim the honours due to a Queen. On the 6th of July 1820 a 'Bill of pains and penalties' was brought into the House of Lords, charging her with unfaithfulness to the King. She was nobly defended by Brougham and Denman; and on the 10th of November the Bill was abandoned, to the great joy of the people, who were all on her side. In the following year she came to the door of Westminster Abbey on the day of her husband's coronation, but was refused admittance by the soldiers on guard. Nineteen days later she died. Even round her coffin, as it was borne from London to Harwich, there was deadly strife between the soldiers and the people.

July 19, 1821 A.D.

In the same month as his wife died, the King visited Ireland, where he was received with joy,—not, however, as the man George Guelph, but as the first British King who had paid a visit of peace to the island. Next month he went to Hanover; and in the August of the following year he stayed for thirteen days in Scotland. There he received the news that one of his chief ministers, the Marquis of Londonderry, —better known as Lord Castlereagh—had committed suicide. The Marquis was succeeded as Foreign Secretary by Mr. George Canning.

In February 1824 the British Government, irritated by outrages on their colonies beyond the Ganges, declared war against Burmah. In the first campaign Sir Archibald Campbell captured the town of Rangoon and the forts at the mouth of the Irrawaddy. A small force under General Morrison seized the province of Aracan during the following year. In 1826 a treaty was made, by which the coasts of Tenasserim and the district of Aracan were given up to Britain.

In 1824 a great rage for joint-stock companies seized the nation. Money was abundant, and men invested it, on the promise of high interest, in schemes of the wildest description. Loans were granted to half the States on the face of the globe. Paper money was issued by the banks to an extent far beyond what was prudent. The natural result was a panic or commercial crisis in 1825, when 50 banks shut their doors, and more than 200 merchants became insolvent.

In the spring of 1827 the Earl of Liverpool, who had been Prime Minister for the last fifteen years, received a stroke of paralysis, and Canning was called to the head of the Government. But this gifted and eloquent statesman, sinking under the heavy load of so great an office, died in the August of the same year. He was succeeded by Lord Goderich.

Early in the reign of George IV. the Greeks rose in revolt against the Turks, who had been grinding them in abject slavery for more than three centuries. The heroic courage of the Suliotes and other Greek mountaineers, among whom the spirit of the ancient race was still alive, won the admiration and sympathy of Europe. Our poet Byron devoted his pen and his fortune to the cause of Greece, and spent the wreck of his short life in her service. In the year 1827 three great Powers of Europe—Russia, France, and Britain—signed a treaty in London, by which they agreed to force Turkey into an acknowledgment of Grecian independence.

Oct. 20, 1827 A.D. Towards the close of the year, the allied fleet under Admiral Codrington, sailing into the harbour of Navarino in the south-west of the Morea, destroyed the whole navy of Turkey in a few hours. Soon afterwards the Turkish soldiers were withdrawn; Greece was formed into an independent kingdom; and Otho, a Bavarian prince, was placed on the newly-erected throne.

The most remarkable political event of this reign was the passing of the Emancipation Bill under the ministry of the Duke of Wellington, who, aided by Mr. Robert Peel as Home Secretary, took office in 1828. Penal laws—necessary at first, but now little needed—had been pressing heavily on the Romanists of Ireland since the Revolution. They now assumed a threatening attitude, and it was evident that a change must be made to preserve the peace of the Empire. In 1828 the Test and Corporation Acts of Charles II. were repealed. But they demanded more than this. In spite of the law forbidding Romanists to sit in Parliament, they returned Daniel O'Connell, an Irish barrister of great popular

1829 A.D. eloquence, as member for the county Clare; and so well did he fight the battle of his Church, that a Bill was passed removing all penal laws against Romanists, and placing them on the same political footing as the Protestant subjects of the Crown.

On the 26th of June 1830 the King died at the age of sixty-eight. He left no heir.

The flatterers of George IV. used to call him 'the first gentleman in Europe.' If a shapely figure, fine taste in dress, and manners of most courtly polish alone make up a gentleman, he had a good claim to the title; but if, as some men think, a true gentleman must have a feeling heart and lead a moral life, then this King deserves not the name.

During this reign Captains Parry and Ross explored the Arctic Seas in search of the North-West Passage. In 1820 the use of broken stones in road-making was introduced by Mr. Macadam. In 1822 the first iron steam-boat was seen on the Thames. In 1824 Mechanics' Institutions were established. In 1825 the Enterprise, under Captain Johnson, made the first steam voyage to India. The Atlantic had already been crossed by steam in 1819. The London University, chartered in 1826, was opened in 1828.

CONTEMPORARY SOVEREIGNS.

FRANCE.	A.D.	PRUSSIA.	A.D.
LOUIS XVIII., ...	died 1825	FREDERIC WILLIAM III.	
CHARLES X.			
		TURKEY.	
SPAIN.		MOHAMMED VI.	
FERDINAND VII., ...	1820		
Revolution.			
		AUSTRIA.	
SWEDEN.		FRANCIS.	
CHAS. JOHN BERNADOTTE.			
		POPES.	
RUSSIA.		PIUS VII., ...	died 1823
ALEXANDER, ...	1825	LEO XII.	
NICHOLAS.			

LEADING AUTHORS UNDER GEORGE IV.

LORD BYRON, ...(1788-1824)—a distinguished poet—lived a debauched life—many of his poems immoral—chief work 'Childe Harold's Pilgrimage,' in the stanza of Spenser—died of fever at Missolonghi in Greece.

DUGALD STEWART, ...(1753-1828)—Professor of Moral Philosophy in Edinburgh—chief works, 'Philosophy of the Human Mind,' and 'Outlines of Moral Philosophy.'

THOMAS BROWN, ...(1778-1820)—successor of Stewart—chief work, 'Class Lectures,' published after his death.

LEADING ARTISTS.

BENJAMIN WEST, ...(1738-1820)—born at Springfield in America—a distinguished historical painter — President of the Royal Academy.

JOHN FLAXMAN, ...(1755-1826)—born at York—a great sculptor—chief works, Illustrations of Homer, Dante, and Æschylus—Professor of Sculpture to the Royal Academy.

SIR THOMAS LAWRENCE, ...(1769-1830)—born in Bristol—called the English Titian—celebrated for his portraits—succeeded Reynolds as State-painter to George III.—elected President of the Royal Academy, 1820.

LEADING INVENTORS, ETC.

SIR WILLIAM HERSCHEL,...(1738-1822)—born in Hanover—at first a musician—the great improver of the reflecting telescope—discovered the planet Uranus in 1781—also volcanoes in the moon, and many satellites—received a pension of £300—died at Slough.

SIR HUMPHREY DAVY,.......(1778-1829)— born at Penzance in Cornwall—son of a wood carver—apprenticed to a surgeon—the inventor of the safety lamp—made great discoveries in chemistry and electricity—wrote 'Salmonia,' and 'Consolations in Travel'—died at Geneva.

CHAPTER VI.

WILLIAM IV.

Born 1765 A.D.—Began to reign 1830 A.D.—Died 1837 A.D.

French Revolution.	The Poor Laws.
First English Railway.	Change of Ministry.
The Cholera.	Municipal Act.
The Reform Bill.	Foreign Policy.
Its changes.	Death of the King.
Abolition of Slavery.	His character.

THE Duke of Clarence, brother of the late King, now ascended the throne, as William IV. In his young days he had seen service in the navy, and he has therefore been called the 'Sailor King.' His wife was Adelaide of Saxe Meiningen.

Soon after his accession a second Revolution occurred in France, when, after three days' fighting in the streets of Paris, Charles X. was driven from the throne, and Louis Philippe, Duke of Orleans, was appointed King of the French. The people of Belgium, influenced by this example, threw off the yoke of Holland, and made Prince Leopold their King. There was at the same time much discontent in Britain, and a loud cry arose for a reform of the House of Commons. The Duke of Wellington, who was opposed to any change of the kind, then resigned in favour of a Whig ministry, of which the chief members were Earl Grey and Lord John Russell.

During this year the first of those railways, which now lie like a net-work of iron over the whole face of the Empire, was opened between Liverpool and Manchester. *Sept. 15, 1830 A.D.*

A new epidemic disease, called *Cholera*, which was noticed first in India, travelling westward, broke out at Sunderland in the October of 1831. Its ravages continued for more than a year, sweeping off nearly 60,000 persons. Since then it has visited Britain twice; but, by active sanitary improvements in sewerage and ventilation, its effects have been much lessened.

The great political event of the reign was the passing of

the Reform Bill. On the 1st of March 1831 Lord John Russell proposed the measure in the House of Commons. It was fiercely opposed in both Houses, especially in the Lords; but the mass of the people were resolved on the change. For fifteen months the struggle went on. Great riots took place in Bristol, Nottingham, and Derby. At one time, indeed, the Bill seemed in peril of being lost. The opposition in the Lords grew so strong that Earl Grey resigned, and the Duke of Wellington was called on to form a Ministry. But this he failed to do; the current of public feeling turned fiercely against him; and the conqueror at Waterloo was obliged to fortify his house against a London mob. Earl Grey was then restored, and the Bill soon became law. The Reform Bills of Scotland and Ireland received the royal assent on the 17th of July, and on the 7th of August.

June 7, 1832 A.D.

Three great changes were thus made: 1. The right of sending members to Parliament was taken away from many places—called pocket or rotten boroughs—in which there were very few voters, and sometimes none residing in the borough. Of this class the most notorious example was Old Sarum, in which there was not a single house. 2. Several towns, which had sprung within the last century into first-class cities, now for the first time received the right of sending members to Parliament. 3. The franchise, or right of voting, was extended more widely among the middle classes. The right of voting for towns was given to the owners, or the tenants of houses worth £10 a year or upwards. For county members all were entitled to vote, who owned land worth £10 a year, or who paid a yearly rent of at least £50 for their holdings.

Ever since the year 1787 a movement to set free all slaves in the British Colonies had been at work in the House of Commons. William Wilberforce, member for the county of York, first brought forward the motion, and through a long life he clung with noble perseverance to the noble work. From time to time the debates were renewed amid great opposition from slaveholders, planters, and merchants. It was not until the question was forty-six years old that the Bill was finally passed

1833 A.D.

£20,000,000 were granted to slave owners as compensation: and the slaves were not set free all at once, but were bound to serve their masters as apprentices for seven years longer. It was thought better, however, to shorten the time of apprenticeship by two years; and in 1838 eight hundred thousand slaves received their freedom. Wilberforce lived only to see the triumph of his life's work. He died in 1833.

In 1834 many changes were made in the Poor Laws. The rate to support the poor had been lately so high as £7,000,000 a year: and a great part of the sum was squandered on the support of strong men and women, who were too idle to work. The new Bill placed the local boards under the superintendence of the Government, and ordered that no aid should be given to able-bodied paupers, unless they chose to go to the poor-houses, and work for their living there.

While this measure was passing through the Houses Earl Grey resigned, having disputed with his colleagues about the Irish Coercion Bill. He was followed as Premier by Viscount Melbourne, with whom were associated Lord John Russell and Lord Palmerston. Towards the close of the year these ministers were thrown out of office, and Sir Robert Peel was called in haste from Italy to form a new Government. But in four months Melbourne returned to the head of affairs.

In 1835 was passed the Municipal Act, by which the Town Councils of England and Wales were reformed. To the rate-payers and freemen was given the right of appointing the councillors, who elected the magistrates from among themselves. Similar changes were made in Scotland and Ireland.

During 1835 and 1836 the Spanish Government was allowed to enlist British soldiers for service against the Carlists. This, and the aid given to the revolted Belgians in 1832, when British ships blockaded the ports of Holland, are almost the only note-worthy points in the foreign policy of the reign.

The King died on the 20th of June 1837, aged seventy-two. His two daughters had died in infancy, one of them on the day of her birth.

The warm heart, the open hand, the free and cordial manner of the sailor-King won the love of his people. He possessed neither brilliant genius nor excellent wisdom, but strong sound sense guided every act of his useful reign.

CONTEMPORARY SOVEREIGNS.

FRANCE. A.D.	PRUSSIA. A.D
CHARLES X.,......dethroned 1830	FREDERIC WILLIAM III
LOUIS PHILIPPE.	
	TURKEY.
SPAIN.	MOHAMMED VI.
REVOLUTION,............until 1833	
ISABELLA II.	AUSTRIA.
	FRANCIS,....................died 1835
SWEDEN.	FERDINAND I.
CHARLES JOHN BERNADOTTE	
	POPES.
RUSSIA.	LEO XII.,......................... 1831
NICHOLAS.	GREGORY XVI.

LEADING AUTHORS UNDER WILLIAM IV.

SIR WALTER SCOTT,...(1771-1832) — a Scottish barrister — wrote ballads and poetical tales—chief poems, 'The Lay of the Last Minstrel,' 'Marmion,' and 'The Lady of the Lake'— more famous as the author of the Waverley Novels, founded chiefly on English and Scottish history.

ADAM CLARKE,............(1762-1832) — an Irishman — a Methodist minister—learned in Oriental languages --chief work, 'A Commentary on the Bible.'

SAMUEL COLERIDGE,...(1772-1834)—born in Devonshire—educated at Cambridge—one of the Lake poets— chief works, the 'Ancient Mariner' and 'Christabel,' an unfinished poem.

FELICIA HEMANS,.......(1793-1835)—a lady-writer of lyric poems, full of the tenderest feeling and the most beautiful imagery. Her 'Songs of the Affections' and her 'Records of Woman' are among her chief works.

CHAPTER VII.

VICTORIA.

Born May 24, 1819 A.D.—Began to reign June 20, 1837 A.D.

Hanover Separated.	The Ameers of Sinde.	Russian War.
Canadian Rebellions.	Sikh War.	Battle of Inkermann.
The Chartists.	Corn Laws Repealed.	Sebastopol Taken.
The Queen's Marriage.	Railway Panic.	China and Persia.
Afghan War.	Irish Riots.	Indian Mutiny.
Syrian War.	Papal Aggression.	Money Crisis.
Chinese War.	The Great Exhibition.	The India Bill.
Repeal Agitation.	Caffre War.	Atlantic Cable.
The Disruption.	Burmese War.	Notes.

ALEXANDRINA VICTORIA, the daughter of Edward Duke of Kent, and the niece of the late King, became Queen at the age of eighteen. She was crowned at Westminster on the 28th of June 1838. Since the Salic law permits no woman to wear the crown of Hanover, by the accession of Victoria that state was severed from the British dominions, and Ernest, Duke of Cumberland, brother of William IV., became its King.

A rebellion, headed by Papineau and Mackenzie, disturbed the Canadas in December 1837. The former leader was defeated in a few days at St. Eustace; the latter attacked Toronto, but was repulsed by Head. In the following year, at the same season, when the fierce frost of the Canadian winter had set in, there was a second rising in Lower Canada; but it was soon suppressed by the energy of Sir John Colborne. To strengthen the Government of the colony, an Act of Parliament was passed in 1840, by which the two Canadas were made one province.

About this time the proceedings of a set of men who called themselves Chartists began to attract notice. They took their name from the People's Charter, a document in which they demanded six sweeping changes in the Constitution:—1. Universal Suffrage,—that every man should have a vote. 2. Vote by ballot. 3. Annual Parliaments. 4. That Members of Parliament should be paid. 5. That every man, whether owning property or not, should be eligible for a seat in Parliament. 6. That the country should be divided into electoral districts. A band of these discontented men, headed by John Frost, who had once been a magistrate, made an unsuccessful attack on Newport in Monmouthshire. For this treason Frost and two others were sentenced to death; but they were afterwards reprieved and transported for life.

On the 10th of February 1840 the Queen was married to Prince Albert of Saxe Coburg and Gotha. The Princess Royal—now Princess Frederic William of Prussia—was born on the 21st of November in the same year; and on the 9th of November 1841 was born Albert Edward, Prince of Wales, the heir apparent to the British throne. Soon after the royal marriage it was decreed in Parliament that, if the Queen shall die before the Prince of Wales come of age, Prince Albert shall rule the Empire as Regent.

From 1839 to 1842 a war raged in Afghanistan. The suspicion that Russia might have evil designs upon our Indian Empire, made it of the highest importance that a Prince friendly to Britain should sit on the throne of Afghanistan; for that state lies between India and Persia, and Persia has always been friendly to the Czars. Accordingly, early in 1839 a British army, under Sir John Keane, entered Afghanistan to replace Shah Shoojah on the throne, which had been usurped by Dost Mohammed. Within a few months the great cities of Candahar, Ghuznee, and Kabool were taken. But the victors were hemmed in at Kabool by a host of wild Afghans under Akbar Khan, the son of Dost Mohammed. Sir William Macnaghten and many officers, being invited to a conference, were basely murdered; and the remnant of the army, leaving Kabool to march through the snow to Jelalabad, a distance of ninety miles, were slaughtered on the road, only one escaping out of many hundreds. Shah Shoojah soon fell by an assassin's hand. But General Pollock, having fought his way nobly through the Khyber Pass, joined Sir Robert Sale and General Nott, and then marched on Kabool, on which the British flag was planted once more amid the peals of martial music. The fortifications of the city were soon destroyed, and

Sept. 15,
1842
A.D.

the British then withdrew from Afghanistan. In 1855 Dost Mohammed made a friendly alliance with Britain.

At the same time there was war in the Levant. The Pacha of Egypt, Mehemet Ali, and his son Ibrahim, had long been troublesome to the Turkish Sultan, and in 1837 the latter defeated the Ottoman troops at Nezib on the Euphrates. The Sultan sought aid from Britain and other states; which was readily granted, because the war had more than once shut the Dardanelles and stopped the Black Sea trade. A British fleet, under Admiral Stopford and Commodore Napier, having previously destroyed Beyrout on the Syrian coast, appeared before the ancient walls of Acre. In three hours that stronghold, the key of all Syria, which had baffled even the mighty Napoleon, yielded to British cannon. Napier then sailed to Alexandria; but the Pacha after a short delay agreed to withdraw his troops from Syria. By a treaty with Turkey, some time afterwards, the Pachalic of Egypt was granted as an inheritance to his family. **Nov. 3, 1840 A.D.**

A dispute arose with China about the trade in opium, a drug which the Chinese love to smoke and chew, although hundreds die from its poisonous effects. The Emperor, alarmed at the growth of the practice, forbade the importation of opium; but British merchants, who made great profits by the trade, still smuggled it into the country. The mandarins in authority seized and destroyed many cargoes of the forbidden drug. Captain Elliot the Commissioner, and other British subjects were imprisoned. War was declared in 1840. British troops soon forced Canton to surrender; and in the north Sir Henry Pottinger, having captured Amoy, marched to the very walls of Nankin. There a peace was concluded, by which the island of Hong Kong was given up to Britain; and, besides Canton, the four ports of Amoy, Foo-choo, Ningpo, and Shanghae were opened to foreign trade. **Aug. 29, 1842 A.D.**

In 1843 riots in opposition to toll-bars took place in Wales. The rioters called themselves 'Rebekah's daughters', from Gen. xxiv. 60, where Rebekah's relatives pray that her seed may possess *the gates* of their enemies; and, to support their assumed sex, they wore women's night-caps and bed gowns.

During the riots, which lasted until the close of the year, every turnpike in South Wales was destroyed. At the same time the agitation in Ireland for a Repeal of the Union reached its crisis. The collection known as the Repeal Rent, which was made at the doors of the Romish chapels in aid of O'Connell, amounted in 1843 to £48,000. Monster meetings were held at Tara, the site of the ancient Irish capital, and other places. Clontarf, the scene of Brian Boru's victory over the Danes, was chosen as a fitting place for one of these ; but the Lord-Lieutenant sent soldiers to occupy the ground. O'Connell and six others were then brought to trial, and sentenced to imprisonment for two years; but they were soon released. O'Connell died at Genoa on the 15th of May 1847, aged seventy-two.

The Disruption in the Church of Scotland occurred in 1843. It was occasioned by certain decisions in the supreme civil tribunals, which overturned sentences that had been passed by the Ecclesiastical Courts of the Church of Scotland. A large party in the Church, considering that her independence was by this means invaded, and her efficiency injured, separated from the State, and formed themselves into the Free Church. About the same time the Church of England was much disturbed by the movements of the Puseyite or Tractarian party, who thought that the forms of worship should be brought nearer to those of the Romish Church. They derived their first name from their leader, Dr. Pusey of Oxford.

During the Afghan war Sinde, a district of 50,000 square miles with a sea coast of 150 miles, lying round the mouths of the Indus, was occupied by British troops. The Ameers or rulers of Sinde objected to this, and an attack was made on the British Residency at Hydrabad. Major Outram, who had only 100 men, retreating skilfully after a gallant defence, joined the main army under Sir Charles Napier. A few days later the British won the battle of Meeanee, and a second victory near Hydrabad completed the conquest of Sinde.

North-east of Sinde, higher up the Indus, lies the great district of the Punjaub, watered by five large rivers, and thence deriving its name, from the Persian words which mean 'five waters.' The country was then held by the warlike Sikhs, who had seized it in the middle of the last century One of their princes, Runjeet Singh, had been a firm friend to the British; but his death in 1839 caused a bloody strife for the throne, during which an unprovoked attack was made on a British force stationed at Moodkee. The Sikhs were repulsed with loss; but they were no mean foes,—they had fine horses, and their gunners were drilled by European officers of artillery. The British army, under Sir Hugh Gough and Sir Henry Hardinge, then moved upon the Sikh camp at Ferozeshah, and took it after two days' hard fighting. The Sikhs fled across the Sutlej. The victories of Aliwal on the 26th of January 1846, and Sobraon a fortnight later, opened the path of the British soldiers to Lahore, the capital of the Punjaub, where a treaty was signed. But in 1849 the war broke out again. The Sikhs, strongly posted at Chillianwalla on the Jhelum, were attacked by Lord Gough on the 13th of January, and a victory was won; but the loss of the British was so severe that their leader was greatly blamed for risking the engagement. However, on the 21st of February at Gujerat Gough utterly routed an immense host of Sikhs, and thus redeemed his fame. The Punjaub was shortly afterwards, by a proclamation of the Governor-General, annexed to our Indian Empire.

The most important political event of Victoria's reign was the Repeal of the Corn Laws. In 1841 the Anti-Corn-Law League was formed in Lancashire in support of Free-trade principles. Its leading spirit was Richard Cobden, a mill-owner of Manchester. Sir Robert Peel, who became Prime Minister in 1841, was at first in favour of high duties on foreign corn, but in 1845 his opinions on the subject changed. All who lived by agriculture, the landowners, the farmers, and the labouring classes, wished to keep foreign grain out of the country, in the mistaken belief that it was their interest, by high duties, to keep up the price of corn grown at home. This long depressed the commerce of the country; but in the end the cause of Free-trade triumphed, and the duty on wheat from abroad was reduced to 1s. a quarter. Two days afterwards Sir Robert Peel resigned, and Lord John Russell became Premier.   June 26, 1846 A.D.

In 1845 a blight fell upon the potato crop, which caused sore famine and fever in Ireland. Generous aid was sent to the starving peasants from Britain and America; but between death and emigration the population was lessened by nearly two millions.

A mania for making railways now seized the nation. Hundreds of companies were started, and everybody bought and sold railway shares. But after the mania came its natural result—the panic, when the opening eyes of the people discovered that half the proposed lines would be utterly useless. Every newspaper was then full of dissolving companies, profitless shares, and bankrupt speculators. The pressure of the crisis was felt most severely in October 1847. However, this gloomy year saw the first practical use of the electric telegraph.

In February 1848 Louis Philippe was driven from his throne, and a Republic established by the third French Revolution. The exiled monarch took refuge in England, where he died at Claremont in 1850. Towards the close of the year Louis Napoleon, son of the ex-King of Holland and nephew of the great Emperor, became President of the French Republic; and, in four years afterwards, Emperor of the French with the title of Napoleon III. The year 1848 was stormy over all Europe. There were tumults in Vienna, in Berlin, and in Rome. There were Chartist riots in England, and a great meeting assembled on the 10th of April on Kennington Common, to escort Feargus O'Connor to the Parliament with a petition embodying their demands. But the streets were filled with 200,000 sturdy citizens, sworn in as special constables, and the astonished Chartists slunk quietly through the day's programme.

In Ireland the more violent members of the Repeal Society, headed by William Smith O'Brien, had formed themselves into the 'Young Ireland Party,' and were bent on war. Rebellious newspapers, of which the cleverest and most violent was the 'United Irishman' edited by John Mitchell, excited the people to arms. Groups of workmen were to be seen every day at ball-practice on the sands or in the fields. But all ended in nothing. A feeble rising under O'Brien and others took place in Tipperary; but it was suppressed by a few policemen. The leaders were soon taken; four of them were condemned to death; but the sentence was afterwards changed to exile. Since then they have been released one by one, or allowed to escape.

A change in the Navigation Laws; a visit of her Majesty to Ireland, where she was heartily welcomed; and the death of Adelaide, the Queen-dowager, were the chief domestic events of 1849.

On the 29th of June 1850 Sir Robert Peel fell from his horse, and four days afterwards he died from the effects of the accident. He was in his sixty-third year. A striking event of the same year was the Papal Aggression, when the Pope, Pius IX., strove, by creating Cardinal Wiseman Archbishop of Westminster, to re-establish in Britain the Romish hierarchy abolished by Elizabeth. The attempt was met with a storm of opposition, which taught Rome how slight a hold she has on the mass of the Anglo-Saxon race.

One of the last hours of Peel's useful life was spent in discussing the plans for the Great Exhibition of the Industry of all Nations. To Prince Albert is due the credit of starting the first idea of this great enterprise. It was indeed a splendid success. A palace of iron and glass—the strongest and the frailest of building materials—designed by the genius of Sir Joseph Paxton, was raised in Hyde Park, enclosing many acres with its walls and overarching lofty trees with its crystal roof. There were gathered articles of every kind from every land; and for five summer months, day after day, wondering thousands thronged the courts of the vast building. Its grand results were two: It gave a great impulse to every branch of our manufactures and our arts; while, by drawing together men of every complexion, costume, and national character, who met under the same roof for the same peaceful end, it could not fail to cause a kindlier feeling among the nations of earth. Similar Exhibitions took place at Dublin in 1853, and at Paris in 1855.

May 1 to Oct. 14, 1851 A.D.

In February 1851 the Russell Ministry, being defeated, resigned; but by the advice of the Duke of Wellington they were restored to office. A war with the Caffres, our troublesome neighbours at the Cape, broke out in the same year; and it was not until 1853 that they were subdued. The Exhibition year was further remarkable for the discovery of gold in Australia, by which great streams of emigrants were drawn from our shores to the 'diggings.'

A second Burmese war broke out in 1852. The governor of Rangoon having ill-treated the commanders of two British vessels, Commodore Lambert was sent by the Indian Government to demand compensation. He was met with an insulting refusal. A second attempt to arrange the difficulty also failed; and a British army then entered Burmah. Martaban on the shore, Rangoon on the eastern branch of the Irrawaddy, and Pegu on the river of the same name were soon captured. A determined effort of the Burmese to recover Pegu was bravely met by Major Hill of the Madras Fusiliers. Notwithstanding these severe losses, the Court of Ava still refused to treat with the Indian Government; and the Province of Pegu was therefore annexed to the British dominions by proclamation.

Early in 1852 Lord Derby and Mr. Disraeli succeeded Lord John Russell in the direction of affairs; but before the close of the year they gave place to a Cabinet, of which the Earl of Aberdeen as Premier, Lord John Russell as Foreign Secretary, and Lord Palmerston as Home Secretary, were the leading members.

On the 14th of September in the same year the 'Iron Duke,' or the 'Hero of a hundred fights,' as he was proudly called by his grateful countrymen, died at Walmer Castle, aged eighty-three. On the 18th of November his coffin was borne with warlike honours to St. Paul's, where lay the dust of Nelson.

There had been no great European war since Waterloo; but Russia having seized the Principalities of Moldavia and Wallachia, which are separated from the rest of the Turkish dominions by the Danube, the balance of power was disturbed. France and Britain formed an alliance in aid of the Sultan, and sent their fleets into the Black Sea. The Russian ambassador soon left London, and war was formally declared on the 28th of March 1854.

The first operation of the war was the bombardment of Odessa. Then followed the noble defence of Silistria by the Turks, who drove the Russian troops across the Danube.

Sir Charles Napier, commanding the Baltic fleet, destroyed the batteries of Bomarsund, and reconnoitred the great fortress of Cronstadt, which guards the approach to the Russian capital.

But the Crimea was the great theatre of war. An army of 56,000 men, under Marshal St. Arnaud and Lord Raglan, landed at Eupatoria on the 14th of September. As they pressed southward along the shore, they found 50,000 Russians lining the steep slopes on the right bank of the Alma. In three hours the passage of the river was forced, and the Russians fell back on their great stronghold. The Allies then took up a position to the south of Sebastopol. Sept. 20, 1854 A.D. Behind the British, some ten miles distant, was the port of Balaklava, where lay their ships and stores. On the 17th of October the city was attacked by land and sea. But the Russians had made good use of their time, and the works, strong before, were now almost impregnable.

A Russian attack on the British lines at Balaklava was nobly repulsed. The brilliant though useless charge of the Light Cavalry Brigade upon the Russian cannon will be long remembered. Near the ruins of Inkermann, on the extreme right of the British position, a still more glorious victory was won. In the dusk of a November morning the sentinels saw the gray-coated Russians close upon them in overwhelming numbers, bent upon forcing the lines. Hastily a few troops ran to the front; volley after volley awoke the camp; officers and men fought shoulder to shoulder; French aid arrived; and, before the short day had closed, the Russians were in full retreat, leaving on the field one-fourth of their number. Oct. 25. Nov. 5.

During the winter the troops suffered greatly from want of food and shelter, although ships laden with abundant stores lay thick in Balaklava harbour. A motion, brought forward by Mr. Roebuck, taxing the Ministry with mismanagement of the war, was passed in the Commons by a majority of 157 votes. The Earl of Aberdeen then resigned, and Lord Palmerston became Premier. More active measures were at once taken. A railway soon ran from Balaklava to the camp; and then was seen the strange spectacle of a locomotive puffing to the field of war with biscuit, beef, and rum, or with a deadly load of shot and shell. There were other novel features in this Russian war, unknown to the heroes of Vittoria and Waterloo. An electric wire passed from the Crimea, under the Black Sea, to the shore near Varna, and thence to London, where every turn in the great struggle was known an hour or two after its occurrence. The leading newspapers, too, had reporters in the camp. Of these the most distinguished was Dr. William Russell, the special correspondent of the 'Times,' whose 'Letters on the War' have made him famous.

On the 2d of March 1855 the Czar Nicholas died; but the war still went on under his son Alexander. An expedition to Kertch and the Sea of Azov, in May 1855, destroyed many Russian ships and towns. Sardinia having joined the Anglo-French alliance, her troops, in conjunction with the French, won a brilliant victory on the banks of the Tchernaya. Twice during the war the French and British leaders were changed. St. Arnaud, dying after the victory of Alma, was followed by Canrobert, who in May 1855 gave place to the victorious Pelissier. In the following month Lord Raglan died of cholera; General Simpson then took the command; but he was soon displaced by Sir William Codrington.

Aug. 16, 1855 A.D.

The Russian earthworks, to which their engineers had learned to trust rather than to granite walls, were forced at last. The French, already masters of the Mamelon, took the Malakoff Tower with a brilliant dash.

Sept. 8.

At the same time a British forlorn-hope seized the Redan; but Russian guns, sweeping it from every side, forced them to retreat with heavy loss. During the next night Gortschakoff led the Russian garrison across the harbour to the northern part of the city; which, however, they held but a short time. Before their flight they sank their ships, which still lie rotting in the water. All the batteries and great dockyards were blown up by the Allies; and the grand fortress of Southern Russia is now a heap of ruins.

During the summer of 1855 Admiral Dundas, who had superseded Sir Charles Napier in the command of the Baltic fleet, inflicted a severe blow upon Russia by the bombardment of Sveaborg.

The Russian war raged also in Circassia, where the distinguished Schamyl fought against the troops of the Czar. Kars was the central point of attack, and was nobly defended by General Williams, until a want of reinforcements compelled him to surrender.

Crippled both in the Baltic and the Black Seas, Russia at last sought for peace; and the final treaty was signed at Paris in March 1856.

Late in 1856 a war with China began. It arose from an outrage offered by the Chinese to a vessel sailing under the British flag. The most remarkable event of the war was the seizure of Canton by the French and British troops. The latest despatches from the East announce that a treaty has been made, throwing all China open to the missionaries and merchants of Europe. About the same time British forces entered Persia—an old ally of Russia—while a British fleet sailed up the Persian Gulf. Herat and Bushire were soon taken, and the Court of Teheran then sued for peace.

However, the topic of greatest interest, since the Russian war, has been the Mutiny of the Sepoys, which still convulses Bengal, although the gallant Colin Campbell—now Baron Clyde of Clydesdale—has done very much to check its violence. Its outbreak at Meerut in the spring of 1857, the story of the greased cartridges, the hideous massacre at Cawnpore, the siege of Delhi, the relief of Lucknow, the death of the heroic Havelock, and the fall of Bareilly are still fresh in every memory; and bitter tears are still dropping in Britain for those whose graves are far away.

The close of 1857 was a gloomy time in the commercial world. Mad speculations having plunged the traders of America into difficulties, the effect was severely felt in Europe. Many long-established houses of business failed. Those that were working without capital, on accommodation bills, speedily fell; and in the crash more than one of our banks came down, ruined by those to whom they had advanced money with reckless imprudence. It was the old story of 1720 and 1797, of 1825 and 1847, told over again—men, rich on paper, dreaming that they are rich in gold.

Early in 1858 Lord Palmerston's Cabinet gave place to a Conservative Ministry, of which the Earl of Derby was Premier, and Mr. Disraeli Chancellor of the Exchequer. The chief political events of their administration were the passing of two Bills,—one for the better government of India, and the other for the admission of Jews into Parliament. By the former, the East India Company ceased to have a political existence on the 1st of September 1858, and the government of India became vested in a Council of Fifteen, presided over by a Secretary of State. By the latter, Baron Rothschild took his seat in the House of Commons as member for the City of London.

Upon the resignation of Lord Derby in June 1859, Lord Palmerston was called to office, with Mr. Gladstone as his Chancellor of Exchequer. Among the first works of the new Cabinet were the enrolment of the Volunteers, and the concluding of an important commercial treaty with France. Chinese treachery led to a renewal of war in that distant land. Storming the forts at the mouth of the Peiho, and beating the Celestials in two battles, an Anglo-French army scaled the walls of Pekin (October 13, 1860), and dictated peace in the palace of the banished Emperor. Within the same month the treaty of Tien-tsin was ratified, —Lord Elgin representing Great Britain. Many of our countrymen took a share in that brilliant campaign of Garibaldi, which opened on the shore of Marsala in Sicily (May 11, 1860), and closed at Naples by the proclamation of Victor Emanuel as king of new-born Italy. Gaeta, where the fallen Bourbon made his last stand, held out for many months.

The census, taken in March 1861, shewed the population of the British Isles to be 29,334,788. The most notable events of that year beyond the circle of our Empire were the opening at Charleston of the American civil war and the death of Count Cavour.

Two heavy blows then fell upon our beloved Queen. March saw her weeping for a mother dead : December saw her a widow. Leaving a blank in the royal home that can never be filled again, Albert, Prince-Consort, died at Windsor of typhoid fever, December 14, 1861. Long shall British Art and Science miss his fostering hand and kindly counsel ! Four sons and five daughters, fair blossoms of nearly twenty-two years of happy married life, remain to console the royal lady, whose crown has now become "a lonely splendour." Her eldest daughter went, four years ago, to grace the Prussian Court as the wife of Prince Frederick William, heir-apparent to that great monarchy.

Chiefly by the exertions of Mr. Rowland Hill, the Penny Post was made general throughout the United Kingdom in 1840 ; since which six times as many letters have passed through the post every year. The Thames Tunnel was completed and opened in 1843. Lord Rosse finished his great telescope in 1844. Many new planets have been since discovered ; amongst them Astrea in 1845, Neptune in 1846, and Victoria in 1850. In 1849 the Queen's Colleges in Ireland were opened at Belfast, Cork, and Galway. The Britannia Tubular Bridge was stretched across the Menai Strait in 1850. The Submarine Telegraph from Dover to Calais in 1851, and that from England to Ireland in 1852, mark the steps which led to the great but as yet unsuccessful Atlantic Cable of 1858. In 1853 the North-West Passage was discovered by Captain M'Clure. In 1858 the Leviathan, or Great Eastern,—the largest ship ever built,—was launched on the Thames, from Mr. Scott Russell's ship-yard. The yacht Fox (Captain M'Clintock), returning in 1859 from the Arctic Seas, brought back the sad news of the death of Sir John Franklin and his gallant band of explorers, who sailed from Greenwich in 1845 in the Erebus and Terror.

CONTEMPORARY SOVEREIGNS.

FRANCE.
A.D.
LOUIS PHILIPPE, dethron'd 1848
REPUBLIC, ceased..............1852
NAPOLEON III.

SPAIN.
ISABELLA II.

SWEDEN.
CHS. JOHN BERNADOTTE, 1844
OSCAR I.

RUSSIA.
NICHOLAS,......................1855
ALEXANDER II.

PRUSSIA.
A.D.
FRED. WILLIAM III., died 1840
FRED. WILLIAM IV.

TURKEY.
MOHAMMED VI..................1839
ABDUL MEDJID.

AUSTRIA.
FERDINAND I.,....................1848
FRANCIS JOSEPH I.

POPES.
GREGORY XVI.,..................1847
PIUS IX.

LEADING AUTHORS UNDER VICTORIA.

ROBERT SOUTHEY,............... (1774–1843)—native of Bristol—chief poems, 'Joan of Arc' and 'Thalaba'—lived near Keswick in Cumberland, hence one of the Lake School — made Poet-laureate in 1813—wrote also a fine 'Life of Nelson,' and several Histories.

THOMAS CAMPBELL,..............(1777–1844)—born and educated in Glasgow—author of 'Pleasures of Hope'— more admired for his warlike ballads, such as 'The Battle of the Baltic' and 'Ye Mariners of England.'

WILLIAM WORDSWORTH,........(1770-1850)—born at Cockermouth—one of the Lake Poets—chief works, 'The Excursion' and the 'White Doe of Rylstone'—Poet-laureate after Southey. Many of his poems describe common events in everyday words.

THOMAS MOORE,..................(1780-1851)—an Irish lyric poet—author of 'Lalla Rookh' a set of Eastern Tales; and of the 'Irish Melodies'—lived chiefly in London—wrote also prose works.

JOHN LINGARD,....................(1769-1851)—a Romish priest—wrote a History of England up to the Revolution — accurate in general though leaning towards Rome.

SAMUEL ROGERS,..................(1762-1855)—a London banker—chief poems, the 'Pleasures of Memory,' and 'Italy.'

LORD MACAULAY,..................(1800-1859)—the finest historian of the day—chief work, 'History of England,' of which four vols. are published, giving the reign of James II. and part of William III., with a sketch of earlier history—distinguished also as the author of 'The Lays of Ancient Rome.'

SIR ARCHIBALD ALISON,.......A Scottish lawyer—author of a History of the French Revolution, and a 'History of Europe' in Napoleon's time.

SIR DAVID BREWSTER,........Editor of the 'Edinburgh Encyclopædia;' begun 1808, ended 1830—wrote 'Letters on Natural Magic' and a 'Life of Newton'—famous for his discoveries in Optics.

SIR E. BULWER LYTTON,......A statesman, novelist, and dramatist—author of 'Rienzi,' and 'Last of the Barons,' &c.; and of the well-known play, 'The Lady of Lyons.'

THOMAS CARLYLE,................An eccentric but talented writer-chief works, 'Sartor Resartus' and a 'History of the French Revolution.

CHARLES DICKENS,...............A distinguished novelist—assumed name Boz—author of 'The Pickwick Papers,' 'Old Curiosity Shop,' 'David Copperfield,' &c.

SHERIDAN KNOWLES, ...Best dramatist of our day—chief works, 'Virginius,' 'William Tell,' the 'Hunchback.'

ALFRED TENNYSON, ...The present Poet-laureate—author of 'The Princess,' 'In Memoriam,' 'Maud,' &c.

WILLIAM M. THACKERAY,...A distinguished novelist and lecturer—assumed name, 'Michael Angelo Titmarsh'—author of 'Vanity Fair,' 'Pendennis,' 'The Newcomes,' 'Lectures on the Four Georges,' &c.

LEADING ARTISTS.

SIR DAVID WILKIE, ...(1785–1841)—born in Fifeshire—famed for his paintings of Scottish peasant life—chief works, his 'Blind Fiddler,' 'Village Festival,' and 'John Knox preaching before Queen Mary.'

SIR FRANCIS CHANTREY,......(1782–1848)—native of Derbyshire—a distinguished sculptor—finest work, 'Monument of Two Sisters in Lichfield Cathedral.'

JOSEPH M. W. TURNER, ...(1775–1851)—one of the best landscape painters of the English School—painted also several historical pictures—died under an assumed name in a humble lodging in London.

LEADING INVENTORS, ETC.

SIR ISAMBARD BRUNEL,.......(1769–1849)—a distinguished engineer—greatest work, 'The Thames Tunnel;' begun 1826, finished 1843.

GEORGE STEPHENSON, ...(1781–1848)—born at Wylam, Northumberland—the great Railway Engineer—inventor of the Locomotive Engine—died at Tapton, aged 67. His son Robert is distinguished as the engineer of the Tubular Bridge over the Menai Strait.

SIR JOSEPH PAXTON, ...Still living—once gardener to the Duke of Devonshire—designer of the Crystal Palace of 1851.

CHAPTER VIII.

THE BRITISH CONSTITUTION AND GOVERNMENT.

The Three Estates.	Making of the Laws.
The Sovereign.	Their Administration.
The Lords.	Various Courts.
The Commons.	Revenue.
The Cabinet.	Expenditure.

THE Three Estates of the British realm are the Sovereign, the Lords, and the Commons. Thus the Constitution is not a pure monarchy, a pure aristocracy, or a pure democracy, but a compound of all three; and in this chiefly lies its strength.

The office of Sovereign is hereditary; and no lingering remnant of barbarism, called a Salic Law, excludes a woman from the British throne. The chief branches of the royal prerogative are: The Sovereign alone can make war or peace; he alone can pardon those who break the laws; he alone can prorogue, dissolve, or call a Parliament; he can prevent a law from passing by refusing to sign it,—but this our Sovereigns seldom or never do; no money can be coined but by his command; all ranks of nobility are created by him. But, while he can do all this, he is bound, as much as any of his subjects, to keep the laws.

Two kinds of Lords sit in the Upper House,—Lords spiritual and Lords temporal. There are thirty Lords spiritual, twenty-six prelates of the Church of England and four Irish prelates—one Archbishop and three Bishops—who hold their seats for a year, and then yield to the next four in order. The number of Lords temporal is unsettled, and can be increased by the Sovereign. They are of five ranks— Dukes, Marquises, Earls, Viscounts, and Barons. Sixteen Scottish and twenty-eight Irish nobles, elected by their brother Peers, sit in the House of Lords, which is on the whole an hereditary body, and is the highest law-court in the Empire.

There are six hundred and fifty-four members in the House of Commons. England and Wales are represented by four hundred and ninety-six; Scotland by fifty-three; and Ireland by one hundred and five. Members are returned by counties, cities, and boroughs, and some of the Universities. The chief power of the Commons has been already noticed more than once. They command all the supplies, and can thus effectually control the Sovereign. No Parliament can sit longer than seven years; and a new one must be called within six months after the accession of a new Sovereign.

The Sovereign rules through his Ministers, the chief of whom form the Cabinet. The Cabinet is now composed of,—

 The First Lord of the Treasury, or the Premier;
 The Lord Chancellor;
 The Lord Privy Seal;
 The President of the Council;
 The Home Secretary;
 The Foreign Secretary;
 The Colonial Secretary;
 The Indian Secretary;
 The War Secretary;
 The Chancellor of the Exchequer;
 The First Lord of the Admiralty;
 The President of the Board of Trade;
 The President of the Poor Law Board;
 The Postmaster General;
 The Chancellor of the Duchy of Lancaster;
 The Chief Secretary for Ireland.

When these are defeated on any important Bill, they generally resign. Then the usual course is for the Sovereign to send for the leader of Opposition, and intrust him with the formation of a new Government. The Cabinet Ministers form, as it were, a Committee of the Privy Council, which is a large body of advisers, selected from the most prominent men in the kingdom.

New laws may be proposed in either House of Parliament. Proposing a law is called bringing in a Bill. Every Bill must be read and passed by a majority of votes three times in each House before it can be laid before the Sovereign for signature. Not until it has gone through these seven stages does the Bill become an Act of Parliament and a law of the land. Money-bills must originate in the Commons. The Lords may reject, but cannot alter them.

The administration of British law is founded on three great principles—the Jury, the Habeas Corpus Act, and the independence of the Judges. In England and Ireland a Grand Jury sit to judge whether the case is fit to go to trial; then a second Jury of twelve decide upon the case, and must be unanimous in their verdict of Guilty or Not Guilty. In Scotland there is no Grand Jury—a Jury of fifteen try the case, and return a verdict of Guilty, Not Guilty, or Not Proven, by a majority of votes.

There are various Courts in which the Statute-law, the Common-law, and the law of Equity are administered. Statute-law is that embodied in Acts of Parliament. Common-law is the law of old custom, and depends on the decision of former cases. The law of Equity applies to those cases in which the Sovereign interferes, through the Lord Chancellor, to prevent injustice arising from the Common-law. The principal English and Irish Courts are those of Chancery, Queen's Bench, Common Pleas, and Exchequer. In Scotland the Court of Session and the High Court of Justiciary are the chief tribunals. In the country justice is administered at Assizes, held generally twice a year by those Judges who go on circuit.

The revenue and expenditure for the year ending March 31st 1858 are subjoined:—

GROSS REVENUE, ...£66,881,513
GROSS EXPENDITURE, ...£70,378,859

Revenue.	Expenditure.
Customs, ...£23,109,104	Interest on National Debt, ...£28,627,103
Excise, ...17,825,000	Army, ...12,915,156
Stamps, ...7,415,719	Navy, ...10,590,000
Taxes, ...3,152,033	Other items, ...18,246,600
Property-tax, ...11,586,114	
Post-Office, ...2,920,000	
Land, ...276,654	
Other sources, ...596,889	

LEADING DATES OF THE BRUNSWICK PERIOD.

GENERAL EVENTS.

	A.D.	
The South Sea Bubble,	1720	George I.
Walpole resigns,	1742	George II.
New Style of reckoning time,	1752	—
Arrest of John Wilkes,	1763	George III.
Trial of Warren Hastings begins,	1788	—
First English Railway opened,	1830	William IV.
Slavery Abolished in British Colonies,	1833	—
The O'Connell State Trials,	1844	Victoria.
The Railway Panic,	1847	—
The Great Exhibition in Hyde Park,	1851	—
Death of Wellington,	1852	—
The Atlantic Cable laid and failed,	1858	—

CONSTITUTIONAL CHANGES.

Riot Act,	1715	George I.
Septennial Act,	1716	—
The American Stamp Act,	1765	George III.
Union of Great Britain and Ireland,	1801	—
Catholic Emancipation Bill,	1829	George IV.
The Reform Bill passed,	1832	William IV
The Corn Laws repealed,	1846	Victoria.
The India Bill,	1858	—

DOMINION ACQUIRED OR LOST.

Conquest of Bengal,	1757	George II.
— Canada,	1759	—
American Independence acknowledged,	1783	George III.
Hong-Kong acquired,	1842	Victoria.
Sinde annexed,	1843	—
The Punjaub taken,	1849	—

WARS, BATTLES, TREATIES, ETC.

James the Pretender in Scotland,	1715	George I.
Battle of Dettingen,	1743	George II.
— Fontenoy,	1745	—
Charles Edward lands in Scotland,	—	—
Battle of Culloden,	1746	—
Peace of Aix-la-Chapelle,	1748	—
Seven Years' War begins,	1756	—

	A.D.	
First Peace of Paris,	1763	George III.
American War begins,	1775	—
Battle of Bunker's Hill,	—	—
— Brandywine River,	1777	—
Siege of Gibraltar,	1779–1783	—
Great French Revolution,	1789–1795	—
Battle of the Nile,	1798	—
Irish Rebellion,	—	—
Treaty of Amiens,	1802	—
Battle of Trafalgar,	1805	—
Peninsular War begins,	1808	—
War with United States,	1812–1814	—
Battle of Vittoria,	1813	—
— Waterloo,	1815	—
Second Peace of Paris,	—	—
Algiers bombarded,	1816	—
Battle of Navarino,	1827	George IV.
— Aliwal,	1846	Victoria.
— Sobraon,	—	—
— Chillianwalla,	1849	—
— Gujerat,	—	—
Russian War begins,	1854	—
Battle of Alma,	—	—
— Balaklava,	—	—
— Inkermann,	—	—
Sebastopol taken,	1855	—
Peace concluded at Paris,	1856	—
The Indian Mutiny begins,	1857	—

GENEALOGY OF THE HOUSE OF BRUNSWICK.

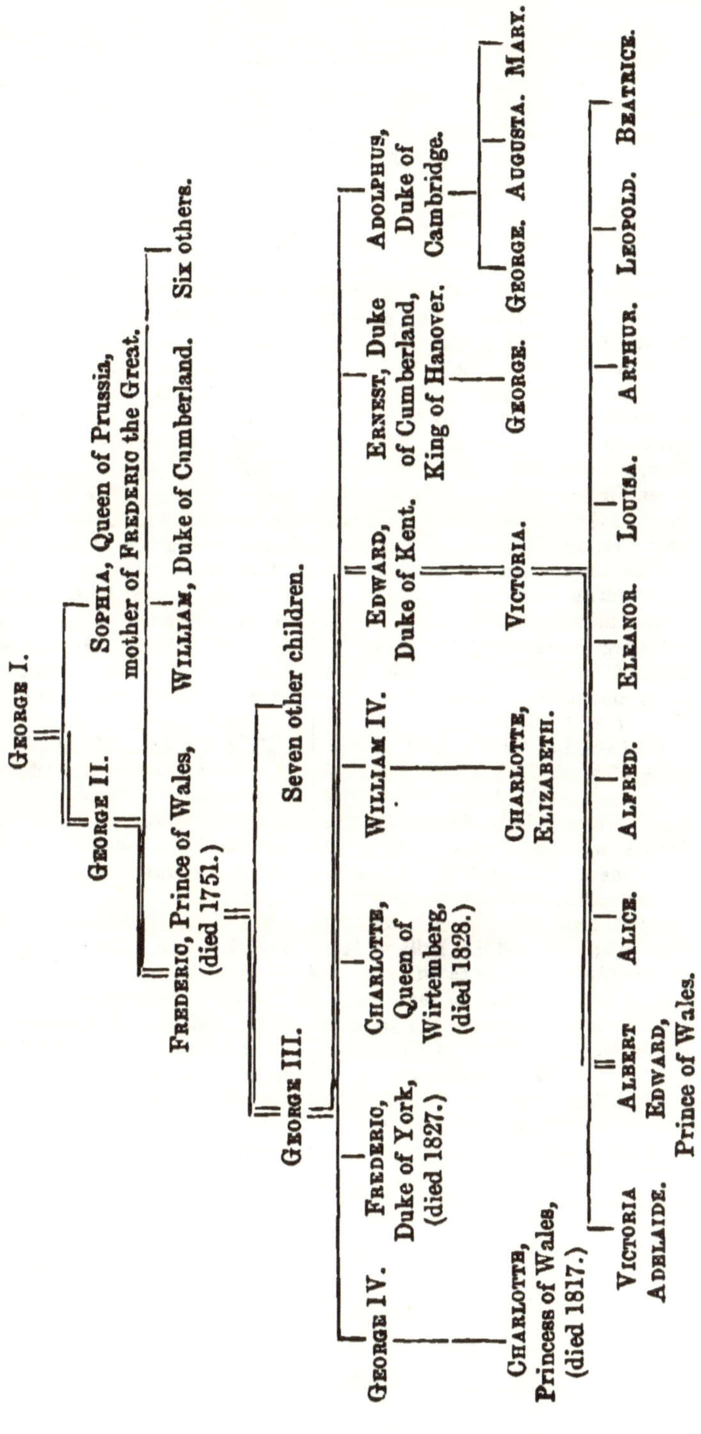

```
GEORGE I.
│
├── GEORGE II.
│   │
│   ├── FREDERIC, Prince of Wales, (died 1751.)
│   │   │
│   │   ├── GEORGE III.
│   │   │   │
│   │   │   ├── GEORGE IV.
│   │   │   │   └── CHARLOTTE, Princess of Wales, (died 1817.)
│   │   │   ├── FREDERIC, Duke of York, (died 1827.)
│   │   │   ├── CHARLOTTE, Queen of Wirtemberg, (died 1828.)
│   │   │   ├── WILLIAM IV.
│   │   │   │   └── CHARLOTTE, ELIZABETH.
│   │   │   ├── EDWARD, Duke of Kent.
│   │   │   │   └── VICTORIA == ALBERT EDWARD, Prince of Wales.
│   │   │   │       ├── VICTORIA ADELAIDE.
│   │   │   │       ├── ALBERT EDWARD, Prince of Wales.
│   │   │   │       ├── ALICE.
│   │   │   │       ├── ALFRED.
│   │   │   │       ├── ELEANOR.
│   │   │   │       ├── LOUISA.
│   │   │   │       ├── ARTHUR.
│   │   │   │       ├── LEOPOLD.
│   │   │   │       └── BEATRICE.
│   │   │   ├── ERNEST, Duke of Cumberland, King of Hanover.
│   │   │   │   └── GEORGE.
│   │   │   ├── ADOLPHUS, Duke of Cambridge.
│   │   │   │   ├── GEORGE.
│   │   │   │   ├── AUGUSTA.
│   │   │   │   └── MARY.
│   │   │   └── Seven other children.
│   └── SOPHIA, Queen of Prussia, mother of FREDERIC the Great.
├── WILLIAM, Duke of Cumberland.
└── Six others.
```

BRITISH COLONIES AND DEPENDENCIES.

EUROPEAN.

GIBRALTAR—A rocky promontory in the south of Spain. Its extremity is called Europa Point. It is the ancient *Calpe*. The rock is 3 miles long and 1500 feet high. The name is derived from *Gibel* a mountain, and *Tarik* a Moorish leader, who landed there in 712 to conquer Spain. It was often taken and retaken by Moors and Spaniards. The British, under Sir George Rooke, aided by the Prince of Hesse Darmstadt, took it from Spain July 24, 1704. It was ceded to Britain by the Treaty of Utrecht. The French and Spaniards besieged it unsuccessfully from June 1779 till February 1783. Rodney brought relief during the siege, but Lord Howe saved the Rock for England. It is very valuable as a naval and military station, being the 'Key of the Mediterranean.'

HELIGOLAND—An islet (1 mile by ⅓ of a mile) 26 miles north-west from the mouth of the Elbe. The name means 'Holy Land,' for the Saxons worshipped the goddess of Earth there. The natives are Frisian. It was chiefly held by the Dukes of Sleswick until 1714; then taken by Denmark; occupied by Britain September 1807; formally ceded by treaty in 1814. In war times, of the greatest value to Britain to secure the German rivers—now prized for its lighthouse, its pilots, and its safe anchorage.

MALTA—Anciently Melita—the scene of Paul's shipwreck. It is about 60 miles south of Sicily. Capital, La Valetta. Given by Charles V. to the Knights of St. John in 1530; often attacked by the Turks; taken by Bonaparte in 1798; retaken by British and Maltese in 1800; then delivered up to Britain by the Maltese. It is the central station of the Mediterranean fleet. Gozo (5 miles to north-west) is a fertile island, but with few inhabitants.

IONIAN ISLANDS—Seven islands to the west of Greece. Cephalonia the largest. The modern Greeks call them Frank Islands. When the Eastern Empire fell in 1453, taken under care of Venice. Seized by France in 1797; then in 1800 under Russia; placed by treaty of 1815 under Britain, who appoints a Lord High Commissioner. Zante produces small grapes, called currants.

THE CHANNEL or NORMAN ISLES—A group in St. Michael's Bay, off Normandy. Jersey the largest. Belonging to Britain since the Conquest; often attacked by the French. Valued for cheap living and healthy climate.

MAN or MONA—An island in the Irish Sea. Taken by Alexander III. of Scotland from the Norwegians in 1270; surrendered to Edward I. in 1289; became the property of the Dukes of Athol in 1735 by inheritance; finally purchased by Britain in 1825. Ruled by officials who are aided by the House of Keys, consisting of 24 chief commoners.

ASIATIC.

ADEN—A town in south-west of Arabia. Taken by the British in 1838. Steamers between Bombay and Suez stop there for coals, &c. Fine coffee produced.

BURMESE COLONIES—Aracan, a district on the north-east of Bay of Bengal and south of Chittagong; conquered by the British in 1826. At the same time was taken **Tenasserim**, close to the Malay Peninsula and south of the Irrawaddy. At the mouth of this river we own **Pegu**, taken in 1853: it produces rice and teak-wood.

CEYLON—An oval island (270 miles by 145) lying south-east of Hindostan. It has always been a Crown Colony. It was occupied by the Portuguese in the 16th century; then by Dutch, from whom we took it about 1796. Native kingdom of Kandy fell in 1815. It produces coffee, sugar, rice, pepper, teak, cinnamon, and gems, especially pearls.

INDIA—The Peninsula of Hindostan, containing three Presidencies,—**Bengal**, **Madras**, and **Bombay**. The chief events in the history of British India are,—Charter granted by Elizabeth in 1600—Settlement at Madras 1648—Bombay acquired by marriage of Charles II. to Catherine of Portugal—Fort-William, Calcutta, erected 1699—Surajah Dowlah of Bengal takes Calcutta in 1756—Clive recovers Calcutta, and wins battle of Plassey, 1757—Warren Hastings made Governor-General in 1773—His wars with Hyder Ali and Tippoo Saib of Mysore—Fall of Seringapatam and death of Tippoo in 1799—Overthrow of the Mahrattas at Assaye by Major-General Wellesley, afterwards Duke of Wellington, September 23, 1803—Afghan War (1839-1842)—Sinde annexed 1843—The Punjaub conquered 1849—Late annexation of Oude—Indian Mutiny 1857—East India Company ceases to rule the Indian Empire September 1, 1858. India is rich in all tropical produce; its owners command the trade of the Eastern Seas; and its possession gives Britain great weight among the nations of the earth.

HONG-KONG—A small island at the mouth of the Canton River. It is 75 miles from Canton. Ceded by the Chinese in 1842. Occupied chiefly by British traders in tea, silk, and opium.

MALACCA—A settlement (40 miles by 25) on the Straits of Malacca, near the southern point of Malaya. Held by Portuguese and then by the Dutch; finally transferred to Britain in 1824 in exchange for possessions in Sumatra.

PENANG or **PRINCE OF WALES' ISLAND**—An island off west coast of Malaya. It was purchased for an annuity of 6000 Spanish dollars from the King of Quedah about 1785. A strip of land opposite, on the Malay shore, was bought in 1802, and is called **Province Wellesley**. Penang is the seat of Government for Malacca and Singapore.

SINGAPORE—An island (26 miles by 18) at the south of the Malay Peninsula. It was bought from the Sultan of Johore in 1819. It produces sugar, cotton, coffee, nutmegs, and pepper; is a great commercial depôt; and is used as a penal settlement for India. It and the last two colonies form the 'Eastern Settlements.'

SARAWAK—A district on the banks of the Sarawak in north-west of Borneo—granted to Sir James Brooke in 1840 by the Sultan of Borneo—withdrawn in 1846, but retaken by British guns. Not now countenanced by the British Government; and yet very valuable, producing antimony ore, diamonds, gold, iron, and all tropic plants; and commanding the trade of the Chinese Sea. **Labuan**, an island (12 miles by 6) at the mouth of Borneo River, taken possession of in 1847. It yields much fine coal.

AUSTRALIAN.

AUSTRALIA—The largest island in the world. Its discovery is claimed by France, England, Holland, and Spain. Called New Holland by Dutch settlers. Its coast was traced by the British navigators, Cook, Furneaux, Bligh, Bass, and Flinders. At Botany Bay, discovered by Cook in 1770, and so called from its beautiful flowers, a penal colony was formed by Britain in 1788. The settlement was called New South Wales; and its capital, Sydney, was built on Port Jackson. In 1829 West Australia was colonized—capital, Perth: in 1834 South Australia—capital, Adelaide: in 1838 North Australia—capital, Victoria. The south-east corner is occupied by the colony of Victoria, whose capital, Melbourne, on Port Philip, was founded in 1837. In 1851 gold was discovered, and a great rush of emigration took place. Chief productions are wool, gold, tallow, and train oil.

VAN DIEMEN'S LAND—An island nearly the size of Ireland, south of Australia. Discovered by Tasman, a Dutch sailor, in 1642—called by him Van Diemen's Land in honour of the Governor of Batavia—now called Tasmania from the discoverer. Found in 1798 to be an island by Bass, who gave his name to the Straits. Regularly occupied by the British in 1803 as a penal colony; declared independent of New South Wales in 1825, and placed under a Lieutenant-Governor and Council. Capital, Hobart Town on the Derwent. Productions similar to those of Australia. Norfolk Island, far to the east of Australia, is under the Government of Tasmania, and used to be only a penal colony. It is now occupied by the Pitcairn Islanders.

NEW ZEALAND—Two large islands, New Ulster and New Munster; and a small one, New Leinster, to the south-east of Australia. Capital, Auckland in New Ulster. Colonized in the present century by the New Zealand Company: recognised as a British Colony in 1841. Enjoys a very temperate climate

---

AFRICAN.

ASCENSION—A small volcanic island half way between Brazil and Guinea. Turtles taken there in abundance. Very useful as an outlying picket of our Empire.

THE CAPE—The southern extremity of Africa. Orange River the northern boundary. Discovered by Bartholomew Diaz in 1487, but he could not land—named Cape of Good Hope by John II. of Portugal, in hope of better fortune next voyage. Doubled by Vasco di Gama in 1497—colonized by the Dutch in 1650, and held by them for 150 years. Taken from the Dutch by the British in 1795, but restored at the Treaty of Amiens—recaptured from the Dutch, who were then allied with France, in January 1806, by Sir David Baird and Sir Home Popham. Port Natal (so called from the coast being discovered on Christmas-day) is outside the bounds of Cape Colony, and was established in 1824. The Cape is the maritime key to India and the East. Produces wheat and wine: beautiful flowers, especially heaths.

GAMBIA and **GOLD COAST**—Settlements dating from the 16th century. The former at the mouth of the Gambia: the latter in Guinea. Chief productions, gold-dust and rice.

MAURITIUS—An island 500 miles east of Madagascar. Capital, Port Louis. Discovered by the Portuguese in 1507, and by them called Cerné. Abandoned. Taken by the Dutch in 1598, and called Mauritius in honour of the Prince of Orange. Again abandoned. Colonized by the French in 1721; they called it Isle of France. Taken from France by British ships in 1810. A naval station: exports sugar, cotton, ebony, indigo.

SIERRA LEONE—The basin of the Rokelle, on western coast of Africa. Means 'Mountains of the Lion.' A settlement in 1787. So unhealthy that it is called 'The white man's grave.'

ST. HELENA—A rocky island (10 miles by 7) in the South Atlantic. Discovered by the Portuguese in 1502; occupied by the Dutch till 1651; then taken by the British. Famous as the prison of Napoleon from 1815 till 1821; his grave till 1840. A station for Indiamen.

Two groups of islets north of Madagascar—the **Seychelles** and the **AmiranteIslands**: were taken from France in 1794. They have a fine climate, safe harbours, and produce spices. **Rodriguez** and the **Chagos** group also belong to Britain.

NORTH AMERICAN.

CANADA—Washed by the St. Lawrence and its Lakes. Discovered by Cabot in 1497. Colonized by the French under Jacques Cartier, who sailed up the St. Lawrence in 1535. Canada is an Indian word meaning 'a collection of huts.' Taken by the British in 1759, when the victor, Wolfe, fell on the plains of Abraham near Quebec. Two insurrections in 1837–38. The two provinces, Upper and Lower Canada, were united in 1840. The capital is unsettled. The Queen has recommended Ottawa, but the Canadians object. Under a Governor-General, a Council of forty-five elected by the Crown, and an Assembly of 130 elected by the Colonists. Chief productions are timber, fish, and furs.

CAPE BRETON—An island off Nova Scotia. Discovered by Cabot. Louisburg taken by the New England Colonists in 1745, and exchanged for Madras in 1749. The island was captured from the French in 1758 and Louisburg was dismantled.

HONDURAS—On eastern side of Yucatan, with a coast line of 270 miles; capital, Belize. Discovered by Columbus in 1502. Honduras means in Spanish 'depth,' from deep water near the shore. Claimed by Britain and Spain. Ceded to Britain in 1763. Since then attacked more than once. Produces mahogany and logwood.

HUDSON'S BAY—Colonized by the Hudson Bay's Company, who trade in furs.

NEW BRUNSWICK—On mainland south of St. Lawrence. Discovered by Cabot. Ceded by France in 1713. Under a Lieutenant-Governor.

NEWFOUNDLAND—An island (420 miles by 300) at the mouth of the St. Lawrence. Supposed to have been discovered by an Icelander in 1001. Visited by Cabot 1497. Valuable for its cod-fisheries. Under a Lieutenant-Governor.

NOVA SCOTIA—A peninsula south of St. Lawrence. Discovered by Cabot. Colonized as a penal settlement by the French in 1598. They called it Acadia. Also by Sir William Alexander in 1623. He called it Nova Scotia. Ceded to Britain by treaty of Utrecht.

PRINCE EDWARD'S ISLAND—Off New Brunswick, (140 miles by 34.) Discovered by Cabot. Taken by fall of Louisburg in 1758. Important as a fishing and trading station.

VANCOUVER'S ISLAND and **BRITISH COLUMBIA**—West on the Pacific shore. The coast was traced for the first time in 1778, by Captain Cook; afterwards more fully in 1788, by Lieutenant John Meares; and in 1793 by George Vancouver. The district has been made suddenly famous in 1858 by the discovery of gold on Fraser River. A Bill has just passed for the formation of a colony.

SOUTH AMERICAN.

BRITISH GUIANA—In north-east of South America. Colonized by the Dutch in 1613. Seized by French in 1783. Taken from the Dutch in 1803. Insurrection of slaves 1823. Settlements on the rivers Berbice, Demerara, and Essequibo, united 1831. Tropical produce.

FALKLAND ISLANDS—Rocky islands 300 miles east of Patagonia. Discovered by Hawkins in 1594. Taken possession of for George III. by Byron in 1765. Claimed by Spain, but afterwards ceded to Britain. Chief value, their fine harbours; especially in East Falkland.

WEST INDIAN.

JAMAICA, or Xaymaca (Indian for plenty of wood and water)—Discovered by Columbus in 1494. Taken from Spain by General Venables and Admiral Penn in 1655. Staple commodities, sugar and rum; produces tropic plants; fine cabinet woods.

TRINIDAD (Spanish for Trinity)—At mouth of Orinoco. Discovered by Columbus in 1498. Colonized by Spaniards in 1588. Attacked by Raleigh 1595. Taken in 1797. Contains mud volcanoes and a lake of pitch. Tropic produce.

Our other West Indian Islands are **Tobago**, taken from the French in 1793; **Grenada** and **St. Vincent**, taken from the same in 1762; **Barbadoes**, colonized by Sir William Courteen in 1625; **St. Lucia** taken from France in 1803, and **Dominica** in 1783; **Montserrat** colonized with **Antigua** in 1632, and **St. Kitts** in 1623, and **Nevis** in 1628; **Anguilla** colonized in 1650, and the **Virgin Islands** in 1666. The **Bahamas**—one of which, San Salvador, was the first American land seen by Columbus—were occupied by the British in 1629, and the **Bermudas** in 1611. These last lie out in the Atlantic. They are healthy and picturesque, and produce fine arrow-root.

NELSONS' SCHOOL SERIES.

THE "STEP BY STEP" SERIES.

Consecutive Number.

1. **Step by Step;** or, The Child's First Lesson-Book. 18mo. PARTS I. and II. Price 2d. each.
2. **Sequel to "Step by Step."** 18mo. Price 4d.
3. **Third Reading-Book.** 18mo, cloth. Price 6d.

All who have experienced the drudgery of teaching children to read will at once perceive the superiority of these books over all others hitherto published. By the system adopted, the task becomes a pleasant one to both pupil and teacher.—*See more fully Preface to "Step by Step."*

New Third Book. "The Four Seasons." 18mo, cloth. Price 6d.

This new volume is intended to be used with the No. III. already published; but where two books cannot be adopted, it may be used alone; and it is recommended for this purpose in preference to the former No. III., as it contains a greater variety of lessons both in poetry and prose.

4. **Fourth Book.** Lessons on Common Things. 18mo, cloth. Price 9d.

SELECTION FROM CONTENTS.

Where does our Food come from?—Oil, Whalebone, and Fur—Greenland—The Breakfast Table—The Damask Table-Cloth—Linen—Cups and Saucers—English Earthenware—Teaspoons—Knives and Forks—Steel, &c. &c.

5. **Fifth Book.** 12mo, cloth. Price 1s.
   New Fifth Book. See Junior Reader, No. I.
6. **Sixth Book.** 12mo. Price 1s.
   New Sixth Book. See Junior Reader, No. II.

"THE PROGRESSIVE READING-BOOKS."

A NEW SERIES OF ENGLISH READERS, DESIGNED TO FOLLOW AFTER No. IV. OF THE "STEP BY STEP" BOOKS.

The object aimed at is to provide a set of books adapted to all classes of Schools and fitted to teach, not only the *art of reading*, but to train the pupil to the *love of reading*.

5. **Junior Reader, No. I.** Post 8vo, cloth. Price 1s. 3d.

SELECTION FROM CONTENTS.

Stories and Fables:—Grumble and Cheery—The Monkey and the Cat—The Stinging Nettle—The Sheep and the Birds—Robinson Crusoe: Crusoe and his Boat—The Footprint on the Sand—Crusoe and the Savages—Crusoe saves Friday, &c. *True Stories:*—The Young Witness—The Gnarled House—The Spider's Web—The Sailor Boy's Prayer, &c. *Stories of Animals, &c.:*—A Tiger Story—A Faithful Dog—The Arab and his Horse—Androcles and the Lion, &c. *Poetry:*—By-and-by—The Voice of Spring—The Spider and the Fly—The Butterfly's Ball—We are Seven, &c. &c.

[*Continued*

NELSONS' SCHOOL SERIES.

6. Junior Reader, No. II. Post 8vo, cloth. Price 1s. 6d.

SELECTION FROM CONTENTS.

MISCELLANEOUS.—*Prose:*—Five Minutes Too Late—The Ploughboy and the Principal—My First Guinea—The Boy makes the Man, &c. *Poetry:*—Work—My Father's at the Helm—The Queen of May—Lord Ullin's Daughter, &c. NATURAL HISTORY, &c.—*Prose:*—Stories of the Shepherd's Dog—The Newfoundland Dog—Wolves in Britain—Robert the Bruce and the Bloodhound, &c. CHIEFLY HISTORICAL.—*Prose:*—Unwritten History—The Coming of the Romans—The Druids—The Sea Kings—Alfred the Great—The Battle of Hastings, &c. *Historical and National Poetry:*—God Save the Queen—The Nation's Prayer—Home—Love of Country—Rule, Britannia—England's Oak, &c. THE HEROES AND TRIUMPHS OF PEACE:—The Art of Printing—Story of Laurence Coster—Story of John Guttenberg—The Printing Machine—The "Times" Printing-Office, &c.

7. The Senior Reader. Post 8vo, cloth, 384 pages. Price 2s. 6d.

SELECTION FROM CONTENTS.

The World we Live in:—Thou art, O God, the life and light—The Earth's Journey Round the Sun—What is Gravitation?—The Stellar Universe—The Air Ocean, &c. *The Land we Live in:*—Britannia—Rise of the English Nation—Pictures of the Olden Time—Scenes from Ivanhoe: The Siege of Torquilstone; Trial by Combat—Rise of Cities—Travelling in the Seventeenth Century, &c. *The Age we Live in:*—Modern London—The Bank of England:—Penny Postage—The Electric Telegraph, &c. *Home and Country Scenes, &c.:*—The Deserted Village—The Skylark—Elegy in a Churchyard—The Cottar's Saturday Night, &c. *Round the World:*—Hymn to the North Star—The North Pole—Adventures in Spitzbergen—Ice, Icebergs, and Glaciers—Greenland and the Greenlanders—Snow and Snow Huts—The Whale Fishery—The Last Search for Franklin—The Siege of Quebec, &c.

8. The Advanced Reader. [*Now Published.*

EXTRA VOLUMES.

9. Readings from the Best Authors. Edited by A. H. BRYCE, LL.D., one of the Classical Masters of the High School, Edinburgh. 12mo, cloth. Price 1s. 6d.

Containing *Historical and Descriptive Selections* from Macaulay—Prescott—W. Irving—W. H. Russell. *Fiction* from Croly—Bulwer Lytton—Scott—Mrs. Stowe—Dickens. *Oratory* from Pitt—Burke—Sheridan—Lord Brougham. *Poetry* from Cowper—Campbell—Scott—Mrs. Hemans—Bell—Macaulay—Rogers—Wordsworth—Goldsmith—Byron—Tennyson, &c. &c.

10. Readings from the Best Authors. SECOND BOOK. Edited by A. H. BRYCE, LL.D. Post 8vo, cloth. Price 2s.

The Extracts which form the Second Book of "Readings from the Best Authors" have been selected mainly with regard to their suitableness as Exercises in Elocution, for the members of middle and upper classes in schools; and thus many of them are of a higher order than the specimens in the first book.

NELSONS' SCHOOL SERIES.

Milton's Paradise Lost and Paradise Regained. With Notes for the Use of Schools. By the Rev. J. EDMONSTON. 12mo, cloth. Price 2s. 6d.

Class-Book of Poetry. Chronologically Arranged. With Critical and Biographical Sketches by D. WILSON, LL.D. 12mo, 495 pages. Price 2s. 6d.

The English Word-Book: A Manual Exhibiting the Sources, Structure, and Affinities of English Words. By JOHN GRAHAM.

 PART I. Prefixes and Postfixes. Illustrated by Parallel Columns in the Primary and Secondary Meanings. In Wrapper. Price 3d.

 PART II. Roots, Derivatives, and Meanings. In Wrapper. Price 6d.

 The two Parts in one volume, cloth, Price 1s.

Word Expositor and Spelling Guide: A School Manual Exhibiting the Spelling, Pronunciation, Meaning, and Derivation of all the Important and Peculiar Words in the English Language. With Copious Exercises for Examination and Dictation. By GEORGE COUTIE, A.M., English Master of Liverpool High School, Liverpool Institute. 12mo, cloth. Price 1s. 3d.

FOR ADVANCED CLASSES.

History of English Literature. In a Series of Biographical Sketches. By WILLIAM FRANCIS COLLIER, LL.D., Author of "School History of the British Empire," "The Great Events of History," &c. 12mo, cloth, 538 pages. Price 3s. 6d.

 "Tracing the origin and progress of our literature from the period of the monkish annalists to our own times, a clear view is given of its development in every branch."—*Witness.*

History of the Church of Christ: With a Special View to the Delineation of Christian Faith and Life. With Notes, Chronological Tables, Lists of Councils, Examination Questions, and other Illustrative Matter. From A.D. 1 to A.D. 313. By the Rev. ISLAY BURNS, M.A., Dundee. Crown 8vo, cloth. Price 5s.

 "It is a book that deserves to be popular. Though oftentimes of a painful nature, the interest throughout is so well sustained that one is irresistibly compelled to read right to the end."—*Spectator.*

 "A very excellent work, suited to general use, and likely to promote not only the higher intelligence, but the more earnest and genial religiousness of attentive readers."—*Nonconformist.*

NELSONS' SCHOOL SERIES.

GEOGRAPHIES.

Modern Geography, for the Use of Schools. By ROBERT ANDERSON, Head Master, Normal Institution, Edinburgh. Foolscap 8vo, cloth. Price 1s. 6d.

    This work has been pronounced, by upwards of one thousand Teachers, to be the best, as well as the cheapest School Geography published.

Exercises in Geography, adapted to Anderson's Geography. 18mo, cloth. Price 6d.

    This work contains about 10,000 Questions and Exercises in Geography, and will be found of great service to both teacher and pupil.

Geography for Junior Classes. By ROBERT ANDERSON, Head Master, Normal Institution, Edinburgh. 18mo, cloth. Price 11d.

Bible Geography. By the Rev. W. G. BLAIKIE, D.D. With Coloured Maps, Price 1s., 12mo, cloth; or with the Maps mounted on Cloth, 1s. 3d.

HISTORIES.

The Great Events of History, from the Beginning of the Christian Era till the Present Time. By W. F. COLLIER, LL.D. 12mo, cloth. Price 2s. 6d.

History of the British Empire. By W. F. COLLIER, LL.D. With Tables of the Leading Events of each Period—Lists of Contemporary Sovereigns—Dates of Battles—Chapters on the Social Changes of each Period, &c. 12mo, cloth. Price 2s.

    "Mr. Collier's book is unrivalled as a School History of the British Empire. The arrangement is admirable."—*English Journal of Education.*

Bible History, in connection with the General History of the World. With Descriptions of Scripture Localities. By the Rev. W. G. BLAIKIE, D.D. 470 pages 12mo, with Maps. Price 3s.

    This volume has been prepared mainly with a view to the instruction of Schools and Families. Its plan differs in many respects from that of any other Bible History.

    1. It follows the great outline of the Bible Narrative,—arranging and classifying the leading facts, *so as to aid eye and memory in grasping the whole.*

    2. It describes briefly the *chief Countries, Towns, and other Scenes of Bible History,* as they occur.

    3. It glances at the *History and Progress of the leading Nations of the World,*—showing what was going on elsewhere while the History of the Bible was being enacted.

History of Scotland. By the Rev. JAMES MACKENZIE. 12mo, cloth. Price 1s. 6d.

NELSONS' SCHOOL SERIES.

CLASSICAL SERIES.

First Latin Reader. By ARCHIBALD H. BRYCE, LL.D., of Trin. Coll., Dublin, one of the Classical Masters in the High School of Edinburgh. Second Edition. 216 pages, 12mo. Price 2s.

This is intended as a First Latin Book, supplying everything which a pupil will require during his first year. It contains—

I. The leading facts and principles of Latin Grammar, with the Inflexions of Substantives, Adjectives, Pronouns, and Verbs, set forth at full length; and also a Synopsis of the Syntax of simple sentences.
II. A numerous set of Simple Exercises, with lists of the words used in them.
III. A Series of easy and interesting Lessons in continuous reading, consisting of a few simple Fables of Phaedrus, &c.
IV. A Vocabulary, in which the quantities of syllables are marked, and the derivation of words given.

The two great features in the plan of the book are—*First*, That pupils are enabled daily, and from the very first, to *make practical use* of grammatical facts and principles so soon as they are learned; and *Secondly*, That acquisitions, when once made, are impressed by constant repetition.

Second Latin Reader. By ARCHIBALD H. BRYCE, LL.D. 384 pages. Price 3s. 6d.

This volume is intended as a Sequel to No. I. It contains—

I. EXTRACTS FROM NEPOS.
II. EXTRACTS FROM CÆSAR.
III. EXTRACTS FROM OVID.
IV. Notes on the above, with Tables for the Declension of Greek Nouns.
V. A System of Syntax, in which the illustrative examples are taken from the Reading Lessons, and to which constant reference is made in the Notes.
VI. A full Vocabulary (proper nouns being inserted), in which are noted peculiarities of Inflexion, Conjugation, and Comparison. Quantities are carefully marked, and derivations given, with frequent illustrations from modern languages.

First Greek Reader. By ARCHIBALD H. BRYCE, LL.D. Third Edition. 222 pages. Price 2s. 6d.

The plan of the Greek Reader is the same as that of the Latin, and seeks to carry out the same principles. As much of the Grammar is given as is deemed absolutely indispensable in a first course; while care has been taken not to overload the text with minutiæ and exceptions, which serve only to confuse and bewilder the beginner. The Extracts for reading are such as to interest and amuse the young, consisting of selections from the Witticisms of Hierocles, from Anecdotes of Famous Men, and from the Fables of Æsop, with a few easy Dialogues of Lucian. A body of Notes is appended to the Reading Lessons, explaining peculiarities of form and of construction.

Horace. Edited by Dr. FREUND, Author of "Latin Lexicon," &c., and JOHN CARMICHAEL, M.A., one of the Classical Masters of the High School, Edinburgh. With Life of Horace, Notes, Vocabulary of Proper Names, and Chronological Table. 12mo, cloth. Price 3s. 6d.

Virgilii Maronis Carmina. Edited by Dr. FREUND. With Life, Notes, and Vocabulary of Proper Names. 12mo, cloth. Price 3s. 6d.

NELSONS' SCHOOL SERIES.

AWARDED THE PRIZE MEDAL AT THE INTERNATIONAL EXHIBITION

NELSON'S WALL MAPS.
EACH 4 FEET BY 4 FEET.
Beautifully Coloured and Mounted on Rollers,
Price 13s. 6d. each.

1. PALESTINE. Divided into Squares of Ten Miles.
2. THE BRITISH ISLANDS in relation to the Continent. Divided into Squares of 100 Miles.
3. ENGLAND. Divided into Squares of 100 Miles.
4. SCOTLAND. Divided into Squares of 100 Miles.
5. EASTERN HEMISPHERE. With Circles at intervals of 1000 English Miles, showing the distance from London.
6. WESTERN HEMISPHERE. Do. Do.
7. EUROPE. Divided into Squares of 1000 English Miles.

The attention of Teachers and others interested in Education is specially invited to these Maps. They will be found to possess advantages for educational purposes over any hitherto published.

Each of the Hemispheres forms a circle four feet in diameter. They are so large that, with the exception of Europe, of which a separate Map is just ready, the Geography of all the countries of the great Divisions of the Globe can be taught from them. Separate Maps of Africa, Asia, Australia, North America, and South America, will not be required in the great majority of schools.

THE FOLLOWING ARE REDUCED COPIES OF THE WALL MAPS:—

NELSON'S SCHOOL MAPS.
Price 1d. each, Plain, with Cover; 2d. each, Coloured; 3d. each, Coloured, and Mounted on Cloth.

1. THE BRITISH ISLANDS in relation to the Continent of Europe.
2. ENGLAND.
3. SCOTLAND.
4. IRELAND.
5. PALESTINE.
6. BIBLE LANDS.
7. EUROPE.

ATLASES.

Nelson's School Atlas. Containing 22 Maps, Full Coloured. 4to, cloth. Price 3s. 6d.

Nelson's Junior Atlas. An entirely New Work, consisting of Reduced Copies of *Nelson's Wall Maps*. Full Coloured. Price 1s. 6d. stiff cover.

Nelson's Shilling Atlas. Containing 16 Maps, plain Stiff wrapper, 4to.